The Essential Historiography Reader

The Essential Historiography Reader

Caroline Hoefferle

Wingate University

Prentice Hall

Boston   Columbus   Indianapolis   New York   San Francisco   Upper Saddle River
Amsterdam   Cape Town   Dubai   London   Madrid   Milan   Munich   Paris   Montréal   Toronto
Delhi   Mexico City   São Paulo   Sydney   Hong Kong   Seoul   Singapore   Taipei   Tokyo

Editorial Director: Craig Campanella
Executive Editor: Jeff Lasser
Editorial Project Manager: Rob DeGeorge
Senior Manufacturing and Operations Manager for Arts & Sciences: Nick Sklitsis
Operations Specialist: Christina Amato
Director of Marketing: Brandy Dawson
Senior Marketing Manager: Maureen E. Prado Roberts
Marketing Assistant: Marissa C. O'Brien
Senior Managing Editor: Ann Marie McCarthy

Senior Project Manager: Denise Forlow
Manager of Central Design: Jayne Conte
Cover Design: Bruce Kenselaar
AV Project Manager: Mirella Signoretto
Full-Service Production, Interior Design, and Composition: Shiny Rajesh/Integra Software Services Pvt. Ltd
Manager, Visual Research: Beth Brenzel
Printer/Binder: RR Donnelley/Harrisonburg
Cover Printer: RR Donnelley/Harrisonburg
Text Font: 10/12 Times Ten

Credits and acknowledgments borrowed from other sources and reproduced, with permission, in this textbook appear on appropriate page within text.

Many of the designations by manufacturers and seller to distinguish their products are claimed as trademarks. Where those designations appear in this book, and the publisher was aware of a trademark claim, the designations have been printed in initial caps or all caps.

Library of Congress Cataloging-in-Publication Data
Hoefferle, Caroline.
   The essential historiography reader / Caroline Hoefferle.
      p. cm.
   Includes bibliographical references.
   ISBN-13: 978-0-321-43762-4 (alk. paper)
   ISBN-10: 0-321-43762-4 (alk. paper)
   1. Historiography–Textbooks.   I. Title.
D13.H5873 2011
907.2–dc22

                            2010017418

10 9 8 7 6 5 4 3 2

Prentice Hall
is an imprint of

www.pearsonhighered.com

ISBN 10:   0-321-43762-4
ISBN 13: 978-0-321-43762-4

*I dedicate this book to my Mike and to all
my friends at Wingate University.*

Contents

Part II
Modern Historiography in the United States   89

Preface

Historiography is an essential component of undergraduate history programs at most American universities, yet few resources are explicitly devoted to supporting historiography education at this level. Having taught the subject to undergraduate history majors for eight years, I have struggled to find appropriate readings every year. While many general historiography texts exist, all are either written for graduate students and are thus too in-depth and complex for most undergraduates, or are too brief and simplistic to help students to thoroughly comprehend the many approaches used by historians over time. Most importantly, historical theories and approaches are often difficult to grasp without actually reading the histories themselves. Some historiography teachers solve this problem by having their students read multiple history books and articles throughout the course of the semester, which may entail the purchase of many books and copyright permissions for many different articles each year. This approach to teaching historiography requires more time and money than many teachers and students desire. I set out to solve these problems by writing and compiling a textbook/reader which not only details the history of historical practice and explains historical theories and philosophies in understandable language, but also provides excerpts to illustrate these historical approaches and help students to identify them in their own writing and in the writings of contemporary historians.

This reader is organized into two main parts. The first part traces contemporary American historical traditions to their roots in ancient Greece and explains how the profession of history emerged and developed in Europe and America through the nineteenth century. The second part focuses more specifically on historiographical developments in the United States since the nineteenth century.

Each chapter is then divided into two sections. In the first section, historical theories, methods, and developments are introduced and explained. Key concepts and historians are noted in the margins, where space is provided for note-taking. The second section contains excerpts from important historians described in the first section. The last excerpt of each chapter, except for Chapter 1, illustrates how one prominent historian applied the approaches mentioned in the first section to the topic of the American Revolution. These excerpts are included so that students can see how historiography and historical context shape the written history of a topic familiar to most American students. All excerpts are taken exactly as they were originally written (or translated as the case may be), including any reference notes they may have originally included. This is done so that the reader can better see the types of sources and methodology used in the excerpts. Questions for consideration are included for each excerpt to help guide student reading and thinking. The Critical Analysis Worksheet provided in Appendix A may additionally help students to take notes on the excerpts and dissect them. By critically analyzing these excerpts, students may gain a deeper understanding of various theoretical frameworks and methodologies, and decide for themselves which of these approaches are the most promising or flawed.

The epilogue discusses trends in American historiography since the 1990s, trends which continue to influence current historians and shape the environment in which history students now live and work. A sample historiographical review essay of the American Revolution is provided in Appendix B to illustrate how one might use the American Revolution excerpts in an actual historiographical essay. An additional bibliography is provided at the end of the book for those who wish to do further research on the topics discussed in each chapter.

The Essential Historiography Reader is by no means an exhaustive discussion of all of the historiographical issues of concern to professional historians, but it aims to help students to understand the theories, philosophies, and methods which have shaped the historical profession in the United States and to think critically about the histories they read as they begin their careers in history.

The following reviewers provided helpful insights and suggestions: Linda Alkana, California State University; Nathan Brooks, New Mexico State University; Marilyn J. Boxer, San Francisco State University; William R. Caraher, University of North Dakota; Charles W. Clark, University of West Georgia; Stephen Englehart, California State Polytechnic University; J. Michael Francis, University of North Florida; George Geib, Butler University; Sharon A. Roger Hepburn, Radford University; Timothy S. Huebner, Rhodes College; Maxine N. Lurie, Seton Hall University; Douglas W. Richmond, University of Texas at Arlington; Judith Mendelsohn Rood, Biola University; George L. Vásquez, San José State University; and Gerrit Voogt, Kennesaw State University.

Introduction

History (with mythology and tradition on the left and right) with an inscription of historians such as Herodotus, Thucydides, and Polybius. In the background a pyramid, the Parthenon, and the Colosseum representing the three civilizations of Egypt, Greece, and Rome. *Source:* Frederick Dielman, *History* (Mosaic, Library of Congress Thomas Jefferson Building, Washington, D.C., 1896), http://www.loc.gov/pictures/item/93510406/ (accessed April 17, 2010).

What kind of history do you like best?
Why do you study history?
Who is your favorite historian?
What kind of historian will *you* be?

Have you ever asked yourself these questions? If you have not already done so, now is the time to find the answers to these questions. And the study of historiography will help you to do just that.

Many of us have never thought deeply about what history is and why we study it. Most of us have learned history by reading primary and secondary sources, memorizing names, dates, and other facts, and using this information to answer historical questions. For some historians, this is good enough: to learn the story (sometimes called "the truth" or "the facts"), enjoy it for what it is, and perhaps learn something from it. Knowing the facts and true story of what happened in the past is important, but memorizing these without understanding how they were created may be a little boring and leave us wondering if this is all there is to the study of history. I would argue that just memorizing facts and unquestioningly accepting what you read misses most of what makes history interesting and valuable, and obscures the true nature of history.

There is so much more to know about the study of history. For example: Who decided what history is and what type of history should be studied in your classes? When did the study of the past become a profession? How do historians choose which topic, method, and theory they apply to their subject? How can we identify different methods and theories used by historians? Has the study of history changed over the years? How does our own view of history fit in with the views of other historians in other times and places? How does our own experience and unique perspective influence our view of what history is and how it should be studied?

Historiography helps us to find the answers to these questions. It helps us to think deeply about the theories and beliefs behind the histories we read, and allows us to get inside the heads of historians. It helps us to realize what we personally can contribute to the study of the past, and it is essential to becoming a well-rounded, reflective, and thoughtful historian.

What Is Historiography and Why Study It?

Although the word "historiography" may sound imposing and scary to some people, it is basically just the history of historical writing. Although this definition is a little vague, historians disagree on a more specific definition of historiography. Two definitions of historiography currently dominate the historical profession in the United States. The first defines historiography simply as a review of various histories which have been written about a certain subject, sort of a history of histories. This type of historiography focuses less on the historical context and philosophies informing histories and more on the findings or information they contain. The second views historiography as the critical examination of the various philosophies, theories, and methods which have been used by historians over time. They would then explain the variation in histories by discussing how each historian was influenced by his or her own specific historical context: the political, cultural, and economic conditions which surrounded historians' personal lives and shaped their histories. While both definitions of historiography are acceptable, *The Essential Historiography Reader* adopts the second definition as its focus.[1]

The most common usage of historiography in the American historical profession today is as a first step in the research process. Since one of the main goals of historical research is to contribute some new information, perspective, or approach to a historical topic, historiographical analysis provides a way to synthesize all of the secondary sources on a particular topic so that one knows what gaps exist in the literature or what one's own perspective might add to the scholarship. Reading

---

[1]Peter Novick, *That Noble Dream: The Objectivity Question and the American Historical Profession* (Cambridge: Cambridge University Press, 1988), 11 and 30.

the secondary sources on a topic and paying attention to their reference notes and bibliographies also provides information on where to start the search for primary sources.

Historians normally summarize and analyze their research of relevant secondary sources in a historiographical review essay, often published at the beginning of a scholarly essay or book. This establishes their expertise on a given topic and allows them to frame their own original research. Historiographical review essays normally introduce the research question or topic under study, and then in chronological order discuss all of the secondary sources which address the question. In analyzing the sources, historians often discuss each monograph's historical context, topic, evidence, thesis, and theory, pointing out especially how each one answers the research question or approaches the topic, and how each monograph relates to the other sources. These essays are then concluded with a discussion of the gaps in scholarship and areas where new perspectives and approaches might contribute to understanding of the topic. This establishes an opening where historians can then introduce their own research and explain how it fits into existing scholarship. An example of a historiographical review essay on the subject of the American Revolution is provided in Appendix B of this reader.

In addition to providing historians with a beginning for their own research, historiography also helps us to understand the inner thinking of other historians in order to comprehend and analyze their methodology and theoretical frameworks. A study of historiography thus helps us to place our own view of history in relation to those of famous historians from other eras, so that we can identify with and learn from our role models and predecessors. It therefore helps us to understand our own philosophy and the unique perspective that we bring to our work. Historiography, consequently, not only helps us to appreciate the practice of history, but helps us to understand ourselves, our own theories of history, and how we fit into the wider scope of the thousands of great historians who have come before us.

What Is History?

Any student of historiography quickly discovers that historians disagree on a number of important issues, and one of the most fundamental differences is on the definition of history itself. Many of us take the word "history" for granted, assuming that everyone knows what we mean by it, that we all share a common definition. The definition of history, however, actually varies considerably, depending upon the perspective and philosophy of the individual. There are a few basic elements of the definition that most historians agree upon. First of all, the word "history" originates as a derivation of *historia*, ancient Greek for "learning through inquiry."[2] The American Historical Association currently defines history as "the never-ending

---

[2]Mark T. Gilderhus, *History and Historians: A Historiographical Introduction*, 5th ed. (New Jersey: Prentice Hall, 2003), 15.

process whereby people seek to understand the past and its many meanings."[3] These broad definitions are a good starting point, but most historians have utilized far more extensive descriptions of history.

     Those historians who agree with defining history as the study of the past may accept all stories about the past, regardless of accuracy or evidence. These historians may include mythopoetic narrative in their definition of history. Consider, for example, the following poem:

Mythopoetic
Narratives

> *...At the time of the night of Makalii*[4]
> *Then began the slime which established the earth*
> *The source of deepest darkness.*
> *Of the depth of darkness, of the depth of darkness,*
> *Of the darkness of the sun, in the depth of night,*
> *It is night, So night was born....*[5]

This is a portion of a creation story from the original inhabitants of Hawaii and describes the earliest history of the earth. A more familiar story about the past might be the following from the Book of Genesis:

> *In the beginning, when God created the heavens and the earth, the earth was a formless wasteland, and darkness covered the abyss, while a mighty wind swept over the waters. Then God said, "Let there be light," and there was light. God saw how good the light was. God then separated the light from the darkness. God called the light "day," and the darkness he called "night." Thus evening came, and morning followed—the first day.*[6]

Classified as mythopoetic narratives, these stories about the past have been transmitted orally and written down at some point. They are distinguished mainly by their inclusion of nonscientific understandings of the universe, including mythical figures, such as gods or spirits and other beings for which science does not have evidence of existence.[7] These narratives consequently are not based on the European or Western notion of science and do not use the scientific method. Whether or not these are actually history, therefore, depends on your definition of history.

---

[3]American Historical Association Professional Division, "Statement on Standards of Professional Conduct" (2004–2005), *American Historical Association*, http://www.historians.org/pubs/Free/ ProfessionalStandards.cfm (accessed August 23, 2009).

[4]Makalii refers to the month of December.

[5]*The Kumulipo*, trans. Queen Liliuokalani (1897) on *Sacred Texts Website* (August 29, 2005), http://www.sacred-texts.com/pac/lku/index.htm (accessed August 23, 2009).

[6]Chapter 1, "Genesis," in *The New American Bible St. Joseph Edition* (New York: Catholic Book Publishing Co., 1992), 4.

[7]"Mythical" here does not imply that these forces do not exist or are somehow inferior to other forces. It denotes that these forces are unseen and therefore difficult to verify scientifically.

According to philosopher M. C. Lemon, there are three primary features of mythopoetic narratives of the past: "a mythical view of space and time; a belief in the eternal recurrence of 'cycles' of events; and following from these beliefs, the absence of any notion of the historic capacity of man to fashion what we call 'progress.'"[8] Mythopoetic stories normally have some moral to the story and are imaginative, or poetic. Often their concept of time is different from the modern notion of time. Rather than abstract and linear units of time, such as hours, days, and decades, some mythopoetic narratives employ a cyclical chronology. Days, events, and the entire past repeat themselves in ongoing cycles related to nature, the cosmos, and the gods. Specific events are sometimes located in time by marking them with the lives of significant persons or cosmic events. In this light, the common Christian method of dating events according to the birth of Jesus of Nazareth (B.C. or A.D.) can be seen as an example of mythopoetic dating. Earlier than that, citizens of the Roman Empire dated their past according to the year of the reigning Roman emperor.

Chinese and other Asian writers too based their histories on the lives of famous rulers from the past, who could be adopted as role models for current and future leaders. Shaped by Confucianism after the second century B.C.E.,[9] Asian historiography was dominated by this moralistic, biographic framework until the nineteenth century.[10] South Asian historiography has long been shaped by a Hindu concept of cyclical time. Viewing the history of the universe as divided into great epochs, consisting of vast amounts of time, Hindus believe that modern history is merely part of the fourth cycle.

Much earlier than that, in the third and fourth millennium B.C.E., ancient Egyptian and Mesopotamian scribes were paid to write annals of the prominent deeds of their rulers and stories about their relationship to the gods, legitimizing their right to rule.[11] For example, the *Epic of Gilgamesh* is a Sumerian mythopoetic story of a ruler and his adventures with gods and other supernatural forces. All of these histories were somewhat cyclical, based on the life and death of a particular ruler. When a new ruler ascended the throne, a new epoch was born.

Mythopoetic histories may also contain elements of linear time. The Judeo-Christian view of time, as expressed in the Bible, is arguably the most linear of these mythopoetic histories. Both the Jewish and Christian biblical concepts of time have a clear beginning with God's creation of the world and a linear progression of time organized around the descendants of Adam. For Christians, the birth of Christ constituted a new era, with years marked according to the year of the Lord Jesus Christ

---

[8]M. C. Lemon, *Philosophy of History: A Guide for Students* (New York: Routledge, 2003), 16.

[9]B.C.E. refers to the now-common chronological designation of "Before the Common Era," which is equivalent to the Christian designation of "Before Christ" (B.C.), but is less religious and Eurocentric in its implications.

[10]Q. Edward Wang and Georg G. Iggers, *Turning Points in Historiography: A Cross-Cultural Perspective* (Rochester, NY: University of Rochester Press, 2002), 6.

[11]Francois Hartog, "The Invention of History: From Homer to Herodotus," *History and Theory* 39 (2000), 384–395.

(Anno Domini in Latin, or A.D.). This era will continue to progress to a specific ending, marked by the Second Coming of Christ, predicted for some date in the future. Judeo-Christian history, however, is also somewhat cyclical in that it included annual cycles of worship, and cycles of human sin, punishment, and reconciliation with God.[12] Regardless of cyclical and linear differences in their sense of time, all peoples around the world seem to have begun with a mythopoetic view of the past. In this way, they can be seen as the original form of history for all peoples.

In many places in the world, mythopoetic narrative is still an acceptable form of history, but beginning in sixth-century Greece, European historians increasingly rejected stories of the past which were not based on verifiable, observable events and forces. Today in the United States, most historians trace their practice back to the ancient Greeks and our definition of history reflects the Greek revolution away from mythopoetic histories. It is important to note, however, that historians in other parts of the world have their own unique historical traditions, and their definitions of history consequently often differ from those of Europeans and Americans.

Even European and American definitions of history, however, have changed over time. Early Greek and European history continued to include supernatural forces until the Renaissance and differed in other ways from our current historical practices. History gradually became secularized and more scientific in the two centuries after the Renaissance, when its definition became the study of how humankind had changed and progressed in linear fashion throughout the ages. In the nineteenth century, European and American historians became increasingly interested in using the scientific method to discover the truth about what really happened in the past. The definition of history consequently included scientific principles, such as maintaining professional objectivity and using written evidence and facts to support conclusions. This definition continues to be the most commonly used in the profession today, but there continues to be disagreements over what history is and is not.

Historical Method   Related to the question of what is history is the question of how it should be studied. Most modern historians can agree on a basic definition of historical method and practice. The American Historical Association states that "the professional practice of history means respecting the integrity of primary and secondary sources while subjecting them to critical scrutiny and contributing in a fair-minded way to ongoing scholarly and public debates over what those sources tell us about the past."[13] Most history textbooks and teachers of methodology courses would add a basic four-step description of the historical method: formulating a historical question or hypothesis, gathering relevant primary and secondary sources, critically analyzing and interpreting those sources, and applying the analysis to answer the historical question.

Historians, however, disagree on many other questions of methodology. They disagree not only on which human experiences are most important to study, but also

---

[12]C. McIntire, "History: Christian Views," in *Encyclopedia of Religion*, vol. 6, 2nd ed., ed. Lindsay Jones (Detroit: MacMillan Reference USA, 2005), 4052.

[13]AHA, "Standards of Professional Conduct."

on how to study them, or more specifically, which historical methods are most valid or appropriate. We cannot study everything that happened in the past, every person, event, institution, country, and period equally, so we must decide what is more important. Should we focus on famous leaders, the "average Joe," or the masses of people? Is one social group, such as men or women or a racial or ethnic group, more important to study than another? Are certain events, such as wars or elections, more important than others? How do we determine what is important? The answers to these questions depend upon our personal philosophy, which is often shaped by the prevailing culture of the society in which we were raised, the priorities of publishers, and the history teachers who trained us.

Providential Philosophy

Speculative Philosophy

Our personal philosophy of the meaning of life, of our role and responsibilities in life, and of how the world really works also has an impact on our historical philosophy, and our historical philosophy helps to determine which historical theories and methods seem most reasonable to us. If we believe that the meaning of life is to fulfill God's plan for us, then we may see the hand of God in the workings of the past and have a "providential" philosophy of history. If we think that our role in life is to improve the world, then we may want to learn from history to improve the world in the present and future, which is a "speculative" philosophy of history. If we think that the world revolves around money, then we may see materialism, or greed, or individual motivation as the main agent driving historical change, but if we think that the world revolves around power, we may see politics and political figures as the main agent of change.

Historical Agency

The issue of historical agency is another source of disagreement among historians. Historical agency refers to whom or what a historian believes to be the primary agent of historical change. Some believe that individuals are free to make their own choices and shape history as they wish. Others believe that social, economic, or cultural forces determine human actions and historical outcomes. Still others believe that supernatural forces are at work. Theories about historical agency greatly shape the methods historians use. For example, if we believe that powerful elites are always the primary agents of change, we may choose a top–down approach, studying famous people by closely analyzing the written documentation they left behind. On the other hand, if we believe that power is in the hands of the large numbers of people, who are the majority of the world's inhabitants, we usually study the masses. Because many of the masses left behind little written evidence, we might need to use a different methodology, quantitatively analyzing information on their lives from census data or some other source. Historical agency, therefore, is an important part of determining a historian's overall methodology and theory of history.

Disagreements over topic, historical agency, and methodology have led to the development of different schools of historical thought over the years. A school of history is an approach to the study of history. Some famous schools of history included in this book are the Empiricist, Progressive, Marxist, Consensus, *Annales*, New left, and Poststructuralist schools. This book will explore these schools of history to help you to identify them when you read them and to select the school which appeals to you the most.

Even as the historical profession emerged in the United States, some historians questioned whether it was possible to be truly objective (meaning unbiased) and

The Objectivity Question scientific about the study of the past. This "objectivity question" is still unresolved. Is history a creative art, and therefore subjective, or is it a "pure" objective science? Some historians and philosophers would argue that all history requires imagination and is therefore somewhat fictional and subjective. These historians are often labeled "skeptics" or "relativists" by other historians who believe that history is nonfiction and scientific. These objectivist or empiricist historians have studied history as a rational analysis and explanation of historical data. Good history in this viewpoint is as objective as possible, and roughly follows the scientific method of raising a historical question, gathering and critically analyzing historical data, making inferences from that data, and drawing logical conclusions. A historian's answer to this question obviously shapes his or her entire approach to history, so the objectivity question is fundamental to any discussion of what history is.

Increasingly, historians have accepted that their questions and approaches are shaped at least to some extent by their own historical context. As E. H. Carr, a British historian, once stated, "History is an unending dialogue between the present and the past."[14] Every new generation of historians asks new questions of the past, questions informed by the current events and experiences shaping their own lives. When and where we are born and live, and our race, class, ethnicity, and gender provide each of us with a unique vantage point or perspective with which to view the world around us and the past. Thus, the generation of American historians who lived through the Civil War asked questions about the causes of the war, the nature of the differences between the North and South, and the nature of slavery. Likewise, historians who lived through the civil rights movement of the 1950s and 1960s asked questions about the origins of racism and revisited questions about the nature and consequences of slavery. Historical context does not alone determine the questions we ask or the topics we choose, but it does influence those choices. Since every historian brings a unique perspective to their study of history, history has constantly evolved over the years, including new topics and exploring old topics with new questions, evidence, and methods.

The Scope of History

In the twentieth century, historians have also disagreed over the scope of historical study. Should it focus only on peoples who have left behind a written record or should it include all peoples, using whatever evidence is available? Should it include the history of things outside of the human experience? A new movement in history, called *Big History* "Big History," urges historians to study the history of the universe and everything in it, because this provides an essential context for any more specific history of human beings. But an individual historian cannot possibly study the history of everything and must therefore decide upon what is most important to study. Many historians leave it

---

[14]E. H. Carr, *What Is History* (Harmondsworth: Penguin, 1964), 30.

to astrophysicists to study the universe and geologists to study the history of the earth, and archeologists and anthropologists to study the history of nonliterate humans. Historians have disagreed on this question for centuries, but once again, this issue shapes every historian's approach to history.

The scope of history is a hotly debated subject, but a discussion of the common differences between history and other disciplines, what history is not, is useful to give us some perspective on the issue. History was not considered its own separate academic discipline until the late nineteenth century. Before that, history was included in other disciplines, such as philosophy, rhetoric, literature, and legal studies. In the late nineteenth century, however, history emerged in the new university systems in Europe and the United States, along with a host of other historical and social sciences. In fact, history shares much in common with these other sciences.

Museum Science and Archeology   Museum science and archeology, for example, are historical sciences as well, but how is history different from these? The methodology and sources of history are what primarily distinguishes it from the other historical sciences. While archeology and museum science rely primarily on material sources, or artifacts, historians rely more on written documents, and focus more on interpreting these documents to understand the chronology of human events, causes and effects, and other patterns, generalizations, or lessons we can draw from past human experience. Despite these slight differences in emphasis, all three historical sciences draw data from each other and often overlap in methods and sources. For example, museums may draw heavily from archeology and history, and historians frequently use archeology to supplement their research.

Geography and Sociology   History also overlaps with other academic disciplines in many ways, but it most closely parallels cultural geography, sociology, and anthropology, and all four of the disciplines have shaped each other as they have evolved since the nineteenth century. All are empirically based and study human societies, but they usually use different methods and approaches. Cultural geographers, for example, typically focus on how geographical features shape societies, while historians generally include a number of other factors, including events, individuals, and other historically specific phenomena. Although sociology may study society in the past and may discuss changes over time, most sociological research investigates a specific society at a particular point in time, either today or in the past. Historians, on the other hand, normally study how society changes over time, and this always entails at least a partial focus on the past. Sociology also tends to focus primarily upon social structures, while history includes a wider range of topics, including individual actions, events, and technology.

Anthropology   Anthropology studies the whole of human experience, tracing the social and cultural evolution of humankind, including prehistoric peoples and the development of humanoid beings on earth. History, on the other hand, focuses primarily on those human beings who have developed writing and left behind texts to analyze. Anthropology is usually more holistic than history, viewing all aspects of society as interrelated. Anthropologists, consequently, tend to study specific individual societies at one point in time to develop the whole picture. Historians typically study one part of society, such as a political or social institution, an individual, or an event, and trace it over time, attempting to answer the questions of what changed and why.

Ethnohistory

Since the latter half of the twentieth century, the lines separating archeology, geography, sociology, anthropology, and history have blurred somewhat. Historical sociology and ethnohistory are hybrid branches of history, which explicitly unite these branches of study, and have become increasingly popular since the 1970s. Historical sociology merged into social history in the United States, and will be discussed in a later chapter, but ethnohistory developed into its own branch of history after the 1950s, when historians and anthropologists working on American Indian history founded the journal *Ethnohistory*. Ethnohistory takes an explicitly interdisciplinary approach, including linguistics and archeology, as well as anthropology and history, to study peoples who left behind few written records. While many historians appreciate the benefits of interdisciplinary approaches, others assert that without document analysis, this is not history. This ongoing argument is shaped by different definitions of history, which are in turn shaped by philosophies of history.

The Philosophy of History

Our own experiences, sense of right and wrong, and beliefs about the meaning of life, and what is valuable to us, all shape our personal philosophies, and our philosophies in turn shape the kind of histories we want to read and write. Although historical philosophy is personal and individualized, we can group different historians into schools of philosophical thought according to why they studied history.

Popular History

For many people, the main reason for studying history is for pleasure. It is intrinsically interesting to learn stories about exciting events and to uncover hidden knowledge from the past. The study of history for history's sake has always been with us and probably always will. The entertainment value of history continues to be extremely important today as the number of films about historical events and figures grows, and audiences make them blockbusters and award-winners. Historical programming on television abounds and history books continue to top book-selling charts. The best-seller and blockbuster histories are usually narratives, or chronological stories, emphasizing the individual characters, the drama, and the exciting events of the past. This is what sells.[15]

Academic History

Academic historians, on the other hand, view this kind of popular history as oversimplified and sensationalized to the point of creating gross distortions about the past. While popular historians are most interested in telling a good story, and helping people to connect with the past and gain a better sense of identification with their heritage, academic historians are generally trained to be more critical in their investigation of the past, attempting to make popular memory as accurate as possible. Obviously, academic historians are often at odds with popular historians.

---

[15]David Starkey, "What History Should We Be Teaching in Britain in the 21st Century?" Plenary lecture given at the Institute of Historical Research Conference on History in British Education (February 14, 2005), *Institute of Historical Research*, http://www.history.ac.uk/education/conference/starkey.html (accessed August 23, 2009).

While popular historians emphasize the entertainment value of history and academic historians emphasize the critical thinking skills and value of knowing the truth about past events, those in control of public education curricula demand additional reasons for requiring students to take history courses. State legislatures and boards of education normally determine history curricula in the United States, but the federal government sometimes intervenes as well. Politicians in the United States have long defended the importance of history, especially U.S. history, in our public education system. They argue that all Americans must be taught the fundamental ideals and institutions of our country so that they can be better citizens, who contribute meaningfully to the democratic system of reforming and improving those institutions. This nationalist justification for the study of history has a long history in itself and has been used by politicians in many countries, seeking to build a sense of national unity and patriotism among their citizens by teaching them their common past. Nationalist philosophies of history usually focus on nation-states and their governments as the topic of study, assuming that political leaders and developments are the most important agents of change. This approach is a natural extension of their goal of providing students with a positive portrait of their government and leaders so that students will feel national pride and have role models of good citizens to follow. It should come as no surprise that national political histories have been the favorite genre of history for politicians and governments for centuries.

This agenda has led to a proliferation of historians who specialize in national histories. In the United States, more historians write about U.S. history than any other nation or topic. Likewise, in other countries, most of their historians focus on their own nation's histories. In the twentieth century, however, increased globalization has led to more interest in studying other nations, and regional and global studies. This trend toward global history is discussed in Chapter 9.

Moral Philosophy
Similar to politicians, religious moralists often view history as essential for providing role models to reinforce good morals and acceptable religious beliefs. Religious leaders need to convince their followers that God exists and that they are indeed guiding the followers in carrying out "God's will." History can be a powerful tool in converting followers to a particular religion by showing God's workings in the past and providing proof that the religious leaders are in fact blessed by God. Religious leaders also look to history to find role models of moral behavior, who conform to their particular religious beliefs, to help teach their followers the proper way to live their lives. Throughout the ages, religious and moral philosophers have used historical role models in this fashion, drawing lessons from the lives of saints and sinners, demonstrating the right and wrong ways to act.

Identity History
Another basic reason for studying history, common to many historians, is the belief that it helps us to understand ourselves, our beliefs, and lives by comparing our lives to those from different times and places. It also helps us to understand our neighbors on this planet. By studying individual and collective histories, we gain a better understanding of the people in our community so that we can better work with them. History gives us a stronger sense of continuity with the past, a feeling of belonging: valuable emotions in a world in which many feel socially isolated and alone.

This is one reason why identity-group histories, such as African American or Native American history, have become so popular. Helping us to identify with others is only one way that history gives us a better sense of perspective. The facts that the past is different from the present, that things change over time, and that historical context shapes our lives in the past and present help us to see that change is possible, and to comprehend how change happens.

History not only helps shape our identity and perspective, but also helps us to improve our lives, allowing us to learn the mechanisms of cause and effect, and learn from the mistakes of those who came before us. This is a very important and ancient reason for the study of history: the desire to apply lessons from the past to improve the future. We need to study history so that we do not "rediscover the wheel" as the saying goes. We can learn from past mistakes and successes, and build upon these historical foundations. Another way of stating this justification was coined by George Santayana: those who forget about the past are condemned to repeat it.

These types of reasons for studying history hint at our hopes of somehow predicting and controlling the future. Policy makers, social activists, and many others who want to change our society to achieve their goals look to history's lessons for how to enact this change. For example, if someone wants to end poverty, they look to the causes (or history) of poverty to understand the problem in order to create better solutions. Motivated to influence change in the present and future, some historians have devoted their lives to studying and understanding patterns of change in the past. *Speculative Philosophy* This speculative philosophy of history has attracted many historians throughout the centuries. For example, Karl Marx studied history in his quest to understand and remedy powerlessness and poverty among the European working classes. Similarly, feminist historians have looked for the roots of powerlessness and inequality among women in order to understand current gender inequality and create a more egalitarian future. Indeed, many people see this desire to use the past to improve the future as the primary reason for learning history.

There is a danger, however, in speculative history. Its assumption that one can predict the future based on patterns of the past can be oversimplified and misguided. The past *is* different from the present, and the exact conditions of the past are never precisely duplicated in the present or future. Since exact historical conditions are never replicated, applying lessons from the past is risky business. For example, you may discover that factors A, B, and C (e.g., the Versailles Peace Treaty, the rise of totalitarian dictators, and global economic crisis) led to World War II, and predict that if factors A, B, and C occur again, we will have another world war. Historians, however, are not all-knowing and all-seeing, so they can never know all of the factors leading up to and shaping the origins of World War II. If even one factor is unaccounted for, or if there is even one new factor shaping conditions in the present and future, the entire equation fails. Arguably, present and future conditions are never identical to those of the past, so these types of equations are always educated guesses at best. Still, educated guesses are better than uneducated guesses, or no attempt to improve the world at all. Given this, speculative history will probably continue to be a popular philosophy of history for many years to come.

One might argue that studying philosophy would help students no matter what profession they choose because all people are and have always been guided by their own personal philosophies, whether they consciously recognize them or not. All humans confront the meaning of life and death at some point in their life. They wonder if they have a purpose in their life and what happens to people when they die. They wonder what really makes the world go around. All of these are philosophical questions, and our answers to these questions profoundly affect the way we view history and why we study it. It makes sense to understand at least our own philosophy, so that we can better define our own approach to history and its relationship to those of other historians. As such, historical philosophy is one of the most important elements in the study of historiography.

How to Study Historiography

The main goal of this reader is to introduce students to different historical philosophies and approaches, and to help them to identify these in their own approaches to history and those of other historians. Students should use the introductions to gain a basic understanding of the historical approaches described in the chapter, and to understand the historical context of the excerpts which follow, using this information to analyze the excerpts. Similar to the analysis of primary sources, the analysis of historical monographs can be compared to the work of a crime scene detective or private investigator. We read carefully, looking for clues to find the hidden meanings underneath the surface. Although all writing is informed by the author's perspective, theories, and purposes, most historians do not bluntly state their personal worldview, philosophy, or historical theories. The historiographer, therefore, must reconstruct the underlying philosophies and theories by looking for clues in the word-choice, organization, or topic of the monograph. This can be a complicated process, but to help students who are new to historiography, this process has been broken down into five basic steps, which are included in the worksheet in *Appendix A*.

The *first* important step in determining the approach or perspective a historian brings to his or her work is to identify her or his historical, social, cultural, and political context. We should find out as much as we can about the authors of our sources in order to appreciate how their own time, place, and preferences might have shaped their historical analyses. The Internet can be an excellent quick reference for finding information on authors. At a minimum, we can discover what other books they may have written, and when and where they lived. This information alone should tell us if the authors are experienced in the field and which philosophies or ideas to which they had access.

The *second* step of determining the topic is relatively easy. Very often the topic of a text is obvious from its title. When the topic is not immediately obvious, authors usually introduce the topic in the first paragraph or two of their work.

The *third* step of uncovering the historian's methodology is more difficult. Most historians use the empirical method of objectively analyzing primary and secondary sources in finding the answer to their question. But there are many different kinds of empirical methodology. For example, social scientific methodology analyzes large amounts quantitative or statistical data to make generalizations about social groups, oral history methods utilize interviews to reconstruct or interpret the past, and Rankean methods closely analyze political records from archives to uncover information about the inner-workings of governments. Often the evidence a historian uses reveals the methodology employed. In most recent histories, the evidence is explicitly included in reference notes. From these, we may ascertain whether the author used primary or secondary sources, and the sort of sources used give us further indication of the approach, methodology, or philosophy of the historian. For example, if the historian uses primarily census records or other quantifiable data, he or she may be a quantitative social historian and historians who had used government documents and other sources written by political figures are probably approaching their topic from a political perspective. This reader will explore many different methods so that students may better identify which methodology is being used.

Monograph   The *fourth* step, finding the thesis, is also often difficult. The thesis is the historian's main argument. In a typical monograph, or historical study focusing on one specific question or topic, it is introduced near the beginning of the work, is supported by evidence throughout, and is proven in the conclusion. In other monographs, however, it is more hidden, emerging only at the end of the work, or is complex, illogical, or contradicts the evidence. Discovering the thesis of a work, however, is essential to understanding and evaluating the overall monograph. This process will not only help us to comprehend the historical philosophy and method, but will help us to recognize them in other monographs we read.

Finally, determining the theory or philosophy at the heart of a historical monograph is often the most difficult step of analyzing this type of source. Most often, historians do not explicitly discuss their personal philosophy, approach, methods, or theories. These may be deduced, however, by analyzing their use of evidence, their interpretation of the evidence, and their thesis, in the context of the author's identity and historical context. For example, if a historian lived in the United States in the 1920s wrote about economic origins of historical developments and included perspectives from multiple segments of society, that historian would most likely be a Progressive historian. On the other hand, if a historian lived in France in the 1980s and analyzed discourses about medieval carnivals in order to reconstruct the meanings of these events, that historian would most likely be labeled a New Cultural historian. This reader will explore the most important philosophies and theories used by historians in the United States so that students will be equipped to identify and understand how these theories and philosophies have shaped the works they read.

This five-step process is designed to simplify the complicated process of critically analyzing secondary sources, which is at the heart of historiographical practice. It is hoped that students will use the worksheet provided to apply this process in making sense not only of the excerpts in this reader, but of all historical works they read. Studying historiography, the theories, philosophies, and approaches of historians throughout time will help in understanding the historical profession in the United States and the overall practice of history itself.

Part I: Historiography in Europe to 1900

Chapter 1

Early Histories

Busts of Herodotus and Thucydides (*Courtesy of the Library of Congress*).

For Europeans, the transition from mythopoetic narrative to stories about the past that we would now recognize as "history" began in sixth-century B.C.E. Greece (Hellas), where a philosophical revolution was taking place. In the midst of nearly continuous wars between the Greeks and the Persian and the various Greek city-states, and a series of civil wars, Greek thinkers strove to bring order to their chaotic world and develop new solutions to age-old questions. Greek philosophers moved beyond merely accepting traditional knowledge as the truth and began to use their own logic and reason to explain the universe. The most famous Greek philosophers, such as Socrates and Aristotle, began using a new inquiry-based method which applied deductive reasoning[1] and observable evidence to all questions. Preserved and transmitted to the rest of Europe and the Mediterranean world by the Greek and Roman empires, their method of asking questions, formulating hypotheses, and testing their theories with observations became the basis for modern Western notions of humanism, rationalism, and the scientific method. This had a revolutionary impact on many fields, but especially on the study of the past. Greco-Roman historians, and their Early Christian and Muslim descendants, now attempted to re-create the human past as accurately as possible by using observable evidence and reason to support their arguments. Their approaches and theories became the foundation for the study of history in the Middle East, Europe, and the United States.

The Greek Revolution

Classical Greeks called the scientific study of the past "historia." The word derives from "histor," which is related to the words for "to see" and "to inquire."[2] In the Greek mind, therefore, historians were considered to be part soothsayers, who study the past to predict the future, and part bards, creating epic poetry in the tradition of Homer. Indeed, *Clio* the Greek muse of history Clio was also the muse of poetry. Many Greeks to this day consider Homer to be their first historian. All we know of him has been handed down through the generations. Homer was supposedly a traveling poet, or bard, who made his living by telling exciting stories to his audiences. The first written copies of these stories appeared in Athens in the sixth century B.C.E., making it difficult to pinpoint the author, much less the accuracy of the stories. The two most famous stories attributed to Homer are *The Iliad* and *The Odyssey*, which told the story of early Greek heroes, gods, goddesses, and the famous Battle of Troy. Homer's stories of the early Greek past were widely known by the fifth century B.C.E. in Greece and spread throughout the Mediterranean world in the next several centuries. As mythopoetic narratives, however, *Homer* Homer's stories bear little resemblance to the kind of history practiced in the United States today. The revolutionary shift in Greek historical thinking took place in the fifth century B.C.E., with the emergence of historians who criticized Homer's lack of observable evidence and applied rationalist methods to their own study of the past.

---

[1]Deductive reasoning starts with a general premise or hypothesis and uses that to deduce specific conclusions. For example, the statement "it is dark outside at night" is a general premise, and from that we could deduce that if an event happened at night, it would have happened in darkness unless artificial light was provided.

[2]Francis Hartog, "The Invention of History: From Homer to Herodotus," *History and Theory* 39 (2000): 384–395, reprinted in Q. Edward Wang and Georg G. Iggers, *Turning Points in Historiography: A Cross-Cultural Perspective* (Rochester, NY: University of Rochester Press, 2002), 28.

Herodotus   Herodotus (c. 484–425 B.C.E.) was the first Greek to break away from the mythopoetic tradition and forge a new path in historiography. Herodotus was born in Halicarnassus, a Greek town on the western coast of modern Turkey, where the revolution in Greek thought began. He lived in Athens and various other Greek cities, where he was exposed to the ideas of Socrates and other leaders of the Greek philosophical revolution. He traveled widely across the Mediterranean, and died sometime after 420 B.C.E. in exile in Thurii, an Athenian colony in southern Italy. Like most of his contemporaries, Herodotus admired Homer, but he criticized Homer for his lack of observable evidence. Like most Greek rationalists of his day, Herodotus attempted to study the world through observable evidence. As a consequence, the primary agents of history in his work were observable forces: human activities and cultures.

Herodotus' only surviving work is *The Histories*, which was written while he was in exile. The Greco-Persian War is the main topic of this work, but it includes chapters on other cultures in the Mediterranean. Rather than focus simply on the political leaders and generals, Herodotus provides extensive descriptions of the various cultures of the Mediterranean, attempting to explain the origin of the wars as a cultural conflict. It is no coincidence that Herodotus chose this event as his subject. He was born in Ionia, where the war began, and this war was the most important event to affect his own life. With little written documentation available, gathering reliable evidence on events from the distant past was difficult, if not impossible. By studying an event which occurred in his own lifetime, in his own region of the world, Herodotus was able to use eyewitness accounts as his evidence, thus making his history more reliable than other stories of past events. Herodotus was interested not only in describing what happened, when, and where, but also in explaining why it happened, another key feature of history as we now know it. Herodotus' methods of gathering evidence and applying it to historical questions about past human events became the foundation for history as it was to be practiced in Western Civilization for the next two thousand years.

While Herodotus may be the father of cultural history in the West, and one of the earliest Greeks to apply scientific methods to the study of the past, it was up to another
Thucydides   Greek, Thucydides (c. 460–400 B.C.E.), to make a clear break from mythopoetic storytelling and question the credibility of his sources. Thucydides was born in Halimous, southwest of Athens in Greece. He lived in Athens when the war with Sparta broke out in 431 B.C.E., lived through the plague, was elected a general, and was banished from Athens after losing an important battle with the Spartans. Exiled in Thrace, he began writing his history of the war between Sparta and Athens, but died in 400 B.C.E. before he could complete his masterpiece *The History of the Peloponnesian War*. It is divided into eight books, chronologically covering the war from its beginning to the twenty-first year of the war. It is primarily a military and political history, but he does set it within the larger context of other events affecting Greece during the war. He includes numerous detailed battlefield accounts and speeches to support his overarching narration of the war.

Even more so than Herodotus, Thucydides studied the actions of men, as opposed to supernatural forces, and used credible, observable evidence to establish a factual account of the past. Thucydides criticized Herodotus not only for his inclusion of unobservable forces, but also for wasting his time studying issues of little importance. For Thucydides, political forces were the driving forces of history, not cultural forces. In his view, the main reason for studying history was speculative: to understand political events, such as the causes and courses of wars, in order to apply this information to making future policy decisions. Like Herodotus, however, Thucydides studied an event (the war between Sparta and Athens), which took place in his own lifetime and in his own region of the world. Reliable eyewitness accounts, therefore, were readily available and could be analyzed and used to re-create a precise account of the event. Thucydides, himself, was an eyewitness in the wars, serving as a military general for part of the conflict. In fact, Thucydides included over thirty speeches in his history, most of which he reconstructed from memory, to tell the story of the war. Thucydides' emphasis on cause and effect, political history, and observable forces greatly influenced ideas about history in Western Civilization.

While Herodotus and Thucydides founded the Western tradition of history, their methods did not immediately dominate the study of the past in Greece or the rest of Europe. Homeric tales and other more entertaining versions of the past continued to be the most popular types of history, while Thucydidean history appealed primarily to the political and scholarly elite. Writing a few generations later in the fourth century B.C.E., the great philosopher Aristotle criticized Thucydidean history as the mere recitation of facts.[3] He considered mythopoetic stories to be more important because they were imaginative and creative, and contained deeper insight to the truth than did dry *Skeptics* factual accounts of the past. Another branch of Greek philosophers, the skeptics, went even further, claiming that since all knowledge is the perception of the individual, no one truth about anything, much less past events, could be discerned. In this view, scientific history was no more factual than mythopoetic history.

Despite these disparaging views, the ideas of Herodotus and Thucydides spread throughout Europe and the Middle East, as the Greek Empire grew under the expansionistic policies of Alexander the Great. As a consequence, Hellenic culture and Hellenic history dominated much of the Mediterranean world and Southwest Asia between the fourth and first century B.C.E.

Roman Historiography

When the Romans engulfed the Greek Empire, they too copied the Greek method of historical inquiry, just as they copied many other Greek practices. Ancient Romans had their own biographical tradition of storytelling, but they eventually adopted some elements of Greek methodology. Roman histories generally focused on Rome's rise to power, attributing its success to the character of its political leaders, fair policies, strong political institutions, and fate.[4]

---

[3]Beverley Southgate, *History: What and Why: Ancient, Modern, and Postmodern Perspectives* (New York: Routledge, 1998), 14.

[4]Ibid., 46–48.

Polybius   Famed Greco-Roman historian, Polybius, directly connects the Greek tradition to Roman historiography. Polybius (c. 200 B.C.E.) was born in Greece, but as a young man lived as a well-treated hostage in Rome, while Rome was overtaking the Greek Empire. A great admirer of Rome, in his great work *The Rise of the Roman Empire* Polybius used the methods of Thucydides to explain and justify Rome's rise to power. He proclaimed this a "universal history," a history of the known world, with the Roman Empire at its center. Like Herodotus and Thucydides, his was essentially a contemporary history and attempted to express a truthful accounting of the subject.

Tacitus   Other Roman historians, such as Tacitus (c. 56–120 C.E.), also professed to maintain strict objectivity in their interpretations. Tacitus' motto, *sine ira et studio*, pledged to write without hatred or political bias.[5] His works, *The Annals* and *The Histories*, however, were clearly influenced by his own personal involvement in the events he described. Tacitus was a senator writing on the lives of the Roman emperors from the death of Augustus to Domitian (14–96 C.E.), and his political opinions clearly shaped his assessment of each ruler. Still, this was a step in the direction of modern notions of objectivity.

Similar to Thucydides, Roman historians focused on political agency and relied heavily on eyewitness accounts and speeches as their evidence. Their emphasis on *Fate* "fate" (also called "destiny" or "fortune"), however, set them apart from the Greek tradition. While they did not go so far as to give agency to specific gods, classical Roman historians considered fate, an unseen, nonobservable supernatural force, to explain certain historical events. By continuing to use the basic methods and ideas of Thucydides and Herodotus, however, Roman historians proved essential in spreading Greek historical methods to the rest of Europe and the farthest reaches of the Roman Empire.

Early Christian Historiography

Western historiography took an even more dramatic turn way from secular history as a result of the emergence and spread of the Christian religion within the Roman Empire. With its epicenter located in the Roman Province of Judea, Christianity was shaped by Judaism, as well as by Greco-Roman culture, but Christian historians added a unique twist to historiography. From the very beginning, history was essential to the Christian religion, just as it was to Judaism. The Gospels and Acts of the Apostles in the Christian Bible (New Testament), similar to the Jewish Bible, are essentially historical narratives.[6] History helped Christians not only to convert new followers and instruct fellow Christians by telling the history of Jesus of Nazareth and his followers, but also to defend Christianity from its enemies and prove that the ideas of the early Christian church were a direct succession from Jesus' apostles. Christians saw the

---

[5]Ibid., 67.

[6]Carl T. McIntire, "History: Christian Views," in *Encyclopedia of Religion*, vol. 6, 2nd ed., ed. Lindsay Jones (Detroit: Macmillan Reference, 2005), 4052.

world as divided into two: good and evil, the sacred and the secular, the age Before Christ (B.C.) and the age of Christ (Anno Domini or A.D.). This duality informed their historical perspectives. These perspectives made Christian history different from its Judaic and Greco-Roman predecessors.

Eusebius   Eusebius (275–339), an early Bishop in the Christian church and confidante of Roman Emperor Constantine, was a leader in shaping this new Christian historical philosophy. Like Greco-Roman histories, Eusebius's *Chronicle* and *Ecclesiastical History* used credible evidence such as eyewitness accounts, speeches, and written documents to support his arguments. Eusebius, however, had a different motive for writing his histories and this clearly showed in his choice of topics and interpretation of events. His *Chronicle* attempted to validate the main events of the Old Testament by aligning them with ancient Egyptian, Assyrian, and Greek chronologies, and placing them all in relation to the life of Christ. His Christian chronology became the basis for the European understanding of ancient history for the next several centuries.[7] Eusebius's *Ecclesiastical History* was similarly influential as it recorded the "official" Christian version of the early history of the Christian church. He saw history as the unfolding of God's will, and the Christian church as predestined to be victorious over its evil enemies and become the official religion of the Roman Empire (as he witnessed in his own lifetime). Like earlier Roman historians, therefore, Eusebius and

Providential   other Christian historians retained a providential philosophy of history, viewing des-
History   tiny as the driving force of historical change. Eusebius's Christian moral philosophy and motivations for writing, however, clearly distinguished his history.

As the Roman Empire crumbled and Christianity struggled to survive and spread, Christian historians continued to emphasize the importance of religion, specifically the power of the Christian God, in the history of mankind. As one of the most important

Augustine   Christian philosophers of all time, Augustine of Hippo in North Africa (354–430) had an enormous impact on Christian historiography. Augustine's *City of God*, written in the fifth century, envisioned all of history as a recurrent conflict between the City of God (the sacred) and the City of this World (the profane).[8] In this way, history was cyclical, but also linear in that God's will for humankind was unfolding from creation toward the Second Coming of Christ (the end). Even more so than Eusebius, Augustine imagined supernatural forces (God and Satan) as primary agents in history. The Augustinian version of the world dominated European scholarship throughout the Middle Ages.

As Christianity spread to the northernmost reaches of the former Roman Empire, Christian monasteries became centers of learning and among the primary producers of history in the Middle Ages. The most important monk-historian in

Bede   England in this period was the "Venerable" Bede (673–735). Bede lived in the eighth century when Christianity was still displacing the original beliefs of the ancient tribes of Britain. He was raised and lived most of his life in monasteries in northern England. There he learned to read and write Latin, and through this language

---

[7]Ernst Breisach, *Historiography: Ancient, Medieval, and Modern*, 2nd ed. (Chicago, IL: University of Chicago Press, 1994), 82.

[8]McIntire, "History," 4053.

of the Roman Empire and the Western Christian church, was able to access many documents relating to the history of the Christian church and prominent people in the British Isles. Bede wanted to preserve the history of the heroes of the Christian church in Britain, and use their lives as role models for other Christians. He spent many years compiling information on the introduction and spread of Christianity in the British Isles, focusing primarily on the role of religious and political leaders. He gathered information from a variety of written and oral sources, examining their reliability in his attempt to present the events as accurately as possible. He completed his *History of the English Church and People* in 731.[9] This work is an excellent representation of Christian historiography and is also important as an early example of a national history. It not only promoted the Christian church, but also promoted an early sense of national unity in England by giving all its citizens common English heroes and a sense of a common past. English Kings quickly realized the powerful potential of his work and had it translated into the English vernacular, making Bede's *History* much more popular than the works of other monks. Bede's *History* shaped English historiography for centuries afterward.

Monmouth

Only a handful of histories in the Greco-Roman tradition were written in Europe in the centuries after Bede. Some were narratives about the past, but were only loosely based on real events and evidence. For example, Geoffrey of Monmouth's (c. 1100–1155) *History of the Kings of England* is more accurately described as historical fiction. He claimed to have written it as a translation of a very old Welsh book, but there is no evidence that the book ever existed. Monmouth's book is most famous for telling the story of King Arthur and the Knights of the Round Table, most of which was pieced together from local legends. Despite its lack of supporting sources, this story continues to be told and believed by many today.

Chronicle

Another more popular form of describing the past in the later Middle Ages was the chronicle. Chronicles were lists of events arranged in chronological order. They originated as calendars, kept by monasteries and businesses. Some of the more famous national chronicles include *The Anglo-Saxon Chronicle* and the *Grandes Chroniques de France*, but most chronicles were more local in focus, often listing events in a specific town or monastery. Chronicles included a variety of facts, such as deaths and successions of popes and other church officials and kings, as well as natural disasters and battles, but they are not narratives, have no explanatory connections between the entries, no explanations of cause and effect, or why things happen, and consequently are not normally considered "history."[10]

Comnena

The Greco-Roman approach to history remained strong, however, in the Byzantine and Islamic empires throughout the Middle Ages. Byzantine historians continued on in the Thucydidean tradition, focusing on political events, observable forces, and evidence. One Byzantine historian, Anna Comnena (1081–1118), was

---

[9]Leo Sherley-Price, *Introduction to a History of the English Church and People.* Revised by R. E. Lathem (Harmondsworth, England: Penguin Books, 1984) (Copyright: Leo Sherley-Price), 15–16.

[10]John Burrow, *A History of Histories: Epics, Chronicles, Romances and Inquiries from Herodotus and Thucydides to the Twentieth Century* (New York: Alfred A. Knopf, 2008), 218–219.

especially notable for being the first female historian in Europe. She was the daughter of Emperor Alexius and her histories focused on the wars and political events of his reign. Although she used Greek methods, she was not too concerned about the reliability of her sources or her own objectivity in interpreting them. Still, her *Alexiad* influenced Byzantine histories for many generations.[11]

In the Middle Eastern and North African areas of the former Roman Empire, Islam replaced Christianity as the dominant religion after 700 C.E. Muslim historians, however, did not always emphasize God (or Al'Lah) as the primary agent in history. Following more directly in the footsteps of Thucydides and Tacitus, Muslim historians stressed human agency in the rise and fall of civilizations. While there were many important Muslim historians, the most famous of these is 'Abd-ar-Rahman Abu Zaid Wali-ad-Din Ibn Khaldun (1332–1395 C.E.). Ibn Khaldun's family originally came from southern Arabia, but had migrated to Spain and finally Tunis in North Africa before he was born.[12]

Ibn Khaldun   Ibn Khaldun was a devout Muslim, and like all Muslim scholars, was trained in the Qur'an. Well-educated, he was a legal scholar, judge, professor, and advisor to rulers at various times in his life. Like his Christian contemporaries, he sought to defend his religion from its critics, legitimize the authority of his political leaders, and glorify God through his work. Unlike many Christian and Muslim scholars, however, he studied secular events and emphasized human agency, specifically group feeling, as the true force behind history. His most famous work was *The Muqaddimah* ("the Introduction"), which explains his historical theories and methodology, and applies them to the history of the Islamic world. Although political forces, such as rulers, wars, taxes, and laws, play an important role in this history, social relationships, ethnic identities, and cultural and economic factors were the driving forces of historical change. While few historians in Western Europe knew of Comnena and Ibn Khaldun, they provide the link between the Greco-Roman historical tradition and those of modern Eastern Europe and the Middle East.

Early Greek, Roman, and Christian histories forged a new way of thinking and writing about the past. Because of their emphasis on rational explanation and observable human events, history emerged in Europe as a practice distinct from poetry and mythology. As such, these early histories laid the foundations for Western historiography.

Herodotus, *The Histories*

Book One

Herodotus of Halicarnassus here displays his inquiry, so that human achievements may not become forgotten in time, and great and marvelous deeds—some displayed by Greeks, some by barbarians—may not be without their glory; and especially to show why the two peoples fought with each other.

---

[11]James V. Spickard et al., *History by the World's Historians* (Boston: McGraw-Hill, 1997), 213.
[12]Ibid., 235.

Learned Persians put the responsibility for the quarrel on the Phoenicians. These people came originally from so-called Red Sea; and as soon as they had penetrated to the Mediterranean and settled in the country where they are today, they took to making long trading voyages. Loaded with Egyptian and Assyrian goods, they called at various places along the coast, including Argos, in those days the most important place in the land now called Hellas [Greece].

Here in Argos they displayed their wares, and five or six days later when they were nearly sold out, a number of women came down to the beach to see the fair. Amongst these was the king's daughter, whom Greek and Persian writers agree in calling Io, daughter of Inachus. These women were standing about near the vessel's stern, buying what they fancied, when suddenly the Phoenician sailors passed the word along and made a rush at them. The greater number got away; but Io and some others were caught and bundled aboard the ship, which cleared at once and made off for Egypt.

This, according to the Persian account (the Greeks have a different story), was how Io came to Egypt; and this was the first in a series of unjust acts...

Such then is the Persian story. In their view it was the capture of Troy that first made them enemies of the Greeks.

As to Io, the Phoenicians do not accept the Persians' account; they deny that they took her to Egypt by force. On the contrary, the girl while she was still in Argos went to bed with the ship's captain, found herself pregnant, and, ashamed to face her parents, sailed away voluntarily to escape exposure.

So much for what Persians and Phoenicians say; I have no intention of passing judgment on its truth or falsity. I prefer to rely on my own knowledge, and to point out who it was in actual fact that first injured the Greeks; then I will proceed with my history, telling the story as I go along of small cities of men no less than of great. For most of those which were great once are small today; and those which used to be small were great in my own time. Knowing, therefore, that human prosperity never abides long in the same place, I shall pay attention to both alike....

Book Two

Cambyses, the son of Cyrus [ruler of the Persian Empire] ... on the ground that he had inherited his father's dominion over the Ionians and Aeloians [Greeks], included them amongst his other subjects in the army he was preparing for an expedition against Egypt.

The next [Egyptian] king after Proteus was Rhampsinitus, who is remembered by the entrance gates which he erected at the western end of the temple of Hephaestus.... Rhampsinitus possessed a vast fortune in silver, so great that no subsequent king came anywhere near it—let alone surpassed it.... Another story I heard about Rhampsinitus was, that at a later period he descended alive into what the Greeks call Hades, and there played dice with Demeter [Greek goddess of grain and fertility], sometimes winning and sometimes losing, and returned to earth with a golden cloth which she had given him as a present. I was told that to mark his descent into the underworld and subsequent return, the Egyptians instituted a festival, which they certainly continued to celebrate in my own day—though I cannot state with confidence that the reason for it is what it was said to be. The priests weave a robe, taking one day only over the process; then they bandage the eyes of one of their number, put the robe into his hands, and lead him to the road which runs to

Source: The Histories, by Herodotus, translated by Aubrey De Sélincourt, revised with introductory matter and notes by John Marincola (Penguin Classics 1954, Second revised edition 1996). Translation copyright 1954 by Aubrey de Sélincourt. This revised edition copyright © John Marincola, 1996. Reproduced by permission of Penguin Books, Ltd.

the temple of Demeter. Here they leave him, and it is supposed that he is escorted to the temple, twenty furlongs from the city, by two wolves which afterwards bring him back to where they found him. Anyone may believe these Egyptian tales, if he is sufficiently credulous; as for myself, I keep to the general plan of this book, which is to record the traditions of the various nations just as I heard them related to me.

The Egyptians say that Demeter and Dionysus [Greek god of wine] are the chief powers in the underworld; and they were also the first people to put forward the doctrine of the immortality of the soul, and to maintain that after death it enters another creature at the moment of that creature's birth. It then makes the round of all living things—animals, birds, and fish— until finally passes once again, at birth, into the body of a man. The whole period of transmigration occupies three thousand years. This theory has been adopted by certain Greek writers some earlier, some later, who have put it forward as their own. Their names are known to me, but I refrain from mentioning them. Up to the time of Rhampsinitus, Egypt was excellently governed and very prosperous; but his successor Cheops (to continue the account which the priests gave me) brought the country into all sorts of misery.... .

Book Seven

The position, then, was that Xerxes was lying with his force at Trachis in Malian territory, while the Greeks occupied the pass known locally as Pylae—though Thermopylae is the common Greek name. Such were the respective positions of the two armies, one being in control of all the country from Trachis northward, the other of the whole mainland to the south. The Greek force which here awaited the coming of Xerxes was made up of the following contingents: 300 hoplites from Sparta, 500 from Tegea, 500 from Mantinea, 120 from Orchomenus in Arcadia, 1000 from the rest of Arcadia; from Corinth there were 400, from Phlius 200, and from Mycenae 80. In addition to these troops from the Peloponnese,

there were the Boeotian contingents of 700 from Thespiae and 400 from Thebes. The Locrians of Opus and the Phocians had also obeyed the call to arms, the former sending all the men they had, the latter one thousand. The other Greeks had induced these two towns to send troops by a message to the effect that they themselves were merely an advance force, and that the main body of the allies was daily expected; the sea, moreover, was strongly held by the fleet of Athens and Aegina and the other naval forces. Thus there was no cause for alarm—for, after all, it was not a god who threatened Greece, but a man, and there neither was nor ever would be a man who was not born with a good chance of misfortune— and the greater the man, the greater the misfortune. The present enemy was no exception; he too was human, and was sure to be disappointed of his great expectations.

The appeal succeeded, and the Opus and Phocis sent their troops to Trachis. The contingents of the various states were under their own officers, but the most respected was Leonidas the Spartan, who was in command of the whole army. Leonidas traced his descent directly back to Heracles, through Anaxandrides, Eurycrates, Polydorus, Alcamenes, Telechles, Archelaus, Agesilaus, Doryssus, Leobotas, Echestratus, Agis, Eurysthenes, Aristodemus, Aristomachus, Cleodaeus—and so to Hyllus, who was Heracle's son. He had come to be king of Sparta quite unexpectedly, for as he had two elder brothers, Cleomenes and Dorieus, he had no thought of himself succeeding to the throne. Dorieus, however, was killed in Sicily, and when Cleomenes also died without an heir, Leonidas found himself next in the succession. He was older than Cleombrotus, Anaxandrides' youngest son, and was, moreover, married to Cleomenes' daughter. The three hundred men whom he brought on this occasion to Thermopylae were chosen by himself, all fathers of living sons. He also took with him the Thebans I mentioned, under the command of Leontiades, the son of Eurymachus. The reason why he made a special point of taking troops from Thebes, and from Thebes only, was that the Thebes were strongly suspected of Persian sympathies, so he called upon them to pay their part in the war in order to see if they would answer the call, or openly refuse to join the confederacy. They did send troops, but their sympathy was nevertheless with the enemy. Leonidas and his three hundred were sent by Sparta in advance of the main army, in order that the sight of them might encourage the other confederates to fight and prevent them from going over to the enemy, as they were quite capable of doing if they knew that Sparta was hanging back; the intention was, when the Carneia was over (for it was that festival which prevented the Spartans from taking the field in the ordinary way), to leave a garrison in the city and march with all the troops at their disposal. The other allied states proposed to act similarly.

On the Spartan side it was a memorable fight; they were men who understood war pitted against an inexperienced enemy, and amongst the feints they employed was to turn their backs in a body and pretend to be retreating in confusion, whereupon the enemy would pursue them with a great clatter and roar; but the Spartans, just as the Persians were on them, would wheel and face them and inflict in the new struggle innumerable casualties. The Spartans had their losses too, but not many. At last the Persians, finding that their assaults upon the pass, whether by divisions or by any other way they could think of, were all useless, broke off the engagement and withdrew.

How to deal with the situation Xerxes had no idea; but just then, a man from Malis, Ephialtes, the son of Eurydemus, came, in hope of a rich reward, to tell the king about track which led over the hills to Thermopylae—and thus he was to prove the death of the Greeks who held the pass… .

In the course of that fight Leonidas fell, having fought most gallantly, and many distinguished Spartans with him—their names I have learned, as those of men who deserve to be remembered; indeed, I have learned the names of all the three hundred. Amongst the Persian dead, too, were many men of high distinction, including two brothers of Xerxes, Habrocomes and Hyperanthes, sons of Darius by Artanes' daughter Phratagune. Artanes, the son of Hystaspes and grandson of Acsames, was Darius' brother; as Phratagune was his only child, his giving her to Darius was equivalent to giving him his entire estate.

There was a bitter struggle over the body of Leonidas; four times the Greeks drove the enemy off, and at last by their valour rescued it. So it went on, until the troops with Ephialtes were close at hand; and then, when the Greeks knew that they had come, the character of the fighting changed. They withdrew again into the narrow neck of the pass, behind the wall, and took up a position in a single compact body—all except the Thebans—on the little hill at the entrance to the pass, where the stone lion in memory of Leonidas stands today. Here they resisted to the last, with their swords, if they had them, and, if not, with their hands and teeth, until the Persians, coming in from the front over ruins of the wall and closing in from behind, finally overwhelmed them with missile weapons.

Of all the Spartans and Thespians who fought so valiantly the most signal proof of courage was given by the Spartan Dieneces. It is said that before the battle he was told by a native of Trachis that, when the Persians shot their arrows, there were so many of them that they hid the sun. Dieneces, however, quite unmoved by the thought of the strength of the Persian army, merely remarked: "This is pleasant news that the stranger from Trachis brings us: if the Persians hide the sun, we shall have our battle in the shade." He is said to have left on record other sayings, too, of a similar kind, by which he will be remembered. After Dieneces the greatest distinction was won by two Spartan brothers, Alpheus and Maron, the sons of Orsiphantus; and of the Thespians the man to gain the highest glory was a certain Dithyrambus, the son of Harmatides.

The dead were buried where they fell, and with them the men who had been killed before those dismissed by Leonidas left the pass. Over them is the inscription, in honour of the whole force:

Four thousand here from Pelops' land

Against three million once did stand

The Spartans have a special epitaph; it runs:

Go tell the Spartans, you who read:
We took their orders, and here lie dead.

>> Questions for Consideration

1. How does Herodotus attempt to be objective and rational, and include multiple perspectives in this history?
2. In what ways might this history be considered mythopoetic? How does Herodotus attempt to move away from mythopoetic storytelling toward a history based on observable forces?
3. How did Herodotus' worldview shape this history? What knowledge does he assume of his readers?

Thucydides, *The History of the Peloponnesian War*

Book One: Introduction

THUCYDIDES the Athenian wrote the history of the war fought between Athens and Sparta, beginning the account at the very outbreak of the war, in the belief that it was going to be a great war and more worth writing about than any of those which had taken place in the past. My belief was based on the fact that the two sides were at the very height of their power and preparedness, and I saw, too, that the rest of the Hellenic world was committed to one side or the other; even those who were not immediately engaged were deliberating on the courses which they were to take later. This was the greatest disturbance in the history of the Hellenes, affecting also a larger part of the non-Hellenic world, and indeed, I might almost say, the whole of mankind. For though I have found it impossible, because of its remoteness in time, to acquire a really precise knowledge of the distant past or even of the history preceding our own period, yet, after looking back into it as far as I can, all the evidence leads me to conclude that these periods were not great periods either in warfare or in anything else.

It appears, for example, that the country now called Hellas[1] had no settled population in ancient times; instead there was a series of migrations, as the various tribes, being under the constant pressure of invaders who were stronger than they were, were always prepared to abandon their own territory. There was no commerce, and no safe communication either by land or sea; the use they made of their land was limited to the production of necessities, they had no surplus left over for

---

[1] In the Greek language, ancient as well as modern, the name of the country is "Hellas," of the people "Hellenes." "Hellas" included all Greek communities, wherever they were established, but here Thucydides is referring more narrowly to the Greek peninsula.

capital, and no regular system of agriculture, since they lacked the protection of fortifications and at any moment an invader might appear and take their land away from them. Thus, in the belief that the day-to-day necessities of life could be secured just as well in one place as in another, they showed no reluctance in moving from their homes, and therefore built no cities of any size or strength, nor acquired any important resources. Where the soil was most fertile there were the most frequent changes of population, as in what is now called Thessaly, in Boeotia, in most of the Peloponnese (except Arcadia), and in others of the richest parts of Hellas. For in these fertile districts it was easier for individuals to secure greater powers than their neighbors, which in any case were more likely than others to attract the attention of foreign invaders.

It is interesting to observe that Attica, because of the poverty of her soil, was remarkably free from political disunity, has always been inhabited by the same race of people. Indeed, this is an important example of my theory that it was because of migrations that there was uneven development elsewhere; for when people were driven out from other parts of Greece by war or by disturbances, the most powerful of them took refuge in Athens, as being a stable society; then they became citizens, and soon made the city even more populous than it had been before, with the result that later Attica became too small for her inhabitants and colonies were sent out to Ionia... .

Different states encountered different obstacles to the course of their development. The Ionians, for instance, were a rapidly rising power; but King Cyrus and his Persians, having eliminated Croesus, invaded the country between the river Halys and the sea, and brought the Ionian cities on the mainland into the Persian Empire. Later Darius, with the aid of the Phoenician navy, conquered the islands as well.

And in the Hellenic states that were governed by tyrants, the tyrant's first thought was always for himself, for his own personal safety, and for the greatness of his own family. Consequently security was the chief political principle in these governments, and no great action ever came out of them-nothing, in fact, that went beyond their immediate local interests, except for the tyrants in Sicily, who rose to great power. So for a long time the state of affairs everywhere in Hellas was such that nothing very remarkable could be done by any combination of powers and that even the individual cities were lacking in enterprise.

Finally, however, the Spartans put down tyranny in the rest of Greece, most of which had been governed by tyrants for much longer than Athens. From the time when the Dorians first settled in Sparta there had been a particularly long period of political disunity; yet the Spartan constitution goes back to a very early date, and the country has never been ruled by tyrants. For rather more than 400 years, dating from the end of the late war, they have had the same system of government, and this has been not only a source of internal strength, but has enabled them to intervene in the affairs of other states.

Not many years after the end of tyrannies in Hellas the battle of Marathon was fought between the Persians and the Athenians. Ten years later the foreign enemy returned with his vast armada for the conquest of Hellas, and at this moment of peril the Spartans, since they were the leading power, were in command of the allied Hellenic forces. In face of the invasion the Athenians decided to abandon their city; they broke up their homes, took to their ships, and became a people of sailors. It was by a common effort that the foreign invasion was repelled; but not long afterwards the Hellenes—both those who had fought in the war together and those

---

Source: The History of the Peloponnesian War by Thucydides, translated by Rex Warner, with an introduction and notes by M. I. Finley (Penguin Classics 1954, Revised edition 1972). Translation copyright © Rex Warner, 1954. Introduction and Appendices copyright © M. I. Finley, 1972. Reproduced by permission of Penguin Books, Ltd. The footnotes are the translator's.

who later revolted from the King of Persia—split into two divisions, one group following Athens and the other Sparta. These were clearly the two most powerful states, one being supreme on land, the other on the sea. For a short time the war-time alliance held together, but it was not long before quarrels took place and Athens and Sparta, each with her own allies, were at war with each other, while among the rest of the Hellenes states that had their own differences now joined one or the other of the two sides. So from the end of the Persian War till the beginning of the Peloponnesian War, though there were some intervals of peace, on the whole these two Powers were either fighting with each other or putting down revolts among their allies. They were consequently in a high state of military preparedness and had gained their military experience in the hard school of danger.

The Spartans did not make their allies pay tribute, but saw to it that they were governed by oligarchies who would work in the Spartan interest. Athens, on the other hand, had in the course of time taken over the fleets of her allies (except for those of Chios and Lesbos) and had made them pay contributions of money instead. Thus the forces available to Athens alone for this war were greater than the combined forces had ever been when the alliance was still intact.

In investigating past history, and in forming the conclusions which I have formed, it must be admitted that one cannot rely on every detail which has come down to use by way of tradition. People are inclined to accept all stories of ancient times in an uncritical way—even when these stories concern their own native countries. Most people in Athens, for instance, are under the impression that Hipparchus, who was killed by Harmodius and Aristogiton, was tyrant at the time, not realizing that it was Hippias who was the eldest and the chief of the sons of Pisistratus, and the Hipparchus and Thessalus were his younger brothers. What happened was this: on the very day that had been fixed for their attempt, indeed at the very last moment, Harmodius and

Aristogeiton had reason to believe that Hippias had been informed of the plot by some of the conspirators. Believing him to have been forewarned, they kept away from him, but, as they wanted to perform some daring exploit before they were arrested themselves, they killed Hipparchus when they found him by the Leocorium organizing the Panathenaic procession.

The rest of the Hellenes, too, make many incorrect assumptions not only about the dimly remembered past, but also about contemporary history. For instance, there is a general belief that the kings of Sparta are each entitled to two votes, whereas in fact they have only one; and it is believed, too, that the Spartans have a company of troops called "Pitanate". Such a company has never existed. Most people, in fact, will not take trouble in finding out the truth, but are much more inclined to accept the first story they hear.

However, I do not think that one will be far wrong in accepting the conclusions I have reached from the evidence which I have put forward. It is better evidence from that of the poets, who exaggerate the importance of their themes, or of the prose chroniclers, who are less interested in telling the truth than in catching the attention of their public, whose authorities cannot be checked, and whose subject-matter, owing to the passage of time, is mostly lost in the unreliable streams of mythology. We may claim instead to have used only the plainest evidence and to have reached conclusions which are reasonably accurate, considering that we have been dealing with ancient history. As for this present war, even though people are apt to think that the war in which they are fighting is the greatest of all wars and, when it is over, to relapse again into their admiration of the past, nevertheless, if one looks at the facts themselves, one will see that this was the greatest war of all.

In this history I have made use of set speeches some of which were delivered just before and others during the war. I have found it difficult to remember the precise words used in the speeches which I listened to myself and my various informants have experienced the same difficulty; so my method has been, while keeping as closely as possible to the general sense of the words that were actually used, to make the speakers say what, in my opinion, was called for by each situation.

And with regard to my factual reporting of the events of the war I have made it a principle not to write down the first story that came my way, and not even to be guided by my own general impressions; either I was present myself at the events which I have described or else I heard of them from eye-witnesses whose reports I have checked with as much thoroughness as possible. Not that even so the truth was easy to discover: different eye-witnesses give different accounts of the same events, speaking out of partiality for one side or the other or else from imperfect memories. And it may well be that my history will seem less easy to read because of the absence in it of a romantic element. It will be enough for me, however, if these words of mine are judged useful by those who want to understand clearly the events which happened in the past and which (human nature being what it is) will, at some time or other and in much the same ways, be repeated in the future. My work is not a piece of writing designed to meet the taste of an immediate public, but was done to last forever.

The greatest war in the past was the Persian War; yet in this war the decision was reached quickly as a result of two naval battles and two battles on land. The Peloponnesian War; on the other hand, not only lasted for a long time, but throughout its course brought with it unprecedented suffering for Hellas. Never before had so many cities been captured and then devastated, whether by foreign armies or by the Hellenic powers themselves (some of these cities, after capture, were resettled with new inhabitants); never had there been so many exiles; never such loss of life—both in the actual warfare and in internal revolutions. Old stories of past prodigies, which had not found much confirmation in recent experience, now became credible. Wide areas, for instance, were affected by violent earthquakes; there were more frequent eclipses of the sun than had ever been recorded before; in various parts of the country there were extensive droughts followed by famine; and there was the plague which did more harm and destroyed more life than almost any other single factor. All these calamites fell together upon the Hellenes after the outbreak of war.

War began when the Athenians and the Peloponnesians broke the Thirty Years Truce which had been made after the capture of Euboea. As to the reasons why they broke the truce, I propose first to give an account of the causes of complaint which they had against each other and of the specific instances where their interests clashed: this is in order that there should be no doubt in anyone's mind about what led to this great war falling upon the Hellenes. But the real reason for the war is, in my opinion, most likely to be disguised by such an argument. What made war inevitable was the growth of Athenian power and the fear which this caused in Sparta. As for the reasons for breaking the truce and declaring war which were openly expressed by each other, they are as follows....

Book Two

Pericles' Funeral Oration

In the same winter the Athenians, following their annual custom, gave a public funeral for those who had been the first to die in the war....Now, at the burial of those who were first to fall in the war Pericles, the son of Xanthippus, was chosen to make the speech. When the moment arrived he came forward from the tomb and, standing on a high platform, so that he might be heard by as many people as possible in the crowd, he spoke as follows:

> I shall begin by speaking about our ancestors, it is only right and proper on such an occasion

to pay them the honor of recalling what they did. In this land of ours there have always been the same people living from generation to generation up till now, and they, by their courage and their virtues, have handled it on to us, a free country. They certainly deserve our praise. Even more so to our fathers deserve it. For to the inheritance they had received they added all the empire we have now, and it was without blood and toil that they handled it down to us of the present generation. And then we ourselves, assembled here today, who are mostly in the prime of life, have, in most direction, added to the power of our empire and have organized our state in such a way that it is perfectly well able to look after itself both in peace and in war....

Let me say that our system of government does not copy the institutions of our neighbors. It is more the case of our being a model to others, than of our imitating anyone else. Our constitution is called a democracy because power is in the hands not of a minority but of the whole people. When it is a question of settling private disputes, everyone is equal before the law; when it is as question of putting one person before another in positions of public responsibility, what counts is not membership of a particular class, but the actual ability which the man possesses. No one, so long as he has it in him to be of service to the state, is kept in political obscurity because of poverty. And, just as our political life is free and open, so is our day-to-day life in our relations with each other. We do not get into a state with our next-door neighbor if he enjoys himself in his own way, nor do we give him the kind of black looks which, though they do no real harm, still do hurt people's feelings. We are free and tolerant in our private lives; but in public affairs we keep to the law. This because it commands our deep respect....

Perhaps I should say a word or two on the duties of women to those among you who are now widowed. I can say all I have to say in a short word of advice. Your great glory is not to be inferior to what God has made you, and the greatest glory of a woman is to be least talked about by men, whether they are praising you or criticizing you. I have now, as the

law demanded, said what I had to say. For the time being our offerings to the dead have been made, and for the future their children will be supported at the public expense by the city, until they come of age. This is the crown and prize which she offers, both to the dead and to their children, for the ordeals which they have faced. Where the rewards of valor are the greatest, there you will find also the best and bravest spirits among the people. And now, when you have mourned for your dear ones, you must depart.

The Plague

In this way the public funeral was conducted in the winter that came at the end of the first year of the war. At the beginning of the following summer the Peloponnesians and their allies, with two-thirds of their total forces as before, invaded Attica, again under the command of the Spartan king Archidamus, the son of Zeuxidamus. Taking up their positions, they set about the devastation of the country.

They had not been many days in Attica before the plague first broke out among the Athenians. Previously attacks of the plague had been reported from many other places in the neighborhood of Lemnos and elsewhere, but there was no record of the disease being so virulent anywhere else or causing so many deaths as it did in Athens. At the beginning the doctors were quite incapable of treating the disease because of their ignorance of the right methods. In fact mortality among the doctors was the highest of all, since they came more frequently in contact with the sick. Nor was any other human art or science of any help at all. Equally useless were prayers made in the temples, consultation of oracles, and so forth; indeed, in the end people were so overcome by their sufferings that they paid no further attention to such things.

The plague originated, so they say, in Ethiopia in upper Egypt, and spread from there into Egypt itself and Libya and much of the territory of the King of Persia. In the city of Athens it appeared suddenly, and the first cases were among the population of Piraeus, where there were no walls at that time, so that it was supposed by them that the Peloponnesians had poisoned the reservoirs. Later, however, it appeared also in the upper city, and by this time the deaths were greatly increasing in number. As to the question of how it could first have come about or what causes can be found adequate to explain its powerful effect of nature, I must leave that to be considered by other writers, with or without medical experience.

>> Questions for Consideration

1. Compare Thucydides' approach to that of Herodotus. How are they similar and different? Which is more similar to the modern histories we read? Whom would you consider the true "Father of History"?

2. Is Thucydides objective in his telling of this conflict or does he side with the Athenians because he was an Athenian general?

3. What kind of evidence does Thucydides use? Why does he use this kind of evidence?

4. What lessons is Thucydides trying to teach us with this history? What is the moral of the story?

Bede, *The Ecclesiastical History of the English Nation*

Preface

To the most glorious King Ceolwolf[1]
Bede the servant of Christ and Priest.

In the meantime, the aforesaid famine distressing the Britons more and more, and leaving to posterity a lasting memory of its mischievous effects, obliged many of them to submit themselves to the depredators; though others still held out, putting their trust in God, when human help failed. These continually made raids from the mountains, caves, and woods, and, at length, began to inflict severe losses on their enemies, who had been for so many years plundering the country. The bold Irish robbers thereupon returned home, intending to come again before long. The Picts then settled down in the farthest part of the island and afterwards remained there, but they did not fail to plunder and harass the Britons from time to time.

Now, when the ravages of the enemy at length abated, the island began to abound with such plenty of grain as had never been known in any age before; along with plenty, evil living increased, and this was immediately attended by the taint of all manner of crime; in particular, cruelty, hatred of truth, and love of falsehood; insomuch, that if any one among them happened to be milder than

---

Source: Bede, *The Ecclesiastical History of the English Nation*, translated by E.M.Sellar (London: George Bell and Sons, 1907): pp. 1–4 and 28–31.

[1]King of Northumbria, cf. V, 23. He succeeded Osric, 729 A.D. In a revolt he was forcibly tonsured, 731, but restored. He voluntarily became a monk in Lindisfarne in 737. The fact that Bede submitted the Ecclesiastical History to him for revision bears witness to this piety and learning.

the rest, and more inclined to truth, all the rest abhorred and persecuted him unrestrainedly, as if he had been the enemy of Britain. Nor were the laity only guilty of these things, but even our Lord's own flock, with its shepherds, casting off the easy yoke of Christ, gave themselves up to drunkenness, enmity, quarrels, strife, envy, and other such sins. In the meantime, on a sudden, a grievous plague fell upon that corrupt generation, which soon destroyed such numbers of them, that the living scarcely availed to bury the dead: yet, those that survived, could not be recalled from the spiritual death, which they had incurred through their sins, either by the death of their friends, or the fear of death. Whereupon, not long after, a more severe vengeance for their fearful crimes fell upon the sinful nation. They held a council to determine what was to be done, and where they should seek help to prevent or repel the cruel and frequent incursions of the northern nations; and in concert with their King Vortigern,[2] it was unanimously decided to call the Saxons to their aid from beyond the sea, which, as the event plainly showed, was brought about by the Lord's will, that evil might fall upon them for their wicked deeds.

Chap. XV. How the Angles, being invited into Britain, at first drove off the enemy; but not long after, making a league with them, turned their weapons against their allies.

In the year of our Lord 449,[3] Marcian, the forty-sixth from Augustus, being made emperor with Valentinian, ruled the empire seven years. Then the nation of the Angles, or Saxons,[4] being invited by the aforesaid king,[5] arrived in Britain with three ships of war and had a place in which to settle assigned to them by the same king, in the eastern part of the island, on the pretext of fighting in defense of their country, whilst their real intentions were to conquer it. Accordingly they engaged with the enemy, who were come from the north to give battle, and the Saxons obtained the victory. When the news of their success and of the fertility of the country, and the cowardice of the Britons, reached their own home, a more considerable fleet was quickly sent over, bringing a greater number of men, and these, being added to the former army, made up an invincible force. The newcomers received of the Britons a place to inhabit among them, upon condition that they should wage war against their enemies for the peace and security of the country, whilst the Britons agreed to furnish them with pay. Those who came over were of the three most powerful nations of Germany-Saxons, Angles, and Jutes. From the Jutes are descended the people of Kent, and of the Isle of Wight, including those in the province of the West-Saxons who are to this day called Jutes, seated opposite to the Isle of Wight. From the Saxons, that is, the country which is now called Old Saxony, came the East-Saxons, the South-Saxons, and the West-Saxons. From the Angles, that is, the country which is called Angulus,[6] and which is said, from that time, to have remained

---

[2]Though he is the subject of many legends, Vortigern is doubtless a historical figure, a ruler of south-eastern Britain. Bede's form of the name, Uurtigernus, is right. It is a British word, meaning "supreme lord" (Rhys).

[3]The date of Marcian's succession is 450.

[4]Bede only professes to give the date of the invasion approximately: cf. V, 24 ("quorum tempore"), I, 23; II, 14; V, 23 ("circiter"), calculating in round numbers apparently. He refers here to their first settlement, which, of course, does not preclude earlier attacks.

[5]I.e., Vortigern.

[6]*Anglia* was believed to be derived from *Angulus*. The country is the modern Schleswig, which the Angles appear to have almost entirely evacuated. For the Continental Saxons, cf. V, 9. It has been supposed that the Jutes came from Jutland, where, at a later period, they mingled with the Danes (*ibid.*), but this is now regarded as doubtful

desert to this day, between the provinces of the Jutes and the Saxons, are descended the East-Angles, the Midland-Angles, the Mercians, all the race of the Northumbrians, that is, of those nations that dwell on the north side of the river Humber, and the other nations of the Angles. The first commanders are said to have been the two brothers Hengist and Horsa. Of these Horsa was afterwards slain in battle by the Britons,[7] and a monument, bearing his name, is still in existence in the eastern parts of Kent. They were the sons of Victgilsus, whose father was Vitta, son of Vecta, son Woden; from whose stock the royal race of many provinces trace their descent. In a short time, swarms of the aforesaid nations came over into the island, and the foreigners began to increase so much, that they became a source of terror to the native themselves who had invited them. Then, having on a sudden entered into league with the Picts, whom they had by this time repelled by force of arms, they began to turn their weapons against their allies. At first, they obliged them to furnish a greater quantity of provisions; and, seeking an occasion of quarrel, protested, that unless more plentiful supplies were brought them, they would break the league, and ravage all the island; nor were they backward in putting their threats into execution. In short, the fire kindled by the hands of the pagans; proved God's just vengeance for the crimes of the people; not unlike that which, being of old lighted by the Chaldeans, consumed the walls and all the buildings of Jerusalem. For here, too, through the agency of the pitiless conqueror, yet by the disposal of the just Judge, it ravaged all the neighboring cities and country, spread the conflagration from the eastern to the western sea, without any opposition, and overran the whole face of the doomed island. Public as well as private buildings were overturned; the priests were everywhere slain before the altars; no respect was shown for office, the prelates with the people were destroyed with fire and sword; nor were there any left to bury those who had been thus cruelly slaughtered. Some of the miserable remnant, being taken in the mountains, were butchered in heaps. Others, spent with hunger, came forth and submitted themselves to the enemy, to undergo for the sake of food perpetual servitude, if they were not killed upon the spot. Some, with sorrowful hearts, fled beyond the seas. Others, remaining in their own country, led a miserable life of terror and anxiety of mind among the mountains, woods and crags.

>> Questions for Consideration

1. How does Bede's approach compare to that of Herodotus and Thucydides? Does he seem to build upon their techniques or is he oblivious to their histories?

2. In what ways is this history "providential"? How does this differ from mythopoetic stories?

3. If you knew nothing about Bede, how could you tell that this history was written by an English Christian?

---

[7]At Aylesford, in Kent. Horsted is the traditional burial-place of Horsa.

Chapter 2

The Evolution of "Modern" History: 1400–1800

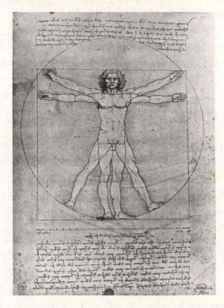

Leondardo da Vinci, *Vitruvian Man* (c. 1490. Ink. Approx. 13 1/2 × 9 5/8 (34.3 × 24.5 cm)) (*Galleria dell'Accademia, Venice/Embassy of Italy*).

Early Greco-Roman history laid the foundations for modern conceptions of history, but as the excerpts from Herodotus and the others clearly show, this form of history was very different from how we in Europe and the United States currently practice history. While many European historians recognized the importance of objectivity and credible, documented sources, they had not yet developed a modern theoretical framework for using them to write history. Many Christian historians even rejected the secular history of Thucydides in favor of providential history, focusing on the work of God in the world. Classical Greco-Roman culture and methods, however, were reborn in Europe during the Renaissance, which shaped everything from art to politics to history. The Renaissance made Greco-Roman historical methods and philosophies popular once again, drawing European attention away from sacred subjects to more secular, human-centered events, creating a more humanist, rational perspective of history. The Renaissance also opened the doors to further questioning of scientific experimentation and Christian worldviews. Spawned by the Renaissance, the Protestant Reformation of the sixteenth century and the Scientific Revolution of the seventeenth century undermined the Roman Catholic Church's control of knowledge in Europe even further, allowing all scholars, including historians, to become more critical of the orthodox Christian worldview which had dominated the region for centuries. By the eighteenth century, "enlightened" European intellectuals had come to see Christian supernatural history as not only unscientific, but unacceptably biased and ignorant. Imitating those in the hard sciences, Enlightenment philosophers applied the scientific method to the study of the humanities, insisting that all of the human experience should be considered rationally and objectively, without any reliance on biases, superstition, or unproven assumptions. They insisted that their versions of the past were superior to all others which had come before them, and that scientific history revealed universal truths about humankind. Between 1400 and 1800, modern practices of history evolved to include a focus on human events, as opposed to those of God or other supernatural forces, a modern sense of time and chronology, a focus on cause and effect and other universal patterns in history, and an insistence on objectivity, reason, and logic.

Renaissance Historians

This four hundred-year-long evolution began in the fourteenth-century Italy with the Renaissance, when scholars gained new access to classical Greco-Roman documents. Greatly impressed with these ancient works, Renaissance humanists consciously imitated classical art, architecture, and philosophy, and applied classical concepts to their own world. In rhetoric and history, Livy, Virgil, and Tacitus were especially admired. While most Renaissance historians remained Christian, their imitation of classical Greco-Roman approaches changed the focus and outlook of their histories to become more secular and rational. For example, instead of seeing the world in Christian terms of simply before Christ and after Christ, Renaissance humanists saw world history as divided into three basic periods: Antiquity, the Middle Ages, and the New Age which began in the fourteenth century.[1] According to this new perspective, antiquity, or classical Greece and Rome, was a golden age of knowledge and advancement, while the Middle Ages were a period of backwardness and darkness as Europeans strayed from the truths of the Greek and Roman philosophers. When Europeans turned back to the path of knowledge set down by Greco-Roman culture, a New Age of science and high culture began.

Bruni　　　The shift toward humanistic history began with Florentine Leonardo Bruni's (1369–1444) *History of the Florentine People.* He read Thucydides and Polybius in their original forms and consciously tried to imitate their style. Bruni influenced two other *Guicciardini*　important Florentines: Francesco Guicciardini (1483–1540) and Niccolo di Bernardo de' Machiavelli (1469–1527). Guicciardini and Machiavelli were employed by the Medici family as diplomats and later wrote their histories in retirement. Guicciardini's most famous work *History of Italy* is a diplomatic history of the relationships between

---

[1]M. C. Lemon, *Philosophy of History: A Guide for Students* (New York: Routledge, 2003), 77.

the various city-states of Italy from 1490 to 1534. His *History* is full of extensive details derived from government documents and complex analysis of multiple causes and effects. Because of this, Guicciardini is sometimes considered to be the Father of Modern History.[2]

Machiavelli   Arguably the most famous writer of the Renaissance, however, was Guicciardini's friend, Machiavelli. A son of a lawyer, Machiavelli worked his way up to become the secretary of the governing council of the Republic of Florence at the turn of the sixteenth century. Although he was primarily interested in politics, Machiavelli used history as a tool to explore how political power is obtained, maintained, and lost. Like other Renaissance scholars, Machiavelli read and adopted the ideas of classical Greco-Roman authors. As an Italian, he especially focused on the works of famous Roman historians, such as Polybius and Livy. His great histories, *History of Florence* (1525) and *Discourses on the First Ten Books of Livy's History of Rome* (1531), explicitly reflect the Roman approach to history. Similar to these classical Roman historians, Machiavelli focused on secular subjects, especially the lives of famous political leaders. He believed that politicians should understand the history of previous leaders so that they could use them as role models and also learn from their mistakes. His philosophy of history, therefore, was explicitly speculative: that is, to learn from the past to improve the future.

In this quest, knowing the truth about the past was especially important. Machiavelli's most important political work *The Prince* (1532) is famous for its realist (some say *cynical*) accounts of the past. He remained objective about even the most brutal and repulsive actions of leaders, analyzing them in terms of their political effectiveness, rather than their morality. Powerful, strong-minded, and knowledgeable men were the main driving force of historical change, but Machiavelli also allowed that sometimes unpredictable changes happen. He relied on the Roman idea of "fortune" as the natural, unpredictable, and uncontrollable agent of change in the world. He did not explicitly deny the presence of God in the world, but by omitting any mention of God in his works, he reshaped his history as a purely secular subject. He also did not see any overarching pattern in history. Humankind was not progressing toward any goal, whether sacred or secular. History to him was simply a series of ups and downs, good leaders and bad, good fortune and bad. Human nature remained the same throughout time and place. Individuals could make history and improve the world through education and decisive action, and fortune or fate had its role, but beyond that, no other forces or patterns were at work in his histories.

Machiavelli and other Renaissance historians, however, seemed to have little sense of the "otherness" of the past, of how peoples and cultures in the past were unique and different from today, but this began to change at the end of the Renaissance. European explorations in the Atlantic, and especially their encounters with the Americas, challenged their belief that the Biblical version of the past was the universal history of the world. The existence of peoples and lands not mentioned in the Bible or in any

---

[2]John Burrow, *A History of Histories: Epics, Chronicles, Romances and Inquiries from Herodotus and Thucydides to the Twentieth Century* (New York: Alfred A Knopf, 2008), 271.

European tradition opened up the possibility that other peoples had their own unique histories and further undermined Christian historical narratives.

Early Modern History

The secular and humanist perspective of the Renaissance began a reorientation in European worldviews, which manifested itself in a number of ways over the next few centuries. The first revolution it spawned was the Protestant Reformation of the sixteenth century. The renewed interest in ancient Greek and Roman texts and questioning of traditional Christian versions of the past led a number of important theologians to research the original written versions of the Old and New Testaments. Their new translations and understandings of these texts contradicted official Roman Catholic teachings. When Catholic Church leaders attempted to force theologians such as Martin Luther to recant their scholarship, Luther and other religious reformers found sympathy among many political leaders who were eager to break with the Catholic Church for political reasons. The Protestant Reformation, as an outgrowth of the Renaissance, shared its critique of traditional versions of the past and encouraged scholars to challenge the Catholic Church's control of knowledge in other ways.

Melanchthon Protestant historians, such as Philip Melanchthon (1497–1560) who was a friend of Martin Luther, supported the Protestant Reformation by publishing new histories of the Catholic Church which exposed the errors of Catholic Christian history and the corruption of Church leaders.[3] Christian history in the Protestant tradition, therefore, became a weapon to destroy the religious and political authority of the Catholic Church and its supporters.

The fifteenth and sixteenth centuries also witnessed the colonization of the Americas and the earliest versions of American history. The first histories of the English colonies in North America followed in the tradition of Renaissance and *John Smith* Protestant Reformation historians. John Smith's *A True Relation of Such Occurrences and Accidents of Note as Hath Hapned in Virginia Since the First Planting of that Colony* (1608) and *General History of Virginia* (1624) were some of the earliest histories of European life in the Americas. Smith himself was an explorer and colonist in Jamestown, Virginia, and used his own experiences as the focus of his histories. Other *Bradford* histories written by Puritan separatists in Plymouth colony, such as William Bradford's *History of Plymouth Plantation* (1646), were similarly participant accounts of the important events of early colonial history. As such, most early American histories were local histories of specific towns or colonies. The first history which looked at the *Douglass* British colonies in North America as a whole was William Douglass's *Summary View, Historical and Political, of the British Settlements in North America* (1747–1750).[4] All of these histories described American history from a European perspective, not

---

[3]Ernst Breisach, *Historiography: Ancient, Medieval, and Modern*, 2nd ed. (Chicago, IL: University of Chicago Press, 1994), 166.
[4]Ibid., 195–198.

even attempting to understand, much less incorporate, the histories of indigenous American nations. Colored with the experiences of the authors and their Protestant, Eurocentric perspectives, and using little evidence other than their own memories, these early histories are more similar to handbooks or primary sources, rather than history as we currently practice it. Early American histories, however, are important in showing how European historical ideas spread to the Americas along with the colonists and supplanted the historical ideas of indigenous peoples just as they supplanted other elements of indigenous life and culture in their conquest of the Americas.

History and the Scientific Revolution

As the Protestant Reformation spread to other countries in Europe and America, it provided shelter to scholars whose research contradicted the Roman Catholic version of the truth. Newly Protestant countries provided asylum for these scholars and published their works to discredit the Catholic Church. Once European scholars mastered the Greco-Roman classics, they began to move beyond them, critiquing and adding on to the knowledge of the ancients. This break with the Renaissance scholars' acceptance of classical knowledge and the consequent development of new worldviews and philosophies, called the Scientific Revolution, began during the Protestant Reformation and spread across Europe and the Americas in the seventeenth century.

Bacon

Empiricism

The most famous heroes of the Scientific Revolution were scholars of the natural world, such as Nicolaus Copernicus, Johannes Kepler, Galileo Galilei, and Isaac Newton, who studied mathematics, astronomy, and physics. The most important philosophers in terms of influence on the study of history, however, were Francis Bacon and Jean Bodin. Bacon (1561–1626), was a member of the English aristocracy and was involved in politics during the reigns of Elizabeth I and James I. Early in life, he began studying the classics and became disillusioned with the limitations of Aristotelian philosophy. Aristotle and other Greco-Roman philosophers had relied too much on human reason and logic, rather than on hard evidence, to support their conclusions. Bacon was especially dissatisfied with Aristotle's deductive reasoning, believing that a more accurate method of reasoning would be inductive reasoning, or observing the data and evidence first, and from this, deriving a general premise or theory.[5] Throughout the rest of his life, he studied and reflected on the nature of knowledge and truth. His main contribution to European knowledge, however, was his advocacy of "experimental philosophy" or "empiricism."[6] He argued that all knowledge must be subjected to experimentation based on observable evidence to prove its reliability and validity. Using the inductive method, he advocated the observation of data or phenomena and the compilation of the data to make generalizations and conclusions.

---

[5]Deductive reasoning begins with a theory or hypothesis and then gathers evidence to prove or disprove the hypothesis.

[6]Lemon, *Philosophy of History*, 110.

He published many books on the subject and laid the foundations for scientific thought in Europe for centuries.

Bodin   Frenchman Jean Bodin (1530–1596) was another political philosopher of the late sixteenth century, but unlike Bacon, Bodin wrote specifically on the topic of history. His most famous work of history *Method for the Easy Understanding of History* (1566) helped to lay the foundations for modern historical practices by describing a scientific method for understanding history. His famous opening statement reveals his understanding that there are different approaches to history:

> Of History, that is, the true narration of things, there are three kinds: Human, natural, and divine.… One depicts the acts of man while leading his life in the midst of society. The second reveals causes hidden in nature and explains their development from earliest beginnings. The last records the strength and power of Almighty God and of the immortal souls, set apart from all else.[7]

By clearly distinguishing the history of God from the history of man, Bodin helped to secularize the history of mankind. Throughout the book, he urged historians to avoid prejudice and anachronism,[8] maintain detachment, stick to the facts, and be aware of the historical context of historians from the past.[9] These rules for the practice of history were essential in shaping European and American ideas about maintaining objectivity and critically analyzing sources of information, but it took another century before most European historians began to adopt them as part of the historical profession.

Vico   One of the few European historians to take Bodin's rules to heart and expand upon them in developing a distinct philosophy of history was Giambattista Vico (1668–1744). Vico was born in Naples, studied civil and church law, and became a professor of rhetoric at the University of Naples. Unlike many other speculative historians of his age, Vico investigated history for its own sake, attempting to understand historical events and actors on their own terms, within the context of their own worldview. In his most famous work *Scienza Nuova* (*New Science*), Vico claimed to have discovered the key to history: that human nature and cultures changed and developed over time, and that the mental world of earlier peoples differed significantly from that of subsequent periods.[10] In order to understand the writings of the past, therefore, historians must first understand the worldview of the culture which produced them and the meaning they attached to the language they used. This idea of the past as a different *Historicism*   world, to be studied in its own terms, is called historicism and is a crucial concept in Western historiography.

Using this historicist method, his "New Science," Vico surmised a universal pattern in history: that all societies advanced through cycles of three ages. The first age of

---

[7]Jean Bodin, *Method for the Easy Comprehension of History*, trans. B. Reynolds (New York: Columbia University Press, [1566] 1945), 15.

[8]"Anachronism" means viewing an event outside of the timeframe or chronology in which it occurred, thus lacking chronological organization.

[9]Lemon, *Philosophy of History*, 119.

[10]Ibid., 129.

human history was the "age of gods and giants," when uncivilized humans were ruled by a few, powerful leaders who organized them into family states, with most of the people completely subjected to their rulers. The second of Vico's ages was the "age of heroes," when the descendents of the noble giants created city-states with aristocratic rulers who subdued their subjects and other city-states through force. The third and final age was the "age of men," when societies were governed by reason and laws. Because of weakness, civil war, corruption, or other factors, societies in the age of men could die and be reborn in the age of gods or heroes. The primary agent of change in all of this was God or Providence.[11] As a Catholic, writing in a Catholic region, this was a natural conclusion for Vico, but it was a departure from the secular trends of his contemporaries. He had little influence on either seventeenth- or eighteenth-century thought, but many current historians now believe that he was the first true philosopher of history, arguing that he was the first to write a theory of history based on abstract principles. Although Vico was virtually unknown to his contemporaries, a number of others began to adopt the scientific approaches of Bodin and Vico in the centuries that followed.[12]

Enlightenment Historians

By the eighteenth century, philosophers in many parts of Europe were using the scientific method to question not only religious beliefs, but all aspects of human life, including politics, economics, and history. This period of philosophic exploration and revolution centered in France, but when German philosophers read the ideas of the French philosophers, they began to refer to the spread of these new ideas about scientific truth as *Aufklärung* or "enlightenment."[13] This term spread to the rest of Europe and America, and has been used to describe these philosophical trends ever since. Enlightenment philosophers considered scientists to be the real heroes of history, and all those who opposed them, especially the Catholic Church, as the enemies of progress and civilization. Enlightenment historians followed in the footsteps of Machiavelli, using reason to create secular histories of human events, but rather than merely imitate the Greco-Romans, they critiqued the classical histories and developed new historical theories.

Progress   The main concept that Enlightenment historians added to European and American perceptions of the past was that of progress. Believing that civilizations advanced with each scientific innovation, enlightened historians saw the past as a long string of advancements toward the present day. Civilizations may struggle with obstacles and setbacks, but overall, knowledge and inventions accumulate over time, steadily and predictably improving the material and mental well-being of the civilization. Logically,

---

[11]Ibid., 127–143.

[12]Ibid., 107.

[13]Robert M. Burns, *Philosophies of History from Enlightenment to Postmodernity* (Malden, MA: Blackwell, 2000), 30.

then, the earliest societies were the least advanced and present-day society is the most advanced.

Another important feature of the Enlightenment was the incredible optimism of the intellectuals of the day, who believed that they had reached the height of civilization, and that they would continue to progress forever. Societies which continued to use science to solve problems would progress, and those with the most scientists and best thinkers would progress faster than other civilizations. In this Eurocentric worldview, European civilization was the most advanced in the entire world because it had moved beyond superstition and ignorance into a period of truth and progress, founded on rationalism and science. In their minds, all the cultures of the world and all of history were relative to the achievements of eighteenth-century Europe in a linear fashion.

Linear Time   Time lines are a perfect example of this linear sense of time. On a time line, Enlightenment philosophers would place the world's earliest civilizations (calling them "ancient") in a spot furthest from eighteenth-century Europe, as most different from themselves. Between the ancient civilizations of Europe and present-day Europe was a time of little progress, where ignorance and superstition prevailed. These were the Dark Ages or Middle Ages, from which Europe had emerged with the Renaissance and Protestant Reformation. Societies which had thrown off the yoke of superstition and now relied on reason and science were "modern"—a concept they invented to describe their own age. If Enlightenment Europe was the pinnacle of advancement, in their eyes, everything else was not as advanced, and hence inferior. While this perspective is obviously Eurocentric and biased to our eyes, their linear sense of time and progress still dominates the modern Western sense of time so much so that it is hard now for us to imagine time differently. It is important, however, to remember how and why this sense of time emerged and understand its historical context.

A number of Enlightenment philosophers used universal histories, which focused on historical trends applicable to all human societies, to support their understanding of this progressive linear past. One of the most famous of these was Frenchman *Voltaire*   François-Marie Arouet (1684–1778), known as Voltaire. He and many other French intellectuals strongly criticized the Roman Catholic Church for its power and corruption. His histories argued that the Catholic Church had kept all of Europe in the Dark

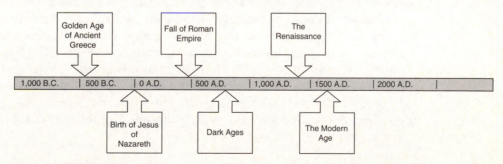

The "Modern" Time line

Ages, and that in order for society to progress, it had to shed the ignorance of superstition (Catholicism) and remove the clergy from power. Society should be led instead by enlightened men, who were not bound by superstition, who were well-educated, and scientific… in other words, men just like him. Like Machiavelli, Voltaire believed in a speculative purpose of history to study the errors of the past in order to teach rulers and leaders how to help their societies to progress. Voltaire's historical works, *Philosophy of History* and *The Age of Louis XIV,* applied the scientific method to historical questions, but relied primarily on reason, rather than empirical evidence, to support his arguments.

Condorcet   Of all the French philosophers, Marie-Jean-Antoine-Nicolas Caritat, the Marquis de Condorcet (1743–1794), wrote the most explicit philosophy of history which most fully demonstrated the concept of progress. A member of the nobility, Condorcet was born in a small town in France, educated at elite colleges, and excelled in the mathematics, philosophy, and political science. Like other French *philosophes,* he was elected to the illustrious Royal Academy of Sciences. He was a strong human rights advocate, supported the newly created U.S. constitution, and was an early leader of the French Revolution. He eventually fell out of favor with the other French revolutionaries and went into hiding in 1794 to avoid imprisonment. While in hiding, he wrote his most important work of history, *Sketch for a Historical Picture of the Progress of the Human Mind* (1793–1794).

Condorcet saw history as a science and applied the scientific method of gathering and ordering facts to ascertain universal truths and patterns from the past and the present world. The overarching pattern of history was a battle between truth and error, in which mankind develops intellectual innovations with which to overcome errors and achieve progress.[14] Like Vico, he saw human nature as essentially universal and so wrote a universal history of mankind. Condorcet argued that humankind traveled through ten stages of history, advancing in a linear fashion from tribal life to agrarian life, and eventually culminating in a final stage of rationalism and scientific truth. This universal history was based solely on a European model and was overly simplistic and despite his understanding of the importance of empirical evidence in history, Condorcet had very little actual documentation or evidence to support his argument because he wrote it while in hiding. He relied instead upon summaries of secondary sources and used deductive reasoning, letting his own logic and reason dictate his conclusions. Condorcet was arrested in 1795 and died soon afterward in prison.

Condorcet's universal theories of progress and the battle between truth and error greatly influenced European and American historians, but some disagreed with the emphasis on finding universal patterns in the past and theories of progress. Johann *Herder*   Gottfried Herder (1744–1803) illustrated this competing view of history. Although he wrote extensively on a variety of subjects, his *Ideas for the Philosophy of History of Humanity* (1784–1791) was the most important to historians. He focused on the development of cultures, or "the Volk," over time. Herder defined the Volk as a group

---

[14]Lemon, *Philosophy of History*, 188–189.

Organicist

of people united by common language, institutions, traditions, and culture. He developed an organicist view of historical change: that like living organisms, the Volk was born, developed, and died.[15] Instead of progress, therefore, he saw a cyclical pattern. He also believed that all cultures in their various phases of change had their own value systems and were worthy of equal attention. Historians, therefore, should not judge the past by present-day standards or some supposedly universal set of values. He inspired many future historians to see that "human history was not a linear progression, but a succession of distinct and heterogeneous civilizations."[16] Herder's organicist and historicist theories of the Volk were to become very influential in the twentieth century.

Wollstonecraft

Similar to Herder, other Enlightenment historians disagreed with the idea that progress was the overarching pattern in universal history. One important dissenter from the progressive view of history was one of the most famous female Enlightenment philosophers, Mary Wollstonecraft (1759–1797). Born in London to a poor family, Wollstonecraft was self-educated, read classical and Enlightenment literature, and established a school for young women. She wrote several books, including her most famous work *Vindication of the Rights of Women* (1792) and her lesser-known *History and Moral View of the Origins and Progress of the French Revolution* (1793). She saw the past as the history of continuity, rather than change, of men's oppression and manipulation of women, looking only to the future as a period of possible progress, equality, and truth for men and women. Arguing against philosophers, such as Jean-Jacques Rousseau, who had asserted that humans were created perfect and society corrupted them, she wrote, "Rousseau exerts himself to prove that all *was* right originally: a crowd of authors that all *is* now right: and I, that all will *be* right."[17] Despite her attempt to include women in the history of the world and her impact on feminism, her ideas were largely ignored by male historians in the nineteenth and twentieth centuries. Male historians, who dominated the field because of their privileged access to higher education and publication, continued to focus on male-oriented subjects and speak of "mankind" as if it represented the experiences of both men and women.

Hume

Other British historians diverged from French ideas of progress even more strongly. Scotsman David Hume (1711–1776) rejected progress completely, viewing all speculations about overarching patterns in the past or future as creations of the human mind, and thus unscientific. He wanted historians to apply Bacon's empirical method, sticking strictly to the facts as expressed in documents and other forms of observable evidence. Similar to Machiavelli's history, Hume's *History of England* (1763) suggested that human nature was unchanging and that history was shaped by many specific influences with neither rhyme nor reason. His greatest contribution to historical practice, however, was his precise use of and reference to specific primary and secondary sources in support of his arguments.

---

[15]Ibid., 222–223.

[16]Isaiah Berlin, *Vico and Herder: Two Studies in the History of Ideas* (New York: Viking Press, 1976), xxv.

[17]Mary Wollstonecraft, *A Vindication of the Rights of Woman* (New York: Penguin, [1792] 1992), 95.

Gibbon   Englishman Edward Gibbon (1737–1794) also rejected simplistic theories of continual progress in the past and any other universal theory of the past. Born into a well-off English family, he briefly converted to Catholicism as a teenager, but quickly renounced it in favor of Deism.[18] Gibbon's aversion to Christian intolerance increased over the years, and his life's work, *The History of the Decline and Fall of the Roman Empire* reflected these views. This masterpiece directly refutes Augustine's version of Christianity within the Roman Empire. Rather than defending Christianity, Gibbon concludes that Christianity corrupted and weakened the Roman Empire, and consequently was indeed the downfall of the Roman Empire. While Gibbon's biases are clear throughout the work, like Hume, he meticulously documents his sources by using reference notes, and his work shows an enormous devotion to thorough research and uncovering the truth as he saw it.

The American Revolution in Historiography

An important political result of Enlightenment ideas was the American Revolution, and many enlightened philosophers and historians analyzed it within an Enlightenment framework. Within the British context, those who approved of political

Whig   and social change were called "Whigs," and described it as a natural result of the progress of the rights and freedoms of men, while Tories (those who opposed the Revolution) wrote of it as an irrational, unfortunate mistake. Irish statesman and

Burke   philosopher Edmund Burke (1729–1797) wrote the standard Whig interpretation of the American Revolution in his political review *The Annual Register* during and after the war. Burke's Whig interpretation of the Revolution was extremely popular among American historians who of course appreciated his positive view of the events.

The first American history of the Revolution was written in 1789 by revolutionary

Ramsay   war hero and South Carolina legislator David Ramsay. His *History of the American Revolution* appeared just as the nation was beginning to take shape and was part of a great literary and cultural effort to create an independent national identity.[19] Although Ramsay plagiarized Burke's accounts of the Revolution, he laid the foundation for nationalist histories of the United States, which characterized the Revolution as forged by a republican consensus, based on long-held beliefs in democracy and liberty unique to the United States.

Warren   Of the participant patriot accounts, however, Mercy Otis Warren's (1728–1814) *History of the Rise, Progress and Termination of the American Revolution* (1805)

---

[18]As a sort of nondenominational, rational worship of a divine Creator, Deism was a common belief among Enlightenment thinkers who rejected the narrowmindedness of Catholicism and Protestantism.

[19]David Ramsay, *The History of the American Revolution in Two Volumes*, ed. Lester H. Cohen (Indianapolis, IN: Liberty Fund, [1789] 1990).

was among the most well-documented and thoroughly argued.[20] She was born in Barnstable, Massachusetts, the child of Colonel James Otis, a leader in the Massachusetts House of Representatives who began agitating against British tyranny long before the Revolution. She married James Warren in 1754 as he began his political career as a leading figure in revolutionary politics. She not only knew many other revolutionary leaders through her relatives and husband, she was also a famous intellectual in her own right. She published a number of plays and poems before beginning her epic history of the American Revolution. Originally three volumes in length, her *History of the Rise, Progress and Termination of the American Revolution* was one of the earliest histories of the American Revolution. As an eyewitness to the Revolution, Warren had access to its leaders and major documents. She infuses her history with her own "observations" or opinions about the events, but these observations are supported by an abundance of historical data: names, dates, speeches, battles, and events. In thirty-one lengthy chapters, she covers the blow-by-blow history of the Revolution, from its origins in colonial America to the creation of the Constitution. She argued that the Revolution was fought to establish a republican political system and liberty, and the American victory proved the logic and popularity of these ideas. While this argument was palatable to most Americans, her assertion that the Constitution weakened the Republic and made it vulnerable to military and monarchical tyranny was less popular.[21] Other patriotic versions, portraying the Constitution, the first presidents, and the leaders of the Revolution only in a positive light, dominated American history for the next century.

The period 1400–1800 witnessed revolutionary developments in the history of European and American thought and helped to create a more "modern" sense of history. The Renaissance, Age of Exploration, Protestant Reformation, Scientific Revolution, and Enlightenment all shaped European perspectives of their past. Whereas earlier historians had presented historical knowledge as revealed by divine authority, modernist historians substituted secular scientific authority as the basis for knowledge of the past. Rather than viewing human nature as unchanging and eternal, historians, beginning with Vico, argued for a universal history emphasizing human development and change over time. Many Enlightenment historians added that human development traveled in a linear trajectory of progress, from primitive to civilized, from an ancient age to the present modern age. Most importantly, historians began to emphasize human reason and empirical methods of inquiry. These broad changes in historical ideas and methods laid the groundwork for the independent discipline of history which would emerge in the nineteenth century.

---

[20]Mercy Otis Warren, *History of the Rise, Progress and Termination of the American Revolution Interspersed with Biographical, Political and Moral Observations*, ed. Lester H. Cohen (Indianapolis, IN: Liberty Fund, [1805] 1989).

[21]Judith B. Markowitz, "Radical and Feminist: Mercy Otis Warren and the Historiographers," *Peace and Change* IV, no. 2 (Spring 1977): 11.

Machiavelli, *The Prince*

Chapter IV: Why the Kingdom of Darius, Conquered by Alexander, Did Not, on Alexander's Death, Rebel Against His Successors.

ALEXANDER the Great having achieved the conquest of Asia in a few years, and dying before he had well entered on possession, it might have been expected, having regard to the difficulty of preserving newly acquired States, that on his death the whole country would rise in revolt. Nevertheless, his successors were able to keep their hold, and found in doing so no other difficulty than arose from their own ambition and mutual jealousies.

If any one think this strange and ask the cause, I answer, that all the Princedoms of which we have record have been governed in one or other of two ways either by a sole Prince, all others being his slaves permitted by his grace and favour to assist in governing the kingdom as his ministers ; or else, by a Prince with his Barons who hold their rank, not by the favour of a superior Lord, but by antiquity of blood, and who have States and subjects of their own who recognize them as their rulers and entertain for them a natural affection. States governed by a sole Prince and by his servants, vest in him a more complete authority; because throughout the land none but he is recognized as sovereign, and if obedience be yielded to any others, it is yielded as to his ministers and officers for whom personally no special love is felt.

Of these two forms of government we see examples in our own days in the Turk and the King of France. The whole Turkish empire is governed by a sole Prince, all others being his slaves. Dividing his kingdom into *sandjaks,* he sends thither different governors whom he shifts and changes at his pleasure. The King of France,

on the other hand, is surrounded by a multitude of nobles of ancient descent, each acknowledged and loved by subjects of his own, and each asserting a pre-eminence in rank of which the King can deprive him only at his peril.

He, therefore, who considers the different character of these two States, will perceive that it would be difficult to gain possession of that of the Turk, but that once won it might be easily held. The obstacles to its conquest are that the invader cannot be called in by a native nobility, nor expect his enterprise to be aided by the defection of those whom the sovereign has around him. And this for the various reasons already given, namely, that all being slaves and under obligations they are not easily corrupted, or if corrupted can render little assistance, being unable, as I have already explained, to influence the people. Whoever, therefore, attacks the Turk must reckon on finding a united people, and must trust rather to his own strength than to divisions on the other side. But if his adversary were once overcome and defeated in the field, so as to be unable to repair his armies, no cause for anxiety would remain, except in the family of the Prince; which being extirpated, there would be no one else to fear; for since all beside are without credit with the people, the invader, as before his victory he had nothing to hope from them, so after it has nothing to dread.

But the contrary is the case in kingdoms governed like that of France, into which, because men who are discontented and desirous of change are to be found everywhere, you may readily procure an entrance by gaining over some Baron of the Realm. Such persons, for the reasons already given, are able to open the way to you for the invasion of their country and to render its conquest easy. But afterwards the effort to maintain

---

Source: Niccolo Machiavelli, *The Prince* (1532), translation by Ninian Hill Thomson (London: Kegan Paul, Trench, 1882): pp. 20–28.

your ground involves you in endless difficulties, as well in respect of those who have helped you, as of those whom you have overthrown. Nor will it be enough to have destroyed the family of the Prince, since all those other Lords remain to put themselves at the head of new movements; whom being unable either to content or destroy, you will lose the State whenever occasion serves them.

Now, if you examine the nature of the government of Darius, you will find that it resembled that of the Turk, and, consequently, that it was necessary for Alexander, first of all, to defeat him utterly and strip him of his dominions; after which defeat, Darius having died, the country, for the causes above explained, was permanently secured to Alexander. And had his successors continued united they might have enjoyed it undisturbed, since there arose no disorders in that kingdom save those of their own creating.

But kingdoms ordered like that of France cannot be retained with the same ease. Hence the repeated risings of Spain, Gaul and Greece against the Romans, resulting from the number of small Princedoms of which these Provinces were made up. For while the memory of these lasted, the Romans could never think their tenure secure. But when that memory was worn out by the authority and long continuance of their rule, they gained a secure hold, and were able afterwards in their contests among themselves, each to carry with him some portion of these Provinces, according as each had acquired influence there; and this because, on the extinction of the line of their old Princes, the people came to recognize no other Lords than the Romans.

Bearing all this in mind, no one need wonder at the ease with which Alexander was able to lay a firm hold on Asia, nor that Pyrrhus and many others should have found difficulty in preserving other acquisitions; since this arose, not from the less or greater merit of the conquerors, but from the different character of the States with which they had to deal.

Chapter V: How to Govern Cities or Princedoms Which Before Their Acquisition Have Lived Under Their Own Laws

WHEN a newly-acquired State has been accustomed, as I have said, to live under its own laws and in freedom, there are three methods whereby it may be held. The first is to destroy it; the second, to go and reside there in person ; the third, to suffer it to live on under its own laws, while subjecting it to a tribute and entrusting its government to a few of its Citizens who will keep the rest your friends. Such a Government, since it is the creature of the new Prince, will see that it cannot stand without his protection and support, and must therefore do all it can to maintain him; and a city accustomed to live in freedom, if it is to be preserved, is more easily controlled through its own citizens than in any other way.

We have examples of all these methods in the histories of the Spartans and the Romans. The Spartans held Athens and Thebes by creating oligarchies in these cities, yet lost them in the end. The Romans, to retain Capua, Carthage and Numantia, destroyed them and never lost them. On the other hand, when they thought to hold Greece as the Spartans had held it, leaving it its freedom, and allowing it to be governed by its own laws, they failed, and had to destroy many cities of that Province before they could secure it. For, in truth, there is no sure way of holding other than by destroying, and whoever becomes master of a City accustomed to live in freedom and does not destroy it, may reckon on being destroyed by it. For if it should rebel, it can always screen itself under the name of liberty and its ancient laws, which no length of time, nor any benefits conferred will ever cause it to forget; and do what you will, and take what care you may, unless the inhabitants be scattered and dispersed, this name, and the old order of things, will never cease to be remembered, but will at once be turned against you whenever misfortune overtakes you, as when Pisa rose against the Florentines after a hundred years of servitude.

If, however, the newly acquired City or Province has been accustomed to live under a Prince, and his line is extirpated, it will be impossible for its inhabitants, used, on the one hand, to obey, and deprived, on the other, of their old ruler, to agree to choose a leader from among themselves; and as they know not how to live as freemen, and are therefore slow to take up arms, a stranger may readily gain them over and attach them to his cause. But in Republics there is a stronger vitality, a fiercer hatred, a keener thirst for revenge. The memory of their former freedom will not let them rest; so that the safest plan is to destroy them, or to go and live there.

>> Questions for Consideration

1. Compare Machiavelli's approach to history with that of Bede. How might their historical contexts (when and where they lived, their occupations, and experiences) explain their differences?

2. What evidence can you find of Renaissance rationalism and admiration of the ancient Greeks and Romans in this excerpt?

3. How do Machiavelli's political ideas shape his history?

Vico, *The New Science*

Book I

The natural law of nations certainly arose with their common customs; nor has the world ever contained a nation of atheists, since all nations originated in some religion. The roots of all religions, moreover, lie in the desire for eternal life, which is natural to all men. This common desire of human nature arises from a common sense, hidden in the depths of the human mind, that the human soul is immortal. The more this sense is secret in origin, the more clearly does it have the following effect: that, in the last throes of death, we hope for a power superior to nature by which death can be overcome, a power which is to be found only in a God who is not identical with, but superior to, nature, i.e., an infinite and eternal mind. But when men stray from this God, they become curious about the future.

Such curiosity, which is forbidden by nature, since it is proper only to a God who is an infinite and eternal mind, occasioned the fall of the two founders of mankind. As a result God based the true religion of the Jews upon worship of His infinite and eternal providence and, as a punishment, because its first authors desired knowledge of the future, condemned the whole human race to work, pain and death. Hence all the false religions arose through idolatry, i.e., the worship of imaginary gods, falsely thought of as beings of supernatural power who supported men in the extremity of their ills. Idolatry shared its birth with that of divination—a vain science of the future, employing certain sensible intimations, believed to be sent to man by the gods. Yet this vain science, in which the vulgar wisdom of all gentile nations must have originated, conceals two great principles of truth: that a divine providence must exist, which governs human beings; and that men must possess free will through which, if they so desire

Source: New Science by Giambattista Vico, translated by David Marsh, Introduction by David Grafton (Penguin Classics, 1999). pp. 81–83, 209–210, and 234–235. Copyright © David Marsh, 1999. Introduction © Anthony Grafton, 1999. Reproduced by permission of Penguin Books Ltd.

and should they make use of it, they can escape that fate which, without such provision, would otherwise be theirs. It follows from this second truth that men can choose whether or not to live in justice. Further proof of this common sense is afforded by the common desire which men naturally have for laws, when they are not influenced against them by feelings of self-interest.

This, and no other, is certainly the human nature which, at all times and in all places, has based its practices upon the following three common senses of mankind: first, that providence must exist; second, that men should beget certain children by certain women, with whom they must share at least the rudiments of a civil religion, in order that children be brought up by their fathers and mothers in a spiritual unity in conformity with the laws and religions amongst which they were born; third, that the dead should be buried. Hence not only has the world never contained a nation of atheists, but neither has it contained a nation in which it has not been the duty of women to adopt the public religion of their husbands. And if there has been no nation which lived in total nakedness, still less has there been one in which bestial and shameless sex and casual matings have been practiced in front of others. Nor, finally, has there been any nation, however barbaric, in which the unburied corpses of its members have been left to rot above ground, for such would be a nefarious state, i.e., a state sinning against the common nature of men. To avoid falling into such a state, all nations preserve their native religions by the observation of inviolate ceremonies and, with refined rites and solemnities, celebrate marriage and burial above all other human practices. This is the vulgar wisdom of mankind, which originated in religions and laws and reached its completion and perfection in the sciences, disciplines and arts....

Book II: Poetic Wisdom

The philosophers and philologists [historians] should all have begun to reason out the wisdom of the ancient gentiles from such first men, stupid, irrational and horrible beasts, that is, from the giants, as taken just now in their proper signification. In his *De ecclesia ante legem*, Father Bouldac says that the giants' names in the scriptures mean "pious, venerable and illustrious men," which can be understood only in reference to the noble giants who, through divination, founded religion among the gentiles and provided the age of the giants with its name. And they ought to have begun from metaphysics, understood as that which seeks to take its proofs not from outside but from within the modifications of the very mind of him who meditates it, for, as we said above, since this world of nations has certainly been made by men, it is within these modifications that they should have sought its principles. And human nature, insofar as it is like that of animals, carries with it this property: that the senses are the only means whereby it knows things.

Hence poetic wisdom, the first wisdom of the gentile world, must have begun in a metaphysics which was not rational and abstract, like that of the learned today, but sensed and imagined, as that of these first men, devoid of reason and wholly composed of powerful senses and vigorous imaginations... must have been. This metaphysics was their own poetry, a faculty which, since they were provided naturally with such senses and imaginations, was innate in them. But it was born into the world of that ignorance of causes which was the mother of their wonder about everything for which... in their all-embracing ignorance, they felt great admiration. This poetry originated in them as a divine poetry because it arose at the time in which they imagined that the causes of the things which they were sensing and admiring were gods... (And this is confirmed today by the Americans, who give the name "god" to everything which exceeds their modest capacity to reason, to whom we may add the ancient Germans who lived by the Sea of Ice, of whom Tacitus relates that they spoke of hearing the sun at night, as it crossed the sea from West to East, and claimed to see the gods. These roughest and simplest of nations enable us to understand much else about the authors of the gentile world who are the subject of our present reasonings.)...

In this mode the first men of the gentile nations, the children as it were, of nascent mankind... created things by means of their own ideas but by a creation which differs infinitely from that of God. For God, in his purest understanding, knows things and creates them in knowing them; whereas, because of their powerful ignorance, men created by dint of a highly corporeal imagination and, this being so, they created with a wonderful sublimity of such quality and magnitude that it perturbed to excess the very men who, by imagining things, created them, whence they were called "poets" which, in Greek, means "creators."... An eternal property of this nature of human things has survived, to which Tacitus gave noble expression: that, when terrified, in vain do men *fingunt simul creduntque* [believe things as they invent them].

Such must have been the natures of the first authors of gentile humanity, a hundred years after the Flood in Mesopotamia and two hundred years after it in the rest of the world....

In commencing our argument, therefore, we lay down as our principle the following philological axiom: that the Egyptians asserted that in the whole previous duration of their world three languages had been spoken, correspondent in number and order to three ages which had elapsed in that world, the ages of the gods, of the heroes and of men; and of these languages they said that the first had been hieroglyphic or sacred or divine, the second had been symbolic or in signs or heroic coats-of-arms, and third had been alphabetic, in order that the needs of daily life might be communicated among men distant from one another. Two golden passages in Homer's *Iliad* are relevant to these three languages, making it clear that the Greeks were in agreement with the Egyptians about them. One is the passage in which Homer relates that Nestor lived through three generations of men who spoke in different languages: Nestor must thus have been a heroic character for the chronology established by the three languages which correspond to the Egyptians' three ages, so that the expression "to live for the years of Nestor" must have meant the same as "to live for the years of the world." The other passage in the *Iliad* is that in which Aeneas tells Achilles that men of a different language began to live in Ilium, after Troy was transferred to the shores of the sea and Pergamum became its citadel. Finally we link to our first principle the tradition, which is also Egyptian, that their Thoth or Mercury invented both laws and letters.

>> Questions for Consideration

1. How does Vico's Christianity shape this history? How does he balance this influence with reason and science?
2. Compare Vico's topic and theory to those of Bede and Machiavelli. What explains the similarities and differences?
3. In what ways might this be considered Enlightenment history?
4. How does your own approach to history compare with Vico's?

Condorcet, *Sketch for a Historical Picture of the Progress of the Human Mind*

Introduction

. . . if one studies [the development of humankind's faculties of thought and sensation] as it manifests itself in the inhabitants of a certain area at a certain period of time and then traces it on from generation to generation, one has the picture of the progress of the human mind. This progress is subject to the same general laws that can be observed in the development of the faculties of the individual, and it is indeed no more than the sum of the development realized in a large number of individuals joined together in society. What happens at any particular moment is the result of what has happened at all previous moments, and itself has an influence on what will happen in the future.

So such a picture is historical, since it is a record of change and is based on the observation of human societies throughout the different stages of their development. It ought to reveal the order of this change and the influence that each moment exerts upon the subsequent moment, and so ought also to show, in the modifications that the human species has undergone, ceaselessly renewing itself through the immensity of the centuries, the path that it has followed, the steps that it has made towards truth or happiness.

Such observations upon what man has been and what he is today, will instruct us about the means we should employ to make certain and rapid the further progress that his nature allows him still to hope for.

Such is the aim of the work that I have undertaken, and its result will be to show by appeal to reason and fact that nature has set no term to the perfection of human faculties; that the perfectibility of man is truly indefinite; and that the progress of this perfectibility, from now onwards independent of any power that might wish to halt it, has no other limit than the duration of the globe upon which nature has cast us. This progress will doubtless vary in speed, but it will never be reversed as long as the earth occupies its present place in the system of the universe, and as long as the general laws of this system produce neither a general cataclysm nor such changes as will deprive the human race of its present faculties and its present resources.

The first stage of civilization observed amongst human beings is that of a small society whose members live by hunting and fishing, and know only how to make rather crude weapons and household utensils and to build or dig for themselves a place in which to live, but are already in possession of a language with which to communicate their needs, and a small number of moral ideas which serve as common laws of conduct; living in families, conforming to general customs which take the place of laws, and even possessing a crude system of government.

The uncertainty of life, the difficulty man experiences in providing for his needs, and the necessary cycle of extreme activity and total idleness do not allow him the leisure in which he can indulge in thought and enrich his understanding with new combinations of ideas. The means of satisfying his needs are too dependent on chance and the seasons to encourage any occupation whose progress might be handed down to later generations, and so each man confines himself to perfecting his own individual skill and talent.

Thus the progress of the human species was necessarily very slow; it could move forward only from time to time when it was favored by exceptional circumstances. However, we see hunting, fishing and the natural fruits of the earth replaced as a source of subsistence by food obtained from animals that man domesticates and that he learns to keep and to breed. Later, a primitive form of agriculture developed; man was no longer satisfied with the fruits or plants that he came across by chance, but learnt to store them, to collect them around his dwelling, to sow or plant them, and to provide them with favorable conditions under which they could spread.

Source: Antoine-Nicolas de Condorcet, *Sketch for a Historical Picture of the Progress of the Human Mind.* Translated by June Barraclough (NY: Noonday Press, 1955, reprinted by Hyperion Press, 1994): pp. 4–11, 103–105. Copyright © 1955 Wiedenfeld & Nicolson. Reprinted by permission of Wiedenfeld & Nicolson, an imprint of Orion Publishing Group.

Property, which at first was limited to the animals that a man killed, his weapons, his nets and his cooking utensils, later came to include his cattle and eventually was extended to the earth that he won from its virgin state and cultivated. On the death of the owner this property naturally passed into the hands of his family, and in consequence some people came to possess a surplus that they could keep. If this surplus was absolute, it gave rise to new needs; but if it existed only in one commodity and at the same time there was a scarcity of another, this state of affairs naturally suggested the idea of exchange, and from then onwards, moral relations grew in number and increased in complexity. A life that was less hazardous and more leisured gave opportunities for meditation or, at least, for sustained observation. Some people adopted the practice of exchanging part of their surplus for labor from which they would then be absolved. In consequence there arose a class of men whose time was not wholly taken up in manual labor and whose desires extended beyond their elementary needs. Industry was born; the arts that were already known, were spread and perfected; as men became more experienced and attentive, quite casual information suggested to them new arts; the population grew as the means of subsistence became less dangerous and precarious; agriculture, which could support a greater number of people on the same amount of land replaced the other means of subsistence; it encouraged the growth of the population and this, in its turn, favored progress; acquired ideas were communicated more quickly and were perpetuated more surely in a society that had become more sedentary, more accessible and more intimate. Already, the dawn of science had begun to break; man revealed himself to be distinct from the other species of animals and seemed no longer confined like them to a purely individual perfection.

As human relations increased in number, scope and complexity, it became necessary to have a method of communicating with those who were absent, of perpetuating the memory of an event with greater precision than that afforded by oral tradition, of fixing the terms of an agreement with greater certainty than that assured by the testimony of witnesses, and of registering in a more enduring manner those respected customs according to which the members of a single society had agreed to regulate their conduct. So the need for writing was felt, and writing was invented. It seems to have been at first a genuine system of representation, but this gave way to a more conventional representation, which preserved merely the characteristic features of objects. Finally by a sort of metaphor analogous to that which had already been introduced into language, the image of a physical object came to express moral ideas. The origin of these signs, like that of words, was ultimately forgotten, and writing became the art of attaching a conventional sign to every idea, to every word, and by so extension, to every modification of ideas and words....

Certain men of genius, humanity's eternal benefactors, whose names and country are for ever buried in oblivion, observed that all the words of a language were nothing but the combinations of a very limited number of primary sounds, but that their number, though very limited, was enough to form an almost limitless number of different combinations. They devised the notion of using visible signs to designate not the ideas or the words that corresponded to ideas, but the simple elements of which words are composed. And here we have the origin of the alphabet.... and this final step assured the progress of the human race for ever.

All peoples whose history is recorded fall somewhere between our present degree of civilization and that which we still see amongst savage tribes; if we survey in a single sweep the universal history of peoples we seem them sometimes making fresh progress, sometimes plunging back into ignorance, sometimes surviving somewhere between these extremes or halted at a certain point, sometimes disappearing from the earth under the conqueror's heel, mixing with the victors or living on in slavery, or sometimes receiving knowledge from some more enlightened people in order to transmit it in their turn to other nations, and so welding an uninterrupted chain between the beginning of historical time and the century in which we live, between the first peoples known to us and the present nations of Europe.

So the picture that I have undertaken to sketch falls into three distinct parts.

In the first our information is based on the tales that travelers bring back to us about the state of the human race among the less civilized peoples, and we have to conjecture the stages by which man living in isolation or restricted to the kind of association necessary for survival, was able to make the first steps on a path whose destination is the use of a developed language. This is the most important distinction and indeed, apart from a few more extensive ideas of morality and the feeble beginnings of social order, the only one separating man from the animals who like him live in a regular and continuous society. We are therefore in this matter forced to rely upon theoretical observations about the development of our intellectual and moral faculties.

In order to carry the history of man up to the point where he practices certain arts, where knowledge of the sciences has already begun to enlighten him, where trade unites the nations and where, finally, alphabetical writing is invented, we can add to this first guide the history of the different societies which have been observed in all their intermediary stages, although none can be traced back far enough to enable us to bridge the gulf which separates these two great eras of the human race.

Here the picture begins to depend in large part on a succession of facts transmitted to us in history, but it is necessary to select them from the history of different peoples, to compare them and combine them in order to extract the hypothetical history of a single people and to compose the picture of its progress.

The history of man from the time when alphabetical writing was known in Greece to the condition of the human race at the present day in the most enlightened countries of Europe is linked by an uninterrupted chain of facts and observations;

and so at this point the picture of the march and progress of the human mind becomes truly historical. Philosophy has nothing more to guess, no more hypothetical surmises to make; it is enough to assemble and order the facts and to show the useful truths that can be derived from their connections and from their totality.

When we have shown all this, there will remain one last picture for us to sketch: that of our hopes, and of the progress reserved for future generations, which the constancy of the laws of nature seems to assure them.... It can even be observed that, according to the general laws of the development of our faculties, certain prejudices have necessarily come into being at each stage of our progress, but they have extended their seductions or their empire long beyond their due season, because men retain the prejudices of their childhood, their country and their age, long after they have discovered all the truths necessary to destroy them.

Finally, in all countries at all times there are different prejudices varying with the standard of education of the different classes of men and their professions. The prejudices of philosophers harm the progress of truth; those of the less enlightened classes retard the propagation of truths already known; those of certain eminent or powerful professions place obstacles in truth's way: here we see three enemies whom reason is obliged to combat without respite, and whom she vanquishes often only after a long and painful struggle. The history of these struggles, of the birth, triumph and fall of prejudices will occupy a great part of this work and will be neither the least important nor the least useful section of it....

The Eighth Stage

.... Intrepid men, inspired by love of glory and passion for discovery, had pushed back further the bounds of the universe for Europe, had shown her new skies and opened up unknown lands. Da Gama had reached India after following the long African coastline with unwearying patience, whilst Columbus, abandoning himself to the waves of the Atlantic Ocean, had discovered that hitherto unknown world which lies to the west of Europe and to the east of Asia.

If this passion, whose restless activity henceforth embraced all objects, presaged great progress for the human race, if noble curiosity animated the heroes of navigation, it was a base, pitiless greed, a stupid, fierce fanaticism that inspired the kings and ruffians who were to profit from their labors. The unfortunate creatures who lived in these new lands were treated as though they were not human beings because they were not Christians. This prejudice, which had an even more degrading effect on the tyrants than on their victims, smothered any feeling of remorse that might have touched these greedy and barbarous men, spewed up from the depths of Europe, and they abandoned themselves to their insatiable thirst for blood and gold. The bones of five million men covered those unfortunate lands where the Portuguese and the Spaniards brought their greed, their superstitions and their wrath. They will lie there to the end of time as a mute witness against the doctrine of the political unity of religion; a doctrine which even to this day finds its apologists amongst us.

For the first time man knew the globe that he inhabited, was able to study in all countries the human race as modified by the long influence of natural causes or social institutions, and could observe the products of the earth or of the sea, in all temperatures and in all climates. The wealth of every kind which these natural resources offer to men, and which is so far from being exhausted that its vast extent is as yet not even suspected; a knowledge of the natural world that can furnish new truths and destroy accredited errors in the sciences; the increased activity of trade which has given new wings to industry and navigation and, by a necessary chain of influence, to all the sciences and to all the arts; and the strength which this activity has given to free nations to resist tyrants, to enslaved people to break their chains or at least to relax the chains of feudalism: all these are also to be numbered amongst the fortunate consequences of these discoveries. But these discoveries will have repaid humanity what they have cost it only when Europe renounces her oppressive and avaricious system of monopoly; only when she remembers that men of all races are equally brothers by the wish of nature and have not been created to feed the vanity and greed of a few privileged nations; only when she calls upon all people to share her independence, freedom and knowledge, which she will do once she is alive to her own true interests. Unfortunately we must still ask ourselves if this revolution will be the honorable fruit of the progress of philosophy or only, as it has hitherto been, the shameful consequence of national jealousies and the excesses of tyranny....

>> Questions for Consideration

1. In what ways is this history progressive and universal?

2. How does Condorcet's classification of the ages of man compare to Vico's? Which do you prefer and why?

3. What evidence of Eurocentrism is evident in this excerpt? Is Condorcet Eurocentric in his discussion of Native Americans?

4. Is this a rational, scientific, and objective history, or are there flaws in his logic and apparent biases present?

Mercy Otis Warren, *History of the Rise, Progress and Termination of the American Revolution*

Chapter I: Introductory Observations

History, the deposite of crimes, and the record of everything disgraceful or honorary to mankind, requires a just knowledge of character, to investigate the sources of action; a clear comprehension, to review the combination of causes; and precision of language, to detail the events that have produced the most remarkable revolutions.

To analyze the secret springs that have effected the progressive changes in society; to trace the origin of the various modes of government, the consequent improvements in science, in morality, or the national tincture that marks the manners of the people under despotic or more liberal forms, is a bold and adventurous work.

The study of the human character opens at once a beautiful and a deformed picture of the soul. We there find a noble principle implanted in the nature of man, that pants for distinction. This principle operates in every bosom, and when kept under the control of reason, and the influence of humanity, it produces the most benevolent effects. But when the checks of conscience are thrown aside, or the moral sense weakened by the sudden acquisition of wealth or power, humanity is obscured, and if a favorable coincidence of circumstances permits, this love of distinction often exhibits the most mortifying instances of profligacy, tyranny, and the wanton exercise of arbitrary sway. Thus when we look over the theater of human action, scrutinize the windings of the heart, and survey the transactions of man from the earliest to the present period, it must be acknowledged that ambition and avarice are the leading springs which generally actuate the restless mind. From these primary sources of corruption have arisen all the rapine and confusion, the depredation and ruin, that have spread distress over the face of the earth from the days of Nimrod to Caesar, and from Caesar to an arbitrary prince of the house of Brunswick.

The progress of the American Revolution has been so rapid, and such the alteration of manners, the blending of characters, and the new train of ideas that almost universally prevail, that the principles which animated to the noblest exertions have been nearly annihilated. Many who first stepped forth in vindication of the rights of human nature are forgotten, and the causes which involved the thirteen colonies in confusion and blood are scarcely known, amidst the rage of accumulation and the taste for expensive pleasures that have since prevailed; a taste that has abolished that mediocrity which once satisfied, and that contentment which long smiled in every countenance. Luxury, the companion of young acquired wealth, is usually the consequence of opposition to, or close connection with, opulent commercial states. Thus the hurry of spirits, that ever attends the eager pursuit of fortune and a passion for splendid enjoyment, leads to forgetfulness; and thus the inhabitants of America cease to look back with due gratitude and respect on the fortitude and virtue of their ancestors, who, through difficulties almost insurmountable, planted them in a happy soil. But the historian and the philosopher will ever venerate the memory of those pious and independent gentlemen, who, after suffering innumerable impositions, restrictions, and penalties, less for political, than theological opinions, left England, not as adventurers for wealth or fame, but for the quiet enjoyment of religion and liberty.

Source: Mercy Otis Warren, *History of the Rise, Progress and Termination of the American Revolution interspersed with Biographical Political and Moral Observations.* (1805) ed. Lester H. Cohen (Indianapolis: Liberty Fund, 1994): pp. 3–16, 167–172, 627–632, 644–646. Reprinted by permission of Liberty Fund, Inc. The original editor, Lester Cohen, translated her old English into modern English, but retained some of her original spellings and they have been preserved in this excerpt.

Chapter IX

They were sensible the step they were about to take, would either set their country on the pinnacle of human glory, or plunge it in the abject state into which turbulent and conquered colonies have been generally reduced. Yet they wisely judged, that this was a proper period to break the shackles, and renounce all political union with the parent state, by a free and bold declaration of the independence of the American States. This measure had been contemplated by some gentlemen in the several colonies, some months before it took place. They had communicated their sentiments to the individual members of congress, but that body had been apprehensive, that the people at large were not prepared to unite in a step so replete with important consequences. But the moment of decision had now arrived, when both the Congress and the inhabitants of the colonies advanced too far to recede.

Richard Henry Lee, Esq., a delegate from the state of Virginia, a gentleman of distinguished ability, uniform patriotism, and unshaken firmness and integrity, was the first who dared explicitly to propose, that this decided measure, on which hung such mighty consequences, should no longer be delayed. This public and unequivocal proposal, from a man of his virtue and shining qualities, appeared to spread a kind of sudden dismay. A silent astonishment for a few minutes seemed to pervade the whole assembly: this was soon succeeded by a long debate, and a considerable division of sentiment on the important question.

After the short silence just observed, the measure proposed by Mr. Lee was advocated with peculiar zeal by John Adams, Esq., of the Massachusetts Bay. He rose with a face of intrepidity and the voice of energy, and invoked the *god of eloquence,* to enable him to do justice to the cause of his country, and to enforce this important step in such a manner, as might silence all opposition, and convince every one of the necessity of an immediate declaration of the independence of the United States of America.

Mr. John Dickinson, of Pennsylvania, took the lead in opposition to the boldness and danger of this decided measure. He had drawn the petition to the king forwarded by Mr. Penn, and though no man was more strenuous in support of the rights of the colonies, he had always been averse to a separation from Britain, and shuddered at the idea of an avowed revolt of the American colonies. He arose on this occasion with no less solemnity than Mr. Adams had recently done, and with equal pathos of expression, and more brilliance of epithet, he invoked the *Great Governor* of the *Universe,* to animate him with powers of language sufficient to exhibit a view of the dread consequences to both countries, that such a hasty dismemberment of the empire might produce. He descanted largely on the happy effects that might probably ensue from more patient and conciliatory dispositions, and urged at least a temporary suspension of a step, that could never be revoked. He declared that it was his opinion, that even policy forbade the precipitation of this measure, and that humanity more strongly dictated, that they ought to wait longer the success of petitions and negotiations, before they formally renounced their allegiance to the king of Great Britain, broke off all connexion with England, plunged alone into an unequal war, and rushed without allies into the unforeseen and inevitable dangers that attended it.

The consequences of such a solemn act of separation were indeed of serious and extensive magnitude. The energy of brilliant talents, and great strength of argument, were displayed by both parties on this weighty occasion. The reasons urging the necessity of decision, and the indubitable danger of delay, were clear and cogent; the objections, plausible, humane, and important: but after a fair discussion of the question, an accurate statement of the reasons for adopting the measure, and a candid scrutiny of the objections against it, grounded either on policy or humanity, a large majority of the members of congress appeared in favor of an immediate renunciation of allegiance to the crown, or any future subjugation to the king of Great Britain.

A declaration of the independence of America, and the sovereignty of the United States, was drawn by the ingenious and philosophic pen of Thomas Jefferson, Esq., a delegate from the state of Virginia. The delegates from twelve of the American States, agreed almost unanimously to this declaration; the language, the principles, and the spirit of which, were equally honorable to themselves and their country. It was signed by John Hancock, then president of congress, on the fourth of July, one thousand seven hundred and seventy-six.

The allegiance of thirteen states at once withdrawn by a solemn declaration, from a government towards which they had looked with the highest veneration; whose authority they had acknowledged, whose laws they had obeyed, whose protection they had claimed for more than a century and a half—was a consideration of solemnity, a bold resolution, an experiment of hazard: especially when the infancy of the colonies as a nation, without wealth, resources, or allies, was contrasted with the strength, riches, and power of Great Britain. The timid trembled at the ideas of final separation; the disciples of passive obedience were shocked by a reflection of a breach of faith to their ancient sovereign; and the enemies to the general freedom of mankind were incensed to madness, or involved in despair. But these classes bore a small proportion to those who resented the rejection of their petitions, and coolly surveyed the impending dangers, that threatened themselves and their children, which rendered it clear to their apprehension, that this step was necessary to their political salvation. They considered themselves no longer bound by any moral tie, to render fealty to a sovereign thus disposed to encroach on their civil freedom, which they could now secure only by a social compact among themselves, and which they determined to maintain, or perish in the attempt.

By the declaration of independence, dreaded by the foes for a time doubtfully viewed by many of the friends of America, everything stood on a new and more respectable footing, both with regard to the operations of war, or negotiations with foreign powers. Americans could now no more be considered as *rebels,* in their proposals for treaties of peace and conciliation with Britain; they were a distinct people, who claimed the rights, the usage, the faith, and the respect of nations, uncontrolled by any foreign power. The colonies thus irretrievably lost to Great Britain, a new face appeared on all affairs both at home and abroad.

America had been little known among the kingdoms of Europe; she was considered only as an appendage to the power of Britain: the principles of her sons were in some respects dissimilar, and their manners not yet wrought up to the standard of refinement reigning in ancient courts: her statesmen in general were unacquainted with the intrigues necessary for negotiations, and the *finesse* usually hackneyed in and about the cabinets of princes. She now appeared in their eyes, a new theater, pregnant with events that might be interesting to the civil and political institutions of nations, that had never before paid much attention to the growth, population, and importance of an immense territory beyond the Atlantic.

The United States had their ambassadors to create, or to transplant from the bar or the compting-house. Their generals were many of them the yeomanry or the tradesmen of the country; their subordinate officers had been of equal rank and fortune, and the army to be governed was composed of many of the old associates of the principal officers, and were equally tenacious of personal liberty. The *regalia* of power, orders of nobility, and the splendor of courts, had been by them viewed only at a distance. The discipline of armies was entirely new; the difficulty of connecting many distinct states to act as it were by one will, the expenses of government in new exigencies, and the waste of war had not yet been accurately calculated by their politicians and statesmen. But their senators, their representatives, and their magistrates, were generally sagacious and vigilant, upright and firm; their officers were brave, their troops in spirits, and with a full confidence in their command in chief: hope was exhilarated by the retreat from Boston, and the repeated successes of their arms at the southward; while new dignity was added to office, and stronger motives for illustrious action, by the rank America had now taken among the nations. Thus, by the declaration of independence they had new ground to tread; the scene of action was changed, genius was called forth from every quarter of the continent, and the public expectation enhanced by the general favorable appearance in all their military operations.

In this situation stood affairs, both in the cabinet and in the field, when lord Howe arrived at Staten Island, with a formidable squadron under his command, on the twelfth of July, one thousand seven hundred and seventy-six. At the head of this hostile arrangement, his lordship came in full confidence of success: yet amid the splendor and parade of war, while he held out his potent arm, he still cherished the delusory hope of peace.

By a pompous declaration, he early announced his pacific powers to the principal magistrates of the several colonies, and promised pardon to all who, in late times, had deviated from their allegiance, on condition, that they would speedily return to their duty, and gave encouragement that they should, on compliance, hereafter reap the benefit of royal favor. Lord Howe observed in his declaration,

> that the commissioners were authorized in his majesty's name to declare any province, colony, county, district, or town, to be at peace of his majesty: and that due consideration should be had to the meritorious services of any who should aid or assist in restoring the public tranquility; that their dutiful representations should be received, pardons granted, and suitable

encouragement to such as would promote the measures of legal government and peace, in pursuance of his majesty's most gracious purposes.*

Congress ordered the declaration to be immediately published in all the American gazettes, that the people of the United States might be fully informed of the terms of peace; that they might see for themselves, that the business of the commissioners was to amuse, disunite, and deceive them; and that those who still continued in suspense, from hopes founded either on the justice or moderation of the court of Great Britain, might now be fully convinced, that their own valor, virtue, and firmness must rescue and preserve the freedom of their country.**

Chapter XXX

We have seen the banners of Albion displayed, and the pendants of her proud navy waving over the waters of the western world, and threatening terror, servitude, or desolation to resisting millions. We have see through the tragic tale of war, all political connexion with Great Britain broken off, the authority of the parent state renounced, and the independence of the American states sealed by the definitive treaty. The mind now willingly draws a veil over the unpleasing part of the drama, and indulges the imagination in future prospects of peace and felicity; when the soldier shall retreat from the field, lay by the sword, and resume the implements of husbandry—the mechanic return to his former occupation, and the merchant rejoice in the prosperous view of commerce; when trade shall not be restricted by the unjust or partial regulations of foreigners; and when the ports of America shall be thrown open to all the world,

---

*This declaration, and the consequent resolves of congress may be seen at large in the public journals of the sessions of one thousand seven hundred and seventy-six. [See Howe's Proclamation, November 30, 1776, in Force, Archives, 5th. ser., 3: 927–928; also see JCC, 5: 567, 574–575, 592–593, 597.]

**The American Congress were not remiss at this time, in exerting their efforts to detach foreigners from the service of Britain, and alluring them to become inhabitants of the United States, by promising them a quiet residence, an allotment of lands, and a security from all interruptions in the enjoyment of their religious opinions, and the investiture of all the privileges of native citizens.

and an intercourse kept free, to reap the advantages of commerce extended to all nations.

The young government of this newly established nation had, by the recent articles of peace, a claim to a jurisdiction over a vast territory, reaching from the St. Mary's on the south, to the river St. Croix, the extreme boundary on the east, containing a line of postroads of eighteen hundred miles, exclusive of the northern and western wilds, but partially settled, and whose limits have not yet been explored. Not the Lycian league, nor any of the combinations of Grecian states, encircled such an extent of territory; nor does modern history furnish any example of a confederacy of equal magnitude and respectability with that of the United States of America.

We look back with astonishment when we reflect, that it was only in the beginning of the seventeenth century, that the first Europeans landed in Virginia, and that nearly at the same time, a few wandering strangers coasted about the unknown bay of Massachusetts, until they found a footing in Plymouth. Only a century and a half had elapsed, before their numbers and their strength accumulated, until they bade defiance to foreign oppression, and stood ready to meet the power of Britain, with courage and magnanimity scarcely paralleled by the progeny of nations, who had been used to every degree of subordination and obedience. ·

The most vivid imagination cannot realize the contrast, when it surveys the vast surface of America now enrobed with fruitful fields, and the rich herbage of the pastures, which had been so recently covered with a thick mattress of woods; when it beholds the cultivated vista, the orchards and the beautiful garden which have arisen within the limits of the Atlantic states, where the deep embrowned, melancholy forest, had from time immemorial sheltered only the wandering savage; where the sweet notes of the feathered race, that follow the track of cultivation, had never chanted their melodious songs: the wild waste had been a haunt only for the hoarse birds of prey, and the prowling quadrupeds that filled the forest.

In a country like America, including a vast variety of soil and climate, producing everything necessary for convenience and pleasure, every man might be lord of his own acquisition. It was a country where the standard of freedom had recently been erected to allure the liberal-minded to her shores, and to receive and to protect the persecuted subjects of arbitrary power, who might there seek an asylum from the chains of servitude to which they had been subjected in any part of the globe. Here it might rationally be expected, that beside the natural increase, the emigrations to a land of such fair promise of the blessings of plenty, liberty, and peace, to which multitudes would probably resort, there would be exhibited in a few years, a population almost beyond the calculation of figures.

The extensive tract of territory above described, on the borders of the Atlantic, had, as we have seen, been divided into several distinct governments, under the control of the crown of Great Britain; these governments were now united in a strong confederacy, absolutely independent of all foreign domination: the several states retained their own legislative powers; they were proud of their individual independence, tenacious of their republican principles, and newly emancipated from the degrading ideas of foreign control, and the sceptred hand of monarchy. With all these distinguished privileges, deeply impressed with the ideas of internal happiness, we shall see they grew jealous of each other, and soon after the peace, even of the powers of the several governments erected by themselves: they were eager for the acquisition of wealth, and the possession of the new advantages dawning on their country, from their friendly connexions abroad, and their abundant resources at home.

At the same time that these wayward appearances began early to threaten their internal felicity, the inhabitants of America were in general sensible, that the freedom of the people, the virtue of society, and the stability of their commonwealth, could only be preserved by the strictest union; and that the independence of the United States must be secured by an undeviating adherence to the principles that produced the revolution.

These principles were grounded on the natural equality of man, their right of adopting their own modes of government, the dignity of the people, and that sovereignty which cannot be ceded either to representatives or to kings. But, as a certain writer has expressed it,

> Powers may be delegated for particular purposes; but the omnipotence of society, if any where, is in itself. Princes, senates, or parliaments, are not proprietors or masters; they are subject to the people, who form and support that society by an eternal law of nature, which has ever subjected a part to the whole.*

These were opinions congenial to the feelings, and were disseminated by the pens of political writers; of Otis, Dickinson, Quincy,[†] and many others, who with pathos and energy had defended the liberties of America, previous to the commencement of hostilities.

On these principles, a due respect must ever be paid to the general will; to the right in the people to dispose of their own moneys by a representative voice; and to liberty of conscience without religious tests; on these principles, frequent elections, and rotations of office, were generally thought necessary, without precluding the indispensable subordination an obedience due to rulers of their own choice. From the principles, manners, habits, and education of the Americans, they expected from their rules, economy in expenditure (both public and private,) simplicity of manners, pure morals,

and undeviating probity. These they considered as the emanations of virtue, grounded on a sense of duty, and a veneration for the Supreme Governor of the universe, to whom the dictates of nature teach all mankind to pay homage, and whom they had been taught to worship according to revelation, and the divine precepts of the gospel. Their ancestors had rejected and fled from the impositions and restrictions of men, vested either with princely or priestly authority: they equally claimed the exercise of private judgment, and the rights of conscience, unfettered by religious establishments in favor of particular denominations.

The writings of the above-named gentleman, previous to the commencement of the war, are still in the hands of many. They expected a simplification of law; clearly defined distinctions between executive, legislative, and judiciary powers: the right of trial by jury, and a sacred regard to personal liberty and the protection of private property, were opinions embraced by all who had any just ideas of government, law, equity, or morals.

These were the rights of men, the privileges of Englishmen, and the claim of Americans; these were the principles of the Saxon ancestry of the British empire, and of all the free nations of Europe, previous to the corrupt systems introduced by intriguing and ambitious individuals.

These were the opinions of Ludlow and Sydney, of Milton and Harrington: these were principles defended by the pen of the learned, enlightened, and renowned Locke; and even Judge Blackstone, in his excellent commentaries on the laws of England, has observed "that trial by jury and the liberties of the people went

---

*See Lessons to a Prince, by an anonymous writer. [David Williams, *Lessons to a Young Prince on the Present Disposition in Europe to a General Revolution: with an Addition of a Lesson on the Mode of Studying and Profiting by the Reflections on the French Revolution by Edmund Burke, by an old States man* (6th. ed. New York, 1791).]

†The characters of Dickenson and Otis are well known, but the early death of Mr. *Quincy* prevented his name from being conspicuous in the history of American worthies. He was a gentleman of abilities and principles which qualified him to be eminently useful, in the great contest to obtain and support the freedom of his country. He had exerted his eloquence and splendid talents for this purpose, until the premature hand of death deprived society of a man, whose genius so well qualified him for the investigation of the claims, and the defense of the rights of mankind. He died on his return from a voyage to Europe, a short time before war was actually commenced between Great Britain and the colonies.

out together." Indeed, most of the learned and virtuous writers that have adorned the pages of literature from generation to generation, in an island celebrated for the erudite and comprehensive genius of its inhabitants, have enforced these rational and liberal opinions.

These were the principles which the ancestors of the inhabitants of the United States brought with them from the polished shores of Europe, to the dark wilds of America: these opinions were deeply infixed in the bosoms of their posterity, and nurtured with zeal, until necessity obliged them to announce the declaration of independence of the United States. We have seen that the instrument which announced the final separation of the American colonies from Great Britain, was drawn by the elegant and energetic pen of Jefferson, with that correct judgment, precision, and dignity, which have ever marked his character.

The declaration of independence, which has done so much honor to the then existing congress, to the inhabitants of the United States, and to the genius and heart of the gentleman who drew it, in the belief, and under the awe, of the Divine Providence, ought to be frequently read by the rising youth of the American states, as a palladium of which they should never lose sight, so long as they wish to continue a free and independent people.

This celebrated paper, which will be admired in the annals of every historian, begins with an assertion, that all men are created equal, and endowed by their Creator with certain unalienable rights, which nature and nature's God entitle them to claim; and, after appealing to the Supreme Judge of the world for the rectitude of their intentions, it concludes in the name of the *good people* of the *colonies*, by their representatives assembled in congress, they publish and declare, that they are and of right ought to be, Free and Independent States: in the *name* of the *people*, the fountain of all just authority, relying on the protection of Divine Providence, they mutually pledged themselves to maintain these rights, with their lives, fortunes, and honor.

These principles the *Sons of Columbia* had supported by argument, defended by the sword, and have now secured by negotiation, as far as the pledges of national faith and honor will bind society to a strict adherence to equity. This however is seldom longer than it appears to be the interest of nations, or designing individuals of influence and power. Virtue in the sublimest sense, operates only on the minds of a chosen few: in their breasts it will ever find its own reward.

In all ages, mankind are governed less by reason and justice, than by interest and passion: the caprice of a day, or the impulse of a moment, will blow them about as with a whirlwind, and bear them down the current of folly, until awakened by their misery, by these they are often led to breaches of the most solemn engagements, the consequences of which may involve whole nations in wretchedness. It is devoutly to be hoped, that the conduct of America will never stand on record as a striking example of the truth of this observation. She has fought for her liberties; she has purchased them by the most costly sacrifices: we have seen her embark in the enterprise, with a spirit that gained her the applause of mankind. The United States have procured their own emancipation from foreign thraldom, by the sacrifice of their heroes and their friends: they are now ushered on to the temple of peace, who holds out her wand, and beckons them to make the wisest improvement of the advantages they had acquired by their patience, perseverance, and valor.

>> Questions for Consideration

1. How is Warren's narrative shaped by the language and ideas of the Enlightenment?

2. Is there any specific evidence in this excerpt indicating that Warren's sex and political identity as an American revolutionary influenced her record of the Revolution?

3. How is Warren responding to Tory histories of the Revolution which portray revolutionaries as radical, irrational, rebels?

Chapter 3

Nineteenth-Century European Historiography

Karl Marx and Leopold von Ranke (*Marx: Courtesy of the Library of Congress. Von Ranke: Public Domain*).

Just as the great intellectual, cultural, and political trends of previous periods transformed historians' views of the past, the tumultuous historical context of the nineteenth century profoundly influenced the development of the historical profession in Europe and the United States. Out of wars of unification and expansion, together with social, economic, political, and intellectual revolutions, history emerged as a newly independent academic discipline in European and American universities. Shaped by these new forces and the legacy of the Enlightenment, historians struggled to validate the importance of their discipline by laying claim to powerful truths and empirical methodology, which justified history's inclusion as a scholarly endeavor. As historians became more prestigious in academia, different schools of thought formed around major historical theories and philosophies. Four of the most influential ideologies shaping European and American historiography in the nineteenth century were Idealism, Marxism, Empiricism, and Romanticism. While each responded to Enlightenment ideals and was popular in the nineteenth century, Empiricism was ultimately the most influential in creating the framework for modern notions of the meaning of history.

Idealism

While France was the hotbed of philosophical innovation in the eighteenth century, Germany witnessed a flowering of philosophical ideas in the nineteenth century. In the nineteenth-century German counter-Enlightenment, Enlightenment theories were questioned and confirmed, revised, or rejected. Since most Enlightenment historical theories were Idealistic in that they focused on abstract, universal patterns, and changes in ideas over time, most nineteenth-century philosophers who grappled with Enlightenment theories can also be considered as Idealists. Some of these theories continued to see God or Providence as the central historical agent and progress as the primary pattern in world history, but others took a more secular path, looking for more observable forces of change and questioning whether any pattern of history really existed.

Hegel   One of the most influential German Idealists was philosophy professor Georg Wilhelm Friedrich Hegel (1770–1831). Hegel agreed with the Enlightenment concept of progress in history, but added that "the history of the world is none other than the progress of the consciousness [or idea] of Freedom…"[1] The Idea, conceptualized of as pure thought, universal consciousness, or God, unfolded its will and was self-realized through time. Human societies and individuals, best represented by their nation-states, merely served the will of the Idea as it unfolded toward the freedom of all mankind. History

Dialectic   unfolded in a sort of divine dialectic. All things in nature (day and night for example) gave rise to their opposite. Similarly, an idea (thesis) in society naturally led an opposing force (antithesis) to challenge the idea. The debate between the two then led to a synthesis which joined elements of both sides. The synthesis in turn became a thesis and set the whole process in motion again. While Hegel wrote little history himself, his philosophies spurred considerable debate among the most prominent historians of his day.

Marxism

Marx   Hegel's most famous student was Karl Marx (1818–1883). Marx was raised in a middle-class Jewish family in Prussia, and he studied law at Bonn and Berlin universities. In Berlin, he associated with the "Young Hegelians," intellectuals interested in using Hegel's "Idea of Freedom" to criticize the Prussian government.[2] Marx not only agreed with Hegel's theory of the rational progress of freedom but also used the idea of dialectical change in his own theories later on in the century. Marx's political and historical theories, however, constantly evolved over the course of his life, leading him further away from Hegelian ideas, toward developing his own revolutionary philosophy.

---

[1]Ernst Breisach, *Historiography: Ancient, Medieval, and Modern*, 2nd ed. (Chicago, IL: University of Chicago Press, 1994), 232.

[2]M. C. Lemon, *Philosophy of History: A Guide for Students* (New York: Routledge, 2003), 238.

His experience with the injustices of industrial capitalism and the lack of democracy in most European governments led him to become more critical of Hegel's theories, especially Hegel's support of the Prussian government and reliance on supernatural explanations for historical change. Marx's outspoken criticism of industrial capitalism and European politics, and involvement in the working-class revolutions of 1848, led him to flee political repression in Germany, Belgium, and France, before English authorities allowed him to settle in London. From there, Marx united with Friedrich Engels, attempting to encourage working-class revolution through the publication of their political, economic, and historical arguments. They hoped to understand the past, especially the creation of industrial capitalism, in order to help workers overthrow the oppressive system and replace it with a system of equality and real freedom. Marxist theory, therefore, was explicitly political, practical, and speculative.

Marx's most famous works are *The Communist Manifesto* (1848) and *Das Kapital* (1867), but he developed his theories in a large body of written materials, much of it unpublished at the time of his death. In these works, he developed a new philosophy

Historical Materialism

called "historical materialism." Explicitly rejecting Idealist philosophies, which are founded upon abstract ideas, Marx argued that real, concrete, observable things should be at the heart of understanding the world. He began his history of capitalism by investigating the material conditions of human beings in the past: how they obtained the basic necessities to live, what they owned, what work they did, and how they produced these necessities. He concluded that each man's relationship to the society's

Mode of Production

mode of production (or socioeconomic class) shaped his life. For example, if the mode of production is industrial, and a man's relationship to this mode is as a worker in an industry, or working class, this condition will shape the rest of his existence: his values, beliefs, behavior, and access to education, political power, and material possessions. Because the bourgeoisie (middle-class entrepreneurs) own and control the means of production, they have greater access to material possessions, education, and political power than the proletariat. This is how material conditions have always shaped life and this is the essence of his concept of materialism.

Superstructure

All of the ideas of human societies, including politics, philosophy, culture, religion, and morality, which Marx called the "superstructure," are determined by socioeconomic structures. Since economic structures, such as the mode of production, change over time, they cause changes in the superstructure, making history and progress. Historical progress occurs in a dialectical fashion through class struggle. The mode of production creates different social relations, or classes. Through technological innovation, the mode of production progresses to a new mode, and the lag between the new mode and the old social relations creates a violent class struggle, as those promoting change battle against the forces defending the existing social order. Marx predicted that eventually, when capitalism had been weakened by its own inherent problems, the proletariat would overthrow the industrial order and establish the next best rational order: a communist society based on equal relations to the mode of production, progress, contentment, and freedom.

Applying this economic theory to history, Marx defined three main eras in human history: ancient society, feudal society, and capitalist (or modern) society. Each epoch

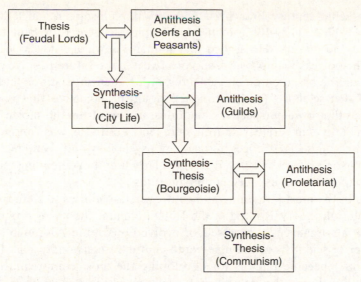

Illustration of the Marxist Dialectic

was defined by their mode of production, and each evolved or progressed to the next because of class struggle. This progress was dialectical in that human beings continually challenged the ideas and forms which came before them and revised and synthesized new ideas. This struggle would continue until the proletariat rose up in revolution to eliminate the bourgeoisie to establish an egalitarian social, economic, and political order, a fourth epoch of socialism. The proletariat, however, had to develop a class consciousness and be aware of their oppression in order to unite to make historical change happen.

History pervades most of Marx's writings, but he wrote few actual histories. The most famous of his histories is *The Eighteenth Brumaire of Louis Napoleon* (1859), which explored the revolutions which occurred in mid-nineteenth-century France. This short work compared the first French Revolution of the eighteenth century to that of 1848–1851, and Napoleon Bonaparte's actions to those of Louis Napoleon in an attempt to better understand the mechanics of revolutions and working-class radicalism. While Marx's theories shook the political world to its foundations in the twentieth century, influencing working-class organizations and communist revolutions across the globe, many historians and philosophers initially ignored his works as radical political tracts, rather than scholarly studies.

Empiricism

Far more influential than Idealism and Marxism in nineteenth-century European and American historiography was Empiricism. Francis Bacon and David Hume's empirical method of using observable evidence dominated the emerging sciences in

Comte

Positivism

the nineteenth century. French mathematician, philosopher, and father of sociology Auguste Comte (1798–1857) built upon empiricist ideas to formulate a new theory he called "positivism." He argued that human knowledge developed through three stages: theological, metaphysical, and positive.[3] In the future positive stage, all knowledge would be based on empirical truths, rather than superstition and prejudices. He asserted that scientists (and historians) should be objective, that is, separate themselves and their own perspectives, emotions, and bias from the subject under study. In this way, they could derive truth from pure facts. Positivism was enormously influential in the emerging social sciences of sociology, psychology, and economics, and those who viewed history as a science found it particularly useful in defending the importance of their discipline as one engaged in finding truths.

Evolution Theory

Darwin

One of the most influential and controversial theories to stem from Empiricism was evolution theory. Rooted in the Enlightenment theory of progress, this theory held that all organisms progressed, or evolved over time. Although this idea guided a number of scientists in the nineteenth century, English naturalist Charles Darwin (1809–1882) became famous for developing the most comprehensive explanation of evolution theory through natural selection. Using a wealth of evidence from a variety of biological organisms from all over the world, Darwin's *On the Origin of Species* (1859) posited that organisms which successfully adapt to their environment survive to procreate, while organisms which remain stagnant and do not adapt eventually die out.

Social Darwinism

Although he meant his theories to explain the evolution of animal species in general, his concept of "survival of the fittest" appealed to many Europeans and Americans eager to support their own theories of racial hierarchy among human beings. By the end of the nineteenth century, historians, politicians, and social theorists (most notably Herbert Spencer) had developed Social Darwinism, arguing that some human societies were more evolved than others. Since most of these theorists were upper-class males of European descent, they naturally saw themselves as the most highly evolved organisms in the world, and placed women, and people of lower classes and other regions of the world, lower down on the evolutionary scale. In this way, they used the idea of "survival of the fittest" to justify patriarchy, imperialism, and segregation. Despite little biological evidence to prove Social Darwinism, the literature of the late nineteenth and early twentieth centuries became infused with these racist, elitist, and sexist concepts, and historical literature was no exception.

Ranke

While evolution theory was one of the most powerful theories to emerge from the nineteenth century in terms of influencing European and American society, the historical profession in Europe and the United States was even more powerfully shaped by an important German empiricist: Leopold von Ranke (1795–1886). The son of a Lutheran minister and Professor at Berlin University for nearly fifty years, Ranke lived through the Napoleonic invasion of Germany and the Prussian state's militarization and unification of the German states. Writing over sixty books on various topics in

---

[3]Robert M. Burns, *Philosophies of History: From Enlightenment to Postmodernity* (Malden, MA: Blackwell, 2000), 100.

European and world history, and using the seminar method in teaching his numerous students, Ranke was at the cutting edge of history in this period and did much to raise the prestige of the discipline. He had tremendous faith in historians to find the truth about the past and to see the past *wie es eigentlich gewesen* ("as it essentially was").[4] His method of reconstructing the past included meticulous, exhaustive research and critical analysis of primary sources (documented with reference notes), disciplined objectivity in interpretations, and gifted historical intuition to draw out the essence of the meaning behind the facts. In some ways, his philosophy of history was both empiricist and Idealist: empiricist in its attempt to reconstruct reality based on specific, individual facts, and Idealist in its attempt to understand the internal essence (spirit or *zeitgeist*) of historical events. Like Hegel and other Idealists, he considered a universal consciousness, or God, to be the main agent guiding history.

Rankean Historicism Ranke's approach has also been termed "historicist," but in a slightly different way than earlier historicists. He agreed with Vico and others that the past must be understood in its own terms, but rather than focusing on universal truths and general patterns in the past, Ranke, like Herder, emphasized specific events and their individual natures.[5] His concept of the "otherness of the past" was strongly influenced by his belief that each historical age and each culture had its own *zeitgeist*, which manifested itself in specific political, religious, and cultural institutions and events. In order to reconstruct this spirit of the past accurately, historians needed to become objective observers, understanding the past within its own context and standards, rather than anachronistically through the lens of present-day values and beliefs. History, then, should be studied to gain this understanding of these past cultures for their own sake, rather than some present-minded speculative reason.

Narrative Ranke's style of writing reflected his view of himself as an objective authority observing his subject from a distance. Like Thucydides and others, he wrote in the narrative style, in which the historian takes on the role of truthful, objective, all-seeing storyteller of the past. These stories focused on specific events and persons, and traced the unfolding of history chronologically, from beginning to end, concluding with the wider meanings, or the moral, of the story. Ranke, however, saw his narratives as no mere fictional story. Although the historian's imagination played a role in organizing and interpreting the primary sources, Ranke stressed the scientific, fact-based nature of his work, and the empirical method as the crucial difference between history and other stories. A critical analysis of his histories, however, clearly shows how his own historical context and philosophy shaped his interpretations, making them less than objective. For example, Ranke's conservative political philosophy is revealed in his focus on the great nation-states as positive historical agents of change and the "thoughts of God."[6]

Ranke's methods, political focus, and emphasis on objectivity, however, helped to validate history as an academic discipline, and he was probably the most important

---

[4]Peter Novick, *That Noble Dream: The "Objectivity Question" and the American Historical Profession* (New York: Cambridge University Press, 1989), 28.

[5]Burns, *Philosophies of History*, 57.

[6]Novick, *That Noble Dream*, 27.

historian to shape the historical profession as it emerged in Europe and the United States in the late nineteenth century. His emphasis on archival research and his seminar teaching method, inviting groups of his best students into his home to analyze historical documents, also appealed to historians across Europe and the United States. As his methods and theories were translated across the ocean, however, the Idealist elements of his philosophy were lost, leaving many Americans to hail him as the champion of nonphilosophical, empirical history.[7]

Droysen

Despite Ranke's fame, one of his contemporaries, German historian Johann Gustav Droysen (1808–1884), lamented Ranke's method of source criticism, which he viewed as too simplistic and concerned only with verifying the authenticity of a document. Droysen was more hermeneutical in his approach, in that he attempted to understand the true meaning of a text as its authors had intended it by interpreting the text

Hermeneutics

in terms of its historical and literary context. Hermeneutics understands that "literal" or "realist" readings of texts are difficult if not impossible. Words often have multiple meanings and in order to understand what an author meant, one must place the words within the context of the whole literary work, and within the cultural and historical context in which the author lived. Understanding the deeper meaning of texts was central to the scientific study of history for Droysen. He believed that this understanding could only be achieved if historians could place themselves in the mental world of the past. Only if historians could understand the worldview of past actors could they truly understand how they perceived historical events.[8] While Droysen's theories made a small impact on German historiography in the nineteenth century, they would take on importance for new cultural historians in the late twentieth century.

Romanticism

Try as they might to be purely objective, positivists and empiricists of the nineteenth century all reflected the historical context in which they wrote. Many historians of the nineteenth century, including Ranke himself, were strongly influenced by the dual trends of Romanticism and nationalism sweeping Europe and the Americas in this period. Romanticism was in some ways a reaction against the cold and clinical approach of Enlightenment rationalism.[9] Romanticists agreed with the benefits of empirical evidence and historicism, but believed that history should express more emotion and creativity, and should read as well as the best literature.

This purpose suited political nationalists, who sought to use emotional appeals to foster patriotism toward the nation-state. The late eighteenth and early nineteenth

---

[7]Ibid., 30.

[8]Philipp Muller, "Understanding History. Hermeneutics and Source Criticism in Historical Scholarship," in *Reading Primary Sources: The Interpretation of Texts from 19th and 20th Century History*, ed. Miriam Dobson and Benjamin Ziemann (New York: Routledge, 2009), 21.

[9]Michael Bentley, "Introduction: Approaches to Modernity: Western Historiography Since the Enlightenment," in *Companion to Historiography* (New Y: Routledge, 1997), 412.

century consequently witnessed the emergence of new nation-states which used romantic nationalism to inspire unity and loyalty among their citizens. By providing a common glorious past with romantic heroes, history played a crucial political role in uniting diverse ethnic groups in each nation-state and gaining loyalty to newly formed republican and democratic governments. An essential part of gaining this loyalty was to prove the historical legitimacy of the new forms of government, the flaws of other forms of government, and the superiority of their nation-state as compared with others. European and American governments funded new history departments to promote this nationalist history, and this in turn fostered the prestige and growth of the historical profession.

Romantic national histories consequently dominated the public schools and book stores in the nineteenth century. These were typically "great man" or "drum and bugle" narratives about heroes from the nation's past: men (and occasionally women) who rallied the troops, destroyed the enemy, and illustrated idealized traits for all citizens to emulate. Romantic nationalists typically used elaborate sentimental prose to sing the praises of their nation's heroes and demonstrate their nation's progress above *Macaulay* and beyond all other nations. In England, Thomas Babington Macaulay (1800–1859) was the exemplar of Romantic nationalist history. Macaulay himself was a politician, serving in the House of Commons for many years, working to liberalize politics, remove religious barriers, and make the government more representative of the will *Whig* of the people. His *History of England* typified the so-called "Whig" interpretation of British history: an eloquent (if flowery and wordy) narrative focusing on high politics, great men, and the inevitable progress of English civilization.

Carlyle Scotsman Thomas Carlyle (1795–1881) carried Romanticism in a slightly different direction later in the century. His works focused more on the great men of history, rather than strictly on politics and government institutions. He asserted,

> …as I take it, Universal History, the history of what man has accomplished in this world, is at bottom the History of the Great Men who have worked here. They were the leaders of men, these great ones; the modelers, patterns, and in a wide sense creators, of whatsoever the general masses of men contrived to do as to attain.[10]

Both men published national histories as well as many biographies of great men throughout the nineteenth century. Both Macaulay and Carlyle used a variety of sources in an attempt at Empiricism, but their works more resemble novels than academic history, and probably because of this were very popular.

History emerged in nineteenth-century Europe as a new discipline and profession distinct from literature and philosophy for the first time. Progress remained the dominant theme for these histories, but professional historians increasingly distinguished their histories from those of amateurs by emphasizing the scientific nature of their empirical method and their objectivity. They increasingly focused on primary sources

---

[10]Thomas Carlyle, *On Heroes, Hero-Worship, and the Heroic in History* (London: Oxford University Press, 1968), 1 as quoted in Breisach, *Historiography*, 254.

and pointedly included them in reference notes. Supported by new nation-states, most historians wrote narratives proclaiming the historical legitimacy of nations by emphasizing the common history of peoples united by the political boundaries of the nation-state as it led the way toward progress. These narrative histories inspired patriotism to nation-states, admiration for national heroes, and esteem for the professional historians who wrote about them. Karl Marx and others strongly dissented against the positive view of the bourgeois nation-state, but even Marx advocated Empiricism and had a progressive view of history overall. With all its flaws and controversies, professional history was born in Europe in the nineteenth century and from there spread to a new nation-state: the United States of America.

Karl Marx, *The Eighteenth Brumaire of Louis Bonaparte*

Hegel says somewhere that that great historic facts and personages recur twice. He forgot to add: "Once as tragedy, and again as farce." Caussidiere for Danton, Louis Blanc for Robespierre, the "Mountain" of 1848–51 for the "Mountain" of 1793–05, the Nephew for the Uncle. The identical caricature marks also the conditions under which the second edition of the eighteenth Brumaire is issued.

Man makes his own history, but he does not make it out of the whole cloth; he does not make it out of conditions chosen by himself, but out of such as he finds close at hand. The tradition of all past generations weighs like an alp upon the brain of the living. At the very time when men appear engaged in revolutionizing things and themselves, in bringing about what never was before, at such very epochs of revolutionary crisis do they anxiously conjure up into their service the spirits of the past, assume their names, their battle cries, their costumes to enact a new historic scene in such time-honored disguise and with such borrowed language. Thus did Luther masquerade as the Apostle Paul; thus did the revolution of 1789-1814 drape itself alternately as Roman Republic and as Roman Empire; nor

did the revolution of 1818 know what better to do than to parody at one time the year 1789, at another the revolutionary traditions of 1793-95. Thus does the beginner, who has acquired a new language, keep on translating it back into his own mother tongue; only then has he grasped the spirit of the new language and is able freely to express himself therewith when he moves in it without recollections of the old, and has forgotten in its use his own hereditary tongue.

When these historic configurations of the dead past are closely observed a striking difference is forthwith noticeable. Camille Desmoulins, Danton, Robespierre, St. Juste, Napoleon, the heroes as well as the parties and the masses of the old French revolution, achieved in Roman costumes and with Roman phrases the task of their time: the emancipation and the establishment of modern bourgeois society. One set knocked to pieces the old feudal groundwork and mowed down the feudal heads that had grown upon it; Napoleon brought about, within France, the conditions under which alone free competition could develop, the partitioned lands be exploited the nation's unshackled powers of industrial production be utilized; while, beyond

Source: Karl Marx, *The Eighteenth Brumaire of Louis Bonaparte* (1852) trans. Daniel de Leon 3rd edition (Chicago: Charles H. Kerr, 1907), pp. 5–11 & 67–71. The reference notes were added by the translator. "Brumaire" refers to the second month of the French Republican calendar. Louis Bonaparte was the nephew of Napoleon, who seized control of France during the uprising of 1848–51.

the French frontier, he swept away everywhere the establishments of feudality, so far as requisite, to furnish the bourgeois social system of France with fit surroundings of the European continent, and such as were in keeping with the times. Once the new social establishment was set on foot, the antediluvian giants vanished, and, along with them, the resuscitated Roman world—the Brutuses, Gracchi, Publicolas, the Tribunes, the Senators, and Caesar himself. In its sober reality, bourgeois society had produced its own true interpretation in the Says, Cousins, Royer-Collards, Benjamin Constants and Guizots; its real generals sat behind the office desks; and the mutton-head of Louis XVIII was its political lead. Wholly absorbed in the production of wealth and in the peaceful fight of competition, this society could no longer understand that the ghosts of the days of Rome had watched over its cradle. And yet, lacking in heroism as bourgeois society is, it nevertheless had stood in need of heroism, of self-sacrifice, of terror, of civil war, and of bloody battle fields to bring it into the world. Its gladiators found in the stern classic traditions of the Roman republic the ideals and the form, the self-deceptions, that they needed in order to conceal from themselves the narrow bourgeois substance of their own struggles, and to keep their passion up to the height of a great historic tragedy. Thus, at another stage of development a century before, did Cromwell and the English people draw from the Old Testament the language, passions and illusions for their own bourgeois revolution. When the real goal was reached, when the remodeling of English society was accomplished, Locke supplanted Habakuk.

Accordingly, the reviving of the dead in those revolutions served the purpose of glorifying the new struggles, not of parodying the old; it served the purpose of exaggerating to the imagination the given task, not to recoil before its practical solution; it served the purpose of rekindling the revolutionary spirit, not to trot out its ghost.

In 1848–51 only the ghost of the old revolution wandered about, from Marrast the "Republicain en gauts jaunes,"[1] who disguised himself in old Bailly, down to the adventurer, who hid his repulsively trivial features under the iron death mask of Napoleon. A whole people, that imagines it has imparted to itself accelerated powers of motion through a revolution, suddenly finds itself transferred back to a dead epoch, and, lest there be any mistake possible on this head, the old dates turn up again; the old calendars; the old names; the old edicts, which long since had sunk to the level of the antiquarian's learning; even the old bailiffs, who had long seemed mouldering with decay. The nation takes on the appearance of that crazy Englishman in Bedlam, who imagines he is living in the days of the Pharaohs, and daily laments the hard work that he must do in the Ethiopian mines as gold digger, immured in a subterranean prison, with a dim lamp fastened on his head, behind him the slave overseer with a long whip, and, at the mouths of the mine a mob of barbarous camp servants who understand neither the convicts in the mines nor one another, because they do not speak a common language. "And all this," cries the crazy Englishman, "is demanded of me, the free-born Englishman, in order to make gold for old Pharaoh." "In order to pay off the debts of the Bonaparte family"—sobs the French nation. The Englishman, so long as he was in his senses, could not rid himself of the rooted thought making gold. The Frenchmen, so long as they were busy with a revolution, could not rid themselves of the Napoleonic memory, as the election of December 10th proved. They longed to escape from the dangers of revolution back to the flesh pots of Egypt; the 2d of December, 1851 was the answer. They have not merely the character of the old Napoleon, but the old Napoleon himself caricatured as he needs must appear in the middle of the nineteenth century.

---

[1] Silk-stocking republican

The social revolution of the nineteenth century cannot draw its poetry from the past, it can draw that only from the future. It cannot start upon its work before it has stricken off all superstition concerning the past. Former revolutions require historic reminiscences in order to intoxicate themselves with their own issues. The revolution of the nineteenth century must let the dead bury their dead in order to reach its issue. With the former, the phrase surpasses the substance; with this one, the substance surpasses the phrase.

The February revolution was a surprise; old society was taken unawares; and the people proclaimed this political stroke a great historic act whereby the new era was opened. On the 2d of December, the February revolution is jockeyed by the trick of a false player, and what is seer to be overthrown is no longer the monarchy, but the liberal concessions which had been wrung from it by centuries of struggles. Instead of society itself having conquered a new point, only the State appears to have returned to its oldest form, to the simply brazen rule of the sword and the club. Thus, upon the "coup de main" of February, 1848, comes the response of the "coup de tête" December, 1851. So won, so lost. Meanwhile, the interval did not go by unutilized. During the years 1848–1851, French society retrieved in abbreviated, because revolutionary, method the lessons and teachings, which—if it was to be more than a disturbance of the surface—should have preceded the February revolution, had it developed in regular order, by rule, so to say. Now French society seems to have receded behind its point of departure; in fact, however, it was compelled to first produce its own revolutionary point of departure, the situation, circumstances, conditions, under which alone the modern revolution is in earnest.

Bourgeois revolutions, like those of the eighteenth century, rush onward rapidly from success to success, their stage effects outbid one another, men and things seem to be set in flaming brilliants, ecstasy is the prevailing spirit; but they are short-lived, they reach their climax speedily, then society relapses into a long fit of nervous reaction before it learns how to appropriate the fruits of its period of feverish excitement. Proletarian revolutions, on the contrary, such as those of the nineteenth century, criticize themselves constantly; constantly interrupt themselves in their own course; come back to what seems to have been accomplished, in order to start over anew; scorn with cruel thoroughness the half measures, weaknesses and meannesses of their first attempts; seem to throw down their adversary only in order to enable him to draw fresh strength from the earth, and again, to rise up against them in more gigantic stature; constantly recoil in fear before the undefined monster magnitude of their own objects—until finally that situation is created which renders all retreat impossible, and the conditions themselves cry out:

"Hic Rhodus, hic salta!"[2]

Every observer of average intelligence; even if he failed to follow step by step the course of French development, must have anticipated that an unheard of fiasco was in store for the revolution. It was enough to hear the self-satisfied yelpings of victory wherewith the Messieurs Democrats mutually congratulated one another upon the pardons of May 2d, 1852. Indeed, May 2d had become a fixed idea in their heads; it had become a dogma with them—something like the day on which Christ was to reappear and the Millennium to begin had formed in the heads of the Chiliasts. Weakness had, as it ever does, taken refuge in the wonderful; it believed the enemy was overcome if, in its imagination, it hocus-pocused him away; and it lost all sense of the present in the imaginary apotheosis of the future, that was at hand, and of the deeds, that it had "in petto," but which it did not yet want to bring to the scratch. The heroes, who ever seek to refute their established incompetence by mutually bestowing their sympathy upon one

---

[2]Here is Rhodes, leap here! An allusion to Aesop's Fables.

another and by pulling together, had packed their satchels, taken their laurels in advance payments and were just engaged in the work of getting discounted "in partibus," on the stock exchange, the republics for which, in the silence of their unassuming dispositions, they had carefully organized the government personnel. The 2d of December struck them like a bolt from a clear sky; and the peoples, who, in periods of timid despondency, gladly allow their hidden fears to be drowned by the loudest screamers, will perhaps have become convinced that the days are gone by when the cackling of geese could save the Capitol.

The constitution, the national assembly, the dynastic parties, the blue and the red republicans, the heroes from Africa, the thunder from the tribune, the flash-lightnings from the daily press, the whole literature, the political names and the intellectual celebrities, the civil and the criminal law, the "liberté, égalité, fraternité," together with the 2d of May 1852—all vanished like a phantasmagoria before the ban of one man, whom his enemies themselves do not pronounce an adept at witchcraft. Universal suffrage seems to have survived only for a moment, to the end that, before the eyes of the whole world, it should make its own testament with its own hands, and, in the name of the people, declare: "All that exists deserves to perish."

It is not enough to say, as the Frenchmen do, that their nation was taken by surprise. A nation, no more than a woman, is excused for the unguarded hour when the first adventurer who comes along can do violence to her. The riddle is not solved by such shifts, it is only formulated in other words. There remains to be explained how a nation of thirty-six millions can be surprised by three swindlers, and taken to prison without resistance.

Let us recapitulate in general outlines the phases which the French revolution of February 24th, 1848, to December, 1851, ran through.

Three main periods are unmistakable:

First—The February period;
Second—The period of constituting the republic, or of the constitutive national assembly (May 4, 1848, to May 29th, 1849);

Third—The period of the constitutional republic, or of the legislative national assembly (May 29, 1849, to December 2, 1851).

The first period, from February 24, or the downfall of Louis Philippe, to May 4, 1848, the date of the assembling of the constitutive assembly—the February period proper—may be designated as the prologue of the revolution. It officially expressed its own character in this, that the government which it improvised declared itself "provisional;" and, like the government, everything that was broached, attempted, or uttered, pronounced itself provisional. Nobody and nothing dared to assume the right of permanent existence and of an actual fact. All the elements that had prepared or determined the revolution—dynastic opposition, republican bourgeoisie, democratic-republican small traders' class, social-democratic labor element—all found "provisionally" their place in the February government.

It could not be otherwise. The February days contemplated originally a reform of the suffrage laws, whereby the area of the politically privileged among the property-holding class was to be extended, while the exclusive rule of the aristocracy of finance was to be overthrown. When, however, it came to a real conflict, when the people mounted the barricades, when the National Guard stood passive, when the army offered no serious resistance, and the kingdom ran away, then the republic seemed self-understood. Each party interpreted it in its own sense. Won, arms in hand, by the proletariat, they put upon it the stamp of their own class, and proclaimed the social republic. Thus the general purpose of modern revolutions was indicated, a purpose, however, that stood in most singular contradiction to everything that, with the material at hand, with the stage of enlightenment that the masses had reached, and under existing circumstances and conditions, could be immediately used. On the other hand, the claims of all the other elements, that had cooperated in the revolution of February, were recognized by the lion's share that they received in the government. Hence, in no period do we find a more motley mixture of high-sounding phrases together with actual doubt and helplessness; of more enthusiastic reform aspirations, together with a more slavish adherence to the old routine; more seeming harmony permeating the whole of society together with a deeper alienation of its several elements. While the Parisian proletariat was still gloating over the sight of the great perspective that had disclosed itself to their view, and was indulging in seriously meant discussions over the social problems, the old powers of society had groomed themselves, had gathered together, had deliberated and found an unexpected support in the mass of the nation—the peasants and small traders—all of whom threw themselves on a sudden upon the political stage, after the barriers of the July monarchy had fallen down.

The second period, from May 4, 1848, to the end of May, 1849, is the period of the constitution, of the founding of the bourgeois republic immediately after the February days, not only was the dynastic opposition surprised by the republicans, and the republicans by the Socialists, but all France was surprised by Paris. The national assembly, that met on May 4, 1848, to frame a constitution, was the outcome of the national elections; it represented the nation. It was a living protest against the assumption of the February days, and it was intended to bring the results of the revolution back to the bourgeois measure. In vain did the proletariat of Paris, which forthwith understood the character of this national assembly, endeavor, a few days after its meeting; on May 15, to deny its existence by force, to dissolve it, to disperse the organic apparition, in which the reacting spirit of the nation was threatening them, and thus reduce it back to its separate component parts. As is known, the 15th of May had no other result than that of removing Blanqui and his associates, i.e. the real leaders of the proletarian party, from the public scene for the whole period of the cycle which we are here considering.

Upon the bourgeois monarchy of Louis Philippe, only the bourgeois republic could follow; that is to say, a limited portion of the bourgeoisie having ruled under the name of the king, now the whole bourgeoisie was to rule under the name of the people. The demands of the Parisian proletariat are utopian tom-fooleries that have to be done away with. To this declaration of the constitutional national assembly, the Paris proletariat answers with the June insurrection, the most colossal event in the history of European civil wars. The bourgeois republic won. On its side stood the aristocracy of finance, the industrial bourgeoisie; the middle class; the small traders' class; the army; the slums, organized as Guarde Mobile; the intellectual celebrities, the parsons' class, and the rural population. On the side of the Parisian proletariat stood none but itself. Over 3,000 insurgents were massacred, after the victory 15,000 were transported without trial. With this defeat, the proletariat steps to the background on the revolutionary stage. It always seeks to crowd forward, so soon as the movement seems to acquire new impetus, but with ever weaker effort and ever smaller results; So soon as any of the above lying layers of society gets into revolutionary fermentation, it enters into alliance therewith and thus shares all the defeats which the several parties successively suffer. But these succeeding blows become ever weaker the more generally they are distributed over the whole surface of society. The more important leaders of the Proletariat, in its councils, and the press, fall one after another victims of the courts, and ever more questionable figures step to the front. It partly throws itself it upon doctrinaire experiments, "co-operative banking" and "labor exchange" schemes; in other words, movements, in which it goes into movements in which it gives up the task of revolutionizing the old world with its own large collective weapons and on the contrary, seeks to bring about its emancipation, behind the back of society, in private ways, within the narrow bounds of its own class conditions, and, consequently, inevitably fails. The proletariat seems to be able neither to find again the revolutionary magnitude within itself nor to draw new energy from the newly formed alliances until all the classes, with whom it contended in June, shall lie prostrate along with itself. But in all these defeats, the proletariat succumbs at least with the honor that attaches to great historic struggles; not France alone, all Europe trembles before the June earthquake, while the successive defeats inflicted upon the higher classes are bought so easily that they need the brazen exaggeration of the victorious party itself to be at all able to pass muster as an event; and these defeats become more disgraceful the further removed the defeated party stands from the proletariat.

True enough, the defeat of the June insurgents prepared, leveled the ground, upon which the bourgeois republic could be founded and erected; but it, at the same time, showed that there are in Europe other issues besides that of "Republic or Monarchy." It revealed the fact that here the Bourgeois Republic meant the unbridled despotism of one class over another. It proved that, with nations enjoying an older civilization, having developed class distinctions, modern conditions of production, an intellectual consciousness, wherein all traditions of old have been dissolved through the work of centuries, that with such countries the republic means only the political revolutionary form of bourgeois society, not its conservative form of existence, as is the case in the United States of America, where, true enough, the classes already exist, but have not yet acquired permanent character, are in constant flux and reflux, constantly changing their elements and yielding them up to one another where the modern means of production, instead of coinciding with a stagnant population, rather compensate for the relative scarcity of heads and hands; and, finally, where the feverishly youthful life of material production, which has to appropriate a new world to itself, has so far

left neither time nor opportunity to abolish the illusions of old.[3]....

[Louis] Bonaparte represents an economic class, and that the most numerous in the commonweal of France—the Allotment Farmer.[4]

As the Bourbons are the dynasty of large landed property, as the Orleans are the dynasty of money, so are the Bonapartes the dynasty of the farmer, i.e. of the French masses. Not the Bonaparte, who threw himself at the feet of the bourgeois parliament, but the Bonaparte, who swept away the bourgeois parliament, is the elect of this farmer class. For three years the cities had succeeded in falsifying the meaning of the election of December 10, and in cheating the farmer out of the restoration of the Empire. The election of December 10, 1848, is not carried out until the "coup d'état" of December 2, 1851.

The allotment farmers are an immense mass, whose individual members live in identical conditions, without, however, entering into manifold relations with one another. Their method of production isolates them from one another, instead of drawing them into mutual intercourse. This isolation is promoted by the poor means of communication in France, together with the poverty of the farmers themselves. Their field of production, the small allotment of land that each cultivates, allows no room for a division of labor, and no opportunity for the application of science; in other words, it shuts out manifoldness of development, diversity of talent, and the luxury of social relations. Every single farmer family is almost self-sufficient; itself produces directly the greater part of what it consumes; and it earns its livelihood more by means of an interchange with nature than by intercourse with society. We have the allotted patch of land, the farmer and his family; alongside of that another allotted patch of land,

---

[3]This was written at the beginning of 1852.

[4]The first French Revolution distributed the bulk of the territory of France, held at the time by the feudal lords, in small patches among the cultivators of the soil. This allotment of lands created the French farmer class.

another farmer and another family. A bunch of these makes up a village; a bunch of villages makes up a Department. Thus the large mass of the French nation is constituted by the simple addition of equal magnitudes—much as a bag with potatoes constitutes a potato-bag. In so far as millions of families live under economic conditions that separate their mode of life, their interests and their culture from those of the other classes, and that place them in an attitude hostile toward the latter, they constitute a class; in so far as there exists only a local connection among these farmers, a connection which the individuality and exclusiveness of their interests prevent from generating among them any unity of interest, national connections, and political organization, they do not constitute a class. Consequently, they are unable to assert their class interests in their own name, be it by a parliament or by convention. They can not represent one another, they must themselves be represented. Their representative must at the same time appear as their master, as an authority over them, as an unlimited governmental power, that protects them from above, bestows rain and sunshine upon them. Accordingly, the political influence of the allotment farmer finds its ultimate expression in an Executive power that subjugates the commonweal to its own autocratic will....

>> Questions for Consideration

1. What specifically makes this a Marxist history (aside from the fact Marx wrote it)?
2. Compare Marx's periodization to that of Condorcet and Vico. Why might they differ?
3. What knowledge does Marx assume of the reader? How does this affect your understanding of his history?

Leopold von Ranke, *History of the Reformation in Germany*

Preface

I see the time approach in which we shall no longer have to found modern history on the reports even of contemporary historians, except in so far as they were in possession of personal and immediate knowledge of facts; still less, on works yet more remote from the source; but on the narratives of eye-witnesses, and the genuine and original documents. For the epoch treated in the following work, this prospect is no distant one. I myself have made use of a number of records which I had found when in the pursuit of another subject, in the Archives of Vienna, Venice, Rome, and especially Florence.

Had I gone into further detail, I should have run the risk of losing sight of the subject as a whole; or in the necessary lapse of time, of breaking the unity of the conception which had arisen before my mind in the course of my past researches.

And thus I proceeded boldly to the completion of this work; persuaded that when an inquirer has made researches of some extent in authentic records, with an earnest spirit and a genuine ardour for truth, though later discoveries may throw clearer and more certain light on details, they can only strengthen his fundamental conceptions of the subject:—for truth can be but one.

Source: Leopold von Ranke, *History of the Reformation in Germany Volume I* (1845–1847), translated by Sarah Austin, Edited by Robert A. Johnson (NY: Frederick Ungar, 1905): vii–xi, 1–2, 40–43. The reference notes here are Ranke's own.

Introduction

View of the Early History of Germany

For purposes of discussion or of instruction, it may be possible to sever ecclesiastical from political history; in actual life, they are indissolubly connected, or rather fused into one indivisible whole.

As indeed there is nothing of real importance in the moral and intellectual business of human life, the source of which does not lie in a profound and more or less conscious relation of man and his concerns to God and divine things, it is impossible to conceive a nation worthy of the name, or entitled to be called, in any sense, great, whose political existence is not constantly elevated and guided by religious ideas. To cultivate, purify and exalt these,—to give them an expression intelligible to all and profitable to all,—to embody them in outward forms and public acts, is its necessary as well as its noblest task.

It is not to be denied that this process inevitably brings into action two great principles which seem to place a nation at variance with itself. Nationality (*i.e.* the sum of the peculiar qualities, habits, and sentiments of a nation) is necessarily restricted within the bounds marked out by neighbouring nationalities; whereas religion, ever since it was revealed to the world in a form which claims and deserves universality, constantly strives after sole and absolute supremacy.

In the foundation or constitution of a State, some particular moral or intellectual principle predominates; a principle prescribed by an inherent necessity, expressed in determinate forms and giving birth to a peculiar condition of society, or character of civilization. But no sooner has a Church, with its forms of wider application, embracing different nations, arisen, than it grasps at the project of absorbing the State, and of reducing the principle on which civil society is founded to complete subjection: the original underived authority of that principle is, indeed, rarely acknowledged by the Church.

At length the universal religion appears, and, after it has incorporated itself with the consciousness of mankind, assumes the character of a great and growing tradition, handed down from people to people, and communicated in rigid dogmas. But nations cannot suffer themselves to be debarred from exercising the understanding bestowed on them by nature, or the knowledge acquired by study, on an investigation of its truth. In every age, therefore, we see diversities in the views of religion arise in different nations, and these again react in various ways on the character and condition of the State. It is evident, from the nature of this struggle, how mighty is the crisis which it involves for the destinies of the human race. Religious truth must have an outward and visible representation, in order that the State may be perpetually reminded of the origin and the end of our earthly existence; of the rights of our neighbors, and the kindred of all the nations of the earth; it would otherwise be in danger of degenerating into tyranny, or of hardening into inveterate prejudice,—into intolerant conceit of self, and hatred of all that is foreign. On the other hand, a free development of the national character and culture is necessary to the interests of religion. Without this, its doctrines can never be truly understood nor profoundly accepted: without incessant alternations of doubt and conviction, of assent and dissent, of seeking and finding, no error could be removed, no deeper understanding of truth attained. Thus, then, independence of thought and political freedom are indispensable to the Church herself; she needs them to remind her of the varying intellectual wants of men, of the changing nature of her own forms; she needs them to preserve her from the lifeless iteration of misunderstood doctrines and rites, which kill the soul.

It has been said, the State is itself the Church, but the Church has thought herself authorized to usurp the place of the State. The truth is, that the spiritual or intellectual life of man—in its intensest depth and energy unquestionably one—yet manifests itself in these two institutions, which come into contact under the most varied forms;

which are continually striving to pervade each other, yet never entirely coincide; to exclude each other, yet neither has ever been permanently victor or vanquished. In the nations of the West, at least, such a result has never been obtained. The Califate may unite ecclesiastical and political power in one hand; but the whole life and character of western Christendom consists of the incessant action and counter-action of Church and State; hence arises the freer, more comprehensive, more profound activity of mind, which must, on the whole, be admitted to characterize that portion of the globe. The aspect of the public life of Europe is always determined by the mutual relations of these two great principles.

Hence it happens that ecclesiastical history is not to be understood without political, nor the latter without the former. The combination of both is necessary to present either in its true light; and if ever we are able to fathom the depths of that profounder life where both have their common source and origin, it must be by a complete knowledge of this combination.

But if this is the case with all nations, it is most pre-eminently so with the German, which has bestowed more persevering and original thought on ecclesiastical and religious subjects than any other. The events of ten centuries turn upon the struggles between the Empire and the Papacy, between Catholicism and Protestantism. We, in our days, stand midway between them.

My design is to relate the history of an epoch in which the politico-religious energy of the German nation was most conspicuous for its growth and most prolific in its results. I do not conceal from myself the great difficulty of this undertaking; but, with God's help, I will endeavour to accomplish it. I shall first attempt to trace my way through a retrospect of earlier times....

Book I.

Attempt to Reform the Constitution of the Empire 1486–1517

....The ideas upon which human society is based are but partially and imperfectly imbued with the divine and eternal Essence from which they emanate; for a time they are beneficient and vivifying, and new creations spring up under their breath. But on earth nothing attains to a pure and perfect existence, and therefore nothing is immortal. When the times are accomplished, higher aspirations and more enlightened schemes spring up out of the tottering remains of former institutions, which they utterly overthrow and efface; for so has God ordered the world.

If the disorders in question were universal, the efforts to put an end to them were not less so. Powers called into life by the necessity of a change, or growing up spontaneously, arose out of the general confusion, and with vigorous and unbidden hand imposed order on the chaos.

This is the great event of the fifteenth century. The names of the energetic princes of that time, whose task it was first to awaken the nations of Europe to a consciousness of their own existence and importance, are known to all. In France we find Charles VII. And Louis XI. The land was at length delivered from the enemy who had so long held divided sway in it, and was united under the standard of the Lilies; the monarchy was founded on a military and financial basis; crafty, calculating policy came in aid of the practical straightforward sense which attained its ends, because it aimed only at what was necessary; all the daring and insolent powers that had bid defiance to the supreme authority were subdued or overthrown: the new order of things had already attained to sufficient strength to endure a long and storm minority.

Henry VII of England, without attempting to destroy the ancient liberties of the nation, laid the foundation of the power of the Tudors on the ruins of the two factions of the aristocracy, with a resolution nothing could shake and a vigour nothing could resist. The Norman times were over;—modern England began. At the same time Isabella of Castile reduced her refractory vassals to submission, by her union with a powerful neighbour, by the share she had acquired in the spiritual power, and by the natural ascendancy of her own grand and womanly character, in which austere domestic virtue and a high chivalrous spirit were so singularly blended. She succeeded in completely driving out the Moors and pacifying the Peninsula. Even in Italy, some stronger governments were consolidated; five considerable states were formed, united by a free alliance, and for a while capable of counteracting all foreign influence. At the same time Poland, doubly strong through her union with Lithuania, climbed to the highest pinnacle of power she ever possessed; while in Hungary, a native king maintained the honour and the unity of his nation at the head of the powerful army he had assembled under his banner.

However various were the resources and the circumstances by which it was surrounded, Monarchy—the central power—was everywhere strong enough to put down the resisting independencies; to exclude foreign influence; to rally the people around its standard, by appealing to the national spirit under whose guidance it acted; and thus to give them a feeling of unity.

In Germany, however, this was not possible. The two powers which might have effected the most were so far carried along by the general tendency of the age that they endeavoured to introduce some degree of order; we have seen with what small success. At the very time in which all the monarchies of Europe consolidated themselves, the emperor was driven out of his hereditary states, and wandered about the other parts of the empire as a fugitive.[1] He was dependent for his daily repast on the bounty of convents, or of the burghers of the imperial cities; his other wants were supplied from the slender revenues of his chancery: he might sometimes be seen traveling along the roads of his own dominions in a carriage drawn by oxen; never—and this he himself felt—was the majesty of the empire dragged about in meaner form: the possessor of a power which, according to the received idea, ruled the world, was become an object of contemptuous pity.

If anything was to be done in Germany, it must be by other means, upon other principles, with other objects, than any that had hitherto been contemplated or employed.

Foundation of a New Constitution.[2]

It is obvious at the first glance, that no attempt at reform could be successful which did not originate with the States themselves. Since they had taken up so strong a position against the two co-ordinate higher powers, they were bound to show how far that position was likely to prove beneficial to the public interests.

It was greatly in their favour that the emperor had sunk into so deplorable a situation.

Not that it was their intention to make use of this to his entire overthrow or destruction; on the contrary, they were determined not to allow him to fall. What for centuries only one emperor had accomplished, and he, in the fullness of his power and by dispensing extraordinary favours (viz. to secure the succession to his son), Frederick III. Achieved in the moment of the deepest humiliation and weakness. The prince-electors met in the year 1486, to choose his son Maximilian king of the Romans. In this measure, Albert Achilles of Brandenburg, took the most prominent and active part. Notwithstanding his advanced age, he came once more in person to Frankfurt: he caused himself to be carried into the electoral chapel on a litter, whence at the close of the proceedings, he presented the scepter;

---

[1]See Unrest, Chronicon austriacum; Hahn. 660–688. Kurz, Oestreich unter Friedrich III, vol. ii.

[2]For an outline of the Germanic Constitution cf. Cambridge Modern History, vol. i., p. 288. Johnson, Europe in the Sixteenth Century, p. 106. Wolf, Deutsche Geschichte im Zeitalter der Gegenreformation, p. 1–113 (more fully).

he was in the act of performing his high function as archchamberlain of the empire, when he expired. It could not escape the electors, that the claims of the house of Austria to the support of the empire were greatly strengthened by this event. Maximilian, the son-in-law of Charles the Bold, who had undertaken to uphold the rights of the house of Burgundy in the Netherlands, encountered there difficulties and misfortunes not much inferior to those which beset his father in Austria, and must, on no account, be abandoned. His election could hardly be regarded as fully accomplished, until the countries which had hitherto maintained a hostile attitude were subjected to him, and thus restored to the empire. It was precisely by determining to send succours in both directions, that the states acquired a two-fold right to discuss internal affairs according to their own judgment. They had rendered fresh services to the reigning house, which could not defend its hereditary possessions without their aid, and their voices must now be heard.

At this moment, too, a coolness arose between the emperor and the pope. There was a large party in Europe which had always regarded the rise of the Austrian power with dislike, and was now greatly offended at the election of Maximilian to the Roman throne. To this party, in consequence of the turn Italian affairs had taken, Pope Innocent VII. belonged. He refused the emperor aid against the Hungarians, and even against the Turks. The imperial ambassador found him, as Frederick complained to the diet, "very awkward to deal with" (*gar ungeschickt*),[3] and could do nothing with him. There was also a difference with the pope about the nomination to the see of Passau, as well as about a newly-imposed tithe. In short, the intervention of the Roman see was, for a moment, suspended.

For the first time, during a long period, we find numerous assemblies of German princes without the presence of a papal legate.

Under these circumstances the deliberations of the States were opened with a better prospect of useful results.

It was evidently not necessary to begin from the beginning; all the elements of a great commonwealth were at hand. The diets had long been regarded as the focus of legislation and of the general government: peace (*Landfriede*) had been proclaimed throughout the realm; an imperial court of justice existed; as long ago as the Hussite war a census had been taken with a view to the general defence of the empire. Nothing remained but to give to these institutions that steady and pervading action which they had hitherto entirely wanted.

To this effect deliberations were incessantly held from the year 1486 to 1489. Ideas embracing the whole land of the German people, and directed to the restoration of its unity and strength, were in active circulation. In order to obtain a more complete and accurate conception of the several important points, we will consider them, not in their historical connection either with each other or with contemporaneous events, but each separately.

The first was the Public Peace, which had again been broken on every side, and now, proclaimed anew in 1486, had been rendered clear by some more precise provisions annexed in 1487; yet it differed little from those which had gone before it. The execution of it was now, as heretofore, left to the tumultuous levy of the neighbourhood within a circle of from six to ten miles (German); nay, the declaration of 1487 expressly declares that a party in whose favour sentence had been pronounced might use force to secure its execution.[4] The only difference was

---

[3]Müller, Rtth. unter Friedrich III. v. 122.

[4]Müller, Rtth. Fr. VI., 115. "Wo aber der, der gewaltige Tate fürneme und übe, das thete uf behapte Urtheil, so solt darüber nyemant dem Bekriegten das mahl Hilf zuzuschicken schuldig seyn." "When, however, anyone, undertaking and exercising acts of violence, does so upon judgment received in his favour, then shall no one be bound to send help thereupon to him who is attacked."

that the co-operation of the pope was no longer invited. There was no further mention of sending papal conservators with peculiar powers of executing justice, in order to the maintenance of the Public Peace. This, however, rendered it doubtful whether the clergy, to whom the pope and the church were much more proximate and formidable than the emperor and the state, would choose to regard themselves as bound by the peace. No other means could be found to obviate this evil than that the emperor should declare, as the bishops had done in regard to their own nobility, that he would put the disobedient out of the favour and protection of the law, and would not defend them from any aggression or injury.

We see what a state of violence, insubordination, and mutual independence still prevailed, and even manifested itself in the laws; and how necessary it was to establish internal regulations, by the firmness and energy of which arbitrary power might be held in check, and the encroachments of an authority which, at the very first meeting of the estates, was regarded as foreign, might be repelled.

The most essential point was to give to the imperial diets more regular forms and greater dignity; and especially to put an end to the resistance offered to their edicts by the cities.

The cities, which were so often hostilely treated by the other estates, and which had interests of so peculiar a nature to defend, held themselves from the earliest period studiously aloof.

During the Hussite war they were even permitted to send into the field a separate municipal army under a captain of their own appointment.[5] In the year 1460 they declined going to council with the princes, or uniting in a common answer to the emperor's proposals.[6] In the year 1474 the deputies refused to approve the Public Peace concluded by the emperor and princes, and obstinately persisted that they would say nothing to it till they had consulted their friends.[7] In 1486 the princes having granted some subsidies to the emperor to which the cities were called upon to contribute, they resisted, and the more strenuously, since they had not even been summoned to the meeting at which the grant was made. Frederick replied that this had not been done, because they would have done nothing without sending home for instructions.

It was evident that this state of things could not be maintained. The imperial cities justly deemed it an intolerable grievance that they should be taxed according to an arbitrary assessment, and a contribution demanded of them as if it were a debt; on the other hand, it was just as little to be endured that they should obstruct every definite decision, and send home to consult their constituents on every individual grant.

So powerful was the influence of the prevailing spirit of the times, that, in the year 1487, the cities came to a resolution to abandon the course they had hitherto pursued.

---

[5]In the year 1431. Datt de Pace Publica, 167.

[6]Protocol in Müller, i., p. 782: with this addition, however, "Sie wolten solch fründlich Fürbringen ihren Fründen berümen." "They would commend so friendly a proposition to their friends."

[7]The answer given by them in Müller, ii., p. 626, is vague and obscure. In the Frankfurt Archives (vol. viii.) it runs thus: "Als die des Friedens nothurftig und begerlich sind, setzen sy (die Städte) in kein Zweifel, E. K. M. (werde) gnediglich darob und daran seyn, dass der vestiglich gehandhabt und gehalten werde: dazu sy aber irenthalb zu reden nit bedacht sind, auch kein Befel haben, untertheniglich bittend, das S. K. M. das also in Gnaden und Guten von in versten und sy als ir allergnedigster Herr bedenken wolle."—"As they have need, and are desirous of peace, they (the cities) make no doubt, your Imperial Majesty will graciously strive to bring about that it be firmly maintained and kept; but beyond this they have no thought of speaking on their own behalf, nor have any command so to do, submissively entreating, that his Imperial Majesty will therefore take this in good and gracious understanding from them, and think of them like their most gracious master."...

>> Questions for Consideration

1. Compare Ranke's periodization and choice of topic to that of Marx: How does Ranke's periodization and topic reflect what he sees as the main driving forces of history and his own conservative German orientation?

2. How might Ranke's religious views have shaped his history? Could his history be considered objective?

3. What evidence does Ranke use? Does this seem empirical to you? Why or why not?

4. What role does *zeitgeist* (the essence, spirit, or set of ideas) play in this history?

Thomas Babington Macaulay, "The Task of the Modern Historian" and "The Revolution of 1688"

"The Task of the Modern Historian" From the essay *on History, Edinburgh Review* (May, 1828)

The perfect historian is he in whose work the character and spirit of an age is exhibited in miniature. He relates no fact, he attributes no expression to his character, which is not authenticated by sufficient testimony. But by judicious selection, rejection, and arrangement, he gives to truth those attractions which have been usurped by fiction. In his narrative a due subordination is observed; some transactions are prominent, others retire. But the scale on which he represents them is increased or diminished, not according to the dignity of the persons concerned in them, but according to the degree in which they elucidate the condition of society and the nature of man. He shows us the court, the camp, and the senate. But he shows us also the nation. He considers no anecdote, no peculiarity of manner, no familiar saying, as too insignificant for his notice, which is not too insignificant to illustrate the operation of laws, of religion, and of education, and to mark the progress of the human mind. Men will not merely be described, but will be made intimately known to us. The changes of manners will be indicated, not merely by a few general phrases, or a few extracts from statistical documents, but by appropriate images presented in every line.

If a man, such as we are supposing, should write the history of England, he would assuredly not omit the battles, the sieges, the negotiations, the seditions, the ministerial changes. But with these he would intersperse the details which are the charm of historical romances. At Lincoln Cathedral there is a beautiful painted window, which was made by an apprentice out of the pieces of glass which had been rejected by his master. It is so far superior to every other in the church, that, according to the tradition, the vanquished artist killed himself from mortification. Sir Walter Scott, in the same manner, has used those fragments of truth which historians have scornfully thrown behind them, in a manner which may well excite their envy.

He has constructed out of their gleanings works which, even considered as histories, are scarcely less valuable than theirs. But a truly great historian would reclaim those materials

---

Source: Thomas Babington Macaulay, "The Task of the Modern Historian" (1828) and *The History of England* (1849) in *Little Masterpieces: Lord Macaulay,* ed. Bliss Perry (NY: Doubleday, Page, and Co., 1906): pp. 15–22 & 166–179.

which the novelist has appropriated. The history of the government and the history of the people would be exhibited in that mode in which alone they can be exhibited justly, in inseparable conjunction and intermixture. We should not then have to look for the wars and votes of the Puritans in Clarendon, and for their phraseology in Old Mortality; for one half of King James in Hume, and for the other half in the Fortunes of Nigel.

The early part of our imaginary history would be rich with coloring from romance, ballad, and chronicle. We should find ourselves in the company of knights such as those of Froissart, and of pilgrims such as those who rode with Chaucer from the Tabard. Society would be shown from the highest to the lowest—from the royal cloth of state to the den of the outlaw; from the throne of the legate to the chimney-corner where the begging friar regaled himself. Palmers, minstrels, crusaders—the stately monastery, with the good cheer in its refectory, and the high-mass in its chapel—the manor-house, with its hunting and hawking—the tournament, with the heralds and ladies, the trumpets and the cloth of gold—would give truth and life to the representation. We should perceive, in a thousand slight touches, the importance of the privileged burgher, and the fierce and haughty spirit which swelled under the collar of the degraded villain. The revival of letters would not merely be described in few magnificent periods. We should discern, in innumerable particulars, the fermentation of mind, the eager appetite for knowledge, which distinguished the sixteenth from the fifteenth century. In the Reformation we should see, not merely a schism which changed the ecclesiastical constitution of England and the mutual relations of the European powers, but a moral war which raged in every family, which set the father against the son, and the son against the father, the mother against the daughter, and the daughter against the mother. Henry would be painted with the skill of Tacitus.

We should have the change of his character from his profuse and joyous youth to his savage and imperious old age. We should perceive the gradual progress of selfish and tyrannical passions, in a mind not naturally insensible or ungenerous; and to the last we should detect some remains of that open and noble temper which endeared him to a people whom he oppressed, struggling with the hardness of despotism and the irritability of disease. We should see Elizabeth in all her weakness, and in all her strength, surrounded by the handsome favorites whom she never trusted, and the wise old statesmen whom she never dismissed, uniting in herself the most contradictory qualities of both her parents—the coquetry, the caprice, the petty malice of Anne—the haughty and resolute spirit of Henry. We have no hesitation in saying, that a great artist might produce a portrait of this remarkable woman, at least as striking as that in the novel of Kenilworth, without employing a single trait not authenticated by ample testimony. In the mean time, we should see arts cultivated, wealth accumulated, the conveniences of life improved.

We should see the keeps, where nobles, insecure themselves, spread insecurity around them, gradually giving place to the halls of peaceful opulence, to the oriels of Longleat, and the stately pinnacles of Burleigh. We should see towns extended, deserts cultivated, the hamlets of fishermen turned into wealthy havens, the meal of the peasant improved, and his hut more commodiously furnished. We should see those opinions and feelings which produced the great struggle against the house of Stuart, slowly growing up in the bosom of private families, before they manifested themselves in parliamentary debates. Then would come the civil war. Those skirmishes, on which Clarendon dwells so minutely, would be told, as Thucydides would have told them, with perspicuous conciseness. They are merely connecting links. But the great characteristics of the age, the loyal enthusiasm of the brave English gentry, the fierce licentiousness of the swearing, dicing, drunken reprobates, whose excesses disgraced the royal cause—the austerity of the Presbyterian Sabbaths in the city, the extravagance of the Independent preachers in the camp, the precise garb, the severe countenance, the petty scruples, the affected accents, the absurd names and phrases which marked the Puritans—the valor, the policy, the public spirit which lurked beneath these ungraceful disguises—the dreams of the raving Fifth-monarchy-man—the dreams, scarcely less wild, of the philosophic republican—all these would enter into the representation, and render it at once more exact and more striking.

The instruction derived from history thus written would be of a vivid and practical character. It would be received by the imagination as well as by the reason. It would be not merely traced on the mind, but branded into it. Many truths, too, would be learned, which can be learned, in no other manner. As the history of states is generally written, the greatest and most momentous revolutions seem to come upon them like supernatural inflictions, without warning or cause. But the fact is, that such revolutions are almost always the consequence of moral changes, which have gradually passed on the mass of the community, and which ordinarily proceed far before their progress is indicated by any public measure. An intimate knowledge of the domestic history of nations is therefore absolutely necessary to the prognosis of political events. A narrative defective in this respect is as useless as a medical treatise which should pass by all the symptoms attendant on the early stage of a disease, and mention only what occurs when the patient is beyond the reach of remedies.

An historian, such as we have been attempting to describe, would indeed be an intellectual prodigy. In his mind, powers, scarcely compatible with each other, must be tempered into an exquisite harmony. We shall sooner see another Shakespeare or another Homer. The highest excellence to which any single faculty can be brought would be less surprising than such a happy and delicate combination of qualities. Yet the contemplation of imaginary models is not an unpleasant or useless employment of the mind. It cannot indeed produce perfection, but it produces improvement, and nourishes that generous

and liberal fastidiousness, which is not inconsistent with the strongest sensibility to merit, and which, while it exalts our conceptions of the art, does not render us unjust to the artist.

"The Revolution of 1688" From the *History of England, Chapter X*

When we compare it [the English Revolution] with those revolutions which have, during the last sixty years, overthrown so many ancient governments, we cannot but be struck by its peculiar character. Why that character was so peculiar is sufficiently obvious, and yet seems not to have been always understood either by eulogists or by censors.

The Continental revolutions of the eighteenth and nineteenth centuries took place in countries where all trace of the limited monarchy of the middle ages had long been effaced. The right of the prince to make laws and to levy money had, during many generations, been undisputed. His throne was guarded by a great regular army. His administration could not, without extreme peril, be blamed even in the mildest terms. His subjects held their personal liberty by no other tenure than his pleasure. Not a single institution was left which had within the memory of the oldest man, afforded efficient protection to the subject against the utmost excess of tyranny. Those great councils which had once curbed the regal power had sunk into oblivion. Their composition and their privileges were known only to antiquaries. We cannot wonder, therefore, that when men who had been thus ruled succeeded in wresting supreme power from a government which they had long in secret hated, they should have been impatient to demolish and unable to construct, that they should have been fascinated by every specious novelty, that they should have proscribed every title, ceremony, and phrase associated with the old system, and that, turning away with disgust from their own national precedents and traditions, they should have sought for principles of government in the writings of theorists, or aped, with ignorant and ungraceful affectation, the patriots of Athens and Rome. As little can we wonder that the violent action of the revolutionary spirit should have been followed by reaction equally violent, and that confusion should speedily have engendered despotism sterner than that from which it had sprung.

Had we been in the same situation; had Strafford succeeded in his favorite scheme of Thorough; had he formed an army as numerous and as well disciplined as that which, a few years later, was formed by Cromwell; had a series of judicial decisions, similar to that which was pronounced by the Exchequer Chamber in the case of ship money transferred to the crown the right of taxing the people; had the Star Chamber and the High Commission continued to fine, mutilate, and imprison every man who dared to raise his voice against the government had the press been as completely enslaved here as at Vienna or at Naples ; had our Kings drawn to themselves the whole legislative power ; had six generations of Englishmen passed away without a single session of Parliament; and had we then at length risen up in some moment of wild excitement against our masters, what an outbreak would that have been! With what a crash, heard and felt to the farthest end of the world, would the whole vast fabric of society have fallen! How many thousands of exiles, once the most prosperous and the most refined members of this great community, would have begged their bread in Continental cities, or have sheltered their heads under huts of bark in the uncleared forests of America! How often should we have seen the pavement of London piled up in barricades, the houses dinted with bullets, the gutters foaming with blood! How many times should we have rushed wildly from extreme to extreme, sought refuge from anarchy in despotism, and been again driven by despotism into anarchy! How many years of blood and confusion would it have cost us to learn the very rudiments of political science! How many childish theories would have duped us! How many rude and ill-poised constitutions should we have set up, only to see them tumble down! Happy would it have been for us if a sharp discipline of half a century had sufficed to educate us into a capacity of enjoying true freedom.

These calamities our Revolution averted. It was a revolution strictly defensive, and had prescription and legitimacy on its side. Here, and here only, a limited monarchy of the thirteenth century had come down unimpaired to the seventeenth century. Our parliamentary institutions were in full vigor. The main principles of our government were excellent. They were not, indeed, formally and exactly set forth in a single written instrument: but they were to be found scattered over our ancient and noble statutes; and, what was of far greater moment, they had been engraven on the hearts of Englishmen during four hundred years. That, without the consent of the representatives of the nation, no legislative act could be passed, no tax imposed, no regular soldiery kept up, that no man could be imprisoned, even for a day, by the arbitrary will of the sovereign, that no tool of power could plead the royal command as a justification for violating any right of the humblest subject, were held both by Whigs and Tories, to be fundamental laws of the realm. A realm of which these were the fundamental laws stood in no need of a new constitution.

But, though a new constitution was not needed, it was plain that changes were required. The misgovernment of the Stuarts, and the troubles which that misgovernment had produced, sufficiently proved that there was somewhere a defect in our polity; and that defect it was the duty of the Convention to discover and to supply.

Some questions of great moment were still open to dispute. Our constitution had begun to exist in times when statesmen were not much accustomed to frame exact definitions. Anomalies, therefore, inconsistent with its principles and dangerous to its very existence, had sprung up almost imperceptibly, and, not having during many years caused any serious inconvenience, had gradually acquired the force of prescription. The remedy for these evils was to assert the rights of the people in such a language as should terminate all controversy, and to declare that no precedent could justify any violation of those rights.

When this had been done it would be impossible for our rulers to misunderstand the law: but, unless something more were done, it was by no means improbable that they might violate it. Unhappily the Church had long taught the nation that hereditary monarchy, alone among our institutions, was divine and inviolable; that the right of the House of Commons to a share in the legislative power was a right merely human, but that the right of the King to the obedience of his people was from above; that the Great Charter was the statute which might be repealed by those who had made it, but that the rule which called the princes of the blood-royal to the throne in order of succession was of celestial origin, and that any Act of Parliament inconsistent with that rule was a nullity. It is evident that, in a society in which such superstitions prevail, constitutional freedom must ever be insecure. A power which is regarded merely as the ordinance of man cannot be an efficient check on a power which is regarded as the ordinance of God. It is vain to hope that laws, however excellent, will permanently restrain a king who, in his own opinion, and in the opinion of a great part of his people, has an authority infinitely higher in kind than the authority which belongs to those laws. To deprive royalty of these mysterious attributes, and to establish the principle that Kings reigned by a right in no respect differing from the right by which freeholders chose knights of the shire, or from the right by which Judges granted writs of Habeas Corpus, was absolutely necessary to the security of our liberties.

Thus the Convention had two great duties to perform. The first was to clear the fundamental laws of the realm from ambiguity. The second was to eradicate from the minds, both of the governors and of the governed, the false and pernicious notion that the royal prerogative was something more sublime and holy than those fundamental laws. The former object was attained by the solemn recital and claim with which the Declaration of Right commences; the latter by the resolution which pronounced the throne vacant, and invited William and Mary to fill it.

The change seems small. Not a single flower of the crown was touched. Not a single new right was given to the people. The whole English law, substantive and adjective, was, in the judgment of all the greatest lawyers, of Holt and Treby, of Maynard and Somers, almost exactly the same after the Revolution as before it. Some controverted points had been decided according to the sense of the best jurists: and there had been a slight deviation from the ordinary course of succession. This was all; and this was enough.

As our Revolution was a vindication of ancient rights, so it was conducted with strict attention to ancient formalities. In almost every word and act may be discerned a profound reverence for the past. The Estates of the Realm deliberated in the old halls and according to the old rules. Powle was conducted to his chair between his mover and his seconder with the accustomed forms. The Sergeant with his mace brought up the messengers of the Lords to the table of the Commons; and the three obeisances were duly made. The conference was held with all the antique ceremonial. On one side of the table, in the Painted Chamber, the managers for the Lords sat covered and robed in ermine and gold. The managers for the Commons stood bareheaded on the other side. The speeches present an almost ludicrous contrast to the revolutionary oratory of every other country. Both the English parties agreed in treating with solemn respect the ancient constitutional traditions of the state. The only question was in what sense those traditions were to be understood. The assertors of liberty said not a word about the natural equality of men and the inalienable sovereignty of the people, about Harmodius or Timoleon, Brutus, the elder or Brutus the younger. When they were told that, by the English law, the crown, at the moment of a demise, must descend to the next heir, they answered that, by the English law, a living man could have no heir. When they were told that there was no precedent for declaring the throne vacant, they produced from among the records in the Tower a roll of parchment, near three hundred years old, on which, in quaint characters and barbarous Latin, it was recorded that the Estates of the Realm had declared vacant the throne of a perfidious and tyrannical Plantagenet. When at length the dispute had been accommodated, the new sovereigns were proclaimed with the old pageantry. All the fantastic pomp of heraldry was there, Clarencieux and Norroy, Portcullis and Rouge Dragon, the trumpets, the banners, the grotesque coats embroidered with lions and lilies. The title of King of France, assumed by the conqueror of Cressy, was not omitted in the royal style. To us, who have lived in the year 1848, it may seem almost an abuse of terms to call a proceeding, conducted with so much deliberation, with so much sobriety, and with such minute attention to proscriptive etiquette, by the terrible name of Revolution.

And yet this revolution, of all revolutions the least violent, has been of all revolutions the most beneficent. It finally decided the great question whether the popular element which had, ever since the age of Fitzwalter and DeMontfort, been found in the English polity, should be destroyed by the monarchical element, or should be suffered to develop itself freely, and to become dominant. The strife between the two principles had been long, fierce, and doubtful. It had lasted through four reigns. It had produced seditions, impeachments, rebellions, battles, sieges, proscriptions, judicial massacres. Sometimes liberty, sometimes royalty, had seemed to be on the point of perishing. During many years one half of the energy of England had been employed in counteracting the other half. The executive power and the legislative power had so effectually impeded each other that the state had been of no account in Europe. The King at Arms, who proclaimed William and Mary before Whitehall Gate, did in truth announce that this great struggle was over; that there was entire union between the throne and the Parliament; that England, long dependent and degraded, was again a power of the first rank; that the ancient laws by which the prerogative was bounded would thenceforth be held as sacred

as the prerogative itself, and would be followed out to all their consequences; that the executive administration would be conducted in conformity with the sense of the representatives of the nation; and that no reform, which the two Houses should, after mature deliberation, propose, would be obstinately withstood by the sovereign. The Declaration of Right, though it made nothing law which had not been law before, contained the germ of the law which gave religious freedom to the Dissenter, of the law which secured the independence of the judges, of the law which limited the duration of Parliaments, of the law which placed the liberty of the press under the protection of juries, of the law which prohibited the slave trade, of the law which abolished the sacramental test, of the law which relieved the Roman Catholics from civil disabilities, of the law which reformed the representative system, of every good law which has been passed during more than a century and a half, of every good law which may hereafter, in the course of ages, be found necessary to promote the public weal, and to satisfy the demands of public opinion.

The highest eulogy which can be pronounced on the revolution of 1688 is this, that it was our last revolution. Several generations have now passed away since any wise and patriotic Englishman has meditated resistance to the established government. In all honest and reflecting minds there is a conviction, daily strengthened by experience, that the means of effecting every improvement which the constitution requires may be found within the constitution itself.

Now, if ever, we ought to be able to appreciate the whole importance of the stand which was made by our forefathers against the House of Stuart. All around us the world is convulsed by the agonies of great nations. Governments which lately seemed likely to stand during ages have been on a sudden shaken and overthrown. The proudest Capitals of Western Europe have streamed with civil blood. All evil passions, the thirst of gain and the thirst of vengeance, the antipathy of class to class, the antipathy of race to race, have broken loose from the control of divine and human laws. Fear and anxiety have clouded the faces and depressed the hearts of millions. Trade has been suspended and industry paralyzed. The rich have become poor; and the poor have become poorer. Doctrines hostile to all sciences, to all arts, to all industry, to all domestic charities, doctrines which, if carried into effect, would, in thirty years, undo all that thirty centuries have done for mankind, and would make the fairest provinces of France and Germany as savage as Congo or Patagonia, have been avowed from the tribune and defended by the sword. Europe has been threatened with subjugation by barbarians, compared with whom the barbarians who marched under Attila and Albion were enlightened and humane. The truest friends of the people have with deep sorrow owned that interests more precious than any political privileges were in jeopardy, and that it might be necessary to sacrifice even liberty in order to save civilization. Meanwhile in our island the regular course of government has never been for a day interrupted. The few bad men who longed for license and plunder have not had the courage to confront for one moment the strength of a loyal nation, rallied in firm array round a parental throne. And, if it be asked what has made us to differ from others, the answer is that we never lost what others are wildly and blindly seeking to regain. It is because we had a preserving revolution in the seventeenth century that we have not had a destroying revolution in the nineteenth. It is because we had freedom in the midst of servitude that we have order in the midst of anarchy. For the authority of law, for the security of property, for the peace of our streets, for the happiness of our homes, our gratitude is due, under Him who raises and pulls down nations at his pleasure, to the Long Parliament, to the Convention, and to William of Orange.

>> Questions for Consideration

1. In what way is Macaulay influenced by Enlightenment thought? In what ways are his theories a departure from it?

2. Compare Macaulay's approach to that of Ranke and Marx. What explains their differences? How might Marx have written about the English Revolution differently?

3. In what ways is this a romantic nationalist or patriotic history? Is Macaulay unduly biased in favor of the English?

Part II: Modern Historiography in the United States

Chapter 4

American History in the Nineteenth Century

Frederick Jackson Turner's Senior History Seminar, 1893–1894 (*Original owned by the University of Wisconsin Archives: Series No. 11/2 Turner, F.J. http://www.library.wisc.edu/etext/ WIReader/Images/WER0563.html. Reproduced Courtesy of the University of Wisconsin-Madison Archives*).

Similar to Europe, ideas of divine progress, Social Darwinism, Romanticism, nationalism, and German empiricism and historicism infused the American historical profession as it emerged in the late nineteenth century. Professionalization was a gradual process by which trained historians, usually university professors, began replacing amateurs and philosophers as the leaders of historical theory and publication.

Ranke had greatly helped to begin this process by advocating the creation of seminars devoted purely to the study of professional historical methods and writing. As his seminar method spread to universities across Europe and the United States, so too did the need to hire qualified history professionals to teach the seminars. Many of these early professionals were trained in German universities and moved back to the United States to head newly created history departments at top universities. While a few history programs existed in the United States earlier in the century, in the 1870s, universities across the country began creating undergraduate and graduate history programs. These academically trained historians worked hard to establish history as a factual science which contributed to civic virtue and supported the authority of the nation-state.[1] This vision of history helped to justify the teaching of history at all levels of the American educational system.

Romanticism and Nationalism

The young nation had a strong demand for nationalistic histories in the century following its Revolution. The founding fathers, including George Washington, Thomas Jefferson, and James Madison, believed that histories, which gave Americans role models of good citizens and showed the Revolution, political leaders, and the nation in a positive light, were necessary to unite citizens in support of the government and instill in them the virtues required to maintain the Republic. Two of the most popular American historians of the nineteenth century, George Bancroft (1800–1891) and Francis Parkman (1823–1893), obliged. Both were Harvard graduates with careers outside of history, but published an abundance of popular histories describing the dramatic and heroic efforts of European Americans in the advancement of liberty and justice. In their eyes, liberty required victory in warfare, courageous adventures, and the conquest of the wilderness. These "drum and bugle" histories were extremely popular and fired the American imagination about its heroic and romantic past.

Bancroft   Bancroft, however, was more than an amateur writing romantic history. Like Macaulay, Bancroft was heavily involved in politics, serving as President Polk's Secretary of the Navy, and later ambassador to Britain and Germany. His positions enabled him to meet many of the leading German and British historians of his day, including Macaulay and Ranke.[2] Trained in theology and philosophy, Bancroft wrote a wide variety of literature, but his historical works reflect the influence of Ranke's empiricism. His life's work was *History of the United States from the Discovery of the American Continent*, which he began in the 1830s and continued to write and revise for the next five decades. Within its ten volumes, Bancroft told the sweeping tale of

---

[1] Bonnie G. Smith, *The Gender of History: Men, Women, and Historical Practice* (Cambridge, MA: Harvard University Press, 1998), 147.

[2] Michael Bentley, "Introduction: Approaches to Modernity: Western Historiography since the Enlightenment," in *Companion to Historiography* (New York: Routledge, 1997), 417.

U.S. history as the unfolding of God's plan for the nation's progress toward liberty and glory.

Bancroft's romantic nationalist approach was tremendously appealing to an American public caught up in the wave of nationalism dominating public discourse in the nineteenth century. Some of the most popular subjects of national histories since that time have been the birth and development of democracy, the American Revolution and Constitution, political elections and intrigues, the Civil War, and foreign diplomacy, including all of the nation's wars and diplomatic institutions. As the central story of the birth of the United States, the American Revolution, with all of its heroes and battles, became part of the foundation of America's national mythology and a favorite topic of nationalist consensus historians.[3] These historians stress the unity and the just cause of the Americans as they rebelled against the evil British in the American Revolution. Like Bancroft, they saw the Revolution as a natural development in the progress of mankind toward greater personal liberty and viewed the Constitution as a high point in the evolution of world history.[4] Nationalist consensus historians perceived the Civil War as merely a temporary aberration from the unified progress of the democracy of the United States. Many drum-and-bugle military histories in the nineteenth and twentieth centuries assumed these theories as they wrote of the glorious battles of the Revolution and Civil War in terms of unified Americans fighting for freedom and liberty. Most of these military and nationalist histories focused on the great men of the wars: the generals, heroes of battles, and political elites. Reflecting the rising nationalism of the age and the increasing power of the United States, these themes of national consensus and the promise of American democracy dominated political history through the early twentieth century, and they remain popular in public histories even today.

Professionalization

By the late nineteenth century, however, amateur history was increasingly criticized by university-trained historians, who wished to establish history as a scientific discipline, independent from rhetoric, philosophy, and literature. One of the most important

American Historical Association

institutions to promote professional history was the American Historical Association (AHA), founded in 1884. Although the majority of its first members were amateur historians, AHA leaders, such as Herbert Baxter Adams and J. Franklin Jameson, sought legitimacy in academia by stressing high standards, objectivity, research and documentation, and the scientific method in the historical profession.[5] By the end of the

---

[3]Linda K. Kerber, "The Revolutionary Generation: Ideology, Politics, and Culture in the Early Republic," in *The New American History*, ed. Eric Foner (Philadelphia: Temple University Press, 1997), 31.

[4]Francis G. Couvares et al., *Interpretations of American History: Patterns and Perspectives*, Vol. I, 7th ed. (New York: The Free Press, 2000), 178.

[5]Ernst Breisach, *Historiography: Ancient, Medieval, and Modern*, 2nd ed. (Chicago: University of Chicago Press, 1994), 287.

nineteenth century, national history written by professional historians began to replace amateur romantic literary histories.

The AHA, as representative of elite professional historians, dominated historical fashions and methodology for the next century. Its Committee of Seven created a national program to reform history curricula in the nation's schools along the lines of Ranke's scientific analysis of documents and the seminar teaching method.[6] Tellingly, Ranke was the first honorary member of the AHA.[7] His brand of history, with its emphasis on objective analysis of primary sources and primacy of political subjects, would dominate the historical profession in the United States for many generations.

The AHA promoted national political history, focusing on national institutions and trends rather than local and regional politics as the most important and relevant topic for academic historians. Professional historians, in the promotion of objective, scientific history, hoped that this would lead to discovering larger, meaningful patterns in history which could aid in understanding the political issues of the day. In this perspective, personal, local, and regional histories were labeled "antiquarian"[8] and irrelevant to the higher goals of professional historians. As such, professional academic historians, such as John Franklin Jameson (1859–1937), encouraged all historical research to focus on national and international problems. As president of the AHA at the turn of the century, and editor of its *American Historical Review* for the next three decades, Jameson had a powerful influence on the historical profession for much of the first half of the twentieth century.

Jameson

Those who wished to focus on personal, local, and regional histories, however, found a home in the Mississippi Valley Historical Association (MVHA), which was founded by the leaders of Midwestern historical societies in 1907.[9] The regional focus of the MVHA remained until the 1940s, when national political trends began to convince even this organization that American political history required a national focus. The experience of the Great Depression and World War II convinced many historians of the need to teach a common national history to understand problems which appeared national in scale and encourage patriotism among American citizens. This final shift to a national focus was reflected in 1964, when the MVHA changed its name to the Organization of American Historians (OAH), and its publication, the *Mississippi Valley Historical Review* became the *Journal of American History.* Currently, the AHA and its journal, the *American Historical Review,* reflects the international and national interests of academic historians in the United States, while the OAH tends to focus more on the history of the United States. They are still the largest, most prestigious professional historical organizations in the United States.

Mississippi Valley Historical Association

Organization of American Historians

---

[6]Smith, *The Gender of History*, 112.

[7]Peter Novick, *That Noble Dream: The "Objectivity Question" and the American Historical Profession* (New York: Cambridge University Press, 1989), 26.

[8]Antiquarian refers to one who studies antiques, or objects of the past, because they admire the artifacts, as opposed to historians who analyze past events to make some meaning of them.

[9]Ian Tyrrell, "Public at the Creation: Place, Memory, and Historical Practice in the Mississippi Valley Historical Association, 1907–1950," *Journal of American History* 94, no. 1 (June 2007): 25.

The Nation's First Professional Historians

Until the creation of professional history programs at the nation's universities in the late nineteenth century, most American historians were amateur historians, with little formal training and full-time jobs unrelated to historical practice. With the advent of professional history degrees in German universities in the mid-nineteenth century, and then in the United States in the late nineteenth century, professional historians emerged and began to forge new standards of historical practice and new definitions of history. Because of sexism and racism in university admissions, however, most professional historians were European American, middle class, and male. While these professional historians strove to achieve high standards of scientific objectivity to distinguish themselves from amateur historians, Eurocentrism and nationalism pervaded their work.

Teutonic Germ Theory

Herbert Baxter Adams (1850–1901) was one of the forty-one founders of the AHA and a leader in bringing Rankean methods to the United States. He was educated in Germany and brought the seminar method to his position as history professor at Johns Hopkins University. Adams also emulated Ranke's focus on the development of political institutions and admiration of German power. He developed a "Teutonic germ theory" as his explanation for the development of democratic institutions in England and America. He claimed that democracy originated among the Teutonic tribes in ancient Germany and they brought their ideas with them to Britain when they conquered and exterminated the "racially inferior Celtic Britons."[10] From there, English colonists brought ideas of democracy with them to the Americas when they conquered American Indians. American political institutions, in his perspective, were a product of natural progress and evolution. Because Adams was one of the founding fathers of the historical profession in the United States and he taught a whole generation of prominent historians, his theories and methods powerfully shaped American historiography.

Turner's Frontier Thesis

The ideas of evolution and progress, and a focus on political institutions, dominated American historical thinking through the middle of the twentieth century, but over the years, historians added new twists to this narrative, refining it as it was told generation after generation. One of the most important contributions to the narrative of American history was Frederick Jackson Turner's "Frontier Thesis." Unlike Adams, Turner (1861–1932) was raised and educated in the Midwest, graduating from the University of Wisconsin and beginning his teaching career there. Although he briefly studied with Adams while getting his PhD at Johns Hopkins, Turner's pride in American institutions led him to emphasize American exceptionalism more than his counterparts. In his famous speech to the AHA in 1893, entitled *The Frontier in American History*, Turner argued that the American sense of democracy was shaped less by its European heritage than by its unique struggle to conquer the Western frontier. The nation's frontiersmen conquered the wilderness, using courage, cunning, and

---

[10]Novick, *That Noble Dream*, 87.

physical prowess, and shaped a new American character, giving its political institutions a distinctive flavor of democracy. The masses of people, struggling with each other and their environment, were Turner's primary agent of historical change and progress. Turner's thesis, therefore, was distinct in at least three ways: He stressed American exceptionalism, struggle and conflict rather than consensus, and the agency of environmental and socioeconomic forces as opposed to great men. Many historians, therefore, view Turner's thesis as "America's declaration of historiographical independence from Europe."[11] This positive view of the American nation was also more appealing to Americans than the Teutonic germ theory, and it quickly became the dominant explanation of the origins of American political institutions.

Underlying both theories was a strong strain of Social Darwinism. Drawing from Enlightenment modernism and Social Darwinian concepts, American historians explained the European conquest and enslavement of American Indians and Africans as the march of progress, the logical result of superior "civilized" nations' domination of inferior "savage" societies. God, Providence, or natural selection, as the agent of historical change, ordained that European civilization control these other societies.

Inevitablist Thesis — Bancroft had reflected this "inevitablist thesis" when he dismissed American Indians as inferior because of their ignorance of civilization and "hereditary idleness."[12] Parkman described them as brave and free, but wild, sinister, jealous, envious, and given to bouts of rage and drunkenness.[13] Despite the lack of evidence to support these racist assumptions, these stereotypes pervaded American history until the 1960s.

Historians of the American South especially revealed the extent of this bias. After the American Civil War (1861–1865), northern and southern white historians disagreed over who was to blame for the war, but agreed that Africans and African Americans were genetically inferior, and that slavery had helped to civilize them. White southern

Phillips — historian Ulrich B. Phillips (1877–1934) exemplified and popularized this racist interpretation of African American history. Sometimes called the "mint-julep" school of

Mint-Julep School — southern history, a reference to the drink associated with the culture of the Old South, he characterized the antebellum period as a golden age for the South, when large plantation owners dominated society with benevolence. Blaming the Civil War on irrational abolitionists, Phillips argued that slavery was unprofitable and would have eventually ended on its own. He and other southern historians portrayed African Americans as happy slaves who were dependent on whites for their livelihood. This school viewed the southern effort during the Civil War as a great "Lost Cause" and termed the conflict "The War of Northern Aggression."

The "traditional" interpretation of Reconstruction was likewise shaped by a white perspective. The authoritative historian on this topic until the 1930s was Columbia

[11]Breisach, *Historiography*, 314.

[12]Gary B. Nash, "The 'Convergence' Paradigm in Studying Early American History in the Schools," in *Knowing, Teaching, and Learning History: National and International Perspectives*, ed. Peter N. Stearns, Peter Seixas, and Sam Wineburg (New York: New York University Press, 2000), 103–104.

[13]Francis Parkman, *The Conspiracy of Pontiac and the Indian War after the Conquest of Canada (1851) in The Works of Francis Parkman* (Boston: Little, Brown, and Co., 1898), 43–49.

professor William A. Dunning (1857–1922). Building on the premise that the South *Dunning* was better off under slavery, the Dunning school portrayed white northerners as "car-*School* pet-baggers" and their southern allies as "scalawags," conspiring to crush white south-erners with moral and political corruption. Dunning argued that white southerners, led by the "courageous" Ku Klux Klan, overthrew the yoke of northern aggression after 1877, ending the disastrous era. These racist inevitablist theories dominated profes-sional historiography in the United States from its birth to the middle of the twentieth century.

A few outspoken writers, however, dissented from the white male consensus in the *Jackson* nineteenth century. Helen Hunt Jackson's (1830–1885) *A Century of Dishonor* (1881) used her first-hand interactions with American Indians to support her argument that European American domination was not inevitable and God-ordained. Analyzing European American primary sources such as presidential speeches, treaties, and other government documents, she demonstrated that the conquest was the result of geno-cidal policies and the dishonest actions of immoral men.

African American writers too rejected the inevitablist thesis of European domi-nation. One of the earliest comprehensive African American histories written by an *Williams* African American was George Washington Williams's (1849–1881) *History of the Negro Race in America* (1882). Although he was not a trained professional historian, Williams's two-volume history of African American contributions to the progress of the United States was as thorough and well-written as any professional history of his day.[14] Famous African American activists Booker T. Washington and W. E. B. Du Bois also published histories of slavery and Reconstruction from their own perspec-tive, revealing the intelligence and courage of African Americans as they struggled to overcome the violence and repression of slavery and racism. Despite their exclu-sion from the history profession, African American women, such as Gertrude Bustill Mossell (1855–1948), also published histories detailing black women's accomplish-ments.[15] These dissenting historians presented voluminous evidence to support their arguments, but were criticized by contemporary professional historians for their "lack of objectivity" on the subject. The inevitablist thesis, therefore, continued to dominate American history until the 1950s.[16]

Social Darwinism and the predominance of men in the professions in the nine-teenth century also limited the active participation of women in the formation of the historical profession in the United States. Many women had followed in the footsteps of Mercy Otis Warren in writing history throughout the nineteenth century, but these histories were ignored by the men who dominated historical associations and history departments. Before they were admitted into professional history programs, hundreds

---

[14]John Hope Franklin, "On the Evolution of Scholarship in Afro-American History," in *The State of Afro-American History: Past, Present, and Future*, ed. Darlene Clark Hine (Baton Rouge, LA: Louisiana State University Press, 1986), 13.

[15]Pero Gaglo Dagbovie, "Black Women Historians from the Late 19th century to the Dawning of the Civil Rights Movement," *Journal of African American History* 89, no. 3 (Summer 2004): 247.

[16]Novick, *That Noble Dream*, 68–69.

of women were amateur historians. Their work, however, was dismissed by most male historians because most women lacked professional credentials and because they generally studied subjects, such as the history of women, and social and cultural trends, which male historians considered unimportant.[17] The numbers of female students in history classes steadily increased, but relatively few were admitted to doctoral programs until the mid-twentieth century. As gender historian Bonnie Smith has found,

> From U.S. professors who maintained that "of course women could not do seminar work," to Oxbridge dons who actively worked to keep them from getting degrees, taking classes, and passing exams, scientific history marked out women as different—less worthy, less competent, and dangerous if intellectual.[18]

Similar to racism, sexism was foundational at the birth of professional history in the United States and shaped its focus and interpretation well into the twentieth century.

Despite the racism and sexism present at the birth of the historical profession in the United States, its claims of scientific objectivity and factual representations of the past convinced Americans of the validity of professional history. Although romantic histories continued to appeal to amateur historians and the general public, and women's and minority histories were produced throughout the century, national consensus political history dominated professional history from the late nineteenth century onward. Both amateur and professional historians in the United States largely ignored Hegelian and Marxist Idealism until the mid-twentieth century, preferring instead to focus on the great progress of the United States and its institutions, as revealed by the words and writings of its political leaders and "great men." Rankean empiricism, mixed in with a heavy dose of American nationalism and Social Darwinism, shaped the American historical profession as it was born in the nineteenth century.

Herbert Baxter Adams, "Saxon Tithing-Men in America"

THE office of Tithing-man has never been satisfactorily explained. New England traditions describe this institution only in its later ecclesiastical form, which was by no means its primitive character even in this country. The oldest people in New England remember the Tithing-man as a kind of Sunday Constable, whose special duty it was, in the old parish meeting-house, to quiet the restlessness of youth and to disturb the slumbers of age. Many are the tales which grandfathers can tell concerning this ancient watchman of the congregation, who saw to it that all persons were attentive except himself, and who occasionally broke the peace by sharply rapping with his tune-book and pointing at some whispering boy, or else by patrolling the aisles to arouse sleeping

---

[17]Smith, *The Gender of History*, 6.

[18]Ibid., 191.

Source: Herbert Baxter Adams. "Saxon Tithing-Men in America. Read before the American Antiquarian Society, October 21, 1881." *John Hopkins University studies—historical and political science* 1:4 (1883): pp. 1–23. The reference notes in this excerpt are in Adams's original manuscript.

saints by means of his black pole, tipped at one end with brass.[1] In some churches there were two or three of these grim, vigilant Tithing-men. It is said that one or two of them sometimes sat under the very shadow of the pulpit, facing the congregation.[2] But more usually one Tithing-man sat at each door of the meeting-house to keep out dogs, and one often sat in the gallery to keep in boys.[3]

From original town records it appears that it was the duty of the early New England Tithing-man, not merely to preserve order in the meeting-house, but to see to it that everyone went to church. The Tithing-man was a kind of ecclesiastical "whipper-in." After looking over the congregation to find if any seats were vacant, the Tithing-man would steal out and explore the horse-sheds, the adjoining fields and orchards, the inns and ordinaries, and even the houses of the village, in order to search out skulkers from divine service. According to the town records of Salem, it is clear that as early as 1644, in that village at least, two men were "appointed euery Lord's day to walke forth in the time of God's worshippe, to take notice of such as either lye about the meeting-howse without attending to the word or ordinances, or that lye at home or in the fields, w'thout giuing good account thereof, and to take the names of such persons & to present them to the Magistrate, whereby they may be accordinglie proceeded against."[4]

A study of the statutes of the mother country, of the period immediately preceding the Puritan migration, shows that the custom of enforcing attendance upon church services was by no means original with the settlers of New England. By an Act[5] passed in the reign of James I., all people were obliged by law to "repaire every Sunday" to church, under penalty of twelve pence for every absence. Upon sufficient information, given of course by the Parish Constable or Tithing-man, the justice of the peace issued a warrant to the church warden to distrain goods, if necessary, in collecting such parish fines. All servants, sojourners, and strangers within a man's gates were brought under the operation of this law, so that the custom of Sunday inspection of every household must have been in vogue in Old England, long before it was revived at Salem. These laws requiring church attendance are of very ancient standing. By the first Act of Elizabeth's reign, "every person and persons inhabiting within this Realme shall diligentlye and faithefully, having

---

[1]This was the old English Tipstaffe, an emblem of the constabulary office, and representing the person of the King. We shall consider the subject of the Tipstaffe or Black Rod more particularly in a paper on "Constables."
By the Province laws of Massachusetts (I. 155, 329) Tithing-men were required to "have a black staffe of two feet long, tipped at one end with brass about three inches, as a badge of their office." We find these black staves mentioned in local town records, e. g., in the town records of Salem, in 1646, i. 147 in the town records of Groton, edited by Dr. Green, i. 19, Item, "toe black staffe," three shillings sixpence. Survivals of these black wands have been seen by the writer in actual use by special constables at Amherst College Commencements, which are still held in the old parish church. The use of wands, with ribbon tips, by ushers, is only an aesthetic transformation of the ancient Tipstaffe. It is said that in some early New England parishes, the Tithing-man's rod was tipped at one end, not with brass, but with a squirrel's tail. This end was used in awakening women. The other end was a deer's hoof, which carried sharp conviction to men and boys.

[2]Blood. History of Temple, N. H., p. 87.

[3]In the town of Salem, the Tithing-men or Constables, used to see to it that no boys escaped from church and that no dogs slunk in. The "Dog Whipper" was a regular institution in certain old English towns, notably in Exeter and Congleton (in Chester). Mr. Edward A. Freeman has called our attention to a curious law of Edgar (see Thorpe's Ancient Laws and Institutes of England, ii. 251), whereby parish priests were to see to it that no dog should enter church, nor yet more a' swine, if it could possibly be prevented!

[4]Town Records of Salem, 131, part 1, 1634–1659, published in the Historical Collections of the Essex Institute, second series, Vol. I.

[5]Statutes of the Realm, 4 Jac. I. c. v.

no lawfull or reasonable Excuse to be absent, endevour themselves to resorte to theyr Parishe Churche or Chappell accustomed upon every Sondaye and other days ordained and used to bee kept as Holy days, and ther tabyde orderlye and soberly during the tyme of the Common Prayer, Preachinges and other Service of God upon payne of punishment by the Censures of the Churche, and also upon payne that every person so offending shall forfeite for every suche oifence twelve pens, to be levied by the Churchewardens of the Parishe to thuse of the Poore."[6] The Church of England and its Puritan reformers can claim no monopoly in this kind of legislation, for it roots far back in the middle ages in the earliest Catholic laws of England against irregular attendance upon conventicles contrary to the Catholic faith, especially against the meetings of Lollards.[7]

In early New England, the execution of the laws for the observance of the Sabbath in other ways than church-going was intrusted to the local Tithing-men. Travel on that day was strictly forbidden. There are many persons still living who can remember that the parish Tithing-man once discharged the pious function of stopping all unnecessary riding and driving on Sunday. An amusing story is told of the writer's grandfather, who was Tithing-man for his parish in Amherst, Massachusetts, and notoriously strict in the discharge of his office both in church and out. Early one Sabbath morning he saw a man driving past his house, with a little hair trunk in the back end of his wagon. Suspecting that the man was upon a journey, the Tithing-man hailed him: "Sir, do you know that travel on Sunday is forbidden by law?" "Yes, sir," said the stranger

in a somewhat melancholy tone. The Tithing-man caught the idea. "Of course," he said, "in case of sickness or death, a Sabbath journey is sometimes permitted." The traveller replied in a subdued manner, "my wife is lying dead in the town just above here." "Oh, well," said the Tithing-man, "you can drive on." The man drove on a safe distance, then looked back and called out: "She has been lying dead for twenty years!"

From the colonial laws of Massachusetts it appears that the functions of the Tithing-man were not restricted to the arrest of "all Saboath breakers," but extended to the inspection of licensed inns for the sake of discovering "disorderly tiplers" on the evening of that day or "at any other time" during the week. He could carry offenders before any magistrate and commit them to prison "as any constable may doe." For Sunday offenders was reserved the special disgrace of imprisonment in the town "cage" which was "set up in the market place."[8] Even by such links as these are the towns of New England bound to old English parish life.[9] The expression jail-bird has some significance in the light of the evolution of prisons from cages. The use of the pillory and the stocks in punishment for drunkenness are similar links of parish habit. The very liquors that New England Tithing-men were instructed to seek out in unlicensed houses or to obtain a satisfactory account of in regular inns, afford as suggestive a commentary upon the English origin of intemperance in New England as does the mention of beer in the Norse sagas of Vineland upon the Teutonic origin of the first white settlers of America. Strong beere, ale, cider, perry,[10] matheglin,[11]

---

[6]Statutes of the Realm. 1 Eliz. c. 2, III.; cf. 23 Eliz. c. i. and 35 Eliz. c. i

[7]Rolls of Parliament, III., 467, 583 ; IV., 24.

[8]Records of Massachusetts, v. 133.

[9]Palgrave, English Commonwealth. Anglo-Saxon Period. Vol. ii., p. clxvi.

[10]A liquor prepared from the juice of pears, like cider from apples.

[11]A fermented liquor made of honey and water boiled together. The name Metheglin is Welsh and is derived from medd (mead) and llyn (liquor). It is one of those familiar household terms which have come down to us from that "exterminated" race, the Kelts. Words like dad, babe, lad, lass, gown, flannel, clout, crock, cabin, basket, bran, flask, mattock, are collectively stronger evidence of Keltic influences surviving in Saxon homes than even the above home-made drink.

rumme, brandy,"[12] these things all have a very English smack. Legislation against the excessive use of these drinks did not begin in New England. The Puritans of Massachusetts struggled against intemperance as did their English fathers before them, and in precisely the same way, by fines and penalties, by laws executed through "Constables, Churchwardens, Headboroughes, Tithingmen, Alecunners and Sydemen," as described in the act of the fourth year of King James I.[13]. . .

Tithings and Tithing-men were no development of New England Puritanism. These institutions for the strict and wholesome government of neighborhoods were transmitted to us from the mother country. We may perhaps discover the first step of the transmission process in the instructions given to Governor Endicott, in 1629, by the Massachusetts Company while they were yet in England. This business association of honorable and enterprising Englishmen, who, according to their own accounts, provided for New England "Ministers, men skylfull in making of pitch, of salt, Vyne Planters,—Wheat, rye, barley, oates,—stones, of all sorts of fruites,"[14] this thoughtful Company provided also the seeds of English self-government in Towns and Tithings. They said to Endicott by letter, "wee hope yow will fynde many religious, discreete, and well ordered persons, wch yow must sett over the rest devyding them into famylies, placing some wth the ministers, and others under such as, ndus honest men (and of their owne calling as neere as may bee) may haue care to see them well educated in their generall callings as Christians, and particuler according to their seuerall trades or fitness in disposition to learne a trade."[15] To any one familiar with the English law of that period concerning the training of servants and apprentices, the above instructions to Endicott, which are repeated over and over again, will appear to be only the natural outgrowth of the family regulations of the mother country.

According to Lambard, the ancient office of Tithing-man was headship of the Frank-pledge. This is not the whole truth for the institutions of Tithing and Tithing-men are older than that of Frank-pledge. Canon Stubbs[16] and George Waitz,[17] the most recent authorities upon English and German constitutional history respectively, maintain that, before the Norman conquest, there is no positive proof of the existence of collective responsibility for crime committed within a Tithing. On the other hand, Palgrave[18] and the older authorities are inclined to discover germs of the system of Frank-pledge even in Anglo Saxon times. By a law of Canute, every freeman who desired to enjoy the privilege of exculpation by the oath of his friends or the protection of Wergeld (money payment for injury) was to be enrolled in a Hundred and in a Tithing; he was to be brought under pledge or "Borh," and this was to hold him to right. The term Frank-pledge is a vulgar corruption of the Saxon Frith-borh or peace-pledge. Whether or no the outgrowth of Saxon beginnings, this institution in Norman times was certainly the collective personal pledge of ten or more men to their lord. The idea of associate responsibility is here of more importance than

---

[12]Records of Massachusetts, v. 240.

[13]Statutes of the Realm, 4 Jac. I. c. v. Cf. I. Jac. I. c. 9.

[14]Records of Massachusetts, i., 24-5.

[15]Ibid. 393 ; cf. 397, 400, 405.

[16]Stubbs' Constitutional History of England, i., 87.

[17]Waitz, Deutsche Verfassungsgeschichte, i., 458 (ed. 1865.) Waitz takes strong ground: "Es gab keine Gesammtbiirgerschaft unter den Angelsachsen, weder fur das AVergeld nock in irgend welchem andern Sinn, weder vor noch nach Aelfreds Zeiten."

[18]Palgrave, English Commonwealth, part ii., cxxiii. "The system was developed between the accession of Canute and the demise of the Conqueror; and it is not improbable that the Normans completed what the Danes had begun."

the mere number, for as many as eighty men were sometimes admitted into one Tithing. Ten was the least number allowed in Frank-pledge.[19] Probably the Normans infused greater energy into the Saxon Tithing and gave to the idea of *Frith-Borh* a more strictly collective sense, as a better surety for the preservation of the peace.[20] The old Saxon Tithing-man certainly became the Borhs-Ealdor (the Borsholder of Lambard) which signifies the same as the Elder or Chief of the Pledge. . . .

The origin of Tithings, and of their multiple the Hundred, is one of the most obscure questions in the early history of English institutions. Blackstone and the earlier writers dispose of the question very summarily by ascribing the above types of local organization to Alfred: "to him," says Blackstone, "we owe that masterpiece of judicial polity, the subdivision of England into tithings and hundreds, if not into counties." The monkish testimony of Ingulph, upon which this widely accepted statement rests, is utterly worthless upon this point. It was customary in the Middle Ages to ascribe every good institution either to Alfred or to Edward the Confessor. If pious monks and popular opinion are to be followed in institutional history, then we must ascribe to King Alfred the origin of trial by jury. As an able critic, presumably Palgrave, said years ago in the Edinburgh Review,[21] if Alfred was really the originator of Hundreds and Tithings, and shires," he must also have been the creator of the common law itself, which only proceeds in conjunction with these divisions." The fact is, Blackstone and the older writers, Coke, Littleton, Bracton, knew really very little about the origin of English institutions. The whole science of institutional history is one of

modern growth and can be pursued only in the light of comparative politics and of comparative jurisprudence, along lines of inquiry opened up by such pioneer investigators as Von Maurer, Hanssen, Nasse, Waitz, Gneist, Stubbs, Freeman, Maine, and specialists in Anglo-Saxon law. The study of Saxon institutions was not possible before the labors of Palgrave, Kemble, Thorpe, and Reinhold Schmid in classifying materials and editing statutes and codices. But with all these modern facilities, it is not easy to trace out to one's entire satisfaction the origin of England's early institutions of law and government.

We find Tithings mentioned in the law of Canute already cited. We can trace back the institution through several Saxon reigns, but finally we lose all trace of it. Among the laws of Edgar, in the ordinance relating to the Hundred it is ordered that if a thief is to be pursued, the fact is to be made known to the Hundredman and he is to inform the Tithing-man, and all are to "go forth to where God may direct them," so that they "do justice on the thief, as it was formerly the enactment of Edmund."[22] Here, if we mistake not, we are upon the historic track of the old Saxon Hue and Cry. We note from the laws of Edgar that "if the hundred pursue a track into another hundred,"[23] warning is to be given to the Hundredman there, so that he may join, in the chase. Following a track from one Hundred into another would seem to imply territorial limits. In the laws of Edgar, it is also prescribed that no one shall take possession of unknown cattle" without the testimonies of the men of the Hundred, or of the Tithing-man."[24] In the laws of Athelstan, among the so-called Judicia

---

[19]Palgrave, ii., cxxv.

[20]Dr. Reinhold Sohmid, in his edition of the Gesetze der Angelsachsen (ed. of 1858, p. 649) calls attention to the fact that we have no evidence of the Normans possessing any such institution as Frank-pledge in Normandy and says : "So weit unsere Kunde von dem Verhaeltniss bis jetzt reicht, bleibt, daher der angelsaechsische Ursprung der Zehntbuergerschaft das Wahrscheinlichere." To this conclusion we had already come before discovering Schmid's note upon "Rechtsbuergschaft," but we gladly rest our results upon his solid authority.

[21]Edinburgh Review (Feb., 1822), p. 289 ; cf. Hallam, Middle Ages, note vi. to ch. viii., part II.

[22]Ancient Laws and Statutes of England, i., 259.

[23]Ibid. 261.

[24]Ancient Laws and Institutes of England, i., 261.

Civitatis Lundonice it is ordered that, in tracing or pursuing a criminal, every man shall render aid, "so long as the track is known; and after the track has failed him, that one man be found [from one Tithing] where there is a large population, as well as from one Tithing where a less population is, either to ride or to go (unless there be need of more.)"[25] This appears to imply a territorial seat even for the Tithing, as an integral part of the Hundred, as well as a varying number of inhabitants within the Tithing itself.

Probably the Saxon Tithing had its origin in the personal association of warriors by tens and hundreds. Such a decimal system of military organization existed among various early Teutonic peoples, if not throughout the whole Aryan family of nations. Even the Jews fought by tens, and fifties, and hundreds. Undoubtedly kinship had originally something to do with the marshalling of hosts. The Homeric warriors fought under patriarchal chiefs. The ancient Germans, according to Tacitus, were arrayed by families and near kinsmen (*familiae et propinquitates*).[26] And it is not at all unlikely that, after the conquest of Britain, the Saxons settled down in Tithings and Hundreds upon somewhat clannish principles. Of course the composition of the host, when levied, would vary from time to time, but a certain idea of territorial permanence would soon attach itself to the Local Tithings and Hundreds from the very fact of the allotment of lands.

>> Questions for Consideration

1. How does Adams's "Teutonic germ theory" shape this history?
2. Is there any evidence of American nationalism or exceptionalism here?
3. In what ways might this history be classified as historicist or empiricist? How does this essay compare to Bancroft's and Ranke's histories? Which seems the most similar to this essay and why?

Frederick Jackson Turner, *The Significance of the Frontier in American History*

In a recent bulletin of the Superintendent of the Census for 1890 appear these significant words: "Up to and including 1880 the country had a frontier of settlement, but at present the unsettled area has been so broken into by isolated bodies of settlement that there can hardly be said to be a frontier line. In the discussion of its extent, its westward movement, etc., it can not, therefore, any longer have a place in the census reports." This brief official statement marks the closing of a great historic movement. Up to our own day American history has been in a large degree the history of the colonization of the Great West. The existence of an area of free land, its continuous recession, and the advance of American settlement westward, explain American development.

---

[25]Ibid. 233, cf. ii., 499 and Schmid, Die Gesetze der Angelsachsen, 161.

[26]Tacitus, Germania, cap. 7. Prof. W. F. Allen, in a note upon this passage, in his edition of the Germania, calls attention to the parallel passage in Caesar, de Bella Galileo, vi., 22, where it is stated that land was assigned gentibus cognationibusque hominum. "From the two passages, it appears that the divisions of land, and military divisions, were alike founded upon Kinship."

Source: A paper read at the meeting of the American Historical Association in Chicago, July 12, 1893. It first appeared in the Proceedings of the State Historical Society of Wisconsin,

(*continued*)

Behind institutions, behind constitutional forms and modifications, lie the vital forces that call these organs into life and shape them to meet changing conditions. The peculiarity of American institutions is, the fact that they have been compelled to adapt themselves to the changes of an expanding people—to the changes involved in crossing a continent, in winning a wilderness, and in developing each area of this progress out of the primitive economic and political conditions of the frontier into the complexity of city life. Said Calhoun in 1817, "We are great, and rapidly—I was about to say fearfully—growing!"[1] So saying, he touched the distinguishing feature of American life. All peoples show development; the germ theory of politics has been sufficiently emphasized. In the case of most nations, however, the development has occurred in a limited area; and if the nation has expanded, it has met other growing peoples whom it has conquered. But in the case of the United States we have a different phenomenon. Limiting our attention to the Atlantic coast, we have the familiar phenomenon of the evolution of institutions in a limited area, such as the rise of representative government; into complex organs; the progress from primitive industrial society, without division of labor, up to manufacturing civilization. But we have in addition to this a recurrence of the process of evolution in each western area reached in the process of expansion. Thus American development has exhibited not merely advance along a single line, but a return to primitive conditions on a continually advancing frontier line, and

a new development for that area. American social development has been continually beginning over again on the frontier. This perennial rebirth, this fluidity of American life, this expansion westward with its new opportunities, its continuous touch with the simplicity of primitive society, furnish the forces dominating American character. The true point of view in the history of this nation is not the Atlantic coast, it is the Great West. Even the slavery struggle, which is made so exclusive an object of attention by writers like Professor von Holst, occupies its important place in American history because of its relation to westward expansion.

In this advance, the frontier is the outer edge of the wave—the meeting point between savagery and civilization. Much has been written about the frontier from the point of view of border warfare and the chase, but as a field for the serious study of the economist and the historian it has been neglected.

The American frontier is sharply distinguished from the European frontier—a fortified boundary line running through dense populations. The most significant thing about the American frontier is, that it lies at the hither edge of free land. In the census reports it is treated as the margin of that settlement which has a density of two or more to the square mile. The term is an elastic one, and for our purposes does not need sharp definition. We shall consider the whole frontier belt including the Indian country and the outer margin of the "settled area" of the census reports. This paper will make no attempt to treat the subject exhaustively; its aim is simply to

---

December 14, 1893, with the following note: "The foundation of this paper is my article entitled 'Problems in American History,' which appeared in *The Ægis*, a publication of the students of the University of Wisconsin, November 4, 1892... It is gratifying to find that Professor Woodrow Wilson—whose volume on 'Division and Reunion' in the Epochs of American History Series, has an appreciative estimate of the importance of the West as a factor in American history—accepts some of the views set forth in the papers above mentioned, and enhances their value by his lucid and suggestive treatment of them in his article in *The Forum* December, 1893, reviewing Goldwin Smith's 'History of the United States.'" The present text is that of the *Report of the American Historical Association* for 1893, 199-227. It was printed with additions in the *Fifth Year Book of the National Herbart Society*, and in various other publications. It retains Turner's original footnotes.

[1]"Abridgment of Debates of Congress," v, p. 706.

call attention to the frontier as a fertile field for investigation, and to suggest some of the problems which arise in connection with it.

In the settlement of America we have to observe how European life entered the continent, and how America modified and developed that life and reacted to Europe. Our early history is the study of European germs developing in an American environment. Too exclusive attention has been paid by institutional students to the Germanic origins, too little to the American factors. The frontier is the line of most rapid and effective Americanization. The wilderness masters the colonist. It finds him a European in dress, industries, tools, modes of travel, and thought. It takes him from the railroad car and puts him in the birch canoe. It strips off the garments of civilization and arrays him in the hunting shirt and the moccasin. It puts him in the log cabin of the Cherokee and Iroquois and runs an Indian palisade around him. Before long he has gone to planting Indian corn and plowing with a sharp stick, he shouts the war cry and takes the scalp in orthodox Indian fashion. In short, at the frontier the environment is at first too strong for the man. He must accept the conditions which it furnishes, or perish, and so he fits himself into the Indian clearings and follows the Indian trails. Little by little he transforms the wilderness, but the outcome is not the old Europe, not simply the development of Germanic germs, any more than the first phenomenon was a case of reversion to the Germanic mark. The fact is, that here is a new product that is American. At first, the frontier was the Atlantic coast. It was the frontier of Europe in a very real sense. Moving westward, the frontier became more and more American. As successive terminal moraines result from successive glaciations, so each frontier leaves its traces behind it, and when it becomes a settled area the region still partakes of the frontier characteristics. Thus the advance of the frontier has meant a steady movement away from the influence of Europe, a steady growth of independence on American lines. And to study this advance, the men who grew up under these conditions, and the political, economic, and social results of it, is to study the really American part of our history.

In the course of the seventeenth century the frontier was advanced up the Atlantic river courses, just beyond the "fall line," and the tidewater region became the settled area. In the first half of the eighteenth century another advance occurred. Traders followed the Delaware and Shawnee Indians to the Ohio as early as the end of the first quarter of the century.[2] Gov. Spotswood, of Virginia, made an expedition in 1714 across the Blue Ridge. The end of the first quarter of the century saw the advance of the Scotch-Irish and the Palatine Germans up the Shenandoah Valley into the western part of Virginia, and along the Piedmont region of the Carolinas.[3] The Germans in New York pushed the frontier of settlement up the Mohawk to German Flats.[4] In Pennsylvania the town of Bedford indicates the line of settlement. Settlements had begun on New River, a branch of the Kanawha, and on the sources of the Yadkin and French Broad.[5] The King attempted to arrest the advance by his proclamation of 1763,[6] forbidding settlements beyond the sources of the rivers flowing

---

[2]Bancroft (1860 ed.), iii, pp. 344, 345, citing Logan MSS.; [Mitchell] "Contest in America," etc. (1752), p. 237.

[3]Kercheval, "History of the Valley"; Bernheim, "German Settlements in the Carolinas"; Winsor, "Narrative and Critical History of America," v, p. 304; Colonial Records of North Carolina, iv, p. xx; Weston, "Documents Connected with the History of South Carolina," p. 82; Ellis and Evans, "History of Lancaster County, Pa.," chs. iii, xxvi.

[4]Parkman, "Pontiac," ii; Griffis, "Sir William Johnson," p. 6; Simms's "Frontiersmen of New York."

[5]Monette, "Mississippi Valley," i, p. 311.

[6]Wis. Hist. Cols., xi, p. 50; Hinsdale, "Old Northwest," p. 121; Burke, "Oration on Conciliation," Works (1872 ed.), i, p. 473.

into the Atlantic, but in vain. In the period of the Revolution the frontier crossed the Alleghanies into Kentucky and Tennessee, and the upper waters of the Ohio were settled.[7] When the first census was taken in 1790, the continuous settled area was bounded by a line which ran near the coast of Maine, and included New England except a portion of Vermont and New Hampshire, New York along the Hudson and up the Mohawk about Schenectady, eastern and southern Pennsylvania, Virginia well across the Shenandoah Valley, and the Carolinas and eastern Georgia.[8] Beyond this region of continuous settlement were the small settled areas of Kentucky and Tennessee, and the Ohio, with the mountains intervening between them and the Atlantic area, thus giving a new and important character to the frontier. The isolation of the region increased its peculiarly American tendencies, and the need of transportation facilities to connect it with the East called out important schemes of internal improvement, which will

be noted farther on. The "West," as a self-conscious section, began to evolve.

From decade to decade distinct advances of the frontier occurred. By the census of 1820[9] the settled area included Ohio, southern Indiana and Illinois, southeastern Missouri, and about one-half of Louisiana. This settled area had surrounded Indian areas, and the management of these tribes became an object of political concern. The frontier region of the time lay along the Great Lakes, where Astor's American Fur Company operated in the Indian trade,[10] and beyond the Mississippi, where Indian traders extended their activity even to the Rocky Mountains; Florida also furnished frontier conditions. The Mississippi River region was the scene of typical frontier settlements.[11]

The rising steam navigation[12] on western waters, the opening of the Erie Canal, and the westward extension of cotton[13] culture added five frontier states to the Union in this period. Grund, writing in 1836, declares: "It appears then

---

[7]Roosevelt, "Winning of the West," and citations there given, Cutler's "Life of Cutler."

[8]Scribner's Statistical Atlas, xxxviii, pl. 13; McMaster, "Hist. of People of U. S.," i, pp. 4, 60, 61; Imlay and Filson, "Western Territory of America" (London, 1793); Rochefoucault-Liancourt, "Travels Through the United States of North America" (London, 1799); Michaux's "Journal," in *Proceedings American Philosophical Society*, xxvi, No. 129; Forman, "Narrative of a Journey Down the Ohio and Mississippi in 1780-'90" (Cincinnati, 1888); Bartram, "Travels Through North Carolina," etc. (London, 1792); Pope, "Tour Through the Southern and Western Territories," etc. (Richmond, 1792); Weld, "Travels Through the States of North America" (London, 1799); Baily, "Journal of a Tour in the Unsettled States of North America, 1796-'97" (London, 1856); Pennsylvania Magazine of History, July, 1886; Winsor, "Narrative and Critical History of America," vii, pp. 491, 492, citations.

[9]Scribner's Statistical Atlas, xxxix.

[10]Turner, "Character and Influence of the Indian Trade in Wisconsin" (Johns Hopkins University Studies, Series ix), pp. 61ff.

[11]Monette, "History of the Mississippi Valley," ii; Flint, "Travels and Residence in Mississippi," Flint, "Geography and History of the Western States," "Abridgment of Debates of Congress," vii, pp. 397 398, 404; Holmes, "Account of the U. S."; Kingdom, "America and the British Colonies" (London, 1820); Grund, "Americans," ii, chs. i, iii, vi (although writing in 1836, he treats of conditions that grew out of western advance from the era of 1820 to that time) Peck, "Guide for Emigrants" (Boston, 1831); Darby, "Emigrants' Guide to Western and Southwestern States and Territories"; Dana, "Geographical Sketches in the Western Country"; Kinzie, "Waubun"; Keating, "Narrative of Long's Expedition"; Schoolcraft, "Discovery of the Sources of the Mississippi River," "Travels in the Central Portions of the Mississippi Valley." and "Lead Mines of the Missouri"; Andreas, "History of Illinois,"' i, 86-99; Hurlbut, "Chicago Antiquities"; McKenney, "Tour to the Lakes"; Thomas "Travels Through the Western Country," etc. (Auburn, N. Y., 1819).

[12]Darby, "Emigrants' Guide," pp. 272 ff; Benton, "Abridgment of Debates," vii, p. 397.

[13]De Bow's *Review*, iv, p. 254; xvii, p. 428.

that the universal disposition of Americans to emigrate to the western wilderness, in order to enlarge their dominion over inanimate nature, is the actual result of an expansive power which is inherent in them, and which by continually agitating all classes of society is constantly throwing a large portion of the whole population on the extreme confines of the State, in order to gain space for its development. Hardly is a new State of Territory formed before the same principle manifests itself again and gives rise to a further emigration; and so is it destined to go on until a physical barrier must finally obstruct its progress."[14]....

At the Atlantic frontier one can study the germs of processes repeated at each successive frontier. We have the complex European life sharply precipitated by the wilderness into the simplicity of primitive conditions. The first frontier had to meet its Indian question, its question of the disposition of the public domain, of the means of intercourse with older settlements, of the extension of political organization, of religious and educational activity. And the settlement of these and similar questions for one frontier served as a guide for the next. The American student needs not to go to the "prim little townships of Sleswick" for illustrations of the law of continuity and development. For example, he may study the origin of our land policies in the colonial land policy; he may see how the system grew by adapting the statutes to the customs of the successive frontiers.[15] He may see how the mining experience in the lead regions of Wisconsin, Illinois, and Iowa was applied to the mining laws of the Sierras,[16] and how our Indian

policy has been a series of experimentations on successive frontiers. Each tier of new States has found in the older ones material for its constitutions.[17] Each frontier has made similar contributions to American character, as will be discussed farther on....

The United States lies like a huge page in the history of society. Line by line as we read this continental page from West to East we find the record of social evolution. It begins with the Indian and the hunter; it goes on to tell of the disintegration of savagery by the entrance of the trader, the pathfinder of civilization; we read the annals of the pastoral stage in ranch life; the exploitation of the soil by the raising of unrotated crops of corn and wheat in sparsely settled farming communities; the intensive culture of the denser farm settlement; and finally the manufacturing organization with city and factory system.[18] This page is familiar to the student of census statistics, but how little of it has been used by our historians. Particularly in eastern States this page is a palimpsest. What is now a manufacturing State was in an earlier decade an area of intensive farming. Earlier yet it had been a wheat area, and still earlier the "range" had attracted the cattleherder. Thus Wisconsin, now developing manufacture, is a State with varied agricultural interests. But earlier it was given over to almost exclusive grain-raising, like North Dakota at the present time.

Each of these areas has had an influence in our economic and political history; the evolution of each into a higher stage has worked political transformations. But what constitutional historian has made any adequate attempt to interpret

---

[14]Grund. "Americans." ii, p. 8.

[15]See the suggestive paper by Prof. Jesse Macy, "The Institutional Beginnings of a Western State."

[16]Shinn, "Mining Camps."

[17]Compare Thorpe, in *Annals American Academy of Political and Social Science*, September, 1891; Bryce, "American Commonwealth," (1888), ii, p. 689.

[18]Compare "Observations on the North American Land Company," London, 1796, pp. xv, 144; Logan, "History of Upper South Carolina," i, pp. 149–151; Turner, "Character and Influence of Indian Trade in Wisconsin," p. 18; Peck, "New Guide for Emigrants" (Boston, 1837), ch. iv; "Compendium Eleventh Census," i, p. xl.

political facts by the light of these social areas and changes?[19]....

And yet, in spite of this opposition of the interests of the trader and the farmer, the Indian trade pioneered the way for civilization. The buffalo trail became the Indian trail, and this became the trader's "trace;" the trails widened into roads, and the roads into turnpikes, and these in turn were transformed into railroads. The same origin can be shown for the railroads of the South, the Far West, and the Dominion of Canada.[20] The trading posts reached by these trails were on the sites of Indian villages which had been placed in positions suggested by nature; and these trading posts, situated so as to command the water systems of the country, have grown into such cities as Albany, Pittsburgh, Detroit, Chicago, St. Louis, Council Bluffs, and Kansas City. Thus civilization in America has followed the arteries made by geology, pouring an ever richer tide through them, until at last the slender paths of aboriginal intercourse have been broadened and interwoven into the complex mazes of modern commercial lines; the wilderness has been interpenetrated by lines of civilization growing ever more numerous. It is like the steady growth of a complex nervous system for the originally simple, inert continent. If one would understand why we are to-day one nation, rather than a collection of isolated states, he must study this economic and social consolidation of the country. In this progress from savage conditions lie topics for the evolutionist.[21]

The effect of the Indian frontier as a consolidating agent in our history is important. From the close of the seventeenth century various intercolonial congresses have been called to treat with Indians and establish common measures of defense. Particularism was strongest in colonies with no Indian frontier. This frontier stretched along the western border like a cord of union. The Indian was a common danger, demanding united action. Most celebrated of these conferences was the Albany congress of 1754, called to treat with the Six Nations, and to consider plans of union. Even a cursory reading of the plan proposed by the congress reveals the importance of the frontier. The powers of the general council and the officers were, chiefly, the determination of peace and war with the Indians, the regulation of Indian trade, the purchase of Indian lands, and the creation and government of new settlements as a security against the Indians. It is evident that the unifying tendencies of the Revolutionary period were facilitated by the previous cooperation in the regulation of the frontier. In this connection may be mentioned the importance of the frontier, from that day to this, as a military training school, keeping alive the power of resistance to aggression, and developing the stalwart and rugged qualities of the frontiersman....

From the time the mountains rose between the pioneer and the seaboard, a new order of Americanism arose. The West and the East began to get out of touch of each other. The settlements from the sea to the mountains kept connection with the rear and had a certain solidarity. But the over-mountain men grew more and more independent. The East took a narrow view of American advance, and nearly lost these men. Kentucky and Tennessee history bears abundant witness to the truth of this statement. The East began to try to hedge and limit westward expansion....

Omitting those of the pioneer farmers who move from the love of adventure, the advance of the more steady farmer is easy to understand. Obviously the immigrant was attracted by the

---

[19]See *post*, for illustrations of the political accompaniments of changed industrial conditions.

[20]"Narrative and Critical History of America," viii, p. 10; Sparks' "Washington Works," ix, pp. 303, 327; Logan, "History of Upper South Carolina," i; McDonald, "Life of Kenton," p. 72; Cong. Record, xxiii, p. 57.

[21]On the effect of the fur trade in opening the routes of migration see the author's "Character and Influence of the Indian Trade in Wisconsin."

cheap lands of the frontier, and even the native farmer felt their influence strongly. Year by year the farmers who lived on soil whose returns were diminished by unrotated crops were offered the virgin soil of the frontier at nominal prices. Their growing families demanded more lands, and these were dear. The competition of the unexhausted, cheap, and easily tilled prairie lands compelled the farmer either to go west and continue the exhaustion of the soil on a new frontier, or to adopt intensive culture. Thus the census of 1890 shows, in the Northwest, many counties in which there is an absolute or a relative decrease of population. These States have been sending farmers to advance the frontier on the plains, and have themselves begun to turn to intensive farming and to manufacture. A decade before this, Ohio had shown the same transition stage. Thus the demand for land and the love of wilderness freedom drew the frontier ever onward. . . .

But the most important effect of the frontier has been in the promotion of democracy here and in Europe. As has been indicated, the frontier is productive of individualism. Complex society is precipitated by the wilderness into a kind of primitive organization based on the family. The tendency is anti-social. It produces antipathy to control, and particularly to any direct control. The tax-gatherer is viewed as a representative of oppression. Prof. Osgood, in an able article,[22] has pointed out that the frontier conditions prevalent in the colonies are important factors in the explanation of the American Revolution, where individual liberty was sometimes confused with absence of all effective government. The same conditions aid in explaining the difficulty of instituting a strong government in the period of the confederacy. The frontier individualism has from the beginning promoted democracy. The frontier States that came into the Union in the first quarter of a century of its existence came in with democratic suffrage provisions, and had reactive effects of the highest importance upon the older States whose peoples were being attracted there. An extension of the franchise became essential. It was *western* New York that forced an extension of suffrage in the constitutional convention of that State in 1821; and it was *western* Virginia that compelled the tide-water region to put a more liberal suffrage provision in the constitution framed in 1830, and to give to the frontier region a more nearly proportionate representation with the tide-water aristocracy. The rise of democracy as an effective force in the nation came in with western preponderance under Jackson and William Henry Harrison, and it meant the triumph of the frontier—with all of its good and with all of its evil elements.[23] An interesting illustration of the tone of frontier democracy in 1830 comes from the same debates in the Virginia convention already referred to. A representative from western Virginia declared:

> But, sir, it is not the increase of population in the West which this gentleman ought to fear. It is the energy which the mountain breeze and western habits impart to those emigrants. They are regenerated, politically I mean, sir. They soon become *working politicians*, and the difference, sir, between a *talking* and a *working* politician is immense. The Old Dominion has long been celebrated for producing great orators; the ablest metaphysicians in policy; men that can split hairs in all abstruse questions of political economy. But at home, or when they return from Congress, they have negroes to fan them asleep. But a Pennsylvania, a New York, an Ohio, or a western Virginia statesman, though far inferior in logic, metaphysics, and rhetoric to an old Virginia statesman, has this advantage, that when he returns home he takes off his coat and takes hold of the plow. This gives him bone and muscle, sir, and preserves his republican principles pure and uncontaminated.

---

[22]*Political Science Quarterly*, ii, p. 457. Compare Sumner, "Alexander Hamilton," chs. ii-vii.

[23]Compare Wilson, "Division and Reunion," pp. 15, 24.

So long as free land exists, the opportunity for a competency exists, and economic power secures political power. But the democracy born of free land, strong in selfishness and individualism, intolerant of administrative experience and education, and pressing individual liberty beyond its proper bounds, has its dangers as well as its benefits. Individualism in America has allowed a laxity in regard to governmental affairs which has rendered possible the spoils system and all the manifest evils that follow from the lack of a highly developed civic spirit. In this connection may be noted also the influence of frontier conditions in permitting lax business honor, inflated paper currency and wild-cat banking. . . .

From the conditions of frontier life came intellectual traits of profound importance. The works of travelers along each frontier from colonial days onward describe certain common traits, and these traits have, while softening down, still persisted as survivals in the place of their origin, even when a higher social organization succeeded. The result is that to the frontier the American intellect owes its striking characteristics. That coarseness and strength combined with acuteness and inquisitiveness; that practical, inventive turn of mind, quick to find expedients; that masterful grasp of material things, lacking in the artistic but powerful to effect great ends; that restless, nervous energy;[24] that dominant individualism, working for good and for evil, and withal that buoyancy and exuberance which comes with freedom—these are traits of the frontier, or traits called out elsewhere because of the existence of the frontier. Since the days when the fleet of Columbus sailed into the waters of the New World, America has been another name for opportunity, and the people of the United States have taken their tone from the incessant expansion which has not only been open but has even been forced upon them. He would be a rash prophet who should assert that the expansive character of American life has now entirely ceased. Movement has been its dominant fact, and, unless this training has no effect upon a people, the American energy will continually demand a wider field for its exercise. But never again will such gifts of free land offer themselves. For a moment, at the frontier, the bonds of custom are broken and unrestraint is triumphant. There is not *tabula rasa*. The stubborn American environment is there with its imperious summons to accept its conditions; the inherited ways of doing things are also there; and yet, in spite of environment, and in spite of custom, each frontier did indeed furnish a new field of opportunity, a gate of escape from the bondage of the past; and freshness, and confidence, and scorn of older society, impatience of its restraints and its ideas, and indifference to its lessons, have accompanied the frontier. What the Mediterranean Sea was to the Greeks, breaking the bond of custom, offering new experiences, calling out new institutions and activities, that, and more, the ever retreating frontier has been to the United States directly, and to the nations of Europe more remotely. And now, four centuries from the discovery of America, at the end of a hundred years of life under the Constitution, the frontier has gone, and with its going has closed the first period of American history.

---

[24]Colonial travelers agree in remarking on the phlegmatic characteristics of the colonists. It has frequently been asked how such a people could have developed that strained nervous energy now characteristic of them. Compare Sumner, "Alexander Hamilton," p. 98, and Adams "History of the United States," i, p 60; ix, pp 240, 241. The transition appears to become marked at the close of the War of 1812, a period when interest centered upon the development of the West, and the West was noted for restless energy. Grund, "Americans," ii, ch. i.

>> Questions for Consideration

1. What evidence does Turner use? How does this reflect his ideas about historical agency?

2. Is there any evidence of racism or sexism in this history? Are all American races and genders treated equally? What assumptions underlay Turner's thesis?

3. Can you detect any evidence of the influence of evolution or Social Darwinist theory here?

4. How does Turner respond to Adams's Teutonic germ theory? What is his alternative theory?

George Bancroft, *History of the United States of America from the Discovery of the Continent*

America Takes Up Arms for Self-Defence and Arrives at Independence.

Chapter 1: America Sustains the Town of Boston. May 1774.

THE hour of the American Revolution was come. The people of the continent obeyed one general impulse, as the earth in spring listens to the command of nature and without the appearance of effort bursts into life. The movement was quickened, even when it was most resisted; and its fiercest adversaries worked with the most effect for its fulfillment. Standing in manifold relations with the governments, the culture, and the experience of the past, the Americans seized as their peculiar inheritance the traditions of liberty. Beyond any other nation, they had made trial of the possible forms of popular representation, and respected individual conscience and thought. The resources of the country in agriculture and commerce, forests and fisheries, mines and materials for manufactures, were so diversified and complete that their development could neither be guided nor circumscribed by a government beyond the ocean. The numbers, purity, culture,

industry, and daring of its inhabitants proclaimed the existence of a people rich in creative energy, and ripe for institutions of their own.

They refused to acknowledge even to themselves the hope that was swelling within them, and yet in their political aspirations they deduced from universal principles a bill of rights, as old as creation and as wide as humanity. The idea of freedom had always revealed itself at least to a few of the wise whose prophetic instincts were quickened by love of their kind, and its growth can be traced in the tendency of the ages. In America, it was the breath of life to the people. For the first time it found a region and a race where it could be professed with the earnestness of an indwelling conviction, and be defended with the enthusiasm that had marked no wars but those for religion. When all Europe slumbered over questions of liberty, a band of exiles, keeping watch by night, heard the glad tidings which promised the political regeneration of the world. A revolution, unexpected in the moment of its coming, but prepared by glorious forerunners, grew naturally and necessarily out of the series of past events by the formative principle of a living belief. And why should man organize resistance to the grand design of Providence? Why should not the consent of the ancestral land

Source: George Bancroft, *History of the United States of America from the Discovery of the Continent* Volume IV (NY: D. Appleton, 1889), pp. 3–5, 426, and 435–452.

and the gratulations of every other call the young nation to its place among the powers of the earth? Britain was the mighty mother who bred men capable of laying the foundation of so noble an empire, and she alone could have trained them up. She had excelled all the world as the founder of colonies. The condition which entitled them to independence was now fulfilled. Their vigorous vitality refused conformity to foreign laws and external rule. They could take no other way to perfection than by the unconstrained development of that which was within them. They were not only able to govern themselves, they alone were able to do so; subordination visibly repressed their energies. Only by self-direction could they at all times employ their collective and individual faculties in the fullest extent of their ever-increasing intelligence. Could not the illustrious nation, which had gained no distinction in war, in literature, or in science, comparable to that of having wisely founded distant settlements on a system of liberty, willingly perfect its beneficent work, now when no more was required than the acknowledgment that its offspring was come of age? Why must the ripening of lineal virtue be struck at, as rebellion in the lawful sons? Why is their unwavering attachment to the essential principle of their existence to be persecuted as treason, rather than viewed with delight as the crowning glory of the country from which they sprung? If the institutions of Britain were so deeply fixed in its usages and opinions that their deviations from justice could not as yet be rectified; if the old continent was pining under systems of authority not fit to be borne, and not ripe for amendment, why should not a people be heartened to build a commonwealth in the wilderness, where alone it was offered a home?

So reasoned a few in Britain, who were jeered at "as visionary enthusiasts." Parliament had asserted an absolute lordship over the colonies in all cases whatsoever, and, fretting itself into a frenzy at the denial of its unlimited dominion, was destroying its recognized authority by its eagerness for more. The majority of the ministers, including the most active and resolute, were bent on the immediate employment of force. Lord North, recoiling from civil war, exercised no control over his colleagues, leaving the government to be conducted by the several departments. As a consequence, the king became the only point of administrative union. In him an approving conscience had no misgiving as to his duty. His heart knew no relenting; his will never wavered. Though America were to be drenched in blood and its towns reduced to ashes, though its people were to be driven to struggle for total independence, though he himself should find it necessary to bid high for hosts of mercenaries from the Scheldt to Moscow, and in quest of savage allies go tapping at every wigwam from Lake Huron to the Gulf of Mexico, he was resolved to coerce the thirteen colonies into submission.

On the tenth of May 1774, which was the day of the accession of Louis XVI, the act closing the port of Boston, transferring the board of customs to Marblehead, and the seat of government to Salem, reached the devoted town. The king was confident that the slow torture which was to be applied to its inhabitants would constrain them to cry out for mercy and promise unconditional obedience. Success in resistance could come only from an American union, which was not to be hoped for, unless Boston should offer herself as a willing sacrifice. The mechanics and merchants and laborers, altogether scarcely so many as thirty-five hundred able-bodied men, knew that they were acting not for a province of America, but for freedom itself. They were inspired by the thought that the Providence which rules the world demanded of them heroic self-denial as the champions of humanity, and they never doubted the fellow-feeling of the continent...

Chapter XXVII. The People of Every American Colony Demand Independence. June–July 1776.

AMERICAN independence was not an act of sudden passion, nor the work of one man or one assembly. It had been discussed in every part of the country by fanners and merchants, by mechanics and planters, by the fishermen and the back-woodsmen; in town-meetings and from the pulpit; at social gatherings and around the camp fires; in newspapers and in pamphlets; in county conventions and conferences of committees; in colonial congresses and assemblies. The decision was put off only to ascertain the voice of the people. Virginia, having uttered her will, and communicated it to her sister colonies, proceeded, as though independence had been proclaimed, to form her constitution. More counselors waited on her assembly than they took notice of: they were aided in their deliberations by the teachings of the law-givers of Greece; by the line of magistrates who had framed the Roman code; by those who had written best in English on government and public freedom. They passed by monarchy and hereditary aristocracy as unessential forms, and looked for the self-subsistent elements of liberty. . . .

Chapter XXVIII. The Resolution and the Declaration of Independence. From the First to the Fourth of July 1776.

ON the morning of the first of July, the day set apart for considering the resolution of independence, John Adams, confident as if the vote had been taken, invoked the blessing of heaven to make the new-born republic more glorious than any which had gone before. His heart melted with sorrow at the sufferings of the array that had been in Canada; he knew that England, having recovered that province, commanded the upper lakes and the Mississippi; that she had a free communication with all the tribes of Indians along the western frontiers, and would induce them by bloodshed and fire to drive in the inhabitants upon the middle settlements, at a time when the coasts might be ravaged by the British navy and a single day might bring the army before New York. Independence could be obtained only by a great expense of life; but the greater the danger, the stronger was his determination, for he held that a free constitution of civil government could not be purchased at too dear a rate. He called to mind the fixed rule of the Romans, never to send

or receive ambassadors to treat of peace with their enemies while their affairs were in a disastrous situation; and he was cheered by the belief that his countrymen were of the same temper and principle.

At the appointed hour, the members, probably on that day fifty in number, appeared in their places; among them, the delegates lately chosen in New Jersey. The great occasion had brought forth superior statesmen men who joined moderation to energy. After they had all passed away, their longevity was remarked as a proof of their calm and temperate nature; full two thirds of the New England representatives lived beyond seventy years some of them to be eighty or ninety. Every colony was found to be represented, and the delegates of all but one had received full power of action. . . .

The resolution of congress changed the old thirteen British colonies into free and independent states. It remained to set forth the reason for this act, and the principles which the new people would own as their guides. Of the committee appointed for that duty, Thomas Jefferson of Virginia had received the largest number of votes, and was in that manner singled out to draft the confession of faith of the rising empire. He owed this distinction to respect for the colony which he represented, to the consummate ability of the state papers which, he had already written, and to that general favor which follows merit, modesty, and a sweet disposition; but the quality which specially fitted him for the task was the sympathetic character of his nature, by which he was able with instinctive perception to read the soul of the nation, and, having collected its best thoughts and noblest feelings, to give them out in clear and bold words, mixed with so little of himself that his country, as it went along with him, found nothing but what it recognized as its own. Born to an independent fortune, he had from his youth been an indefatigable student. "The glow of one warm thought was worth more to him than money." Of a hopeful temperament and a tranquil, philosophic cast of mind, always temperate in his mode of life and decorous in his manners, he was a perfect master of his passions, he was of a delicate organization, and fond of elegance; his tastes were refined; laborious in his application to business or the pursuit of knowledge, music, the most spiritual of all pleasures of the senses, was his favorite recreation; and he took a never-failing delight in the varied beauty of rural life, building himself a home in the loveliest region of his native state. He was a skilful horseman, and with elastic step would roam the mountains on foot. The range of his studies was very wide; he was not unfamiliar with the literature of Greece and Rome; had an aptitude for mathematics and mechanics, and loved especially the natural sciences; scorning nothing but metaphysics. British governors and officials had introduced into Williamsburg the prevalent free-thinking of Englishmen of that century, and Jefferson had grown up in its atmosphere; he was not only a hater of priestcraft and superstition and bigotry and intolerance, he was thought to be indifferent to religion; yet his instincts all inclined him to trace every fact to a general law, and to put faith in ideal truth; the world of the senses did not bound his aspirations, and he believed more than he himself was aware of. . . . Just thirty-three years old, married, and happy in his family, affluent, with a bright career before him, he was no rash innovator by his character or his position; if his convictions drove him to demand independence, it was only because he could no longer live with honor under the British "constitution, which he still acknowledged to be better than all that had preceded it." His enunciation of general principles was fearless, but he was no visionary devotee of abstract theories; the nursling of his country, the offspring of his time, he set about the work of a practical statesman, and the principles which he set forth grew so naturally out of previous law and the facts of the past that they struck deep root and have endured. . . .

From the fullness of his own mind, without consulting one single book, yet having in memory the example of the Swiss and the manifesto of the United Provinces of the Netherlands, Jefferson drafted the declaration, in which, after citing the primal principles of government, he presented the complaints of the United States against England in the three classes of the iniquitous use of the royal prerogative, the usurpation of legislative power over America by the king in parliament, and the measures for enforcing the acts of the British parliament. He submitted the paper separately to Franklin and to John Adams, accepted from each of them one or two verbal, unimportant corrections, and on the twenty-eighth of June reported it to congress, which, on the second of July, immediately after adopting the resolution of independence, entered upon its consideration. During the remainder of that day, and the next two, the language, the statements, and the principles of the paper were closely scanned.

All other changes and omissions in Jefferson's paper were either insignificant or much for the better, rendering its language more terse, more dispassionate, and more exact; and, in the evening of the fourth day of July, New York still abstaining from the vote, twelve states, without one negative, agreed to this "Declaration by the Representatives of the United States of America in Congress assembled. . . .

This immortal state paper was "the genuine effusion of the soul of the country at that time," the revelation of its mind, when, in its youth, its enthusiasm, its sublime confronting of danger, it rose to the highest creative powers of which man is capable. The bill of rights which it promulgates is of rights that are older than human institutions, and spring from the eternal justice. Two political theories divided the world: one founded the commonwealth on the advantage of the state, the policy of expediency, the other on the immutable principles of morals; the new republic, as it took its place among the powers of the world, proclaimed its faith in the truth and reality and unchangeableness of freedom, virtue, and right. The heart of Jefferson in writing the declaration, and of congress in adopting it, beat for all humanity; the assertion of right was made for the entire world of mankind and all coming generations, without any exception whatever; for the proposition which admits of exceptions can never be self-evident. As it was put forth in the name of the ascendant people of that time, it was sure to make the circuit of the world, passing everywhere through the despotic countries of Europe; and the astonished nations, as they read that all men are created equal, started out of their lethargy, like those who have been exiles from childhood, when they suddenly hear the dimly remembered accents of their mother tongue. . . .

Finally, the declaration was not only the announcement of the birth of a people, but the establishment of a national government; a most imperfect one, it is true, but still a government, in conformity with the limited constituent powers which each colony had conferred upon its delegates in congress. The war was no longer a civil war; Britain was become to the United States a foreign country. Every former subject of the British king in the thirteen colonies now owed primary allegiance to the dynasty of the people, and became a citizen of the new republic; except in this, everything remained as before; every man retained his rights; the colonies did not dissolve into a state of nature, nor did the new people undertake a social revolution. The management of the internal police and government was carefully reserved to the separate states, which could, each for itself, enter upon the career of domestic reforms. But the states which were henceforth independent of Britain were not independent of one another: the United States of America, presenting themselves to mankind as one people, assumed powers over war, peace, foreign alliances, and commerce.

>> Questions for Consideration

1. What evidence can you find here that indicates this is a romantic national consensus history?

2. In what ways might this history be considered an extension of Enlightenment history?

3. How could this history be used to support the emerging myth of American exceptionalism and of heroic founding fathers?

4. How is Bancroft responding to critics of the American Revolution, who claimed that it was unnatural and violent, led by a few irrational and irresponsible radicals and traitors?

5. How does Bancroft's history compare to that of Mercy Otis Warren, an actual observer of the Revolution? What might account for the differences?

Chapter 5

Conflict and Consensus: The Progressive Challenge to American History and the Consensus Response

W. E. B. Du Bois (*Courtesy of the Library of Congress*).

Although professional historians continued to apply nationalist consensus approaches throughout the twentieth century, new theories grew increasingly attractive after 1890. These theories were born and shaped in the intellectual currents of turn-of-the-century America and Europe. The most important current of this era was Progressivism, which began as a reaction against the political corruption, social chaos, and economic turmoil of the late nineteenth century. It attacked corruption in politics and big business, demanding reforms to make the government more democratic and responsive to the needs of the people. The new social science disciplines took a lead in this movement, using the methods of economics, political science, sociology, and history to explore the roots of the problems and suggest possible solutions. Influenced by Pragmatism and to a much smaller extent Marxism, many Progressive intellectuals saw economic factors, such as class inequalities, capitalism, and imperialism, as the root of most of these problems, and concluded that greater government regulation was necessary to control these potentially destructive forces and ensure the continued progress of the nation. Influenced by Progressivism, some historians successfully challenged the original consensus version of U.S. history, but consensus historians remained in the academy and fought back. While World War I and the Great Depression seemed to favor the Progressive's critical view of the U.S. government and capitalism, World War II had the reverse effect. Progressive historians were labeled as traitors because of their continued criticisms of the U.S. government, and consensus history once again came into vogue with a vengeance. By the 1950s, consensus nationalist history once again dominated the academy.

Relativism, Pragmatism, and Progressivism

One of the most influential American philosophies of the twentieth century was Pragmatism. Led by John Dewey, Charles Sanders Peirce, and William James, Pragmatists argued that all knowledge was provisional and that a community of scientists must constantly test all hypotheses to find truth.[1] While Pragmatic scientists and philosophers continued to believe in progress and in the ability of humans to understand everything through reason and logic, they added that this progress was accomplished through conflict, rather than consensus or unity, and that it resulted from human actions rather than ideas or the hand of God.

New theories of relativity which emerged in the sciences in the first decades of the twentieth century also influenced many Pragmatists. In the physical sciences, Albert
Einstein   Einstein's *General Theory of Relativity* (1913) overthrew Newtonian and Euclidean theories which had dominated the sciences for centuries. Einstein's theory of relativity was complex, but most relevant to historians; it questioned observable reality and "absolute simultaneity," or the existence of a common time frame or reality shared by all natural phenomena.[2] This implied the existence of multiple realities, perspectives, and truths for every moment in time, thus rendering impossible any attempt to re-create any event objectively and exactly. Widespread disillusionment with prewar values and ideology following World War I made Americans and Europeans particularly

---

[1]James T. Kloppenberg, "Pragmatism and the Practice of History: From Turner and Du Bois to Today," *Metaphilosophy* 35, no. 1/2 (January 2004): 202.

[2]Ernst Breisach, *Historiography: Ancient, Medieval and Modern*, 2nd ed. (Chicago: University of Chicago Press, 1995), 137.

receptive of these theories. Pragmatists used these theories to bolster their claim that truth was man-made, and therefore relative to one's individual perspective. While not all Progressive historians were Pragmatists, and few were pure relativists, these theories did influence many Progressive histories in the 1920s and 1930s.

James   The Pragmatist historical sensibility first emerged in the late 1880s at Harvard University when William James (1842–1910) introduced this approach in his philosophy and psychology courses.[3] James was influential in exposing Frederick Jackson Turner to Pragmatist philosophy and a critique of "traditional" history. These new theories shaped Turner's argument that economic and social forces drove American history. While still convinced of the superiority and exceptionalism of American political institutions and progress, Turner played an important role in shaping a new generation of historians who would study politics through the lens of economic and social forces.

Du Bois   William James also taught W. E. B. Du Bois (1868–1963), arguably the most important African American intellectual of all time. He convinced Du Bois to take a Pragmatic approach to the study of American history. Du Bois graduated from Harvard University with a PhD in history focusing on the African slave trade. Afterward he studied race relations and African American culture following the Civil War, which resulted in the publication of his most famous work *The Souls of Black Folk* (1903). This work directly challenged the Dunning interpretation of Reconstruction by showing how African American powerlessness following the Civil War and the violence and hatred of southern whites caused the failure of Reconstruction policies. His writings in general emphasized how racism and the conflicting economic interests of white and black Americans shaped international and national politics. Du Bois helped to spearhead a revival of African American interest and pride in their heritage and culture, and this encouraged many black intellectuals to uncover more knowledge about their history.

Woodson   Professional historian Carter G. Woodson (1875–1950) was another major figure in this cultural revival. Like Du Bois, Woodson was the son of American slaves and graduated with a PhD in history from Harvard University. In addition to publishing his own histories, he helped to found the Association for the Study of Negro Life and History in 1915 and the *Journal of Negro History* in 1916.[4] He continued to promote the history of all aspects of African American life throughout the first half of the twentieth century, but few white historians knew of his work. Outside of the traditionally black colleges, few universities had classes in African American history and few doctoral advisors assigned topics in this field prior to the 1950s. White historians, even many fellow Progressives, disregarded African American history as being racially biased in favor of African Americans. As a consequence, it was easily marginalized, and almost all of it was published privately or in the *Journal of Negro History*.

---

[3]Kloppenberg, "Pragmatism and the Practice of History," 203.

[4]John Hope Franklin, "On the Evolution of Scholarship in Afro-American History," in *The State of Afro-American History: Past, Present, and Future*, ed. Darlene Clark Hine (Baton Rouge, LA: Louisiana State University Press, 1986), 14. The *Journal of Negro History* was renamed the *Journal of African American History* in 2002.

Robinson   Another famous Progressive historian, James Harvey Robinson, was John Dewey's colleague at Columbia University in the early twentieth century and applied his Pragmatic philosophy to writing a new history. In fact, he entitled his manifesto of this approach *The New History* (1912), which shaped the interpretations of another generation of historians. He emphasized the interpretive nature of history, arguing that not only is truth relative, but it changes according to the constantly increasing amount of historical knowledge. All conclusions were therefore tentative, because they would eventually be supplanted by new conclusions based on accumulated evidence.[5] As a Progressive reformer, Robinson wanted to use history to help people understand themselves and the contemporary world. Along with Charles Beard and Dewey, he helped to found the New School for Social Research in 1918 to bring the study of history to Americans who lacked access to higher education.[6]

Beard   Charles Beard (1874–1978) also worked with John Dewey at Columbia University and was greatly influenced by his Pragmatism. Arguably the most famous of the Progressive historians, Beard was born in Indiana, but studied at Oxford University, where he encountered socialist political theories. This socialism led Beard to see American capitalism from a much more critical perspective than many of his contemporaries. Beard then completed his studies at Columbia University, where his encounter with Pragmatism led him to see all knowledge as conditional and relative to the individual truth-seeker. Historiographer Ernst Breisach summarizes Beard's subjectivism and relativism: "Beard denied that the past could be grasped as an external object, that historians could face it with impartiality, that the multitude of events had any inner structure, and that the past could be intellectually conquered by man."[7] When Beard was elected president of the American Historical Association in 1935, he applied Pragmatic relativism to the historical profession in his inaugural presidential address. He argued that the "noble dream" of purely objective scientific history was nothing more than a dream and that all historians are shaped by their own time and place in history.[8] While Beard brought historical relativism to the wider historical profession, he and other Progressive historians never gave up on the search for historical truth.

Although these historical theories attracted some interest from professional historians, his economic and political history attracted even more attention (and consternation) from Americans outside of academia. His controversial study *An Economic Interpretation of the Constitution of the United States* (1913) argued that rather than having the national interests or ideas of liberty at heart, the authors of the Constitution and the nation's founders were guided primarily by selfish economic interests. This interpretation offended many patriotic Americans, who dismissed him as an un-American socialist, but he influenced generations of historians who would no longer view the nation's political history with rose-colored glasses. In fact, in the 1930s,

---

[5]Kloppenberg, "Pragmatism and the Practice of History," 205.

[6]Ibid., 206.

[7]Breisach, *Historiography*, 332.

[8]Charles Beard, "That Noble Dream," *The American Historical Review* 41, no. 1 (October 1935): 74–87.

Beard's texts became the standard for colleges across the nation. He had become the most influential historian of his day.

Ritter Beard   Charles Beard's wife, Mary Ritter Beard (1856–1958), was also influenced by Pragmatic Progressive ideas and brought these to her histories of women. Like other wives of professional historians in the nineteenth and twentieth centuries, Mary helped her husband to write and publish his histories, but unlike other wives, Mary had a professional career of her own. She graduated from De Pauw University, where she met Charles and joined him in courses at Oxford and Columbia universities. Mary, however, chose to devote herself to raising children and feminist and labor activism, rather than pursue her PhD. As she investigated social history, the glaring omission of women from existing histories presented an important challenge: to write women back into history.

One element of Progressivism which particularly shaped Mary Beard's history was the feminist movement, which had been demanding reform of women's employment and suffrage. Like other Progressives, she sought to support these reform efforts by writing histories of how these issues had evolved in the past and investigating the roots of the problems of women's social and economic inequality. In *Woman as Force in History* (1946), Mary Beard used the modern feminist movement and the discussions about the role of women in World War II as a starting point for her discussion of women's role in history. Through the critical analysis of secondary sources on women's roles in America, Europe, and the World, she wrote of the important political, economic, and social roles of women throughout the ages, convincingly arguing against the idea that women were merely shadows and subjects of men.[9] Although other women had become professional historians before her and other feminists' published histories, Mary Beard is often seen as the Mother of American women's history because of this work.

Mary and Charles Beard also wrote a number of popular American history textbooks in the 1920s and 1930s. These textbooks brought together political, social, and economic history and were remarkable for their emphasis on economic forces and inclusion of women's history. *The Rise of American Civilization* (1927) was a best-selling textbook for many years and is a good example of their approach. It emphasized the conflict between capitalist and agrarian interests throughout American history. It treated the Civil War as an economic struggle between the northern capitalists and southern agrarians, with northern industrial capitalism victorious. Unlike many conservative historians of their time, the Beards labeled American expansionism as imperialist and unabashedly discussed the negative aspects of this force in American history. Unlike Marx, however, the Beards explained the positive consequences of capitalism as well as the negative, and they did not anticipate a communist revolution in this country. They argued that the working classes benefited from America's expanding economy through economic opportunities and class mobility, and that these factors thwarted the growth of working-class radicalism.[10] While this critical interpretation of

---

[9]Mary Beard, *Woman as Force in History: A Study in Traditions and Realities* (New York: Macmillan, 1946).

[10]Charles A. Beard and Mary R. Beard, *The Rise of American Civilization*, Vol. II (New York: Macmillan, 1927). Revised edition 1933, reprinted 1947, 395.

American history was popular following World War I, it was heavily criticized as unpatriotic and Marxist during the upsurge of nationalism and anticommunism in the 1940s.

Schlesinger, Jr.   Charles Beard's student Arthur M. Schlesinger, Sr. (1888–1965) carried Progressive history into the middle of the twentieth century, as he continued to publish and teach for the next fifty years. His son, Harvard historian Arthur M. Schlesinger, Jr. (1918–2007), carried on the Progressive tradition with his publications in the middle and late twentieth century. His work *The Age of Jackson* (1945) had a Progressive thesis, asserting that reform movements were the key to American progress and improvement. His sense of history, however, evolved over the course of the century. In *The Cycles of American History* (1986), he elaborated on the role of liberal reform and developed an overarching pattern to American history. Rather than seeing progress as a continuous pattern throughout history, he argued that America went through alternating periods of liberalism and progress, and conservatism and retrenchment. His ideas had enormous influence, not only in the historical world, but also in the political arena.[11]

A Return to Consensus

Despite its popularity in the early twentieth century, Progressive history came under attack during and after World War II, and retreated during the 1950s. As Western scholars attacked moral and ideological relativism as part of the West's battle with totalitarian Nazism and communism, the American historical profession attacked Progressive historians, including the Beards, for their relativist ideas and their criticism of the U.S. government. Charles Beard's outspoken opposition to U.S. intervention in World War II only added fuel to the fire which consumed his reputation in the 1940s. Subsequent historians, such as Oscar Handlin, denied that Beard was even a historian at all.[12] In this climate, nationalist consensus history regained its dominant position in the academy.

Hofstadter   World War II also accentuated Americans' sense of exceptionalism, and historians sought to comprehend historical reasons for why the United States was the strongest most stable nation in the world. Richard Hofstadter (1916–1970) and other historians in the 1950s came to the conclusion that what made America unique was its lack of dissent and universal consensus on democratic ideals and effective government. These new consensus historians of the 1940s and 1950s saw their Progressive mentors as unduly influenced by the political context of their time period, warping their perspective and making them overemphasize the economic and social divisions *Neoconsensus* in American society. In *The American Political Tradition and the Men Who Made It* *School* (1948), Hofstadter laid down the foundations for the neoconsensus school of history, arguing that the success and progress of the United States was due to its unique democratic system, which encouraged and fostered consensus among liberals, conservatives, and other groups within society. This "counter-progressive" school minimized conflict

---

[11]John Patrick Diggins, "Arthur M. Schlesinger, Jr.," *OAH Newsletter*, May 2007, 19.

[12]Breisach, *Historiography*, 292.

and difference in American history and emphasized homogeneity, compromise, and positive progress.

This conservative trend in historiography reflected the wider cultural trend in the United States following World War II. The nation's people desired a return to "normalcy" following the disruptive years of the two world wars and the Great Depression. Values, fashions, and ideas from the late nineteenth century were once again appealing to Americans. The increasing suspicion of and opposition to communism which followed only increased the appeal of the late nineteenth century, as Americans sought to defend "traditional" American values from communistic ideas which had infiltrated the country in the early twentieth century. In this anticommunist context, Progressive ideas, like any ideas which bore any resemblance to Marxism or communism, were considered not only unfashionable, but treasonous. As a consequence, conservative consensus history blossomed and dominated the era.

Boorstin   Consensus historians wrote on a variety of topics and shaped a new generation of Americans' views of their past. Louis Hartz (1919–1986) and Daniel Boorstin (1913–2004) helped to firmly establish consensus theories in the profession in the 1950s.[13] Boorstin was born in Georgia and graduated from Harvard and Yale universities. Rejecting relativism, he asserted the importance of objectivity and empiricism. He and many other consensus historians found the American Revolution and political tradition especially important in their research. Arguing that the American Revolution was a conservative movement to protect democratic rights, he downplayed any disagreements or differences among Americans during or after the war, and saw unity of purpose and mission as the great driving force in American history.

Morgan   Edmund S. Morgan's (1916–) *Birth of the Republic 1763–1789* (1956) stressed the agreement of Americans on protecting traditional principles of protection of property and liberty, and human equality. Intellectual historians in the 1960s, such as *Bailyn*   Bernard Bailyn (1922–) and Gordon S. Wood (1933–), agreed that Americans were united behind a common ideology, but stressed the radicalism of the Revolution and *Wood*   Constitution.[14] They pointed to republicanism as the dominant ideology guiding this period in U.S. history. Wood's "republican synthesis" theory dominated ideological interpretations of the Revolution through the 1980s. These consensus historians effectively silenced Progressive history in the 1950s, guiding American historiography back to the national political history reminiscent of the nineteenth century. While the works of Morgan, Bailyn, and Wood have evolved greatly since the 1950s, all three are still considered leading experts on the American Revolution to this day.

Although the conservative consensus thesis retained its hold over America's popular memory, Progressive historians had created a strong alternative perspective which enormously influenced American historiography. Shaped by Marxism, Pragmatism,

---

[13]Louis Hartz, *The Liberal Tradition in America: An Interpretation of American Political Thought since the Revolution* (New York: Harcourt Brace, 1955) and Daniel Boorstein, *The Americans* (Harmondsworth: Penguin, 1965).

[14]Bernard Bailyn, *The Ideological Origins of the American Constitution* (Cambridge: Harvard University Press, 1967) and Gordon Wood, *The Radicalism of the American Revolution* (New York: A.A. Knopf, 1992).

and the social, economic, and political forces which gave rise to the Progressive movement, Progressive historians exposed the economic and social origins of modern institutions, revealed economic and class conflicts, and questioned the objectivity of the profession. Political history remained dominant, but Progressives successfully revised American history to include more social and economic factors. Their longest-lasting impact on American history, however, was to demonstrate the importance of diversity and conflict in American history. In the second half of the twentieth century, their theories would regain popularity and shape a variety of new approaches.

W. E. Burghardt Du Bois, *The Souls of Black Folk*

Of the Dawn of Freedom

The problem of the twentieth century is the problem of the color-line,—the relation of the darker to the lighter races of men in Asia and Africa, in America and the islands of the sea. It was a phase of this problem that caused the Civil War; and however much they who marched South and North in 1861 may have fixed on the technical points, of union and local autonomy as a shibboleth, all nevertheless knew, as we know, that the question of Negro slavery was the real cause of the conflict. Curious it was, too, how this deeper question ever forced itself to the surface despite effort and disclaimer. No sooner had Northern armies touched Southern soil than this old question, newly guised, sprang from the earth,—What shall be done with Negroes? Peremptory military commands this way and that, could not answer the query; the Emancipation Proclamation seemed but to broaden and intensify the difficulties; and the War Amendments made the Negro problems of today.

It is the aim of this essay to study the period of history from 1861 to 1872 so far as it relates to the American Negro. In effect, this tale of the dawn of Freedom is an account of that government of men called the Freedmen's Bureau,—one of the most singular and interesting of the attempts made by a great nation to grapple with vast problems of race and social condition.

The war has naught to do with slaves, cried Congress, the President, and the Nation; and yet no sooner had the armies, East and West, penetrated Virginia and Tennessee than fugitive slaves appeared within their lines. They came at night, when the flickering camp-fires shone like vast unsteady stars along the black horizon: old men and thin, with gray and tufted hair; women with frightened eyes, dragging whimpering hungry children; men and girls, stalwart and gaunt,—a horde of starving vagabonds, homeless, helpless, and pitiable, in their dark distress. Two methods of treating these newcomers seemed equally logical to opposite sorts of minds. Ben Butler, in Virginia, quickly declared slave property contraband of war, and put the fugitives to work; while Fremont, in Missouri, declared the slaves free under martial law. Butler's action was approved, but Fremont's was hastily countermanded, and his successor, Halleck, saw things differently. "Hereafter," he commanded, "no slaves should be allowed to come into your lines at all; if any come without your knowledge, when owners call for them deliver them." Such a policy was difficult to enforce; some of the black refugees declared themselves freemen, others showed that their masters had deserted them, and still others were captured with forts and plantations. Evidently, too, slaves were a source of strength to

Source: W.E.B. Du Bois, *The Souls of Black Folk* (Chicago: A. C. McClurg & Co., 1903): pp. 13–22, 26–36, & 38–40.

the Confederacy, and were being used as laborers and producers. "They constitute a military resource," wrote Secretary Cameron, late in 1861; "and being such, that they should not be turned over to the enemy is too plain to discuss." So gradually the tone of the army chiefs changed; Congress forbade the rendition of fugitives, and Butler's "contrabands" were welcomed as military laborers. This complicated rather than solved the problem, for now the scattering fugitives became a steady stream, which flowed faster as the armies marched.

Then the long-headed man with care-chiselled face who sat in the White House saw the inevitable, and emancipated the slaves of rebels on New Year's, 1863. A month later Congress called earnestly for the Negro soldiers whom the act of July, 1862, had half grudgingly allowed to enlist. Thus the barriers were levelled and the deed was done. The stream of fugitives swelled to a flood, and anxious army officers kept inquiring: "What must be done with slaves, arriving almost daily? Are we to find food and shelter for women and children?"

It was a Pierce of Boston who pointed out the way, and thus became in a sense the founder of the Freedmen's Bureau. He was a firm friend of Secretary Chase; and when, in 1861, the care of slaves and abandoned lands devolved upon the Treasury officials, Pierce was specially detailed from the ranks to study the conditions. First, he cared for the refugees at Fortress Monroe; and then, after Sherman had captured Hilton Head, Pierce was sent there to found his Port Royal experiment of making free workingmen out of slaves. Before his experiment was barely started, however, the problem of the fugitives had assumed such proportions that it was taken from the hands of the over-burdened Treasury Department and given to the army officials. Already centres of massed freedmen were forming at Fortress Monroe, Washington, New Orleans, Vicksburg and Corinth, Columbus, Ky., and Cairo, Ill., as well as at Port Royal. Army chaplains found here new and fruitful fields;

"superintendents of contrabands" multiplied, and some attempt at systematic work was made by enlisting the able-bodied men and giving work to the others.

Then came the Freedmen's Aid societies, born of the touching appeals from Pierce and from these other centres of distress. There was the American Missionary Association, sprung from the Amistad, and now full-grown for work; the various church organizations, the National Freedmen's Relief Association, the American Freedmen's Union, the Western Freedmen's Aid Commission,—in all fifty or more active organizations, which sent clothes, money, school-books, and teachers southward. All they did was needed, for the destitution of the freedmen was often reported as "too appalling for belief," and the situation was daily growing worse rather than better.

And daily, too, it seemed more plain that this was no ordinary matter of temporary relief, but a national crisis; for here loomed a labor problem of vast dimensions. Masses of Negroes stood idle, or, if they worked spasmodically, were never sure of pay; and if perchance they received pay, squandered the new thing thoughtlessly. In these and other ways were camp-life and the new liberty demoralizing the freedmen. The broader economic organization thus clearly demanded sprang up here and there as accident and local conditions determined. Here it was that Pierce's Port Royal plan of leased plantations and guided workmen pointed out the rough way. In Washington the military governor, at the urgent appeal of the superintendent, opened confiscated estates to the cultivation of the fugitives, and there in the shadow of the dome gathered black farm villages. General Dix gave over estates to the freedmen of Fortress Monroe, and so on, South and West. The government and benevolent societies furnished the means of cultivation, and the Negro turned again slowly to work. The systems of control, thus started, rapidly grew, here and there, into strange little governments, like that of General Banks in Louisiana, with its ninety thousand black subjects, its fifty thousand guided laborers, and its annual budget of one hundred thousand dollars and more. It made out four thousand pay-rolls a year, registered all freedmen, inquired into grievances and redressed them, laid and collected taxes, and established a system of public schools. So, too, Colonel Eaton, the superintendent of Tennessee and Arkansas, ruled over one hundred thousand freedmen, leased and cultivated seven thousand acres of cotton land, and fed ten thousand paupers a year. In South Carolina was General Saxton, with his deep interest in black folk. He succeeded Pierce and the Treasury officials, and sold forfeited estates, leased abandoned plantations, encouraged schools, and received from Sherman, after that terribly picturesque march to the sea, thousands of the wretched camp followers.

Three characteristic things one might have seen in Sherman's raid through Georgia, which threw the new situation in shadowy relief: the Conqueror, the Conquered, and the Negro. Some see all significance in the grim front of the destroyer, and some in the bitter sufferers of the Lost Cause. But to me neither soldier nor fugitive speaks with so deep a meaning as that dark human cloud that clung like remorse on the rear of those swift columns, swelling at times to half their size, almost engulfing and choking them. In vain were they ordered back, in vain were bridges hewn from beneath their feet; on they trudged and writhed and surged, until they rolled into Savannah, a starved and naked horde of tens of thousands. There too came the characteristic military remedy: "The islands from Charleston south, the abandoned rice-fields along the rivers for thirty miles back from the sea, and the country bordering the St. John's River, Florida, are reserved and set apart for the settlement of Negroes now made free by act of war." So read the celebrated "Field-order Number Fifteen."

All these experiments, orders, and systems were bound to attract and perplex the government and the nation. Directly after the Emancipation Proclamation, Representative Eliot had introduced a bill creating a Bureau of Emancipation; but it was never reported. The following June a committee of inquiry, appointed by the Secretary of War, reported in favor of a temporary bureau for the "improvement, protection, and employment of refugee freedmen," on much the same lines as were afterwards followed. Petitions came in to President Lincoln from distinguished citizens and organizations, strongly urging a comprehensive and unified plan of dealing with the freedmen, under a bureau which should be "charged with the study of plans and execution of measures for easily guiding, and in every way judiciously and humanely aiding, the passage of our emancipated and yet to be emancipated blacks from the old condition of forced labor to their new state of voluntary industry."

Some half-hearted steps were taken to accomplish this, in part, by putting the whole matter again in charge of the special Treasury agents. Laws of 1863 and 1864 directed them to take charge of and lease abandoned lands for periods not exceeding twelve months, and to "provide in such leases, or otherwise, for the employment and general welfare" of the freedmen. Most of the army officers greeted this as a welcome relief from perplexing "Negro affairs," and Secretary Fessenden, July 29, 1864, issued an excellent system of regulations, which were afterward closely followed by General Howard. Under Treasury agents, large quantities of land were leased in the Mississippi Valley, and many Negroes were employed; but in August, 1864, the new regulations were suspended for reasons of "public policy," and the army was again in control.

Meanwhile Congress had turned its attention to the subject; and in March the House passed a bill by a majority of two establishing a Bureau for Freedmen in the War Department. Charles Sumner, who had charge of the bill in the Senate, argued that freedmen and abandoned lands ought to be under the same department, and reported a substitute for the House bill attaching the Bureau to the Treasury Department. This bill passed, but too late for action by the House.

The debates wandered over the whole policy of the administration and the general question of slavery, without touching very closely the specific merits of the measure in hand. Then the national election took place; and the administration, with a vote of renewed confidence from the country, addressed itself to the matter more seriously. A conference between the two branches of Congress agreed upon a carefully drawn measure which contained the chief provisions of Sumner's bill, but made the proposed organization a department independent of both the War and the Treasury officials. The bill was conservative, giving the new department "general superintendence of all freedmen." Its purpose was to "establish regulations" for them, protect them, lease them lands, adjust their wages, and appear in civil and military courts as their "next friend." There were many limitations attached to the powers thus granted, and the organization was made permanent. Nevertheless, the Senate defeated the bill, and a new conference committee was appointed. This committee reported a new bill, February 28, which was whirled through just as the session closed, and became the act of 1865 establishing in the War Department a "Bureau of Refugees, Freedmen, and Abandoned Lands."

This last compromise was a hasty bit of legislation, vague and uncertain in outline. A Bureau was created, "to continue during the present War of Rebellion, and for one year thereafter," to which was given "the supervision and management of all abandoned lands and the control of all subjects relating to refugees and freedmen," under "such rules and regulations as may be presented by the head of the Bureau and approved by the President." A Commissioner, appointed by the President and Senate, was to control the Bureau, with an office force not exceeding ten clerks. The President might also appoint assistant commissioners in the seceded States, and to all these offices military officials might be detailed at regular pay. The Secretary of War could issue rations, clothing, and fuel to the destitute, and all abandoned property was placed in the hands

of the Bureau for eventual lease and sale to ex-slaves in forty-acre parcels ...

Thus did the United States government definitely assume charge of the emancipated Negro as the ward of the nation. It was a tremendous undertaking. Here at a stroke of the pen was erected a government of millions of men,—and not ordinary men either, but black men emasculated by a peculiarly complete system of slavery, centuries old; and now, suddenly, violently, they come into a new birthright, at a time of war and passion, in the midst of the stricken and embittered population of their former masters. Any man might well have hesitated to assume charge of such a work, with vast responsibilities, indefinite powers, and limited resources. Probably no one but a soldier would have answered such a call promptly; and, indeed, no one but a soldier could be called, for Congress had appropriated no money for salaries and expenses....

The act of 1866 gave the Freedmen's Bureau its final form,—the form by which it will be known to posterity and judged of men. It extended the existence of the Bureau to July, 1868; it authorized additional assistant commissioners, the retention of army officers mustered out of regular service, the sale of certain forfeited lands to freedmen on nominal terms, the sale of Confederate public property for Negro schools, and a wider field of judicial interpretation and cognizance. The government of the unreconstructed South was thus put very largely in the hands of the Freedmen's Bureau, especially as in many cases the departmental military commander was now made also assistant commissioner. It was thus that the Freedmen's Bureau became a full-fledged government of men. It made laws, executed them and interpreted them; it laid and collected taxes, defined and punished crime, maintained and used military force, and dictated such measures as it thought necessary and proper for the accomplishment of its varied ends. Naturally, all these powers were not exercised continuously nor to their fullest extent; and yet, as General Howard has said, "scarcely any subject that has to be legislated upon in civil society failed, at one time or another, to demand the action of this singular Bureau."

To understand and criticize intelligently so vast a work, one must not forget an instant the drift of things in the later sixties. Lee had surrendered, Lincoln was dead, and Johnson and Congress were at loggerheads; the Thirteenth Amendment was adopted, the Fourteenth pending, and the Fifteenth declared in force in 1870. Guerrilla raiding, the ever-present flickering after-flame of war, was spending its forces against the Negroes, and all the Southern land was awakening as from some wild dream to poverty and social revolution. In a time of perfect calm, amid willing neighbors and streaming wealth, the social uplifting of four million slaves to an assured and self-sustaining place in the body politic and economic would have been a herculean task; but when to the inherent difficulties of so delicate and nice a social operation were added the spite and hate of conflict, the hell of war; when suspicion and cruelty were rife, and gaunt Hunger wept beside Bereavement,—in such a case, the work of any instrument of social regeneration was in large part foredoomed to failure. The very name of the Bureau stood for a thing in the South which for two centuries and better men had refused even to argue,—that life amid free Negroes was simply unthinkable, the maddest of experiments.

The agents that the Bureau could command varied all the way from unselfish philanthropists to narrow-minded busybodies and thieves; and even though it be true that the average was far better than the worst, it was the occasional fly that helped spoil the ointment.

Then amid all crouched the freed slave, bewildered between friend and foe. He had emerged from slavery,—not the worst slavery in the world, not a slavery that made all life unbearable, rather a slavery that had here and there something of kindliness, fidelity, and happiness,—but withal slavery, which, so far as human aspiration and desert were concerned, classed the black man and the ox together. And the Negro knew full well that, whatever their deeper convictions may have been, Southern men had fought with desperate energy to perpetuate this slavery under which the black masses, with half-articulate thought, had writhed and shivered. They welcomed freedom with a cry. They shrank from the master who still strove for their chains; they fled to the friends that had freed them, even though those friends stood ready to use them as a club for driving the recalcitrant South back into loyalty. So the cleft between the white and black South grew. Idle to say it never should have been; it was as inevitable as its results were pitiable. Curiously incongruous elements were left arrayed against each other,—the North, the government, the carpet-bagger, and the slave, here; and there, all the South that was white, whether gentleman or vagabond, honest man or rascal, lawless murderer or martyr to duty.

Thus it is doubly difficult to write of this period calmly, so intense was the feeling, so mighty the human passions that swayed and blinded men. Amid it all, two figures ever stand to typify that day to coming ages,—the one, a gray-haired gentleman, whose fathers had quit themselves like men, whose sons lay in nameless graves; who bowed to the evil of slavery because its abolition threatened untold ill to all; who stood at last, in the evening of life, a blighted, ruined form, with hate in his eyes;—and the other, a form hovering dark and mother-like, her awful face black with the mists of centuries, had aforetime quailed at that white master's command, had bent in love over the cradles of his sons and daughters, and closed in death the sunken eyes of his wife,—aye, too, at his behest had laid herself low to his lust, and borne a tawny man-child to the world, only to see her dark boy's limbs scattered to the winds by midnight marauders riding after "damned Niggers." These were the saddest sights of that woeful day; and no man clasped the hands of these two passing figures of the present-past; but, hating, they went to their long home, and, hating, their children's children live today....

Such was the dawn of Freedom; such was the work of the Freedmen's Bureau, which, summed up in brief, may be epitomized thus: for some fifteen million dollars, beside the sums spent before 1865, and the dole of benevolent societies, this Bureau set going a system of free labor, established a beginning of peasant proprietorship, secured the recognition of black freedmen before courts of law, and founded the free common school in the South. On the other hand, it failed to begin the establishment of good-will between ex-masters and freedmen, to guard its work wholly from paternalistic methods which discouraged self-reliance, and to carry out to any considerable extent its implied promises to furnish the freedmen with land. Its successes were the result of hard work, supplemented by the aid of philanthropists and the eager striving of black men. Its failures were the result of bad local agents, the inherent difficulties of the work, and national neglect....

The passing of a great human institution before its work is done, like the untimely passing of a single soul, but leaves a legacy of striving for other men. The legacy of the Freedmen's Bureau is the heavy heritage of this generation. To-day, when new and vaster problems are destined to strain every fibre of the national mind and soul, would it not be well to count this legacy honestly and carefully? For this much all men know: despite compromise, war, and struggle, the Negro is not free. In the backwoods of the Gulf States, for miles and miles, he may not leave the plantation of his birth; in well-nigh the whole rural South the black farmers are peons, bound by law and custom to an economic slavery, from which the only escape is death or the penitentiary. In the most cultured sections and cities of the South the Negroes are a segregated servile caste, with restricted rights and privileges. Before the courts, both in law and custom, they stand on a different and peculiar basis. Taxation without representation is the rule of their political life. And the result of all this is, and in nature must have been, lawlessness and crime. That is the large legacy of the Freedmen's Bureau, the work it did not do because it could not.

>> Questions for Consideration

1. In what way is this essay shaped by Du Bois's experiences and beliefs about racial equality? What evidence is there of objectivity in this excerpt?
2. How is Du Bois responding to the Dunning school of Reconstruction history here?
3. Compare this essay with Turner's thesis. What explains the similarities and differences?
4. Based on this essay, is Du Bois arguing that race, economic motivation, or culture is the main historical agent of change? Defend your answer.

Charles and Mary Beard, *The Rise of American Civilization*

The Clash of Metropolis and Colony

CONCERNING the origin of the American Revolution there are as many theories as there are writers of sagas. The oldest hypothesis, born of the conflict on American soil, is the consecrated story of school textbooks: the Revolution was an indignant uprising of a virtuous people, who loved orderly and progressive government, against the cruel, unnatural, and unconstitutional acts of King George III. From the same conflict arose, on the other side, the Tory interpretation: the War for Independence was a violent outcome of lawless efforts on the part of bucolic downs, led by briefless pettifoggers and smuggling merchants, to evade wise and moderate laws broadly conceived in the interest of the English-speaking empire. Such were the authentic canons of early creeds....

On taking up any work dealing with the American Revolution it is necessary, therefore, to inquire about the assumptions upon which the author is operating. Is he preparing to unite the English-speaking peoples in the next world war? Does he have in mind some Teutonic or Hibernian concept of American polity? Or is he desirous of discovering how the conflict arose without any reference to the devices of current politicians? As for this book, the purpose is simple, namely, to inquire into the pertinent facts which conditioned the struggle between the men who governed England and those who ruled the thirteen colonies—on the theory that only adolescents allow ancient grudges to affect their judgments in matters international....

In the thousands of complaints, appeals, petitions, memorials, rulings, vetoes, decisions, and instructions recorded in the papers of the Crown agencies for controlling American trade and industry are disclosed the continuous conflict of English and American forces which hammered and welded thirteen jealous colonies into a society ready for revolution. The subjects of controversy were definite and mainly economic in character. Colonial laws enacted in the interest of local business enterprises but contrary to English regulations were often set aside by royal disallowance; sometimes blanket orders were issued to colonial governors instructing them not to permit the enactment of any legislation adverse to English commercial undertakings. Colonial populism was struck down by vetoes, warnings, and

finally parliamentary action against paper money. To these great sources of economic antagonism was added incessant wrangling between assemblies and governors over salaries and allotments to royal officers, over land titles and land grants, over quitrents due to the Crown or to proprietors, over bankruptcy acts designed to ease the burdens of American debtors at the expense of English creditors, and over efforts of the colonists to promote trade at the cost of their neighbors or of England.

American business and agricultural enterprise was growing, swelling, beating against the frontiers of English imperial control at every point. Colonial assemblies and English royal officials were serving as the political knights errant in a great economic struggle that was to shake a continent.

Considered in the light of the English and provincial statutes spread over more than a hundred years, in the light of the authentic records which tell of the interminable clashes between province and metropolis, the concept of the American Revolution as a quarrel caused by a stubborn, king and obsequious ministers shrinks into a trifling joke. Long before George III came to his throne, long before Grenville took direction of affairs, thousands of Americans had come into collision with British economic imperialism, and by the middle of the eighteenth century, far-seeing men, like Franklin, had discovered the essence of the conflict.

In a letter written in 1754, six years before the accession of George III, the philosopher of Poor Richard set forth the case in terms that admitted of no misinterpretation. With reference to matters of politics, he declared that royal governors often came to the New World merely to make their fortunes; that royal officers in the provinces were frequently men of small estate subservient to the governors who fed them; and

Source: Charles A. Beard and Mary R. Beard, *The Rise of American Civilization Volume I The Agricultural Era* (NY: Macmillan, 1927): pp. 189–191, 201–203, 211–214, 220–221, 233–235, 258–259, 264–267, & 296. This excerpt is taken from a college history textbook, and as such, does not use reference notes as other monographs normally would.

that the Americans in reality bore a large share of English taxes in the form of enhanced prices for English goods thrust upon them by monopolistic laws. Turning to questions of commercial economy, Franklin insisted that the acts of Parliament forbidding Americans to make certain commodities forced them to purchase such goods in England, thus pouring more tribute into the English chest; that statutes restraining their trade with foreign countries compelled them to buy dearer commodities in England, adding that golden stream to the same treasury; that, since the Americans were not allowed to stop the importation and consumption of English "superfluities," their "whole wealth centers finally among the Merchants and Inhabitants of Britain." In short, in enumerating grievances that had flourished for many a decade, Franklin gave a clue to the friction which was soon to burst into an agrarian war.

In a larger sense the American Revolution was merely one battle in the long political campaign that has been waged for more than two centuries on this continent. The institutions of metropolis and colony and the issues of their dispute were analogous to the institutions and issues that have figured in every great national crisis from that day to this. On the side of the mother country, a Crown and Parliament sought to govern all America somewhat after the fashion of the President and Congress under the federal Constitution of 1787. The central British government regulated the interstate and foreign commerce of the thirteen colonies in the interest of the manufacturing and commercial classes of England; it directed the disposal of western lands; it struck down paper money and controlled the currency; it provided for a common defense and conducted the diplomacy of the continent. With a view to protecting practical interests, the British Crown and judiciary nullified acts of local legislatures similar in character to those declared void long afterward by Chief Justice Marshall.

On the American side of the colonial conflict, the agent of local power was the popular assembly which aspired to sovereignty and independence, placing all rights of person and property at the disposal of passing majorities. It authorized the issue of paper money; passed bankruptcy acts in the interest of debtors; stayed the collection of overdue obligations; sought to control the sale of western lands, and assumed the power of regulating local trade and industry. The British government brought heavy pressure upon it; an explosion resulted. For a decade the state legislature was sovereign, and it worked its will in matters of finance, currency, debts, trade, and property. Then followed the inevitable reaction in which were restored, under the aegis of the Constitution and under American leadership, agencies of control and economic policies akin to those formerly employed by Great Britain. In a word, the American Revolution was merely one phase of a social process that began long before the founding of Jamestown and is not yet finished....

During the seven years of the French and Indian War, American merchants, planters, and farmers had been unusually prosperous; produce of every kind had brought high prices and the specie disbursed by the quartermasters had stimulated economic activity in every field. The estates acquired by war profiteers were numerous and large; many merchants had suddenly risen, complained the lieutenant governor of New York, "from the lowest rank of the people to considerable fortunes and chiefly by illicit trade in the last war." But in the swift reaction that followed inflated prices collapsed, business languished, workmen in the towns were thrown out of employment, farmers and planters, burdened by falling prices, found the difficulties of securing specie steadily growing.

By the new imperial program the evils of depression were aggravated. It struck a blow at the West India trade, that fruitful source of business and specie. It put a stop to colonial paper money, thus sharply contracting the currency. It required the payment of the new taxes in coin into the British treasury, putting another drain on the depleted resources of the colonists.

It harassed American merchants by irritating searches and seizures, filling them with uncertainty and dismay, and adding to the confusion of business. Moreover, all the colonies, not merely the commercial North, were now thrown into distress; all classes, too, disfranchised and unemployed workmen of the towns as well as farmers, planters, and merchants. This is significant; it was the workmen of the commercial centers who furnished the muscle and the courage necessary to carry the protests of the merchants into the open violence that astounded the friends of law and order in England and America and threatened to kindle the flames of war. In fact, the greeting accorded to the Grenville program in America astounded the governing classes on both sides of the water. Before the Sugar Act was passed, Boston merchants, hearing rumors of the impending legislation, had organized a committee, presented a memorial to the legislature, and entered into correspondence with merchants in other colonies. Likewise in New York, commercial men had begun to draw together in anticipation of trouble. When the drastic terms of the Sugar Law and the sweeping provisions of the Stamp Act became known, the wrath of the people knew no bounds. Merchants, lawyers, and publishers held conferences and passed resolutions condemning British measures and policies. Patriotic women flocked to associations, pledged themselves not to drink tea, and, besides refusing to purchase British goods, set to work spinning and weaving with greater energy than ever "from sunrise to dark." The maidens of Providence bound themselves to favor no suitors who approved the Stamp Act.

Artisans and laborers, hundreds of them rendered idle by the business depression, formed themselves into societies known as "Sons of Liberty." Feeling their way toward that political power which was to come in the early nineteenth century, they leaped over the boundaries of polite ceremony. They broke out in rioting in Boston, New York, Philadelphia, and Charleston; they pillaged and razed the offices of stamp agents; they burned stamps in the streets; they assailed the houses of royal officers; in Boston the residence of the lieutenant governor was pried open, his chambers sacked, and his property pitched out into the streets. In fact, the agitation, contrary to the intent of the merchants and lawyers, got quite beyond the bounds of law and order. As Gouverneur Morris remarked, "the heads of the mobility grow dangerous to the gentry, and how to keep them down is the question." Indeed, the conduct of the mechanics and laborers was so lawless that it is difficult to paint a picture of the scene in tones subdued enough for modern Sons and Daughters of the Revolution.

In the colonial assemblies, of course, protests against British policies took on the form of legal arguments and dignified resolutions. The Virginia House of Burgesses declared that attempts to tax the people of the Old Dominion, except through the local legislature, were illegal, unconstitutional, and unjust" a declaration supported by a moving speech of Patrick Henry in which he warned George III about the fate of Caesar and Charles I, silencing dissent by the exclamation, "If this be treason, make the most of it!" Not content with formal protests, the Massachusetts assembly appealed for concerted action, inviting the other legislatures to send delegates to a congress in New York to consult about the circumstances of America and to consider a general plan for obtaining relief.

With surprising alacrity, nine colonies responded to the summons, and in the autumn of 1765 the Stamp Act Congress was duly called to order in New York. After the usual preliminaries, the Congress agreed to a definite profession of faith embodied in a set of solemn resolutions: Englishmen cannot be taxed without their consent; the colonists from the nature of things cannot be represented in Parliament; they can only be taxed by their local legislatures; the Stamp Act tends to subvert their rights and liberties; and other acts imposing duties on the colonists and regulating their trade are grievous and burdensome. This creed was then supplemented by an appeal made to the king and Parliament, begging for the abolition of several objectionable measures. Going beyond "humble supplication," the insurgents gave an effective drive to their demands by a well-timed economic stroke a general boycott of English goods, which had a deadly effect, within a few months driving the imports rapidly to the lowest point reached in thirty years. With a cry of anguish English merchants set upon Parliament demanding a repeal of the Stamp Act, which yielded no revenue and ruined their business.... .

Every few days Boston was filled with alarm over the landing of goods in defiance of law, over forcible seizures by revenue authorities, and over forcible recaptures accompanied by assaults on officers. In June, 1768, when John Hancock's sloop Liberty reached Boston with a cargo of wine, temper was high. The collector who went on board to enforce the law was pitched into the cabin of the ship and most of the wine was taken off in spite of his cries. When the customs board ordered the seizure of the vessel, a mob replied by attacking the revenue officers and stoning their houses. When regulars were brought into the city to restore order, the remedy proved to be worse than the disease. Even school children now emulated their elders by jeering soldiers and officers; indeed, one of the first Americans killed in the conflict was a school boy shot by an informer who resented childish ridicule.

This affair was shortly followed by the "Boston Massacre" of March, 1770, starting in comedy as some youths threw snowballs and stones at a small body of British regulars and ending in tragedy with the killing and wounding of several citizens. "The Boston people are run mad," lamented the governor. "The frenzy was not higher when they banished my pious great-grandmother, when they hanged the Quakers, when they afterwards hanged the poor innocent witches." In other colonies the storm also raged. Two years after the "Massacre," John Brown, of Providence, the richest merchant in the town, at the head of an armed mob, boarded the revenue

cutter, Gaspee, which had run ashore while chasing a smuggler; after seizing the crew, the rioters set the ship on fire.

During these operations in defiance of the law, merchants were organizing non-importation associations and bringing a stringent boycott to bear on the English government. Once more women came to the rescue by denying themselves English goods and by working hard with their wheels and looms to supply the deficiency. "The female spinners kept on spinning six days of the week," caustically remarked a high Tory, "and on the seventh the Parsons took their turns and spun out their prayers and sermons to the long thread of politics." Townshend had aroused passions that were soon to challenge British supremacy on the field of battle.

While radicals were agitating, merchants drawing up resolutions, and women spinning, colonial assemblies were learning the lessons of cooperation.

Independence and Civil Conflict

From beginning to end, the spirit of the Congress was civic rather than martial. Every debate was haunted by a dread of military power, the delegates seeming to fear a triumphant American army almost as much as they did the soldiers of George III. At no time did a dictator attempt to seize the helm of the government. Washington might have made himself master of the scene with ease, but the operation was foreign to the spirit of that Virginia gentleman. When, upon occasion, sovereign powers were conferred upon him by the Congress, he always returned them in due time unsullied by personal ambitions. Even in the most crucial hour there arose in the Congress no tyrannical committee of public safety such as ruled France in the darkest days of her revolution.

Nor were the proceedings of the Congress especially dramatic. Usually there were not more than twenty or thirty members in attendance; and in such an assembly the stormy eloquence of a Marat would have been comic. Although the lawyers present consumed weeks and months in displaying their logical capacities, the Congress was, on the whole, more like a village debating society than the Convention which carried France through the Reign of Terror. Moreover, it met in the little town of Philadelphia, with its twenty thousand inhabitants dominated by Quakers, not in a Paris crowded by half a million people soldiers, priests, noblemen, merchants, artisans, raging Amazons, and passionate radicals. When, in the sultry days of 1776, it discussed the Declaration of Independence, no throngs pressed into the galleries to intimidate the wavering, no tumultuous mob stormed the doors clamoring for a decision. As a rule its transactions had the air of timidity and negotiation instead of resolution and mastery, disputes, vacillation, and delays marking its operations from session to session.

Its incompetence was not all due, however, as its critics have alleged, to mere perversity of human nature. The members of the Congress labored under the gravest of difficulties. Unlike the party of Cromwell or the national assembly of France, they could not take over an administrative machine that was already organized and working. Exactly the opposite was true; they had to create everything national out of a void a government, a treasury, an army, even a bookkeeping system, and agencies for buying supplies.

Unlike the English and French revolutionists, they had no centuries of national tradition behind them no nationwide class informed by a historic solidarity of interests to which they could appeal for support with assurance. Instead, they were largely dependent from the first day to the last upon the good graces of state assemblies and governors for troops, money, supplies, and the enforcement of their resolutions. And in the best of times the states were in arrears on everything; almost on the eve of Yorktown, Washington recorded that hardly one had put one-eighth of its quota of men at the service of the Revolution.

To make matters worse, the Congress itself was beset by the sectional jealousies which divided the states. Everything had to be viewed with an eye to its effect on the commercial or the planting interests. Among the members was no dominant majority invincibly united for a specific end, no single person moved to grasp large powers and enforce by sheer strength of will the acts of the Congress. All business had to be done by committees and on every important committee each state usually had at least one member.

Administration as well as legislation was controlled by commissions: foreign affairs, finance, supplies, and other matters of prime significance were entrusted to boards. Even the treasury was supervised by a committee until near the end of the struggle, when dire necessity forced the appointment of Robert Morris as superintendent of finance. Yet this is the body that gave voice to the national revolutionary movement, directed war, conducted foreign relations, made treaties, won independence, created a government, and nourished the germs of American nationality.…

Whether they formed a majority of the populace or not the revolutionary masses assumed obligations and engineered activities of the first magnitude. Far and wide, through many agencies, they prosecuted with unremitting fervor an agitation in favor of the patriot cause. Independent state constitutions were established. The Tory opposition was suppressed or kept under strict surveillance. All the ordinary functions of government were discharged, at least in a fashion the administration of justice, the levy of taxes, the maintenance of order, and the enactment of enlightened and humane legislation. To these obligations were joined stern duties connected with the war: raising quotas of men and money, collecting and forwarding supplies, promoting the sale of Continental bonds, and cooperating with the Congress in the restraint of speculators and profiteers. Furthermore, since the fighting spread up and down the coast, most of the states were called upon at one time or another to raise local forces and meet the enemy on their own soil.

Intense and wide must have been the agitation carried on by the patriots. Hundreds of pamphlets, bundles of faded letters, files of newspapers, and collections of cartoons, broadsides, and lampoons reveal an intellectual ferment comparable to that which marked the course of the Puritan revolution in England more than a hundred years before. Notices of public meetings held to cheer the leaders in the forum and the armies in the field bear witness to the tumult of opinion that marked the progress of the American cause. Entries in diaries tell of heated debates in taverns where "John Presbyter, Will Democrack, and Nathan Smuggle," to use the Tory gibe, roundly damned the king and his "minions" and put the fear of battle and sudden death into the hearts of royalists and lukewarm subjects. Letters open the doors of private houses, disclosing families and their friends at dinner or seated by fireplaces in lively debate on the fortunes of the day and the tasks ahead. In the familiar correspondence of husbands and wives, such as the letters of John and Abigail Adams or of James and Mercy Warren, are revealed the springs of faith and affection that fed the currents of action.…

In this mass movement in which preachers, pamphleteers, committees, lawyers, and state governments advanced the revolutionary cause, women in every section played their customary role of backing up their fighting men with all the intensity of emotion and loyalty to their kind that war had always inspired in the "gentle" sex, except among a few pacific Quakers. Lysistrata, summoning her sisters to strike against the arbitrament of arms, was a character in fiction created by the mind of man. The revolutionary records seem to indicate patriot valor on the part of women commensurate in fervor with that of men.

Nearly every male leader of the rebellion had a wife, sister, or daughter actively at work in the second line of defense. Propaganda of the pen was waged by Mercy Warren, sister of James Otis and wife of James Warren, who wrote satires and farces in the elaborate style of the day, scoring loyalists and praising liberty offering these as replies to the British playwrights and the actors who were delighting New York crowds with their caricatures of the patriots. Women were also to be found among the publishers and editors of newspapers, encouraging the writers of stirring pleas for independence, trying to make the pen as mighty as the sword.

In every branch of economy that kept the social order intact and the army supplied, to the degree that it was, women were industrious laborers and energetic promoters. They had long formed the majority of the workers in the textile industry and throughout the war the whirr of their wheels and the clank of their looms were heard in the land as they spun and wove for soldiers and civilians alike. Letters of the time reveal them sowing, reaping, and managing the affairs of farm as well as kitchen. They gave lead from their windows and pewter from their shelves to be melted into bullets, united in a boycott of English luxuries, combined to extend the use of domestic manufactures, canvassed from door to door when money and provisions for the army were most needed.

As non-combatants it was often women's obligation to face marauding soldiers; Catherine Schuyler, setting the torch to her own crops in her fields near Saratoga before the advancing British troops and watching with composure the roaring flames that devoured her food with theirs, proved how courageously women could fight in their way. In the wake of the British armies, South and North, they labored to restore their ruined homes and hold together the fragments of their family property for the veterans when they should return.

Stern disciplinarians they were too, in their steadfastness to the faith. They formed committees to visit profiteers and warn them against extortion. In one instance they seized a supply of tea in the hands of a stubborn merchant and sold it over the counter at a price fixed by themselves. "Madam," said John Adams to Mrs. Huston at Falmouth, "is it lawful for a weary traveler to refresh himself with a dish of tea, provided it has been honestly smuggled or paid no duties?" The answer was decisive. "No, sir, we have renounced all tea in this place, but I'll make you coffee." There was no redress. "I must be weaned," lamented the wayfarer, "and the sooner the better." The young ladies of Amelia County, Virginia, were reported to have formed an agreement "not to permit the addresses of any person, be his circumstances or situation in life what they will, unless he has served in the American armies long enough to prove by his valor that he is deserving of their love."

It would be a mistake, however, in portraying this widespread movement of the people, to represent the patriot masses facing the enemy in solid array. The contrary is the truth. Everywhere the supporters of the Revolution were divided into conservative and radical wings, the former composed mainly of merchants and men of substance and the latter of mechanics and yeomen-farmers, sometimes led by men of the other group. In Massachusetts an insurgent left wing drew up a state constitution pleasing to the politicians but was not strong enough to force its adoption. By a skillful combination, the aristocracy of "wealth and talents" defeated the plan and substituted a system which safeguarded the rights and privileges of property at every bastion. Morison describes the instrument briefly: "The Constitution of 1780 was a lawyers' and merchants' constitution, directed toward something like quarterdeck efficiency in government and the protection of property against democratic pirates." ...

Indeed, in nearly every branch of enlightened activity, in every sphere of liberal thought, the American Revolution marked the opening of a new humane epoch. Slavery, of course, afforded a glaring contrast to the grand doctrines of the Revolution, but still it must be noted that Jefferson and his friends were painfully aware of the anachronism; that Virginia prohibited the slave trade in 1778 a measure which the British Crown had vetoed twenty years before; that a movement for the abolition of slavery appeared among the new social forces of the age; and that it was the lofty doctrines of the Revolution which were invoked by Lincoln when in the fullness of time chattel bondage was to be finally broken. If a balance sheet is struck and the rhetoric of the Fourth of July celebrations is discounted, if the externals of the conflict are given a proper perspective in the background, then it is seen that the American Revolution was more than a war on England. It was in truth an economic, social, and intellectual transformation of prime significance the first of those modern world-shaking reconstructions in which mankind has sought to cut and fashion the tough and stubborn web of fact to fit the pattern of its dreams.

>> Questions for Consideration

1. What evidence of Pragmatism and Progressivism can you detect in this excerpt?
2. How do the Beards deal with the question of objectivity?
3. In what ways does this text include women's history? Does it do it effectively? How might this reflect the influence of the feminist suffrage movement?
4. In what ways are the Beards responding to Bancroft's version of the American Revolution?

Daniel J. Boorstin, *The Genius of American Politics*

The American Revolution: Revolution without Dogma

We are accustomed to think of the Revolution as the great age of American political thought. It may therefore be something of a shock to realize that it did not produce in America a single important treatise on political theory. Men like Franklin and Jefferson, universal in their interests, active and spectacularly successful in developing institutions, were not fertile as political philosophers.

In the present chapter I shall offer some explanations of this fact and shall explore some of its significance for our later political life. I shall be trying to discover why, in the era of our Revolution, a political theory failed to be born. But my inquiry will not be entirely negative. I will seek those features of the Revolution, those positive ideas and attitudes, which actually have done much to reinforce our sense of "givenness."

We have been slow to see some of the more obvious and more important peculiarities of our Revolution because influential scholars on the subject have cast their story in the mold of the French Revolution of 1789. Some of our best historians have managed to empty our Revolution of much of its local flavor by exaggerating what it had in common with that distinctively European struggle. This they have done in two ways.

First, they have stressed the international character of the intellectual movement of which the French Revolution was a classic expression — the so-called "Enlightenment." They speak of it as a "climate of opinion" whose effects, like the barometric pressure, could no more be escaped in America than in Europe.

Second, they have treated ours as only a particular species of the genus "Revolution" — of what should perhaps more properly be called *revolution Europaensis*.

The effect of all these has been to emphasize — or rather exaggerate — the similarity of ours to all other modern revolutions.

In so doing, historians have exaggerated the significance of what is supposed to have been the ideology of the Revolution. Such an emphasis has had the further attraction to some "liberal" historians of seeming to put us in the main current of European history. It has never been quite clear to me why historians would not have found our revolution significant enough merely as a victory of constitutionalism.

Some Peculiarities of Our Revolution

The most obvious peculiarity of our American Revolution is that, in the modern European sense of the word, it was hardly a revolution at all. The Daughters of the American Revolution, who have been understandably sensitive on this subject, have always insisted in their literature that the American Revolution was no revolution but merely a colonial rebellion. The more I have looked into the subject, the more convinced I have become of the wisdom of their naïvetè. "The social condition and the Constitution of the Americans are democratic," De Tocqueville observed about a hundred years ago. "But they have not had a democratic revolution." This fact is surely one of the most important of our history.... .

The feature of which I want to direct your attention might be called the "conservatism" of the Revolution. If we understand this characteristic, we will begin to see the Revolution as an illusion of the remarkable continuity of American history. And we will also see how the attitude of

Source: Daniel J. Boorstin, "The American Revolution: Revolution without Dogma," in *The Genius of American Politics* (Chicago: University of Chicago Press, 1953), 66–69, 80–89, 92–98. © The University of Chicago Press. Reprinted by permission of the University of Chicago Press.

our Revolutionary thinkers has engraved more deeply in our national consciousness a belief in the inevitability of our particular institutions, or, in a word, our sense of "givenness."

The character of our Revolution has nourished our assumption that whatever institutions we happened to have here (in this case the British constitution) had the self-evident validity of anything that is "normal." We have thus casually established the tradition that it is superfluous to the American condition to produce elaborate treaties on political philosophy or to be explicit about political values and the theory of community.

I shall confine myself to two topics. First, the manifesto of the Revolution, namely, the Declaration of Independence; and, second, the man who has been generally considered the most outspoken and systematic political philosopher of the Revolution, Thomas Jefferson. Of course, I will not try to give a full account of either of them. I will attempt only to call your attention to a few facts which may not have been sufficiently emphasized and which are especially significant for our present purpose. Obviously, no one could contend that there is either in the man or in the document nothing of the cosmopolitan spirit, nothing of the world climate of opinion. My suggestion is simply that we do find another spirit of at least equal, and perhaps overshadowing, importance and that this spirit may actually be more characteristic of our Revolution.

First, then, for the Declaration of Independence. Its technical, legalistic, and conservative character, which I wish to emphasize, will appear at once by contrast with the comparable document of the French Revolution. Ours was concerned with a specific event, namely, the separation of these colonies from the mother-country. But the French produced a "Declaration of the Rights of Man and the Citizen." When De Tocqueville, in his *Ancien Régime* (Book I, chap iii), sums up the spirit of the French Revolution, he is describing exactly what the American Revolution was not:

The French Revolution acted, with regard to things of this world, precisely as religious revolutions have acted with regard to things of the others. It dealt with the citizen in the abstract, independent of particular social organizations, just as religions deal with mankind in general, independent of time and place. It inquired, not what were the particular rights of the French citizens, but what were the general rights and duties of mankind in reference to political concerns....

In contrast to all this, our Declaration of Independence is essentially a list of specific historic instances. It is directed not to the regeneration but only to the "opinions" of mankind. It is closely tied to time and place; the special affection for "British brethren" is freely admitted; it is concerned with the duties of a particular king and certain of his subjects....

Even if we took only the first two paragraphs or preamble, which are the most general part of the document, and actually read them as a whole, we could make a good case for their being merely a succinct restatement of the Whig theory of the British Revolution of 1688.

To be understood, its words must be annotated by British history. This is among the facts which have led some historians (Guizot, for example) to go so far as to say the English revolution succeeded twice, once in England and once in America.

The remaining three-quarters—the unread three-quarters—of the documents is technical and legalistic. That is, of course, the main reason why it remains unread. For it is a bill of indictment against the king, written in the language of British constitutionalism. "The patient sufferance of these Colonies" is the point of departure. It carefully recounts that the customary and traditional forms of protests, such as "repeated Petitions," have already been tried.

The more the Declaration is reread in context, the more plainly it appears a document of imperial legal relations rather than a piece of high-flown political philosophy. The desire to remain true to the principles of British constitutionalism up to the better end explains why, as has been often remarked, the document is directed against the king, despite the fact that the practical grievances were against Parliament; perhaps also why at this stage there is no longer an explicit appeal to the rights of Englishmen. Most of the document is a bald enumeration of George III's failure, excesses, and crimes in violation of the constitution and laws of Great Britain. One indictment after another makes sense only if one presupposes the framework of British constitutionalism. How else, for example, could one indict a king "for depriving us in many cases, of the benefits of Trial by Jury"?

We can learn a great deal about the context of our Revolutionary thoughts by examining Jefferson's own thinking down to the period of the Revolution. We need not stretch a point or give Jefferson a charismatic role, to say that the flavor of his thought is especially important for our purposes. He has been widely considered the leading political philosopher of the Revolution. Among other things, he was, of course, the principal author of the Declaration of Independence itself; and the Declaration has been taken to be the climax of the abstract philosophizing of the revolutionaries. Because he is supposed to be the avant-garde of revolutionary thought, evidence of conservatism and legalism in Jefferson's thought as a whole is especially significant.

We now are beginning to have a definitive edition of Jefferson's papers (edited by Julian P. Boyd and published by the Princeton University Press), which is one of the richest treasures ever amassed for the historian of a particular period. This helps us use Jefferson's thought as a touchstone. Neither in the letters which Jefferson wrote nor in those he received do we discover that he and his close associates—at least down to the date of the Revolution—showed any conspicuous interest in political theory. We look in vain for general reflections on the nature of government or constitutions. The manners of the day did require that a cultivated gentleman be acquainted with certain classics of political thought; yet we lack evidence that such works were read with more than a perfunctory interest. To be sure, when Jefferson prepares a list of worthy books for a young friend in 1771, he includes references to Montesquieu, Sidney, and Bolingbroke; but such references are rare. Even when he exchanges letters with Edmund Pendleton on the more general problems of institutions, he remains on the level of legality and policy, hardly touching political theory. Jefferson's papers for the Revolutionary period (read without the hindsight which has put the American and the French revolutions in the same era of world history) show little evidence that the American Revolution was a road to higher levels of abstract thinking about society. We miss any such tendency in what Jefferson and his associates were reading or in what they were writing.

On the other hand, we find ample evidence that the locale of early Jeffersonian thought was distinctly *colonial*; we might even say *provincial*. And we begin to see some of the significance of that fact in making the limits of political theorizing in America. By 1776, when the irreversible step of revolution was taken, the colonial period in the life of Jefferson and the other Revolutionary thinkers was technically at an end; but by then their minds had been congealed, their formal education completed, their social habits and the case of their political thinking determined. The Virginia society of the pre- Revolutionary years had been decidedly derivative, not only in its culture, its furniture, its clothes, and its books, but in many of the ideas and—what is more to our purpose—in perhaps most of its institutions.…

The importance of this colonial framework in America, as I have already suggested, was to be enormous, not only from the point of view of Revolutionary thought, but in its long-term effect on the role of political theory in American life. The legal institutions which Americans considered their own and which they felt bound to master were largely borrowed. Jefferson and John

Adams, both lawyers by profession, like their English contemporaries, had extracted much of their legal knowledge out of the crabbed pages of Coke's *Institutes....* During the very years when the Revolution was brewing, Jefferson was every day talking the language of the common law. We cannot but be impressed not only, as I have remarked, at the scarcity in the Jefferson papers for these years of anything that could be called fresh inquiry into the theory of government but also by the legalistic context of Jefferson's thought. We begin to see that the United States was being born in an atmosphere of legal rather then philosophical debate. Even apart from those technical materials with which Jefferson earned his living, his political piece themselves possess a legal rather than a philosophical flavor....

Jefferson's philosophic concern with politics by the outbreak of the Revolution (actually only the end of his thirty-third year) was the enthusiasm of a reflective and progressive colonial lawyer for the traditional rights of Englishmen. To be sure, Jefferson did go further than some of his fellow-lawyers in his desire for legal reform—of feudal tenures, of entails, of the law of inheritance, of criminal law, and of established religion—yet even these projects were not, at least at that time, part of a coherent theory of society. They remained discrete reforms, "improvements" on the common law.

Jefferson's willingness to devote himself to purification of the common law must have rested on his faith in those ancient institutions and a desire to return to their essentials. This faith shines through those general maxims and mottoes about government which men took seriously in the eighteenth century and which often imply much more than they say. Jefferson's personal motto, "Rebellion to Tyrants Is Obedience to God," expresses pretty much the sum of his political theory—if, indeed, we should call it a "theory"—in this epoch. It was this motto (which Jefferson probably borrowed from Franklin, who offered it in 1776 for the Seal of the United States) that Jefferson himself proposed for

Virginia and which he used on the seal for his own letters. But when we try to discover the meaning of the slogan to Jefferson, we find that it must be defined by reference less to any precise theology than to certain convictions about the British constitution. For who, after all, was a "tyrant"? None other than one who violated the sacred tenets of the United States seal: figures of "Hengist and Horsa, the Saxon chiefs from whom we claim the honor of being descended, and whose political principles and form of government we have assumed" (quoted by John Adams to Mrs. Adams, August 14, 1776; *Familiar Letters* [New York, 1875], p. 221).

In the Revolutionary period, when the temptations to be dogmatic were greatest, Jefferson did not succumb. The awareness of the peculiarity of America had not yet by any means led Jefferson to a rash desire to remake all society and institutions. What we actually discern is a growing tension between his feeling of the novelty of the American experience, on the other hand, and his feeling of belonging to ancient British institutions, on the other....

Revolution without Dogma: A Legacy of Institutions

We begin to see how far we would be misled, were we to cast American events of this era in the mold of European history. The American Revolution was in a very special way conceived as both a vindication of the British past and an affirmation of an American future. The British past we contained in the ancient and living institutions rather than in doctrines; as the American future was never to be contained in a theory. What British institutions meant did not need to be articulated; what America might mean was still to be discovered. This continuity of American history was to make a sense of "givenness" easier to develop; for it was this continuity which had made a new ideology of revolution seem unnecessary.

Perhaps the intellectual energy which American Revolutionaries economized because they were not obliged to construct a whole theory of institutions was to strengthen them for their encounter with nature and for their solution of practical problems. The effort which Jefferson, for example, did not care to spend on the theory of sovereignty he was to give freely to the revision of the criminal law, the observation of the weather, the mapping of the continent, the collection of fossils, the study of the Indian language, and the doubling of the national area.

The experience of our Revolution may suggest that the sparseness of American political theory, which has sometimes been described as a refusal of American statesmen to confront their basic philosophical problems, has been due less to a conscious refusal than to a simple lack of necessity. As the British colonists in America had forced on them the need to create a nation, so they had forced on them the need to be traditional and empirical in their institutions. The Revolution, because it was conceived as essentially affirming the British constitution, did not create the kind of theoretical vacuum made by some other revolutions.

The colonial situation, it would seem, had provided a *ne plus ultra* beyond which political theorizing did not need to range. Even Jefferson, the greatest and most influential theorist of the Revolution, remained loath to trespass that boundary, except under pressure: the pressure of a need to create a new federal structure. Mainly in the realm of federalism were new expedients called for. And no part of our history is more familiar than the story of how the framers of the federal Constitution achieved a solution: by compromise on details rather than by agreement on a theory....

The Revolution itself, as we have seen, had been a kind of affirmation of faith in ancient British institutions. In the greater part of the Institutional life of the community the Revolution thus required no basic change. If any of this helps to illustrate or explain our characteristic lack of interest in political philosophy, it also helps to account for the value which we still attach to our inheritance from the British constitution: trial by jury, due process of law, representation before taxation, habeas corpus, freedom from attainder, independence of the judiciary, and the rights of free speech, free petition, and free assembly, as well as our narrow definition of treason and our antipathy to standing armies in peacetime. It also explains our continuing—sometimes bizarre, but usually fortunate—readiness to think of these traditional rights of Englishmen as if they were indigenous to our continent.

>> Questions for Consideration

1. What does Boorstin mean by his reference to "our sense of givenness"? How does this relate to his thesis on the nature of the American Revolution?

2. How might Boorstin's approach to the American Revolution reflect his own conservative political values and the U.S. government's attempt to protect the country from radical political ideologies such as communism and socialism?

3. How does Boorstin respond to the idea of American exceptionalism?

4. Weigh Boorstin's argument against the Beards'. On which points to they disagree? Which has more evidence and seems more accurate?

Chapter 6

Marxism, *Annales*, and the New Left

A student-led demonstration against racism and the war in Vietnam (CORBIS-NY).

Just as it had in the 1950s, historical perspectives in the 1960s shifted again in response to a changing political and cultural climate. The repressiveness of Cold War culture, the Vietnam War, and the civil rights movement led to the rise of a New Left in Europe and the United States which challenged the conservative status quo. The New Left in England and the United States was a group of intellectuals who sought a third path between Soviet communism and American capitalism. They were influenced by Marxism, but wanted to apply it in new ways to fit the social and economic conditions of the 1960s and 1970s. Like Progressives, New Left historians demonstrated the negative consequences of capitalism and imperialism in the past and exposed the long history of class conflict. More explicitly Marxist, however, New Left historians looked for reasons for the lack of communist revolutions in the United States and Britain, focusing more intently on the history of capitalism and working-class culture, experiences, and organizations.

Marxist Historiography in the Twentieth Century

Gramsci

While Marxist historiography was largely ignored in the United States prior to the 1960s, Marxist histories written in the early twentieth century would become especially influential to the international New Left. Marxist history became the official history of communist Soviet Union and Eastern Europe, and flourished in some areas of Western Europe, where Marxist historians struggled to distance themselves from the brutal legacy of Stalinist communism but stay true to Marx's focus on class struggle. A prominent theme in twentieth-century Marxist historiography explored why the working classes had not developed a revolutionary consciousness and had not overthrown the bourgeoisie in other areas of the world. In this quest, Italian Marxist sociologist Antonio Gramsci (1891–1937) had a tremendous influence on many historians. Gramsci explored the ways in which the superstructure, particularly cultural institutions such as churches and schools, operated to shape class consciousness and prevent revolutions. He argued that capitalism maintained control through cultural hegemony, imposing bourgeoisie values and culture on the masses. This counterrevolutionary culture explained the lack of revolution in Western Europe and North America. Gramscist theories would become especially popular among the international New Left as well as new cultural historians.

Hobsbawm

English historians discovered Gramsci in the 1950s and 1960s. While most English historians in the 1950s remained conservative and focused on political events in the distant past, a new postwar generation of historians was more attracted to Marxist approaches and more recent history. Two of the most famous British Marxist historians of the twentieth century were Eric J. Hobsbawm and E.P. Thompson. Hobsbawm (1917–) was a longtime member of the British Communist Party, graduated from Cambridge University with a PhD in history on a British socialist society, and was a professor at the University of London for most of his career. He dominated English Marxist historiography for the remainder of the twentieth century, remaining true to the political goals of Marxism, as well as setting the standards for Marxist theory and historical methods.[1] He asserted that the upper strata of the working class became identified with the bourgeoisie and controlled labor unions, making them less revolutionary and more reformist. Both Hobsbawm and Thompson were founding members of the Communist Party Historians' Group in Britain in 1946. They published the influential history journal *Past and Present*, which is still being published today. Reflecting the influence of both Gramscist Marxism and new interdisciplinary methods, this group sought to "understand the dynamics of whole societies" and "connect political events to underlying forces."[2] This journal became a focal point for neo-Marxists in Britain and

---

[1]Hobsbawm has a lengthy publication record on many different subjects, ranging from revolutions, to labor movements, to terrorism, and he continues to publish regularly. His works include, for example, *Labouring Men: Studies in the History of Labour* (1964), *Bandits* (1969), *The Age of Extremes* (1994), and *On History* (1997).

[2]Geoff Eley, *A Crooked Line: From Cultural History to the History of Society* (Ann Arbor: University of Michigan Press, 2005), 31.

the United States in the 1960s and helped to give birth to a New Left, which would soon break with the Communist Party.

The French *Annales*

While Marxism was foundational to the international New Left, a new French school of history, called the *Annales*, was also enormously influential. French scholars led by Marc Bloch (1886–1944) and Lucien Febvre (1878–1956) began exploring new methods to describe the totality of the human experience in the 1920s. They rejected the dominance of political and diplomatic history and sought a more holistic approach to history, using an interdisciplinary social scientific approach to understand the history of human cultures and societies from multiple perspectives. Bloch and Febvre forged this new approach in their journal *Annales d'histoire economique et sociale*, first published in 1929. Dubbed the *Annales* school, these historians strove to move beyond narrow political and diplomatic history, which they saw as too brief and short-lived to tell us much about the human condition overall, or to provide complete information about the nature of change and continuity in human history. Instead, they studied broader agents of change, such as changes in the environment, demographics, and technology.

Bloch   Bloch, for example, studied the structures of feudal society, investigating intersections of cultural, economic, political, and social relationships through a sort of anthro-
Febvre   pological approach. Febvre, on the other hand, investigated the impact of geography on social, political, economic, and cultural history. He became especially interested in understanding the unique psychological mentality of different groups of peoples in the past. He called upon historians to recover the mental worlds of past peoples instead of anachronistically assuming that they saw the world in the same way that we do in the present.[3]

The Annales school, like most other elements of European society, was unfortunately disrupted during World War II, and Bloch was eventually executed as a member of the French Resistance. After the war, Febvre forged ahead and founded a new research center, with a new journal *Annales: Economies, societies, civilization.* This propelled the *Annales* school to the forefront of French historiography and influenced historians elsewhere in the world.

Braudel   The work of second-generation *Annalistes*, such as Fernand Braudel (1902–1985), especially generated enormous interest. Braudel was Febvre's student and synthesized the approaches of both Bloch and Febvre. Braudel was born and raised in France, but spent several years in Brazil with French anthropologist Claude Lévi-Strauss, helping to create the University of São Paolo. When he returned to France during World War II, he was captured and was a prisoner of war from 1940 to 1945. Following the war, he was elected to replace Febvre at the Collège de France and

---

[3]Marc Bloch, *The Historians Craft* (New York: Vintage, 1984) and Lucien Febvre, *A New Kind of History: From the Writings of Febvre* (New York: Harper and Row, 1973).

went on to found the famous "Sixième Section" for economic and social sciences. He became a leading social and economic historian in Europe and the United States for the next twenty years.

Braudel's *The Mediterranean World in the Age of Philip II* (1949) stands out as the most famous completed *Annaliste* history. In this lengthy two-volume masterpiece, Braudel focused on the continuities of life in the Mediterranean region, analyzing political, social, economic, intellectual, and geographic perspectives to create a total history. Studying demographics, the climate, and geography of civilizations, Braudel conceived of time as moving at three different paces or layers for different historical phenomena. For example, the history of how humans relate to their environment, or geographical time, changed almost imperceptibly over long cycles he termed the *longue durée* or the long duration. Other historical phenomena changed at faster rates, revolving in ten-to-fifty year cycles, such as economic and demographic shifts, or *conjonctures*. The tip of the historical iceberg, specific events, political, diplomatic, and biographical history, which he termed *histoire événementielle* could be studied in shorter periods and represented a more linear sequence of events. With Braudel as its new leader, the *Annales* school shaped historical approaches in Europe and the United States throughout the 1960s and 1970s.

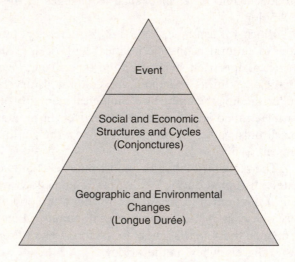

The English New Left

While *Annaliste* history became popular everywhere, it was especially influential in England, where many neo-Marxists were beginning to explore new approaches to history. Calling themselves the "New Left," these intellectuals rejected the totalitarian brutality of Soviet communism and sought to forge a new path between communist Marxism and conservative procapitalist theories. While some communist historians, such as Hobsbawm, remained a member of the Communist Party, many others followed the lead of E.P. Thompson (1924–1993), who renounced his Communist Party

Thompson

membership in 1958 in reaction to Soviet aggression in Hungary. Thompson was born in Oxford, England, and studied at Cambridge University, where he joined the Communist Party. After leaving the Communist Party, he helped to found *The New Left Review*, which became the leading publisher of New Left histories in the 1960s and continues to be a leader in radical publications today. As a leader in radical activist causes, Thompson never held a long-term ranking position as a university professor, but rather taught more informally in the newly created Open University for most of his career. Breaking away from communist Marxism, Thompson and other New Left historians forged a new path, merging Marxist and *Annaliste* methods, as they wrote history "from the bottom-up."

Thompson's most famous work by far was *The Making of the English Working Class* (1963). This work focused on the formation of working-class consciousness in the late eighteenth and early nineteenth centuries. Influenced by Gramsci and Febvre, Thompson focused on the culture and mental world of the working class, and, like Braudel, looked for continuities in the past, as well as changes. Rather than perceiving the working class as merely victims of industrialization, he saw them as historical agents in their own right, responding to changing conditions, and maintaining their own distinct culture through it all. *The Making of the English Working Class* influenced a whole generation of English and American historians and was seminal in establishing New Left history in academia in the United States and Britain in the 1960s.

New Left Historians in the United States

While the British New Left influenced its American counterpart, and both shared a common origin in Cold War politics, the American New Left was additionally shaped by the civil rights movement and the Vietnam War. Similar to the English New Left, American New Left historians had ties to the Old Left. Howard Zinn and Eugene Genovese, for example, had been members of the American Communist Party.[4] While this exposure to Marxism influenced their critique of American class conflict, the American civil rights movement and Vietnam War also shaped their historical perspectives. American New Left history, as a consequence, not only was critical of capitalism and class interests, but also included a new interest in diplomatic history and racial conflict.

The Cold War and especially the Vietnam War inspired many historians to explore American diplomatic history from a more critical perspective. Previous consensus historians had written from the perspective of the U.S. government, and their findings showed a clear pro-American bias. New Left historians, who were deeply suspicious of the capitalist U.S. government, were much more critical of America's relationship with other countries. A leader in New Left diplomatic history was

---

[4]Ernst Breisach, *Historiography: Ancient, Medieval, and Modern*, 2nd ed. (Chicago: University of Chicago Press, 1994), 419.

Williams   William Appleman Williams (1921–1990), professor at the University of Wisconsin. He laid the groundwork for the New Left interpretation of foreign politics with his *Tragedy of American Diplomacy* (1959). Contrary to the consensus belief that American foreign policy was guided by democratic ideals, he argued that economic motives had guided American foreign policy at least since the end of the nineteenth century. The imperialistic search for foreign markets shaped most foreign policy goals in the twentieth century, leading the United States into war after war, including the Cold War.

Kolko   Other historians of the Cold War, such as Walter La Feber and Joyce and Gabriel Kolko, were similarly critical of American actions in the Cold War. The Kolkos made the strongest New Left argument against American foreign policy in *The Limits of Power: World and United States Foreign Policy, 1945–1954* (1968). Reducing all American foreign policy in this period to the materialistic quest for imperial domination, the Kolkos blamed American greed and capitalism for financing counterrevolutions against communism, which caused political unrest across the globe, as well as the Cold War.

Realist   New Left historians were immediately attacked as being biased by communist anti-American ideologies. Claiming a more objective perspective, self-styled "realist" historians interpreted the Cold War in terms of *Realpolitik*, a Machiavellian view of power politics based solely on national interests. They argued that both the United States and Soviet Union rightfully acted in their own best interests in the Cold War. The Cold War was simply an unavoidable result of conflicting national interests. Hans J. Morgenthau's *In Defense of the National Interest: A Critical Examination of American Foreign Policy* (1951) first articulated the realist school of thought on the Cold War, but his ideas became even more popular in the 1970s and 1980s. Consensus, New Left, and realist theories continue to shape diplomatic history to this day.

Lynd   Equally as important as the Vietnam War in shaping the American New Left was the African American civil rights movement of the 1950s and 1960s. Staughton Lynd (1929–) was a civil rights and antiwar activist, and an early leader of the American New Left. His activism sparked his interest in the effects of imperialism, capitalism, and racism. Influenced by neo-Marxism, he took the Beards' argument a step forward, asserting that "the United States Constitution represented, not the triumph of capitalism over a landed aristocracy (like the French Revolution and the American Civil War), but a compromise or coalition between men of wealth in the cities and men of wealth on the land."[5] In *Class Conflict, Slavery, and the United States Constitution* (1967), he argued that the planter aristocracy and mercantile elite joined together to create a government to guarantee the rights and privileges of the upper class and prevent the independence movement from becoming an internal social revolution as well as a political revolution. He argued that slavery was a divisive issue even before the Constitution was created and the continued existence of the institution was a clear

---

[5]Staughton Lynd, "Beyond Beard," in *Towards a New Past: Dissenting Essays in American History* Vintage Books edition, ed. Barton J. Bernstein (New York: Random House, 1969), 53.

indication of how the elites who created the Constitution betrayed the foundational ideals of the Declaration of Independence and the Revolution. Despite the positive reception of this work, Lynd's civil rights and antiwar activism on campus led his academic career to stall. Eventually, he went to law school and became a lawyer for the remainder of his career.

Many other historians were inspired by the civil rights movement, as well as other social justice movements of the 1960s, to look at history from the ground-up and to look at the past from the perspectives of marginalized peoples who had been left out
Zinn of "traditional" history. Howard Zinn (1922–2010) was probably the most well-known of these New Left historians. Disillusioned by his experience in the U.S. military, active in the movement against the Vietnam War, and inspired by the civil rights movement, he consciously studied the histories of marginalized groups and activists in order to inspire and support progressive movements. He met Lynd while they taught at Spelman University, and both became heavily involved in the civil rights movement there. Zinn lost his job because of this activism, which further radicalized his perspective on the past and present.

Zinn's life's work is synthesized in his most famous textbook *A People's History of the United States* (1980). This text illustrates many of the different applications of New Left social and political history. He challenges the white, elite, male-focus of dominant narratives of U.S. history by telling the story of the United States from the bottom-up, that is, from the perspective of Native Americans, African Americans, Asian Americans, working-class and poor Americans, and women. His social histories bear the strong imprint of Marxist theory, in that he seeks to understand the mechanisms of oppression as they have operated in the United States to control the working classes and other marginalized people in the interests of preserving capitalism and preventing a socialist revolution. Like many other New Left social historians, it is obvious that Zinn sees history as the key to understanding the history of social injustice in order to eliminate it.

While New Left historians applied their theories to a wide variety of subjects, they had an especially important impact on the historiography of the American Revolution. Seeking to uncover the role of the masses in the Revolution, historians such as Gary
Lemisch B. Nash, Edward Countryman, and Jesse Lemisch explored how the working-class "rabble" contributed to the Revolution. Similar to Zinn, Lemisch (b. 1936) is an especially prominent New Left historian to this day. He was born to a working-class Jewish family in New York and graduated from Yale University in 1963, with his dissertation on the role of seamen in the American Revolution, which he published in 1968. This work sought to uncover the hidden history of the inarticulate masses who helped to precipitate the American Revolution, but did not immediately benefit from its success. His article-length form of this dissertation was named one of the most important articles ever published in the prestigious journal of early American history, the *William and Mary Quarterly*. He was a self-consciously radical historian and a member of the radical Students for a Democratic Society (SDS) organization. Because of his activism, he too lost his position at the University of Chicago, ostensibly because of his admitted use of history in support of radical causes. The SDS chapter there protested the

dismissal as hypocritical, arguing that another University of Chicago professor, Daniel Boorstin, had boasted of using his writing and teaching to oppose communism.[6] While Lemisch continued to teach at less research-oriented universities and publish sporadically, his ability to research and publish more innovative histories of this sort was greatly diminished.

Perspectivalism   Despite their use of Marxist theory, New Leftists were divided over the issue of objectivity. Most New Leftists sought the objective truth in their works, but many were admittedly perspectival. Perspectivalism argues that all truth and all history is a matter of perspective. One person may see one perspective of an event, while another person may see a different, but equally valid perspective of that same event. For example, a roomful of students might be listening to the same professor, but when they are asked what the professor said, each may have a different answer, depending on their own unique perspective and what information they thought was important. Perspectivalists believed that earlier histories had been tainted by white male elitism and sought to uncover the real truths of history written from multiple perspectives. Some believed that perspectivalism would result in the most objective and truthful histories, while others argued that perspectivalism was relativism in another disguise.

Another more hotly debated issue was whether historians should be guided by their ideological commitments. Some, such as Howard Zinn and Staughton Lynd, argued that while historians should be committed to uncovering the truth, they should focus on uncovering those truths which would be most useful to social groups then struggling for peace and justice. For example, historians who were opposed to the Vietnam War should focus their attention on exploring the origins and course of the war to understand it and thus better confront it. Other leftist historians, such as Eugene Genovese, however, argued that while all history is value-laden, explicitly ideologically motivated history should be disregarded by the profession as biased and unreliable.[7] This debate continued to plague the historical profession throughout the 1990s.

While New Left historians sharply disagreed with each other on many issues, they contributed important new approaches to American historiography and began the shift away from consensus history. Influenced not only by the Vietnam War and the civil rights movement, but also by Marxism and *Annales* approaches, New Left historians explored American history from a fresh, radical perspective, uncovering much new material as they wrote history "from the bottom-up." Many of these historians continue to write radical history to this day despite strong criticism from neoconservatives and those more comfortable with nationalist consensus histories. New Left history has made a lasting impact on the academy and remains relevant today.

---

[6]Jim O'Brien, "'Be Realistic, Demand the Impossible': Staughton Lynd, Jesse Lemisch, and a Committed History," *Radical History Review* 82 (December 2002):71.

[7]Lynd, "Beyond Beard," 432.

Fernand Braudel, *The Mediterranean and the Mediterranean World in the Age of Philip II*

The Peninsulas: Mountains, Plateaux, and Plains

The five peninsulas of the inland sea are very similar. If one thinks of their relief they are regularly divided between mountains—the largest part—a few plains, occasional hills, and wide plateaux. This is not the only way in which the land masses can be dissected, but let us use simple categories. Each piece of these jigsaw puzzles belongs to a particular family and can be classified within a distinct typology. So, rather than consider each peninsula as an autonomous entity, let us look at the analogies between the materials that make them up. In other words let us shuffle the pieces of the jigsaw and compare the comparable. Even on the historical plane, this breakdown and reclassification will be illuminating....

To tell the truth, the historian is not unlike the traveller. He tends to linger over the plain, which is the setting for the leading actors of the day, and does not seem eager to approach the high mountains nearby. More than one historian who has never left the towns and their archives would be surprised to discover their existence. And yet how can one ignore these conspicuous actors, the half-wild mountains, where man has taken root like a hardy plant; always semi-deserted, for man is constantly leaving them?

How can one ignore them when often their sheer slopes come right down to the sea's edge?[1]

Mountains, civilizations, and religions. The mountains are as a rule a world apart from civilizations, which are an urban and lowland achievement. Their history is to have none, to remain almost always on the fringe of the great waves of civilization, even the longest and most persistent, which may spread over great distances in the horizontal plane but are powerless to move vertically when faced with an obstacle of a few hundred metres. To these hilltop worlds, out of touch with the towns, even Rome itself, in all its years of power, can have meant very little,[2] except perhaps through the military camps that the empire established for security reasons in various places on the edges of unconquered mountain lands: hence León, at the foot of the Cantabrian mountains, Djemilah, facing the rebellious Berber Atlas, Timgad and the annex at Lambaesis, where the *IIIa legio augusta* encamped. Neither did Latin as a language take root in the hostile massifs of North Africa, Spain or elsewhere, and the Latin or Italic house type remained a house of the plains.[3] In a few places it may have infiltrated locally, but on the whole the mountains resisted it.

Later, when the Rome of the Emperors had become the Rome of Saint Peter, the same problem remained. It was only in places where its action

---

Source: Excerpts from pp. 25, 29–30, 34–5, 38–41, 170 from *The Mediterranean and the Mediterranean World in the Age of Philip II* Volume I by Fernand Braudel. Copyright © Librairie Armand Colin 1966. English translation copyright © 1972 by Wm. Collins Sons Ltd. and Harper & Ros Publishers, Inc. Reprinted by permission of HarperCollins Publishers.

[1] Cf. a letter from Villegaignon to the king of France in 1552; "The entire sea coast, from Gaietta to Naples and from Naples to Sicily, is bounded by high mountains, at the feet of which lies a beach open to all the winds of the sea, as you would say that the coast of Picardy is open to the sea-winds, except that your coast has rivers along which one might retreat, and here there are none", Abbé Marchand's communication, "Documents pour l'histoire du règne de Henri II", in *Bulletin hist. et phil. Du Comité des travaux hist. et scient.*, 1901, p. 565–8.

[2] In Baetica, Rome was much more successful in the lowlands, and along the rivers, than on the plateaux, G. Niemeier, *Siedlungsgeogr. Untersuchungen in Niederandalusien*, Hamburg, 1935, p. 37. In the mountainous northwest of Spain with the added difficulty of distance, Rome penetrated late on and with little success, R. Konetzke, *Geschichte des spanischen und portugiesischen Volkes*, Leipzig, 1941, p. 31.

[3] Albert Dauzat, *Le village et le paysan de France*, 1941, p. 52.

could be persistently reinforced that the Church was able to tame and evangelize these herdsmen and independent peasants. Even so it took an incredibly long time. In the sixteenth century the task was far from complete, and this applies to Islam and Catholicism alike, for they both met the same obstacles: the Berbers of North Africa, protected by the mountain peaks, were still hardly at all, or very imperfectly, won over to Muhammad. The same is true of the Kurds in Asia;[4] while in Aragon, in the Valencia region or round Granada, the mountains were, conversely, the zone of religious dissidence, a Moslem stronghold,[5] just as the high, wild, "suspicious" hills of the Lubéron protected the strongholds of the Vaudois.[6] Everywhere in the sixteenth century, the hilltop world was very little influenced by the dominant religions at sea level; mountain life persistently lagged behind the plain....

Mountain freedom.[7] There can be no doubt that the lowland, urban civilization penetrated to the highland world very imperfectly and at a very slow rate. This was as true of other things as it was of Christianity. The feudal system as a political, economic, and social system, and as an instrument of justice failed to catch in its toils most of the mountain regions and those it did reach it only partially influenced. The resistance of the Corsican and Sardinian mountains to lowland influence has often been noted and further evidence could be found in Lunigiana, regarded by Italian historians as a kind of mainland Corsica, between Tuscany and Liguria.[8] The observation could be confirmed anywhere where the population is so inadequate, thinly distributed, and widely dispersed as to prevent the establishment of the state, dominant languages, and important civilizations.

A study of the vendetta would lead one towards a similar conclusion. The countries where the vendetta was in force—and they were all mountainous countries—were those that had not been moulded and penetrated by mediæval concepts of feudal justice,[9] the Berber countries, Corsica,

---

[4]Comte de Sercey, *op. cit.,* p. 104: "One can see however, (since they dance) that the Kurdish women, although Moslem, are not kept in seclusion".

[5]See below, sections on the Moriscos, (Part II, ch. V and Part III, ch. III).

[6]Lurmarin, Cabrières, Mérindol and about twenty other hill towns in the heart of the Lubéron, where there was abundant wild life—foxes, wolves and boars—were Protestant strongholds, J. L. Vaudoyer, *Beautés de la Provence, Paris, 1926, p. 238. And there were the Vaudois of the Savoy states and in the Apennines in the kingdom of Naples. "Catharism", wrote Marc Bloch, "had dwindled to an obscure sect of mountain shepherds",* Annales d'hist.sociale, 1940, p. 79.

[7]As observed by contemporaries; Loys Le Roy, *De l'excellence du gouvernement royal,* Paris, 1575, p. 37, writes "A country covered with mountains, rocks, and forests, fit only for pasture, where there are many poor men, as is most of Switzerland, is best suited for democracy...The lands of the plain, where there are greater numbers of rich and noble men, are better suited to an aristocratic form of government". Jean Bodin, in *Les six livres de la République* (English translation, *The Six Books of the Commonwealth,* by Knolles, 1606, facs. Edition Harvard, 1962, p. 694) reports that Leo Africanus was astonished by the robust physique of the mountain folk of Mount Megeza, while the plain-dwellers were smaller men. "This force and vigour doth cause the mountaineers to love popular liberty...as we have said of the Swissers and Grisons". The Middle Ages in Corsica, says Lorenzi de Bradi, *La Corse inconnue,* 1927, p. 35, were a great period for liberty. "The Corsican would not suffer any man to rob him of the product of his labour. The milk from his goat and the harvest from his field were his alone." And H. Taine in his *Voyage aux Pyrénées, 1858, p. 138, says "freedom took root here deep in the past, a gruff and wild sort of freedom".*

[8]Arrigo Solmi, "La Corsica" in *Arch. St. di Corsica*, 1925, p. 32.

[9]For a general picture, see the penetrating but legalistic work by Jacques Lambert, *La vengeance privée et les fondements du droit international,* Paris, 1936. In the same order of ideas, cf. Michelet's remark on the Dauphiné, where "feudalism (never) exerted the same influence as it did upon the rest of France." And Taine again: *op. cit.,* p. 138, "These are the *fors* of Béarn, in which it is said that in Béarn in the old days there was no *seigneur"*. On blood feuds in Montenegro and upper Albania, see Ami Boué, *La Turquie d'Europe,* Paris, 1840, II, p. 395 and 523.

and Albania, for example. Marc Bloch,[10] writing about studies of Sardinia, points out that during the Middle Ages the island was an "extensively manorialized, but not feudalized society" as a result of having been "long isolated from the great currents which swept the continent". This is putting the accent on the insularity of Sardinia, and it is quite true that it has been a decisive factor in Sardinian history. But the mountains are an equally important factor, just as responsible for the isolation of the people of Sardinia as the sea, if not more so; even in our own time they have produced those cruel and romantic outlaws, at Orgosolo and elsewhere, in revolt against the establishment of the modern state and its *carabinieri*. This moving phenomenon has been portrayed by anthropologists and film directors. "He who does not steal", says a character in a Sardinian novel, "is not a man".[11] "Law?" says another, "I make my own laws and I take what I need."[12]

In Sardinia, as in Lunigiana and Calabria, and everywhere where observation (when it is possible) reveals a hiatus between the society and the broad movements of history—if social archaisms (the vendetta among others) persisted, it was above all for the simple reason that mountains are mountains: that is, primarily an obstacle, and therefore also a refuge, a land of the free. For there men can live out of reach of the pressures and tyrannies of civilization: its social and political order, its monetary economy. Here there was no landed nobility with strong and powerful roots (the "lords

of the Atlas" created by the Maghzen were of recent origin); in the sixteenth century in Haute-Provence, the country nobleman, the "*cavalier salvatje*", lived alongside his peasants, cleared the land as they did, did not scorn to plough and till the ground, or to carry wood and dung on the back of his donkey. He was a constant irritation "in the eyes of the Provençal nobility, who are essentially city-dwellers like the Italians".[13] Here there were no rich, well-fed clergy to be envied and mocked; the priest was as poor as his flock.[14] There was no tight urban network so no administration, no towns in the proper sense of the word, and no gendarmes either we might add. It is only in the lowlands that one finds a close-knit, stifling society, a prebendal clergy, a haughty aristocracy, and an efficient system of justice. The hills were the refuge of liberty, democracy, and peasant "republics".

"The steepest places have been at all times the asylum of liberty", writes the learned Baron de Tott in his *Memoirs*.[15] "In traveling along the coast of Syria, we see despotism extending itself over all the flat country and its progress stopt towards the mountains, at the first rock, at the first defile, that is easy of defence; whilst the Curdi, the Drusi, and the Mutuali, masters of the Lebanon and Anti-Lebanon, constantly preserve their independence."[16] A poor thing was Turkish despotism—ruler indeed of the roads, passes, towns, and plains, but what can it have meant in the Balkan highlands, or in Greece and Epirus, in the mountains of Crete

---

[10]Marc Bloch, *Feudal Society*, (trans. L. Manyon), London, 1961, p. 247. See also his useful remarks on Sardinia, "La Sardaigne" in *Mélanges d'histoire sociale*, III, p. 94.

[11]Maurice Le Lannou, "Le bandit d'Orgosolo", *Le Monde*, 16/17 June, 1963. The film was directed by vittorio de Seta, the anthropological study carried out by Franco Caguetta, French transl.: *Les Bandits de'Orgosolo*, 1963; the novels mentioned are by Grazia Deledda, *La via del male,* Rome, 1896; *Il Dio dei viventi*, Rome, 1922.

[12]*Ibid.*

[13]Fernand Benoit, *La Provence et le Comtat Venaissin,* 1949, p. 27.

[14]For the high Milanese, see S. Pugliese, "Condizioni economiche e finanziarie della Lombardia nella prima meta del secolo XVIII" in *Misc. di Storia italiana*, 3rd series, vol. xxi, 1924.

[15]*Mémoires sur les Turcs et les Tartares*, (Eng. Trans. *Memoirs of the Baron de Tott on the Turks and Tartars*... London 1785, I, p. 398): "asylum of liberty, or," he adds, "the haunt of tyrants." This was in connection with the Genoese installations in the Crimea.

[16]*Ibid.*, Preliminary Discourse, I, 11.

where the Skafiotes defied, from their hilltops, all authority from the seventeenth century onward, or in the Albanian hills, where, much later, lived 'Ali Pasha Tepedelenli? Did the Wali Bey, installed at Monastir by the Turkish conquest of the fifteenth century, ever really govern? In theory his authority extended to the Greek and Albanian hill-villages, but each one was a fortress, an independent enclave and on occasion could become a hornets' nest.[17] It is hardly surprising, then, that the Abruzzi, the highest, widest, and wildest part of the Apennines, should have escaped Byzantine rule, the rule of the Exarchs of Ravenna, and finally the domination of Papal Rome, although the Abruzzi lie directly behind the city and the Papal State ran north through Umbria as far as the Po valley.[18] Nor is it astonishing that in Morocco the *bled es siba*, lands unsubdued by the sultan, should be essentially mountain regions.[19]

Sometimes this freedom of the hills has survived into our own time and can be seen today in spite of the immense weight of modern administration. In the Moroccan High Atlas, notes Robert Montagne,[20] "the villages which are ranged along the sunny banks of the mountain torrents, near immense walnut trees watered by the turbulent Atlas streams, have no *chikhs'* or *Khalifats'* houses. It is impossible to distinguish between a poor man's house and a rich man's. Each of these little mountain cantons forms a separate state, administered by a council. The village elders, all clad alike in brown wool garments, meet on a terrace and discuss for hours on end the interests of the village. No one raises his voice and it is impossible from watching them to discover which is their president." All this is preserved, if the mountain canton is sufficiently high and sufficiently inaccessible, away from the main roads, which is a rare case today but was less so in former times before the expansion of road systems. This is why the Nurra, although connected to the rest of the island of Sardinia by an easily accessible plain, remained for a long time out of the reach of roads and traffic. The following legend was inscribed on an eighteenth century map by the Piedmontese engineers: "Nurra, unconquered peoples, who pay no taxes!"[21]

>> Questions for Consideration

1. What is the main agent of historical change here? What specific evidence supports this?

2. What does Braudel mean by claiming that historians "linger over the plain"? Do you agree with him?

3. Explain his thesis on "Mountain Freedom" in your own words.

---

[17]Cf. Franz Spnda in Werner Benndorf, *Das Mittelmeerbuch.* 1940, p. 209–210.

[18]A. Philippson, "Umbrien und Etrurien", in *Geogr. Zeitung,* 1933, p. 452.

[19]Further examples: Napoleon was unable to control the mountains round Genoa, a refuge for deserters, in spite of the searches organized (Jean Borel, *Gênes sous Napoléon Ier*, 2nd ed. 1929, p. 103). In about 1828, the Turkish police were powerless to prevent outbreaks of brigandage by the peoples of Mt. Ararat (Comte de Sercey, *op. cit.*, p. 95); they seem to be equally unsuccessful today in protecting the mountain's forest wealth from the ravages of the flocks (Hermann Wenzel, "Agrargeographische Wandlungen in der Türkei", in *Geogr. Zeitschr.* 1937, p. 407). Similarly in Morocco: "In reality, in southern Morocco, the sultan's authority did not reach beyond the plain", writes R. Montagne, *op. cit.*, p. 134.

[20]*Ibid.,* p. 131.

[21]M. Le. Lannou, *Pâtres et paysans de la Sardaigne*, 1941, p. 14, n. 1.

E. P. Thompson, *The Making of The English Working Class*

THIS BOOK HAS a clumsy title, but it is one which meets its purpose. *Making*, because it is a study in an active process, which owes as much to agency as to conditioning. The working class did not rise like the sun at an appointed time. It was present at its own making.

Class, rather than classes, for reasons which it is one purpose of this book to examine. There is, of course, a difference. "Working classes" is a descriptive term, which evades as much as it defines. It ties loosely together a bundle of discrete phenomena. There were tailors here and weavers there, and together they make up the working classes.

By class I understand an historical phenomenon, unifying a number of disparate and seemingly unconnected events, both in the raw material of experience and in consciousness. I emphasise that it is an *historical* phenomenon. I do not see class as a "structure", nor even as a "category", but as something which in fact happens (and can be shown to have happened) in human relationships.

More than this, the notion of class entails the notion of historical relationship. Like any other relationship, it is a fluency which evades analysis if we attempt to stop it dead at any given moment and anatomise its structure. The finest-meshed sociological net cannot give us a pure specimen of class, any more than it can give us one of deference or of love. The relationship must always be embodied in real people and in a real context. Moreover, we cannot have two distinct classes, each with an independent being, and then bring them *into* relationship with each other. We cannot have love without lovers, nor deference without squires and labourers. And class happens when some men, as a result of common experiences (inherited or shared), feel and articulate the identity of their interests as between themselves, and as against other men whose interests are different from (and usually opposed to) theirs. The class experience is largely determined by the productive relations into which men are born—or enter involuntarily. Class-consciousness is the way in which these experiences are handled in cultural terms: embodied in traditions, value-systems, ideas, and institutional forms. If the experience appears as determined, class-consciousness does not. We can see a *logic* in the responses of similar occupational groups undergoing similar experiences, but we cannot predicate any *law*. Consciousness of class arises in the same way in different times and places, but never in *just* the same way.

There is today an ever-present temptation to suppose that class is a thing. This was not Marx's meaning, in his own historical writing, yet the error vitiates much latter-day "Marxist" writing. "It", the working class, is assumed to have a real existence, which can be defined almost mathematically—so many men who stand in a certain relation to the means of production. Once this is assumed it becomes possible to deduce the class-consciousness which "it" ought to have (but seldom does have) if "it" was properly aware of its own position and real interests. There is a cultural superstructure, through which this recognition dawns in inefficient ways. These cultural "lags" and distortions are a nuisance, so that it is easy to pass from this to some theory of substitution: the party, sect, or theorist, who disclose class-consciousness, not as it is, but as it ought to be.

But a similar error is committed daily on the other side of the ideological divide. In one form, this is a plain negative. Since the crude notion of class attributed to Marx can be faulted without difficulty, it is assumed that any notion of class is a pejorative theoretical construct, imposed upon the evidence. It is denied that class has happened at all. In another form, and by a curious inversion, it is possible to pass from a dynamic to a static view of class. "It"—the working class—exists, and can be defined with some accuracy as a component of the social structure. Class-consciousness, however, is a bad thing, invented by displaced intellectuals, since everything which disturbs the harmonious co-existence of groups performing different "social roles" (and which thereby retards economic growth) is to be deplored as an "unjustified disturbance-symptom".[1] The problem is to determine how best "it" can be conditioned to accept its social role, and how its grievances may best be "handled and channelled".

If we remember that class is a relationship, and not a thing, we cannot think in this way. "It" does not exist, either to have an ideal interest or consciousness, or to lie as a patient on the Adjustor's table. Nor can we turn matters upon their heads, as has been done by one authority who (in a study of class obsessively concerned with methodology, to the exclusion of the examination of a single real class situation in a real historical context) has informed us:

> Classes are based on the differences in legitimate power associated with certain positions, i.e. on the structure of social roles with respect to their authority expectations.... An individual becomes a member of a class by playing a social role relevant from the point of view of authority.... He belongs to a class because he occupies a position in a social organization; i.e. class membership is derived from the incumbency of a social role.[2]

The question, of course, is how the individual got to be in this "social role", and how the particular social organization (with its property-rights and structure of authority) got to be there. And these are historical questions. If we stop history at a given point, then there are no classes but simply a multitude of individuals with a multitude of experiences. But if we watch these men over an adequate period of social change, we observe patterns in their relationships, their ideas, and their institutions. Class is defined by men as they live their own history, and, in the end, this is its only definition.

If I have shown insufficient understanding of the methodological preoccupations of certain sociologists, nevertheless I hope this book will be seen as a contribution to the understanding of class. For I am convinced that we cannot understand class unless we see it as a social and cultural formation, arising from processes which can only be studied as they work themselves out over a considerable historical period. This book can be seen as a biography of the English working class from its adolescence until its early manhood. In the years between 1780 and 1832 most English working people came to feel an identity of interests as between themselves, and as against their rulers and employers. This ruling class was itself much divided, and in fact only gained in cohesion over the same years because certain antagonisms were resolved (or faded into relative insignificance) in the face of an insurgent working class. Thus the working-class presence was, in 1832, the most significant factor in British political life....

I am seeking to rescue the poor stockinger, the Luddite cropper, the "obsolete" hand-loom weaver, the "utopian" artisan, and even the deluded follower of Joanna Southcott, from the enormous condescension of posterity. Their crafts and traditions may have been dying. Their hostility to the new industrialism may have been backward-looking. Their communitarian ideals may have been fantasies. Their

---

[1]An example of this approach, covering the period of this book, is to be found in the work of a colleague of professor Talcott Parsons: J.J. Smelser, *Social Change in the Industrial Revolution* (1959).

[2]R. Dahrendorf, *Class and Class Conflict in Industrial Society* (1959), pp. 148–9.

insurrectionary conspiracies may have been foolhardy. But they lived through these times of acute social disturbance, and we did not. Their aspirations were valid in terms of their own experience; and, if they were casualties of history, they remain, condemned in their own lives, as casualties.

Our only criterion of judgement should not be whether or not a man's actions are justified in the light of subsequent evolution. After all, we are not at the end of social evolution ourselves. In some of the lost causes of the people of the Industrial Revolution we may discover insights into social evils which we have yet to cure. Moreover, this period now compels attention for two particular reasons. First, it was a time in which the plebeian movement placed an exceptionally high valuation upon egalitarian and democratic values. Although we often boast our democratic way of life, the events of these critical years are far too often forgotten or slurred over. Second, the greater part of the world today is still undergoing problems of industrialization, and of the formation of democratic institutions, analogous in many ways to our own experience during the Industrial Revolution. Causes which were lost in England might, in Asia or Africa, yet be won.

Exploitation

JOHN THELWALL was not alone in seeing in every "manufactory" a potential centre of political rebellion. An aristocratic traveler who visited the Yorkshire dales in 1792 was alarmed to find a new cotton-mill in the "pastoral vale" of Aysgarth—"why, here now is a great flaring mill, whose back stream has drawn off half the water of the falls above the bridge":

> With the bell ringing, and the clamour of the mill, all the vale is disturb'd; treason and leveling

systems are the discourse; and rebellion may be near at hand.

The mill appeared as symbol of social energies which were destroying the very "course of Nature". It embodied a double threat to the settled order. First, from the owners of industrial wealth, those upstarts who enjoyed an unfair advantage over the landowners whose income was tied to their rent-roll:

> If men thus start into riches; or if riches from trade are too easily procured, woe to us men of middling income, and settled revenue; and woe it has been to all the Nappa Halls, and the Yeomanry of the land.

Second, from the industrial working population, which our traveler regarded with an alliterative hostility which betrays a response not far removed from that of the white racialist towards the coloured population today:

> The people, indeed, are employ'd; but they are all abandon'd to vice from the throng.... At the times when people work not in the mill, they issue out to poaching, profligacy and plunder...[3]

The equation between the cotton-mill and the new industrial society, and the correspondence between new forms of productive and of social relationship, was a commonplace among observers in the years between 1790 and 1850. Karl Marx was only expressing this with unusual vigour when he declared: "The hand-mill gives you society with the feudal lord: the steam-mill, society with the industrial capitalist." And it was not only the mill-owner but also the working population brought into being within and around the mills which seemed to contemporaries to be "new". "The instant we get near the borders of the manufacturing parts of Lancashire", a rural magistrate wrote in 1808, "we meet a fresh race of beings, both in

---

[3]The Torrington Diaries, ed. C.B. Andrews (1936), III, pp. 81–2.

point of manners, employments and subordination ..."; while Robert Owen, in 1815, declared that "the general diffusion of manufactures throughout a country generates a new character in its inhabitants ... an essential change in the general character of the mass of the people."

Observers in the 1830s and 1840s were still exclaiming at the novelty of the "factory system". Peter Gaskell, in 1833, spoke of the manufacturing population as "but a Hercules in the cradle"; it was "only since the introduction of steam as a power that they have acquired their paramount importance" The steam-engine had "drawn together the population into dense masses" and already Gaskell saw in working-class organizations as " 'imperium in imperio' of the most obnoxious description".[4] Ten years later Cooke Taylor was writing in similar terms:

The steam-engine had no precedent, the spinning-jenny is without ancestry, the mule and the power-look entered on no prepared heritage: they sprang into sudden existence like Minerva from the brain of Jupiter.

But it was the human consequence of these "novelties" which caused this observer most disquiet:

As a stranger passes through the masses of human beings which have accumulated round the mills and print works ... he cannot contemplate these "crowded hives" without feeling of anxiety and apprehension almost amounting to dismay. The population, like the system to which it belongs, is NEW; but it is hourly increasing in breadth and strength. It is an aggregate of masses, our conceptions of which clothe themselves in terms that express something portentous and fearful ... as of the slow rising and gradual swelling of an ocean which must, at some future and no distant time, bear all the elements of society aloft upon its bosom, and float them Heaven knows whither. There are mighty energies slumbering in these masses.... The manufacturing population is not new in its formation alone: it is new in its habits of thought and action, which have been formed by the circumstances of its condition, with little instruction, and less guidance, from external sources...[5]

For Engels, describing the *Condition of the Working Class in England* in 1844 it seemed that "the first proletarians were connected with manufacture, were engendered by it...the factory hands, eldest children of the industrial revolution, have from the beginning to the present day formed the nucleus of the labour Movement".

However different their judgments of value, conservative, radical, and socialist observers suggested the same equation: steam power and the cotton-mill=new working class. The physical instruments of production were seen as giving rise in a direct and more-or-less compulsive way to new social relationships, institutions, and cultural modes. At the same time the history of popular agitation during the period 1811–50 appears to confirm this picture. It is as if the English nation entered a crucible in the 1790s and emerged after the Wars in a different form. Between 1811 and 1813, the Luddite crisis; in 1817 the Pentridge Rising; in 1819, Peterloo; throughout the next decade the proliferation of trade, union activity, Owenite propaganda, radical journalism, the Ten Hours Movement, the revolutionary crisis of 1831–2; and, beyond that, the multitude of movements which made up Chartism. It is, perhaps, the scale and intensity of this multiform popular agitation which has, more than anything else, given rise (among contemporary observers and historians alike) to the sense of some catastrophic change.

---

[4]P. Gaskell, *The Manufacturing Population of England* (1833), p. 6; Asa Briggs, "The Language of 'Class' in Early Nineteenth-century England", in *Essays in Labour History,* ed. Briggs and Saville (1960), p. 63.

[5]W. Cooke Taylor, *Notes of a Tour in the Manufacturing Districts of Lancashire (1842),* pp. 4–6.

Almost every radical phenomenon of the 1790s can be found reproduced tenfold after 1815. The handful of Jacobin sheets gave rise to a score of ultra-radical and Owenite periodicals. Where Daniel Eaton served imprisonment for publishing Paine, Richard Carlile and his shop-men served a total of more than 200 years imprisonment for similar crimes. Where Corresponding Societies maintained a precarious existence in a score of town, the post-war Hampden Clubs or political unions struck root in small industrial villages. And when this popular agitation is recalled alongside the dramatic pace of change in the cotton industry, it is natural to assume a direct casual relationship. The cotton-mill is seen as the agent not only of industrial but also of social revolution, producing not only more goods but also the "Labour movement" itself. The industrial Revolution, which commenced as a description, is now invoked as an explanation.

From the time of Arkwright through to the Plug Riots and beyond, it is the image of the "dark, satanic mill" which dominates our visual reconstruction of the Industrial Revolution. In part, perhaps, because it is a dramatic visual image—the barrack-like buildings, the great mill chimneys, the factory children, the clogs and shawls, the dwellings clustering around the mills as if spawned by them. (It is an image which forces one to think first of the industry, and only secondly of the people connected to it or serving it.) In part, because the cotton-mill and the mill-town— from the swiftness of its growth, ingenuity of its techniques, and the novelty or harshness of its discipline—seemed to contemporaries to be dramatic and portentous: a more satisfactory symbol for debate on the "condition-of-England" question than those anonymous or sprawling manufacturing *districts* which figure even more often in the Home Office "disturbance books". And from this both a literary and an

historical tradition is derived. Nearly all the classic accounts by contemporaries of conditions in the Industrial Revolution are based on the cotton industry—and, in the Taylor, Engels, to mention a few. Novels such as *Michael Armstrong* or *Mary Barton* or *Hard Times* perpetuate the tradition. And the emphasis is markedly found in the subsequent writing of economic and social history.

But many difficulties remain. Cotton was certainly the pace-making industry of the Industrial Revolution,[6] and the cotton-mill was the pre-eminent model for the factory-system. Yet we should not assume any automatic, or over-direct, correspondence between the dynamic of economic growth and the dynamic of social or cultural life. For half a century after the "breakthrough" of the cotton-mill (around 1780) the mill workers remained as a minority of the adult labour force in the cotton industry itself. In the early 1830s the cotton handloom weavers alone still outnumbered all the men and women in spinning and weaving mills of cotton, wool, and silk combined.[7] Still, in 1830, the adult male cotton-spinner was no more typical of that elusive figure, the "average working man," than is the Coventry motor-worker of the 1960s.

The point is the importance, because too much emphasis upon the newness of the cotton-mills can lead to an underestimation of the continuity of political and cultural traditions in the making of working-class communities. The factory hands, so far from being the "eldest children of the industrial revolution", were late arrival. Many of their ideas and forms of organization were anticipated by domestic workers, such as the woolen workers of Norwich and the West County, or the small-ware weavers of Manchester. And it is questionable whether factory hands—except in the cotton districts—"formed the nucleus of the Labour Movement" at any time before the late 1840s (and, in some northern and Midland

---

[6]For an admirable restatement of the reasons for the primacy of the cotton industry in the Industrial Revolution, see E.J. Hobsbawm, *The Age of Revolution (1962)*, ch. 2.

[7]Estimates for U.K., 1833. Total adult labour force in all textile mills, 191,671. Number of cotton hand-loom weavers, 213,000. See below, p. 327.

towns, the years 1832–4, leading up to the great lock-outs). Jacobinism, as we have seen, struck root most deeply among agitation as the factory hands. And in many towns the actual nucleus from which the labour movement derived ideas, organization, and leadership, was made up of such men as shoemakers, weavers, saddlers and harnessmakers, booksellers, printers, building workers, small tradesmen, and the like. The vast area of radical London between 1815 and 1850 drew its strength from no major heavy industries (shipbuilding was tending to decline, and the engineers only made their impact later in the century) but from the host of smaller trades and occupations.[8]

Such diversity of experiences has led some writers to question both the notions of an "industrial revolution" and of a "working class". The first discussion need not detain us here.[9] The term is serviceable enough in its usual connotations. For the second, many writers prefer the term working *classes*, which emphasize, within the portmanteau phrase. And in this they echo the complaints of Francis Place:

> If the character and conduct of the working-people are to be taken from reviews, magazines, pamphlets, newspapers, reports of the two Houses of parliament and the factory Commissioners, we shall find them all jumbled together as the "lower orders", the most skilled and the most prudent workmen, with the most ignorant and imprudent labourers and paupers, though the difference is great indeed, and indeed in many cases will scarce admit of comparison.[10]

Place is, of course, right: the Sunderland sailor, the Irish navy, the Jewish costermonger, the inmate of an east Anglian village workhouse, the compositor on the *Times*—all might be seen by

their "betters" as belonging to the "lower classes" while they themselves might scarcely understand each others' dialect.

Nevertheless, when every caution has been made, the outstanding fact of the period between 1790 and 1830 is the formation of "the working class". This is revealed, first, in the growth of class-consciousness: the consciousness of an identity of interests as between all these diverse groups of working people and as against the interests of other classes. And, second, in the growth of corresponding forms of political and industrial organization. By 1832 there were strongly based and self-conscious working-class institutions—trade unions, friendly societies, educational and religious movements, political organizations, periodicals—working-class intellectual traditions, working-class structure of feeling.

The making of the working class is a fact of political and cultural, as much as economic, history. It was not the spontaneous generation of the factory system. Not should we think of an external force—the "industrial revolution"—working upon some nondescript undifferentiated raw material of humanity, and turning it out at the other end as a "fresh race of beings". The changing productive relations and working conditions of the Industrial Revolution were imposed, not upon raw material, but upon the free-born Englishman—and the free-born Englishman as Paine had left him or as the Methodists had moulded him. The factory hand or stockinger was also the inheritor of Bunyan, of remembered village rights, of notions of equality before the law, of craft indoctrination and the creator of political traditions. The working class made itself as much as it was made.

---

[8]Cf. Hobsbawm, op. cit., ch. 2.

[9]There is a summary of this controversy in E. E. Lampard, *Industrial Revolution* (American Historical Association, 1957). See also Hobsbawm, op. cit., ch. 2.

[10]Cit. M.D. George, *London Life in the Eighteenth Century* (1930), p. 210.

>> Questions for Consideration

1. Who or what is the historical agent in this history? Where in this excerpt does it indicate Thompson's view of historical agency?

2. What evidence of Marxist, Gramscist, and *Annaliste* influence is there in this excerpt?

3. A common criticism of this work is that it omits any consideration of women's experiences. Do you think this criticism is justified?

Jesse Lemisch, "Jack Tar in the Streets"

HERE comes Jack Tar, his bowed legs bracing him as if the very Broadway beneath his feet might begin to pitch and roll.[1] In his dress he is, in the words of a superior, "very nasty and negligent", "his black stockings ragged, his long, baggy trousers tarred to make them waterproof.[2]

Bred in "that very shambles of language," the merchant marine, he is foul-mouthed, his talk alien and suspect.[3] He is Jolly Jack, a bull in a china shop, always, in his words, "for a Short Life and a Merry one," and, in the concurring words of his superiors, "concerned only for the

---

Source: Jesse Lemisch, "Jack Tar in the Streets: Merchant Seamen in the Politics of Revolutionary America," *William and Mary Quarterly*, Third Series 25: 3 (July 1968): 371–384, 387, 389–391, 393–400 & 405–407 (with footnotes). Copyright © Jesse Lemisch.

[1]His walk was sometimes described as a "waddle," *New-York Gazette*; or *the Weekly Post-Boy*, Sept. 3, 1759. Seamen were often called Jack Tar in England and in the colonies, for example, *ibid.*, Oct. 15, 1770. The term was used more or less interchangeably along with "seaman," "sailor," and "mariner," with the latter frequently connoting "master" (as in Panel of Jurors [n.d.], New York Supreme Court, Pleadings P-2689, Office of County Clerk, Hall of Records, New York City, where seven of ten "mariners" are identifiable as captains by comparison with such sources as *The Burghers of New Amsterdam and the Freemen of New York, 1675–1866* [New-York Historical Society, *Collections*, XVIII (New York, 1886)], *passim; N.-Y. Gaz.; Weekly Post-Boy, passim*; and the especially valuable list of privateer captains in Stuyvesant Fish, *The New York Privateers, 1756–1763* [New York, 1945], 83–90). In this article Jack Tar is a merchant seaman, a "sailor" is in the Royal Navy, and a "mariner" is the captain of a merchant vessel. If a source calls a man a "mariner" or a "sailor" I have had to have evidence that he was in fact a merchant seaman before I would count him as one. For a useful discussion of terms see I. M. V., "Note," *Mariner's Mirror*, VII (1921), 351.

[2][George Balfour], "Memorandum," *Mariner's Mirror*, VIII (1922), 248. For the seaman's dress see *Abstracts of Wills on File in the Surrogate's Office, City of New York* (N.-Y. Hist. Soc., Coll., XXV–XLI [New York, 1893–1909]), VI, III; descriptions of dress scattered throughout Admiralty Group, Class 98, Piece II-14, Public Record Office. Hereafter cited as Adm. 98/II-14; *N.-Y. Gaz.; Weekly Post-Boy,* Dec. 10, 1759, Oct. 14, Dec. 16, 1762, Nov. 3, 1763, Mar. 6, June 26, 1766, Oct. 1, 1767, Jan. 29, 1770, July 6, 1772; Samuel Eliot Morison, *John Paul Jones* (Boston, 1959), 72. A pair of useful illustrations appears in *Mariner's Mirror*, IX (1923), 128.

[3]J. R. Hutchinson, *The Press-Gang, Afloat and Ashore* (New York, 1913), 29. See *The Acts and Resolves…of the Province of Massachusetts Bay…* (Boston, 1869–1922), III, 318–319, for an act of Feb. 10, 1747, prescribing the stocks and whipping for seamen guilty of "profane cursing or swearing." For a landsman's version of some seamen's dialogue, see *N.-Y. Gaz.; Weekly Post-Boy*, Dec. 10, 1767.

present…incapable of thinking of, or inattentive to, future welfare," "like froward Children not knowing how to judge for themselves."[4]

Clothes don't make the man, nor does language; surely we can do better than these stereotypes. Few have tried. Maritime history, as it has been written, has had as little to do with the common seaman as business history has had to do with the laborer. In that mischianza of mystique and elitism, "seaman" has meant Sir Francis Drake, not Jack Tar; the focus has been on trade, exploration, the great navigators, but rarely on the men who sailed the ships.[5] Thus we know very little about Jack. Samuel Eliot Morison is one of the few who have tried to portray the common seaman. In an influential anecdote in *The Maritime History of Massachusetts* Morison has described a "frequent occurrence" in early New England. A farmer's boy, called by the smell or the sight of the sea, suddenly runs off; three years later he returns as a man, marries the hired girl, and lives "happily ever after." This experience, Morison tells us, was "typical of the Massachusetts merchant marine,"

where the "old salt" was almost non-existent and where there never was "a native deep-sea proletariat." The ships were sailed by wave after wave of "adventure-seeking boys," drawn by high wages and *wanderlust*. If they recovered, they took their earnings, married, and bought a farm; if not, these "young, ambitious seamen culled from the most active element of a pushing race" stayed on and rose to become masters in a merchant marine distinguished from its class-ridden European counterparts by easy mobility.[6]

To a fleeing apprentice, dissatisfied with the "bondage" of work ashore,[7] to a runaway slave, the sea might appear the only real shelter. Men with no experience at sea tried to pass for seamen and before long discovered that they had indeed become seamen. Others *were* seamen, apprenticed in one vessel and fled to another. Still others, deserted soldiers, bail-jumpers, thieves, and murderers, had gotten into trouble with the law.[8] And others went to sea entirely unwillingly, originally impressed—perhaps from jail—into the navy, or tricked into the merchant

---

[4]Robert E. Peabody, "The Naval Career of Captain John Manley of Marblehead," Essex Institute, *Historical Collections*, XLV (1909), 25; Ralph D. Paine, *The Ships and Sailors of Old Salem* (New York, 1909), 23; John Cremer, *Ramblin' Jack.…* ed. R. Reynell Bellamy (London, 1936), 38–39; Congressman Edward Livingston, Apr. 10, 1798, United States, Congress, *Debates and Proceedings in the Congress of the United States…* (Washington, D. C., 1834–1856), 5th Cong., 2d sess., 1388. Hereafter cited as *Annals of Congress*; Colvill to Admiralty, Nov. 12, 1765, Adm. 1/482.

[5]The bibliography is endless: a typical recent instance is Edmund O. Sawyer, *America's Sea Saga* (New York, 1962), foreword, 185, "a tale of unending courage" by a retired lieutenant colonel who now lives in Hollywood where he "plays an active role in the relentless crusade against the Communist conspiracy." Although there is much of use in *American Neptune*, the magazine's definition of maritime history has been too genteel, dwelling too often on such matters as ship design and construction, yachting, reminiscences, and model-building. On the other hand, even the W. P. A. Writer's Program neglected the seamen in *Boston Looks Seaward* (Boston, 1941) and in *A Maritime History of New York* (Garden City, N. Y., 1941).

[6]Samuel Eliot Morison, The Maritime History of Massachusetts (Boston, 192I), 105–107, iii; see also Morison, John Paul Jones, 22–23.

[7]The term is used by Fox, *Adventures*, 18, describing his situation in 1775. In an interesting passage *ibid.*, 17–19, he sees in the movement for independence a cause of a general "spirit of insubordination" among American youth at the time. For another runaway, see Bushnell, *Adventures of Hawkins*, 10, 60–61.

[8]See *N.-Y. Gaz.; Weekly Post-Boy*, Sept. 3, Dec. 10, 1759, Oct. 14, Dec. 16, 1762, July 2I, Oct. 6, Nov. 3, 1763, Mar. 29, May 10, 24, July 19, Sept. 6, 20, 1764, Apr. 4, 18, June 27, 1765, June 29, July 6, 1772; *New-York Journal: or the General Advertiser*, May 13, 1773. For a Negro seaman see log of *Hunter*, Sept. 8, 1758, Adm. 51/465. Some Negro seamen were free and some received their freedom as a reward for service in warships. Benjamin Quarles, *The Negro in the American Revolution* (Chapel Hill, 196i), 84; Robert McColley, *Slavery and Jeffersonian Virginia* (Urbana, 1964), 89.

(continued)

service by crimps.[9] These were the floaters who drifted and slipped their moorings, the suicides, the men whose wives—if they had wives—ran off with other men; the beneficiaries in their wills—when they left wills—were innkeepers.[10] Hitherto, argued a proponent of a United States navy in 1782, the merchant marine had been "the resource of necessity, accident or indulgence."[11]

The merchant marine was a place full of forces beyond the seaman's control: death and disease, storms, and fluctuations in employment. Indeed, the lack of "old salts" in Morison's merchant marine might reflect a sombre irony: was the average seaman young because mobility rapidly brought him to another trade or because seamen

died young?[12] A man in jail, said Dr. Johnson, was at least safe from drowning, and he had more room, better food, and better company. The Quaker John Woolman was one of the few sensitive enough to see that if the "poor bewildered sailors" drank and cursed, the fault lay not so much in themselves as in the harsh environment and the greed of employers. Nor was the road up through the hawse-hole so easy as Morison asserts. That the few succeeded tells us nothing of the many; only the successful left autobiographies.[13] Perhaps the sons of merchants and ship-masters made it, along with the captain's brother-in-law[14] and those who attended schools of navigation,[15] but what of the "poor lads bound apprentice" who

---

But Negroes also served at sea and in related maritime trades as part of their bondage and were sometimes advertised as "brought up from his Infancy to the sea." William Waller Hening, *The Statutes at Large...of Virginia* (Richmond, 1809–1823), XI, 404; *N.-Y. Gaz.; Weekly Post-Boy,* Mar. 26, 1761, July 7, Aug. 18, Nov. 17, 1763; Samuel Hallett in American Loyalists: Transcripts of the Commission of Enquiry into the Losses and Services of the American Loyalists...1783–1790, XIX, 207, New York Public Library; George William Edwards, *New York as an Eighteenth Century Municipality,* 1731–1776 (New York, 1917), 178.

[9]For crimps, see Hutchinson, *Press-Gang,* 48–49. Hohman, *Seamen Ashore,* 273–274, dates the development of crimping in America between 1830 and 1845, but there were crimps in Norfolk in 1767. See Captain Jeremiah Morgan to Governor Francis Fauquier, Sept. 11, 1767, Adm. 1/2116, Library of Congress transcript.

[10]*N.-Y. Gaz.; Weekly Post-Boy,* Sept. 30, 1773; *The King v. Jane the Wife of Thomas Dun,* Indictment for Bigamy, filed Oct. 26, 1763, N. Y. Supreme Court, Pleadings K-41. Although no statistical conclusions are possible, to a surprising extent the beneficiaries in a sample of seamen's wills are not wives but rather brothers and sisters, friends and innkeepers, *Abstracts of Wills,* VI, 111, 226; VII, 12, 38, 148, 397; VIII, 98; XI, 194.

[11]*Independent Chronicle* (Boston), Sept. 5, 1782.

[12]For some reflections on mortality in the merchant marine see Ralph Davis, *The Rise of the English Shipping Industry in the Seventeenth and Eighteenth Centuries* (London, 1962), 156. As late as the 1840's Massachusetts seamen, with an average age at death of 42.47 years, died younger than farmers, clergymen, lawyers, physicians, blacksmiths, carpenters, merchants, and laborers. Only painters, fishermen, manufacturers, mechanics, and printers are listed as having shorter lives in Lemuel Shattuck *et al., Report of the Sanitary Commission of Massachusetts, 1850* (Cambridge, Mass., 1948), 87. For employment see *N. Y. Journal or Gen. Adv.,* Oct. 5, 1775; Thomas Paine, *The Complete Writings,* ed. Philip S. Foner (New York, 1945), I, 33; in addition, a kind of unemployment is built into the profession; a seaman ashore is generally unemployed. See Hohman, *Seamen Ashore,* 209.

[13]Quoted in Davis, *Rise of English Shipping,* 154; John Woolman, *The Journal of John Woolman and a Plea for the Poor* (New York, 1961), 206, 192–193, 196. For comments on elitism in the writings of Morison and of other historians of early America, see Jesse Lemisch, "The American Revolution Seen from the Bottom Up," in Barton J. Bernstein, ed., *Towards a New Past: Dissenting Essays in American History* (New York, 1968), 3–45.

[14]Barney, ed., *Memoir,* 10. For the relative prospects of the sons of merchants and masters as opposed to others in the English merchant marine, see Davis, *Rise of English Shipping,* 117.

[15]For such schools see Boston Registry Department, Records Relating to the Early History of Boston (Boston, 1876–1909), XIII, 2, 204; Carl Bridenbaugh, *Cities in Revolt* (New York, 1955), 377.

troubled Woolman, those whose wages went to their masters? What of the seamen in Morison's own Boston who died too poor to pay taxes and who were a part of what James Henretta has called "the bottom" of Boston society?[16]

Admiralty law treated seamen in a special way, as "wards." Carl Ubbelohde says that seamen favored the colonial Vice Admiralty Courts as "particular tribunals in case of trouble," and Charles M. Andrews and Richard B. Morris agreed that these courts were "guardians of the rights of the seamen." The benefits of being classified as a "ward" are dubious, but, regardless of the quality of treatment which admiralty law accorded to seamen, it certainly does not follow that, all in all, the colonial seaman was well treated by the law. Indeed, if we broaden our scope to include colonial law generally, we find an extraordinarily harsh collection of laws, all justifying Olmsted's later claim that American seamen "are more wretched, and are governed more by threats of force than any other civilized laborers of the world."[17] There are laws providing for the whipping of disobedient seamen and in one case for their punishment as "seditious"; laws prohibiting seamen in port from leaving their vessels after sundown and from travelling on land without certificates of discharge from their last job; laws empowering "every free white person" to catch runaway seamen.[18]

These harsh or at best paternalistic laws[19] add up to a structure whose purpose is to assure a ready supply of cheap, docile labor.[20] Obedience, both at sea and ashore, is the keystone.[21] Charles Beard at his most rigidly mechanistic would doubtless have found the Constitution merely mild stuff alongside this blatantly one-sided class legislation. Today's historians of the classless society would do well to examine the preambles of these laws, written in a more candid age, by

---

[16]Woolman, *Journal*, 195; *Bethune v. Warner*, May 27, 1724, Admiralty Court, Boston, Minute Book II (1718–1726), 177, Office of Clerk, Supreme Judicial Court, Suffolk County, Mass.; Boston Reg. Dept., *Records of Boston*, XIV, 88–89, 94–95; Henretta, "Economic Development," 85; see also Jackson T. Main, *The Social Structure of Revolutionary America* (Princeton, 1965), 74.

[17]Carl Ubbelohde, *The Vice-Admiralty Courts and the American Revolution* (Chapel Hill, 1960), 20, 159–160; Charles M. Andrews, introduction to Dorothy S. Towle, ed., *The Records of the Vice Admiralty Court of Rhode Island*, 1716–1752 (Washington, 1936), 60; Richard B. Morris, *Government and Labor in Early America* (New York, 1946), 232, 256; Olmsted, *Journey*, 287. Ubbelohde, Morris, and Andrews do not contend that the seaman was well treated by the law in an overall sense. Ubbelohde and Morris show that the seaman was better treated in Vice Admiralty Courts than in courts of common law; but when the focus moves to colonial legislation the hostility of the law emerges as the central fact for the seaman.

[18]Hening, *Statutes of Virginia*, IV, 107–108; VI, 26; E. B. O'Callaghan, ed., *Laws and Ordinances of New Netherland*, 1638–1674 (Albany, 1868), 11–12. This law also prevented landsmen from going aboard vessels without authorization from the director of the West India Company. On June 13, 1647, two seamen convicted of tearing down a copy of this law attached to their vessel's mainmast were sentenced to be chained to a wheelbarrow and employed at hard labor on bread and water for three months. I. N. P. Stokes, *The Iconography of Manhattan Island, 1498–1909* (New York, 1915–1928), IV, 87. Thomas Cooper, ed., *The Statutes at Large of South Carolina* (Columbia, 1836–1840), III, 736.

[19]Eugene T. Jackman, "Efforts Made Before 1825 to Ameliorate the Lot of the American Seaman: With Emphasis on his Moral Regeneration," *American Neptune*, XXIV (1964), 109, describes legislation for seamen after the Revolution as "paternalistic." As late as 1897 the Supreme Court declared that "seamen are treated by Congress, as well as by the Parliament of Great Britain, as deficient in that full and intelligent responsibility for their acts which is accredited to ordinary adults." Hohman, *Seamen Ashore*, 214.

[20]Morris, *Government and Labor*, 230, agrees with this statement in a somewhat more limited form.

[21]See Deposition of Commander Arthur Tough [1742], Gertrude MacKinney, ed., *Pennsylvania Archives*, 8th Ser. (Harrisburg, 1931–1935), IV, 2993.

legislatures for which, even by Robert Brown's evidence, most seamen could not vote.[22]

Thus if we think of Jack Tar as jolly, childlike, irresponsible, and in many ways surprisingly like the Negro stereotype, it is because he was treated so much like a child, a servant, and a slave. What the employer saw as the necessities of an authoritarian profession were written into law and culture: the society that wanted Jack dependent made him that way and then concluded that that was the way he really was.[23]

II

Constantly plagued by short complements, the Royal Navy attempted to solve its manning problems in America, as in England, by impressment.[24] Neil Stout has recently attributed these shortages to "death, illness, crime, and desertion" which were in turn caused largely by rum and by the deliberate enticements of American merchants.[25] Rum and inveiglement certainly took a high toll, but to focus on these two causes of shortages

---

[22]Robert E. Brown, *Middle-Class Democracy and the Revolution in Massachusetts, 1691–1780* (Ithaca, 1955), 27–30, acknowledges that the "city proletariat" constituted "the largest disfranchised group" and strongly implies that itinerant sea-men could not vote. Even so, Brown has stated the case too optimistically. By including propertied captains under the ambiguous label "mariner," he has disguised the fact, legible in his own evidence, that the "mariners" who could vote were captains and the common seamen could not. See John Cary, "Statistical Method and the Brown Thesis on Colonial Democracy, With a Rebuttal by Robert E. Brown," *Wm. and Mary Qtly.*, 3d Ser., XX (1963), 257. For Brown's acknowledgement of the error see *ibid.*, 272. Arthur M. Schlesinger, *The Colonial Merchants and the American Revolution, 1763–1776* (New York, 1918), 28, includes seamen in a list of those who were "for the most part, unenfranchised." For an assertion that "sailors" could vote based on evidence that *masters* could compare Jacob R. Marcus, *Early American Jewry* (Philadelphia, 1953), II, 231, and B. R. Carroll, ed., *Historical Collections of South Carolina* (New York, 1836), II, 44X.

[23]For examples of the similarity between life at sea and life on the plantation compare Morris, *Government and Labor*, 230, 247, 256, 262, 274, and McColley, *Slavery and Jeffersonian Virginia*, 103. For Frederick Olmsted's comments on the similarity, based on his own experience at sea in 1843–1844, see *The Cotton Kingdom*, ed. Arthur M. Schlesinger (New York, 1953), 453. For the image of the seaman in literature see Harold F. Watson, *The Sailor in English Fiction and Drama, 1550–1880* (New York, 1931), 159–160, and passim.

[24]For shortages which led to impressment see, for example, Capt. Thos. Miles to Admiralty, Jan. 31, 1705/6, Adm. 1/2093; Lord Cornbury to Lords of Trade, Oct. 3, 1706, E. B. O'Callaghan, ed., *Documents Relative to the Colonial History of the State of New York* (Albany, 1853–1887), IV, 1183–1185; Captain A. Forrest to Lt. Gov. Spencer Phips, Oct. 26, 1745, Adm. 1/1782. For a detailed record of such shortages see items headed "The State and Condition of His Majesty's Ships and Sloops" appearing frequently, scattered throughout Admirals' Dispatches, Adm. 1/480–486. For impressment in the colonies see Neil R. Stout, "Manning the Royal Navy in North America, 1763–1775," *American Neptune*, XXIII (1963), 174–185, and Neil R. Stout, The Royal Navy in American Waters, 1760–1775 (unpubl. Ph.D. diss., University of Wisconsin, 1962), 359–395; R. Pares, "The Manning of the Navy in the West Indies, 1702–63," Royal Historical Society, *Transactions*, 4th Ser., XX (1937), 31–60; Dora Mae Clark, "The Impressment of Seamen in the American Colonies," in *Essays in Colonial History Presented to Charles McLean Andrews by his Students* (New Haven, 1931), 198–224; Jesse Lemisch, Jack Tar vs. John Bull: The Role of New York's Seamen in precipitating the Revolution (unpubl. Ph.D. diss., Yale University, 1962), 12–51. Two useful accounts primarily dealing with impressment in England may be found in Hutchinson, *Press-Gang*, passim, and Daniel A. Baugh, *British Naval Administration in the Age of Walpole* (Princeton, 1965), 147–240.

[25]Stout, "Manning the Royal Navy," 176–177, suggests the possibility of other causes when he notes that desertion was high "whatever the causes," but he mentions no cause other than rum and inveiglement. The Admiralty made the seamen's "natural Levity" another possible reason for desertion. Admiralty to Gov. Thomas on Impressments, 1743, *Pennsylvania Archives*, 1st Ser. (Philadelphia, 1852–1856), I, 639; see also *Massachusetts Historical Society, Journals of the House of Representatives of Massachusetts* (Boston, 1919–), XX, 84, 98; Colvill to Admiralty, Aug. 8, 1765, Adm. 1/482; Pares, "Manning the Navy," 31, 33–34.

is unfairly to shift the blame for impressment onto its victims. The navy itself caused shortages. Impressment, said Thomas Hutchinson, caused desertion, rather than the other way around.[26] Jack Tar had good reasons for avoiding the navy. It would, a young Virginian was warned, "cut him and staple him and use him like a Negro, or rather, like a dog"; James Otis grieved at the loss of the "flower" of Massachusetts's youth "by ten thousands" to a service which treated them little better than "hewers of wood and drawers of water." Discipline was harsh and sometimes irrational, and punishments were cruel.[27] Water poured into sailors' beds, they went mad, and died of fevers and scurvy.[28] Sickness, Benjamin Franklin noted, was more common in the navy than in the merchant service and more frequently fatal.[29] In a fruitless attempt to prevent desertion, wages were withheld and men shunted about from ship to ship without being paid.[30] But the accumulation of even three or four years' back wages could not keep a man from running.[31] And why should it have? Privateering paid better in wartime, and wages were higher in the merchant service; even laborers ashore were better paid.[32]

Impressment angered and frightened the seamen, but it pervaded and disrupted all society, giving other classes and groups cause to share a common grievance with the press-gang's more direct victims: just about everyone had a relative

[26]Hutchinson to Richard Jackson, June 16, 1768, G. G. Wolkins, "The Seizure of John Hancock's Sloop 'Liberty,' " *Massachusetts Historical Society, Proceedings*, LV (Boston, 1923), 283.

[27]Freeman, Washington, I, x99; James Otis, *The Rights of the British Colonies Asserted and Proved* (Boston, 1764) in Bernard Bailyn, ed., *Pamphlets of the American Revolution, 1750–1776* (Cambridge, Mass., 1965), I, 464. Flogging was universal and men received as many as 600 and 700 lashes. Colvill to Admiralty, Nov. 12, 1765, Adm. 1/482. For obscenity the tongue was scraped with hoop-iron. There were punishments for smiling in the presence of an officer. One captain put his sailors' heads in bags for trivial offenses. Hutchinson, *Press-Gang*, 31–36. And, of course, the captain might go mad, as did Captain Robert Bond of *Gibraltar*. Admiral Gambier to Admiralty, Oct. 17, 1771, Adm. 1/483, log of *Gibraltar*, Feb. 10, 14, 1771, Adm. 51/394.

[28]Log of *Arethusa*, Dec. 28, 1771, Adm. 51/59; Petition of Jeremiah Raven, [fall 1756], Letters as to Admission of Pensioners to Greenwich Hospital, 1756–1770, Adm. 65/81, an excellent source for the discovery of the effects of service in the navy on health. See also the items headed "Weekly Account of Sick and Wounded Seamen" in Admirals' Dispatches, for example, Admiral Gambier to Admiralty, May 6, June 10, July 20, 27, 1771, Adm. 1/483; Nov. 9, 1771, Aug. 29, 1772, Adm. 1/484.

[29]Remarks on Judge Foster's Argument in Favor of…Impressing Seamen, Jared Sparks, ed., *The Works of Benjamin Franklin*, II (Boston, 1844), 333. Sparks gives this no date; John Bigelow, ed., *The Complete Works of Benjamin Franklin* (New York, 1887–1888), IV, 70, dates it 1767; Helen C. Boatfield of the Papers of Benjamin Franklin, Yale University, dates it post-1776.

[30]Pares, "Manning the Navy," 31–38; Roland G. Usher, Jr., "Royal Navy Impressment during the American Revolution," *Mississippi Valley Historical Review*, XXXVII (1950–1951), 686. At the time of the Mutiny at the Nore the crew of one ship had not been paid in 15 years, Hutchinson, Press-Gang, 44.

[31]Mr. William Polhampton to Lords of Trade, Mar. 6, 1711, O'Callaghan, ed., Docs. Rel. Col. Hist. N. Y., V, 194. A seaman who deserted his ship would leave an "R"—for "run"—written against his name in the ship's book. See Hutchinson, *Press- Gang*, 151, for a song which urges seamen to flee the press-gang and "leave 'em an R in pawn!"

[32]Peter Warren to Admiralty, Sept. 8, 1744, Adm. 1/2654; Mr. William Polhampton to Lords of Trade, Mar. 6, 1711, O'Callaghan, ed., *Docs. Rel. Col. Hist. N. Y., V*, 194; Admiralty to Thomas, 1743, *PA. Arch.*, 1st Ser., I, 638–639; Morris, *Government and Labor*, 247–248. The navy's most imaginative response to the problem was sporadic and abortive attempts to limit the wages given to merchant sea-men, but the inviting differential remained. When the navy offered bounties for enlistment, this merely served to induce additional desertions by men who could pick up a month's pay simply by signing up. Pares, "Manning the Navy," 33–34; Hutchinson, Press-Gang, 22, 48–49; Remarks on Judge Foster's Argument, Sparks, ed., *Works of Franklin*, II, 333; *N.-Y. Gaz.; Weekly Post-Boy*, Mar. 31, Apr. 21, 1755, Mar. 11, 1771.

at sea.[33] Whole cities were crippled. A night-time operation in New York in 1757 took in eight hundred men, the equivalent of more than one-quarter of the city's adult male population.[34] Impressment and the attendant shortage of men may have been a critical factor in the stagnancy of "the once cherished now depressed, once flourishing now sinking Town of Boston."[35] H.M.S. *Shirley*'s log lists at least ninety-two men pressed off Boston in five months of 1745–1746; *Gramont* received seventy-three pressed men in New York in three days in 1758; *Arethusa* took thirty-one in two days off Virginia in 1771.[36] Binges such as these left the communities where they occurred

seriously harmed. Preachers' congregations took flight, and merchants complained loudly about the "many Thousands of Pounds of Damage."[37] "Kiss my arse, you dog," shouted the captain as he made off with their men, leaving vessels with their fires still burning, unmanned, finally to be wrecked.[38]

Boston was especially hard-hit by impressment in the 1740's, with frequent incidents throughout the decade and major explosions in 1745 and 1747. Again and again the town meeting and the House of Representatives protested, drumming away at the same themes: impressment was harmful to maritime commerce and to the economic life of the city in general and illegal if

---

[33]At least in Pennsylvania and New Jersey, according to the *Independent Chronicle* (Boston), Sept. 5, 1782.

[34]Three thousand men participated in this massive operation. Three or four hundred of those seized were released. Lord Loudoun to Pitt, May 30, 1757, Gertrude S. Kimball, ed., *Correspondence of William Pitt* (New York, 1906), I, 69; Paul L. Ford, ed., *The Journals of Hugh Gaine, Printer* (New York, 1902), II, 8–9; May 20, 1757, *The Montresor Journals* (N.-Y. Hist. Soc., *Coll.*, XIV [New York, 1882]), 150–151; Benjamin Cutter, *History of the Cutter Family of New England* (Boston, 1870), 67; Evarts B. Greene and Virginia D. Harrington, *American Population before the Federal Census of 1790* (New York, 1932), 101, 1756 census.

[35]Boston is so described in a petition of the town meeting to the House of Representatives, Mar. II, 1745/6, Mass. Hist. Soc., *Mass. House Journals*, XXII, 204. This petition is but one of many attributing the depletion of Boston's population in part to impressment. For a table indicating a downward trend in Boston's population after 1743 see Stuart Bruchey, ed., *The Colonial Merchant: Sources and Readings* (New York, 1966), II. I am indebted to Joel Shufro, a graduate student at the University of Chicago, for the suggestion of a connection between impressment and the decline of Boston.

[36]Log of Shirley, Dec. 25, 1745–May 17, 1746, Adm. 51/4341; log of *Gramont*, Apr. 25–27, 1758, Adm. 51/413; log of *Arethusa*, Mar. 19–20, 1771, Adm. 51/59. Shirley's haul was not mentioned in the *Boston Evening Post* or in the records of any American governmental body. Here is but one instance in which the serious grievance of 92 Americans has previously gone unnoticed. Such grievances are none—the less real and play a causal role despite their invisibility to historians. On the other hand, overdependence on British sources is apt to be extremely misleading. Either because of sloppiness or because of the clouded legality of impressment, official records seem more often to ignore the practice or to distort it than to complement information from American sources. Admiral Charles Hardy neglected to mention the massive press in New York in 1757 in his correspondence with the Admiralty. See May–June 1757, Adm. 1/481. The absence of impressment in Triton's Prize's log in 1706, Adm. 50/1014, is contradicted in Lord Cornbury to Lords of Trade, Oct. 3, 1706, O'Callaghan, ed., *Docs. Rel. Col. Hist. N. Y.*, IV, 1183–1185. Sometimes logs show what seems to be purposeful distortion: Diana, whose log, Apr. 15, 1758, Adm. 51/4162, reveals only that she "saluted with 9 Guns" *Prince of Orange* privateer, in fact pressed her hands, *Montresor Journal*, 152. In another instance St. John "received on board a Boat Load of Ballast," log, July I6, 1764, Adm. 51/3961, which seems in fact to have consisted of hogs, sheep, and poultry stolen from the people of Martha's Vineyard, *Newport Mercury*, July 23, 1764. See below n. 69.

[37]*Boston Evening Post*, Sept. 3, 1739, July 6, 1741.

[38]Deposition of Nathaniel Holmes, July 18, 1702, Deposition of John Gullison, July 17, 1702, Lt. Gov. Thomas Povey to Lords Commissioners for Trade and Plantations, July 20, 1702, Colonial Office Group, Class 5, Piece 862, Public Record Office. Hereafter cited as C.O. 5/862; *Boston Evening Post*, Dec. 14, 1747; *N.-Y. Gaz.; Weekly Post-Boy*, Jan. I4, 1771.

not properly authorized.[39] In all this the seaman himself becomes all but invisible. The attitude towards him in the protests is at best neutral and often sharply antagonistic. In 1747 the House of Representatives condemned the violent response of hundreds of seamen to a large-scale press as "a tumultuous riotous assembling of armed Seamen, Servants, Negroes, and others...tending to the Destruction of all Government and Order." While acknowledging that the people had reason to protest, the House chose to level *its* protest against "the most audacious Insult" to the governor, Council, and House. And the town meeting, that stronghold of democracy, offered its support to those who took "orderly" steps while expressing its "Abhorence of such Illegal Criminal Proceedings" as those undertaken by the seamen "and other persons of mean and Vile Condition.[40]

Protests such as these reflect at the same time both unity and division in colonial society. All kinds of Americans—both merchants and seamen—opposed impressment, but the town meeting and the House spoke for the merchant, not the seaman. They opposed impressment not for its effect on the seaman but for its effect on commerce. Thus their protests express antagonism to British policy at the same time that they express class division. These two themes continue and develop in American opposition to impressment in the three decades between the Knowles Riots of 1747 and the Declaration of Independence.

From the beginning, impressment's most direct victims—the seamen—were its most active opponents. Bernard Bailyn's contention that "not a single murder resulted from the activities of the Revolutionary mobs in America" does not hold up if extended to cover resistance to impressment; there were murders on both sides. Perhaps the great bulk of incidents of this sort must remain forever invisible to the historian, for they often took place out of sight of friendly observers, and the only witness, the navy, kept records which are demonstrably biased and faulty, omitting the taking of thousands of men.[41] But even the visible records provide a great deal of information. This much we know without doubt: seamen did not go peacefully. Their violence was purposeful, and sometimes they were articulate. "I know who you are," said one, as reported by John Adams and supported by Thomas Hutchinson. "You are the lieutenant of a man-of-war, come with a pressgang to deprive me of my liberty. You have no right to impress me. I have retreated from you as far as

---

[39]See, for example, Mass. Hist. Soc., *Mass. House Journals*, XVIII, 202; XX, 98–99; XXII, 76–77, 204–205.

[40]*Ibid.*, XXIV, 212; Boston Reg. Dept., *Records of Boston*, XIV, I27. Bridenbaugh, *Cities in Revolt*, 117, sees the law of 1751 for suppressing riots as in part a response to the Knowles Riots; he calls the law "brutal" even for its own day and a "triumph for the reactionaries."

[41]Bailyn, ed., *Pamphlets*, I, 58L. Six Englishmen of varying ranks were killed while pressing in the 1760's. In addition to the incidents just discussed in which a lieutenant of marines was murdered on June 8, 1764, while pressing at New York and in which John Adams's clients-to-be, accused of murdering a lieutenant off Cape Ann Apr. 22, 1769, got off with justifiable homicide in self-defense, four sailors were shot to death at New York, Aug. 18, 1760. Cadwallader Colden to Lords of Trade, Aug. 30, 1760, O'Callaghan, ed., *Docs. Rel. Col. Hist. N. Y.*, VII, 446; *The King v. Osborn Greatrakes* and the *King v. Josiah Moore*, Oct. 24, 28, 30, Nov. II-17, 1760, New York Supreme Court Minute Book (1756–1761), 1–16, 200, 209, 215; *The King v. Ship Sampson*, Examination of Hugh Mode, Pilot, taken Aug. 19, 1760, N. Y. Supreme Court, Pleadings K-304; Capt. J. Hale to Admiralty, Aug. 28, 1760, Adm. 0/1895; Weyman's *N.-Y. Gaz.*, Aug. 25, 1760; Dawson, *Sons of Liberty*, 51–54. Governor Cadwallader Colden called the last incident murder, but the jury refused to indict. For some instances of Americans killed while resisting impressment see deposition of William Thwing, Nathaniel Vaill, and Thomas Hals, July 15, 1702, C.O. 5/862; Governor Hunter to Secretary St. John, Sept. 12, 1711, O'Callaghan, ed., *Docs. Rel. Col. Hist. N. Y.*, V, 254–255 (conviction of murder); Bridenbaugh, *Cities in Revolt*, 114–115; *N.-Y. Gaz.; Weekly Post-Boy*, Aug. 7, 1760. There is every reason to suppose that this list is partial. See above n. 57.

I can. I can go no farther. I and my companions are determined to stand upon our defence. Stand off."[42] (It was difficult for Englishmen to fail to see impressments in such terms—even a sailor *doing* the pressing could feel shame over "fighting with honest sailors, to deprive them of their liberty.")[43]

Ashore, seamen and others demonstrated their opposition to impressment with the only weapon which the unrepresentative politics of the day offered them—riot. In Boston several thousand people responded to a nighttime impressment sweep of the harbor and docks with three days of rioting beginning in the early hours of November 17, 1747. Thomas Hutchinson reported that "the lower class were beyond measure enraged." Negroes, servants, and hundreds of seamen seized a naval lieutenant, assaulted a sheriff and put his deputy in the stocks, surrounded the governor's house, and stormed the Town House where the General Court was sitting. The rioters demanded the seizure of the impressing officers, the release of the men they had pressed, and execution of a death sentence which had been levied against a member of an earlier press-gang who had been convicted of murder. When the governor fled to Castle William—some called it "abdication"—Commodore Knowles threatened to put down what he called "arrant rebellion" by bombarding the town. The governor, who, for his part, thought the rioting a secret plot of the upper class, was happily surprised when the town meeting expressed its "Abhorence" of the seamen's riot.[44]

After the French and Indian War press riots increased in frequency. Armed mobs of whites and Negroes repeatedly manhandled captains, officers, and crews, threatened their lives, and held them hostage for the men they pressed. Mobs fired at pressing vessels and tried to board them; they threatened to burn one, and they regularly dragged ships' boats to the center of town for ceremonial bonfires.

Long before 1765 Americans had developed beliefs about impressment, and they had expressed those beliefs in words and deeds. Impressment was bad for trade and it was illegal. As such, it was, in the words of the Massachusetts House in 1720, "a great Breach on the Rights of His Majesties Subjects." In 1747 it was a violation of "the common Liberty of the Subject," and in 1754 "inconsistent with Civil Liberty, and the Natural Rights of Mankind."[45] Some felt in 1757 that it was even "abhorrent to the English Constitution."[46] In fact, the claim that impressment was unconstitutional was wrong. (Even *Magna Charta* was no protection. *Nullus liber homo capiatur* did not apply to seamen.)[47] Instead impressment indicated to Benjamin Franklin "that the constitution is yet imperfect, since in so general a case it doth not secure liberty, but destroys it." "If impressing seamen is of right by common law in Britain," he also

---

[42]"Inadmissable Principles" [1809], Adams, ed., *Works of Adams,* IX, 318, quotes Michael Corbet, commenting that Corbet displayed "the cool intrepidity of a Nelson, reasoned, remonstrated, and laid down the law with the precision of a Mansfield." Hutchinson, *History of Massachusetts-Bay,* ed. Mayo, III, 167n, notes that Corbet and his companions "swore they would die before they would be taken, and that they preferred death to slavery."

[43]"Inadmissable Principles" [1809], Adams, ed., *Works of Adams,* IX, 317–318.

[44]Hutchinson, *History of Massachusetts-Bay,ed.* Mayo, II, 330–331, 333; Mass. Hist. Soc., *Mass. House Journals,* XXIV, 212; Bridenbaugh, *Cities in Revolt,* 115–117; Boston Reg. Dept., *Records of Boston,* XIV, 127; William Shirley to Lords of Trade, Dec. 1, 1747, Lincoln, ed., *Correspondence of Shirley,* I, 412–419, is the best single account. Shirley says that only the officers responded to his call for the militia.

[45]Mass. Hist. Soc., *Mass. House Journals,* 11, 300–301; Freeman, Washington, I, 199; N.Y. Gaz.; *Weekly Post-Boy,* Aug. 12, 1754.

[46]Mass. Hist. Soc., *Mass. House Journals,* XXXIII, Pt. ii, 434.

[47]Hutchinson, *Press-Gang,* 5–7.

remarked, "slavery is then of right by common law there; there being no slavery worse than that sailors are subjected to."[48]

For Franklin, impressment was a symptom of injustice built into the British Constitution. In *Common Sense* Tom Paine saw in impressment a reason for rejecting monarchy. In the Declaration of Independence Thomas Jefferson included impressment among the "Oppressions" of George III; later he likened the practice to the capture of Africans for slavery. Both "reduced [the victim] to…bondage by force, in flagrant violation of his own consent, and of his natural right in his own person."[49]

Despite all this, and all that went before, we have thought little of impressment as an element in explaining the conduct of the common man in the American Revolution.[50] Contemporaries knew better. John Adams felt that a tactical mistake by Thomas Hutchinson on the question of impressment in 1769 would have "accelerated the revolution…. It would have spread a wider flame than Otis's ever did, or could have done."[51]

III

The seamen's conduct in the 1760's and 1770's makes more sense in the light of previous and continued impressment. What may have seemed irrational violence can now be seen as purposeful and radical. The pattern of rioting as political expression, established as a response to impressment, was now adapted and broadened as a response to the Stamp Act. In New York General Gage described the "insurrection" of October 31, 1765, and following as "composed of great numbers of Sailors." The seamen, he said, were "the only People who may be properly Stiled Mob," and estimates indicate that between a fifth and a fourth of New York's rioters were seamen. The disturbances began among the seamen—especially former privateersmen—on October 31. On November 1 they had marched, led primarily by their former captains; later they rioted, led by no one but themselves. Why? Because they had been duped by merchants, or, if not by merchants, then certainly by lawyers. So British officials believed—aroused by these men who meant to use

---

[48]Sparks, ed., *Works of Franklin*, II, 338, 334. For opposition to impressment on the part of the Genevan democrat, Jean Louis De Lolme, and by the British radical John Wilkes, see Robert R. Palmer, *The Age of the Democratic Revolution* (Princeton, 1959), I48. *N.-Y. Gaz.; Weekly Post-Boy*, Dec. 3I, 1770; *Annual Register…for 1771* (London, 1772), 67, 68, 70–71; R. W. Postgate, *That Devil Wilkes* (New York, 1929), 182; Percy Fitzgerald, *The Life and Times of John Wilkes* (London, 1888), II, 120.

[49]Paine, *Writings*, ed. Foner, I, 11. For later attacks on impressment by Paine see *ibid.,* I, 449, II, 476. The complaint in the Declaration of Independence alludes to impressment after the outbreak of fighting: "He has constrained our fellow Citizens taken Captive on the high Seas to bear Arms against their Country, to become the executioners of their friends and Brethren, or to fall themselves by their Hands." Carl L. Becker, *The Declaration of Independence* (New York, 1958), 190, 156, 166. Thomas Jefferson to Dr. Thomas Cooper, Sept. 10, 1814, Andrew A. Lipscomb and Albert Ellery Bergh, eds., *The Writings of Thomas Jefferson*, XIV (Washington, 1907), 183.

[50]James Fulton Zimmerman, *Impressment of American Seamen* (New York, 1925), esp. 11–17, treats the practice as almost non-existent before the Revolution, giving the pre-revolutionary phenomenon only the briefest consideration, and concluding, on the basis of speculative evidence, that impressment was rare in the colonies. The author does not understand the Sixth of Anne and thinks it was repealed in 1769. Clark, "Impressment of Seamen," in *Essays to Andrews*, 202; Paine, *Ships and Sailors of Salem*, 65; George Athan Billias, *General John Glover and his Marblehead Mariners* (New York, 1960), 31; Bridenbaugh, *Cities in Revolt*, 114–117, 308–310; Bernhard Knollenberg, *Origin of the American Revolution: 1759–1766* (New York, 1961), 12, 179–181, all see impressment as contributing in some way to the revolutionary spirit.

[51]Adams, ed., *Works of Adams*, II, 226n. Neil Stout, "Manning the Royal Navy," 182–184, suggests that impressment did not become a "great issue" of the American Revolution because American "radicals" did not *make* an issue of it and especially because of the failure of John Adams's attempt to make a "*cause celebre*" in 1769. Stout's approach sides with the navy and minimizes the reality of impressment as a grievance. Its implication is that the seaman had in fact no genuine grievance and that he acted in response to manipulation.

them, the seamen themselves had nothing more than plunder on their minds. In fact, at that point in New York's rioting when the leaders lost control, the seamen, who were then in the center of town, in an area rich for plunder, chose instead to march in an orderly and disciplined way clear across town to do violence to the home and possessions of an English major whose provocative conduct had made him the obvious political enemy. Thus the "rioting" was actually very discriminating.[52]

Seamen and non-seamen alike joined to oppose the Stamp Act for many reasons,[53] but the seamen had two special grievances: impressment and the effect of England's new attitude toward colonial trade. To those discharged by the navy at the end of the war and others thrown out of work by the death of privateering were added perhaps twenty thousand more seamen and fishermen who were thought to be the direct victims of the post-1763 trade regulations.[54] This problem came to the fore in the weeks following November 1, 1765, when the Stamp Act went into effect. The strategy of opposition chosen by the colonial leadership

---

[52]General Gage to Secretary Conway, Nov. 4, Dec. 21, 1765, Clarence Edwin Carter, ed., *The Correspondence of General Thomas Gage…1763–1775* (New Haven, 1931), I, 70–71, 79; *N.-Y. Gaz.; Weekly Post-Boy*, Nov. 7, 1765, estimates that there were four to five hundred seamen in the mob; Nov. 1, 7, 1765, *Montresor Journal*, 336, 339, estimates the total mob at "about 2000" and is the only source describing the participation of a professional group other than seamen, estimating 300 carpenters; R. R. Livingston to General Monckton, Nov. 8, 1765, Chalmers Manuscripts, IV, New York Public Library, for a note signed "Sons of Neptune"; Lieutenant-Governor Colden to Secretary Conway, Nov. 5, 9, 1765, O'Callaghan, ed., *Docs. Rel. Col. Hist. N. Y.*, VII, 771–774; *New York Mercury*, Nov. 4, 1765. For additional information on the leadership of privateer captains, especially Isaac Sears, see William Gordon, *History of the Rise, Progress, and Establishment of the United States of America* (London, 1788), I, 185–186. The navy continued to press during the crisis. See log of *Guarland*, Apr. 22, 1766, Adm. 51/386; Apr. 21, 1766, *Montresor Journal*, 361. Impressment also limited the navy's activities against the rioting. "As most of our men are imprest," wrote a captain in answer to a governor's re-quest for men to put down a mob, "there is a great risque of their deserting." Marines were needed as sentries to keep them from deserting. Archibald Kennedy to Cadwallader Colden, Nov. 1, 1765, *The Letters and Papers of Cadwallader Colden* (N.-Y. Hist. Soc., *Coll.*, L-LVI [New York, 1918–1923]), VII, 85–86.

[53]For a fuller account of the seamen's opposition to the Stamp Act see Lemisch, "Jack Tar vs. John Bull," 76–I28.

[54]*N.-Y. Gaz.; Weekly Post-Boy*, May 19, 1763; "Essay on the trade of the Northern Colonies," *ibid.*, Feb. 9, 1764. Even admirals were worried about the prospects of postwar unemployment, Colvill to Admiralty, Nov. 9, 1762, Adm. 1/482. During the French and Indian War 18,000 American seamen had served in the Royal Navy, *Annual Register…for 1778* (London, 1779), 201, and a large additional number had been privateersmen. Fifteen to twenty thousand had sailed in 224 privateers out of New York alone, 5670 of them in 1759, Fish, *New York Privateers*, 4, 54–82; Bridenbaugh, *Cities in Revolt*, 62. A New York merchants' petition of Apr. 20, 1764, expressed the fear that seamen thrown out of work by the Sugar Act might drift into foreign merchant fleets, *Journal of the Votes and Proceedings of the General Assembly of the Colony of New York* (New York, 1764–1766), II, 742–743. On the eve of the Revolution maritime commerce employed approximately 30,000–35,000 American seamen, Carman, ed., American Husbandry, 495–496; John Adams to the President of Congress, June 16, 1780, Francis Wharton, ed., *The Revolutionary Diplomatic Correspondence of the United States* (Washington, 1889), III, 789. I am presently assembling data which will allow more detailed statements on various demographic matters involving seamen, such as their numbers, comparisons with other occupations, their origins and permanence. For some further quantitative information on seamen in various colonial ports, see in addition to the sources cited immediately above, Evarts B. Greene and Richard B. Morris, *A Guide to the Principal Sources for Early American History (1600–1800) in the City of New York*, 2d ed., rev. (New York, 1953), 265; E. B. O'Callaghan, ed., *The Documentary History of the State of New York*, I (Albany, 1849), 493; Governor Clinton's Report on the Province of New York, May 23, 1749, Report of Governor Tryon on the Province of New York, June 11, 1774, O'Callaghan, ed., *Docs. Rel. Col. Hist. N. Y.*, VI, 511, VIII, 446; Main, *Social Structure*, 38–39; Benjamin W. Labaree, *Patriots and Partisans* (Cambridge, Mass., 1962), 5; John R. Bartlett, ed., *Records of the Colony of Rhode Island and Providence Plantations…* (Providence, 1856–1865), VI, 379.

was to cease all activities which required the use of stamps. Thus maritime trade came to a halt in the cities.[55] Some said that this was a cowardly strategy. If the Americans opposed the Stamp Act, let them go on with business as usual, refusing outright to use the stamps.[56] The leaders' strategy was especially harmful to the seamen, and the latter took the more radical position—otherwise the ships would not sail. And this time the seamen's radicalism triumphed over both colonial leadership and British officials. Within little more than a month the act had been largely nullified. Customs officers were allowing ships to sail without stamps, offering as the reason the fear that the seamen, "who are the people that are most dangerous on these occasions, as their whole dependance for a subsistence is upon Trade," would certainly "commit some terrible Mischief." Philadelphia's customs officers feared that the seamen would soon "compel" them to let ships pass without stamps. Customs officers at New York yielded when they heard that the seamen were about to have a meeting.[57]

Customs officers had worse luck on other days. Seamen battled them throughout the 1760's and 1770's. In October 1769 a Philadelphia customs officer was attacked by a mob of seamen who also tarred, feathered, and nearly drowned a man who had furnished him with information about illegally imported goods. A year later a New Jersey customs officer who approached an incoming vessel in Delaware Bay had his boat boarded by armed seamen who threatened to murder him and came close to doing so.

Many of these animosities flared in the Boston Massacre. What John Adams described as "a motley rabble of saucy boys, negroes and molattoes, Irish teagues and out landish jack tarrs," including twenty or thirty of the latter, armed with clubs and sticks, did battle with the soldiers. Their leader was Crispus Attucks, a mulatto seaman; he was shot to death in front of the Custom House.[58] One of the seamen's reasons for being there has been too little explored. The Massacre grew out of a fight between workers and off-duty soldiers at a ropewalk two days before.[59] That fight, in

---

[55]See, for example, James and Drinker to William Starkey, Oct. 30, 1765, James and Drinker Letterbook; *N.-Y. Gaz.; Weekly Post-Boy*, Dec. 19, 1765.

[56]See, for example, *N.-Y. Gaz.; Weekly Post-Boy*, Nov. 28, Dec. 5, 1765. For a fuller account of this dispute, see Jesse Lemisch, "New York's Petitions and Re-solves of December 1765: Liberals vs. Radicals," New-York Historical Society, *Quarterly*, XLIX (1965), 313–326.

[57]Edmund S. and Helen M. Morgan, *The Stamp Act Crisis* (Chapel Hill, 1953), 162. For a fuller account of the nullification of the Stamp Act, see *ibid.*, 159–179. The seamen's strategy may have been more effective in bringing about repeal than was the strategy of the leaders. Commenting on Parliament's secret de-bates, Lawrence Henry Gipson, "The Great Debate in the Committee of the Whole House of Commons on the Stamp Act, 1766, as Reported by Nathaniel Ryder," *Pennsylvania Magazine of History and Biography*, LXXXVI (1962), 10–41, notes that merchant pressure was only the "ostensible cause" of repeal and that many members were influenced by the violent resistance in America. I am indebted to E. S. Morgan for calling Ryder's notes to my attention.

[58]On the participation of seamen in the Boston Massacre see testimony of Robert Goddard, Oct. 25, 1770; Ebenezer Bridgham, Nov. 27, 1770; James Bailey, Nov. 28, Dec. 4, 1770; James Thompson, Nov. 30, 1770; all in Wroth and Zobel, eds., *Legal Papers of Adams*, III, 57–58, 103–106, 114–115, 115n–120n, 188, 189n, 268–269; also Frederick Kidder, *History of the Boston Massacre*, March 5, 1770 (Albany, 1870), 288. For Adams's description, see Wroth and Zobel, eds., *Legal Papers of Adams,* III, 266. For Attucks see testimony of James Bailey, Nov. 28, 1770, of Patrick Keeton, Nov. 30, 1770, *ibid.*, III, II4–II5, 115n–I20n, 191–192, 262, 268–269; Kidder, Boston Massacre, 29n–30n, 287; Hutchinson, *History of Massachusetts-Bay*, ed. Mayo, III, 196; Boston Herald, Nov. 19, 1890 [sic.]; John Hope Franklin, *From Slavery to Freedom* (New York, 1956), 127.

[59]Lt. Col. W. Dalrymple to Hillsborough, Mar. 13, 1770, C.O 5/759, Pt. 3, Library of Congress photostat; Capt. Thos. Rich to Admiralty, Mar. 11, 1770, Adm. 1/2388; Morris, *Government and Labor*, 190–192.

turn, grew out of the long-standing practice in the British army of allowing off-duty soldiers to take civilian employment. They did so, in Boston and elsewhere, often at wages which undercut those offered to Americans—including unemployed seamen who sought work ashore—by as much as 50 per cent.[60] In hard times this led to intense competition for work, and the Boston Massacre was in part a product of this competition. Less well known is the Battle of Golden Hill, which arose from similar causes and took place in New York six weeks before. In January 1770 a gang of seamen went from house to house and from dock to dock, using clubs to drive away the soldiers employed there and threatening anyone who might rehire them.[61] In the days of rioting which followed and which came to be called the Battle of Golden Hill, the only fatality was a seaman, although many other seamen were wounded in the attempt to take vengeance for the killing.[62] The antipathy between soldiers and seamen was so great, said John Adams, "that they fight as naturally when they meet, as the elephant and Rhinoceros."[63]

Other historians have seen the colonial seamen—and the rest of the lower class—as mindless and manipulated, both before and after 1765.[64] The seeming implication behind this is that the seamen who demonstrated in colonial streets did so as much out of simple vindictiveness or undisciplined violence as out of love of liberty. Certainly such motivation would blend well with the traditional picture of the seaman as rough and ready. For along with the stereotype of Jolly Jack—and in part belying that stereotype—is bold and reckless Jack, the exotic and violent.[65] Jack *was* violent; the conditions of his existence were violent. Was his violence non-political? Sometimes. The mob of seventy to eighty yelling, club-swinging, out-of-town seamen who tried to breakup a Philadelphia election in 1742 had no interest in the election; they had been bought off with money and liquor.[66]

Other violence is not so clear-cut. Edward Thompson has seen the fighting out of significant

---

[60]*The Times,* Broadsides, 1770-2I, New-York Historical Society, New York City; Morris, *Government and Labor,* 190n.

[61]*N.-Y. Gaz.; Weekly Post-Boy,* Feb. 5, 1770, reports on the gang of seamen which went from dock to dock turning out soldiers. *The Times,* N.-Y. Hist. Soc. Broadsides, 1770–21 describes what could only be the same group and adds the threat of vengeance.

[62]*N.-Y. Gaz.; Weekly Post-Boy,* Jan. 22, Feb. 5, 1770; Dawson, *Sons of Liberty,* 177n; William J. Davis, "The Old Bridewell," in Henry B. Dawson, *Reminiscences of the Park and its Vicinity* (New York, 1855), 61. Thomas Hutchinson noted the death of the seaman and believed that the Battle of Golden Hill "encouraged" Boston, thus leading to the Boston Massacre, Hutchinson, *History of Massachusetts- Bay,* ed. Mayo, III, 194.

[63]Wroth and Zobel, eds., *Legal Papers of Adams,* III, 262. See also John Shy, *Toward Lexington* (Princeton, 1965), 309.

[64]For a further discussion see Lemisch, "American Revolution," in Bernstein, ed., *Towards a New Past, passim.* Bailyn, ed., *Pamphlets,* 581, is not entirely clear on the situation *after* 1765. He denies that "Revolutionary mobs" in America were in fact "revolutionary" and questions their "meliorista spirations."

[65]For rough and ready Jack see Watson, *Sailor in English Fiction,* 45, 159–160; Hohman, *Seamen Ashore,* 217.

[66]135 *Pa. Archives,* 8th Ser., IV, 2971, 2987, 2995–2998, 3009; "Extracts from the Gazette, 1742," Labaree *et al.,* eds., *Papers of Benjamin Franklin,* II, 363–364. Yet even these men can be shown to have had some ideas; their shouts, which included attacks on "Broad-brims," "Dutch dogs," and "You damned Quakers,... Enemies to King GEORGE," are similar to those of the European "Church and King" rioters. See Rude, *Crowd in History,* 135–448; E. J. Hobsbawm, *Primitive Rebels* (New York, 1965), 110, 118, 120–123.

social conflict in eighteenth-century England "in terms of Tyburn, the hulks and the Bridewells on the one hand; and crime, riot, and mob action on the other."[67] Crime and violence among eighteenth-century American seamen needs reexamination from such a perspective. Does "mutiny" adequately describe the act of the crew which seized *Black Prince*, renamed it *Liberty*, and chose their course and a new captain by voting? What shall we call the conduct of 150 seamen who demanded higher wages by marching along the streets of Philadelphia with clubs, unrigging vessels, and forcing workmen ashore? If "mutiny" is often the captain's name for what we have come to call a "strike," perhaps we might also detect some significance broader than mere criminality in the seamen's frequent assaults on captains and thefts from them.[68] Is it not in some sense a political act for a seaman to tear off the mast a copy of a law which says that disobedient seamen will be punished as "seditious"?

Impressment meant the loss of freedom, both personal and economic, and, sometimes, the loss of life itself. The seaman who defended himself against impressment felt that he was fighting to defend his "liberty," and he justified his resistance on grounds of "right."[69] It is in the concern for liberty and right that the seaman rises from vindictiveness to a somewhat more complex awareness that certain values larger than himself exist and that he is the victim not only of cruelty and hardship but also, in the light of those values, of injustice. The riots ashore, whether they be against impressment, the Stamp Act, or competition for work express that same sense of injustice. And here, thousands of men took positive and effective steps to demonstrate their opposition to both acts and policies.

Two of England's most exciting historians have immensely broadened our knowledge of past and present by examining phenomena strikingly like the conduct and thought of the seamen in America. These historians have described such manifestations as "sub-political" or "pre-political," and one of them has urged that such movements be "seriously considered not simply as an unconnected series of individual curiosities, as footnotes to history, but as a phenomenon of general importance and considerable weight in modern history."[70] When Jack Tar went to sea in the American Revolution, he fought, as he had for many years before, quite literally, to protect his life, liberty, and property. It might be extravagant to call the seamen's conduct and the sense of injustice which underlay it in any fully developed sense ideological or political; on the other hand, it makes little sense to describe their ideological content as zero. There are many worlds and much of human history in that vast area between ideology and inertness.

---

[67]E. P. Thompson, *The Making of the English Working Class* (New York, 1964), 60.

[68]Deposition of Thomas Austin, Dec. 10, 1769, in Hutchinson to Hillsborough, Dec. 20, 1769, C.O. 5/759, Pt. 2, Library of Congress Transcript; *Pennsylvania Packet* (Philadelphia), Jan. 16, 1779; *Colonial Records of Pennsylvania 1683–1790* (Harrisburg, 1852–1853), XI, 664–665; J. Thomas Scharf and Thompson Westcott, *History of Philadelphia, 1609–1884* (Philadelphia, 1884), I, 403. For some crimes of seamen against masters see *The King v. John Forster*, Indictment for Petty Larceny, filed Oct. 23, 1772, N. Y. Supreme Court, Pleadings K-495; Deposition of Cap. Elder and Examination of John Forster, sworn Oct. 20, 1772, N. Y. Supreme Court, Pleadings K-457; *N.-Y. Gaz.; Weekly Post-Boy*, Feb. 2, 1764.

[69]See above, 390.

[70]Thompson, *Making of the English Working Class*, 55, 59, 78; Hobsbawm, *Primitive Rebels*, 2, 7, 10.

>> Questions for Consideration

1. How does Lemisch clarify the reality of life as a seaman as opposed to stereotypical characterizations? How is this important to his overall thesis on their role in the American Revolution?

2. What specific evidence can you find of Marxist and Progressive influences in this excerpt? In what ways is he self-consciously applying E. P. Thompson's approaches to the topic of the American Revolution?

3. What kinds of evidence does Lemisch use? Why do you think he uses so many reference notes to support his argument?

4. In what ways is Lemisch constructing a "bottom-up" history of the American Revolution? How might this approach reflect Lemisch's own left-wing political values? Contrast this excerpt to Boorstin's: How do their different political values lead them to different approaches and conclusions?

Chapter 7

New Social History

John Hope Franklin (*AP Wide World Photos*).

While only a minority of historians were truly New Leftists, many non-Marxist working-class, female and minority historians, newly admitted to the profession in larger numbers, were especially attracted to the New Left's emphasis on social history. Similar to New Leftists, new social historians were greatly influenced by the social movements of the 1950s and 1960s. Many of these historians participated in the movements. For example, more than forty historians, including John Hope Franklin and William Leuchtenburg, joined Martin Luther King Jr. in his famous Selma March in 1965.[1] These movements advocated equal rights for African Americans and other racial minorities, women, and homosexuals. Among other things, these social groups demanded and gained access to higher education in the 1960s. As a consequence, universities and history programs became much more diverse. Once women and minorities became college students, however, they began demanding reforms to an educational system which clearly reflected the biases of the elite white males who had created and dominated it for two centuries.

---

[1] Peter Charles Hoffer, *Past Imperfect: Facts, Fictions, Fraud—American History from Bancroft and Parkman to Ambrose, Bellesiles, Ellis, and Goodwin* (New York: Public Affairs, 2004), 73.

After much struggle, they created new courses on race and gender. As more women and minorities entered graduate schools, and as more women and minorities were needed to teach the new African American and women's history courses, interest and publications in these fields blossomed in the 1970s. In historiography, new social history reflected these larger social, political, and intellectual trends.

Carr   While many new social historians were inspired by E. P. Thompson's history from the bottom-up, another British historian, E. H. Carr (1892–1982), became just as influential. His *What Is History?* (1961) became standard reading for history students in Europe and the United States in the 1960s and had a tremendous impact on that generation of historians. He argued that the main goal of history was to help us to understand the present and shape the future.[2] American historian Alice Kessler-Harris asserts that Carr's views were extremely appealing to a generation embroiled in the Vietnam War and the civil rights movement. His view that all history is laden with the values and historical context of its authors offended those who believed that objectivity should be the goal of historians, but appealed to those who believed that historians in the past had distorted their findings to justify imperialism, racism, and nationalism.[3] Carr saw long-term social and economic forces as the primary agent of historical causation and change, and he was thus a motivating force in the trend toward socioeconomic histories, which would dominate the historical profession from the 1960s to the 1980s.

In the United States, new social historians exposed the biases of many earlier histories written by elite white males, and like their Progressive predecessors argued that all history was shaped by the perspective of historians. New social historians created an avalanche of new studies of peoples left out of most traditional histories: the illiterate, the poor, women, children, immigrants, and racial and religious minorities. They not only showed how political events affected the masses, but how social and economic trends, and the masses, affected politics. New social history was less explicitly theoretical and more empirical than New Left history, and as a consequence was much more acceptable to the mainstream historical profession. New social history not only resulted in a new focus for the American historical profession, but also encouraged the use of new methods borrowed from the social sciences. The desire to comprehend large-scale social and economic processes led many social historians to turn to the methods used by economists, sociologists, psychologists, anthropologists, geographers, and political scientists. Rooted in positivism and empiricism, social scientific methods helped historians to be more mathematically precise and use more empirical data to support their arguments. Social history consequently became less focused on narrative, and more analytical and scientific. Employing an array of approaches and methods borrowed from the New Left, the *Annales* school, and the social sciences, new social historians replaced narrative-based consensus history as the new orthodoxy and remain prominent in the profession to this day.

---

[2]Richard J. Evans, "Prologue: What Is History Now," in *What Is History Now*, ed. David Cannadine (London: Palgrave Macmillan, 2002), 2.

[3]Alice Kessler-Harris, "What Is Gender History Now?" in *What Is History Now*, ed. David Cannadine (London: Palgrave Macmillan, 2002), 97–98.

Race Histories

Stampp

Shaped by the rising civil rights movement and America's renewed commitment to equality following World War II, new theories of race relations arose to challenge the "mint julep" school of thought on African Americans. Kenneth Stampp (1946–1983) was a path-breaker in this field. He emphasized the essential similarity of black and white Americans, and blamed the harshness and cruelty of slavery for the different historical trajectories of the two races. A white American raised in Wisconsin, Stampp was influenced by Charles Beard's histories and carried this concern with economic and social history with him throughout his career at the University of California at Berkeley. While controversial at the time, Stampp's antiracist *Peculiar Institution* (1954) laid the foundation for new interpretations of African American history over the next several decades.

Genovese

Another innovative history of slavery was the award-winning *Roll, Jordan, Roll: The World the Slaves Made* (1974), by Eugene Genovese (b. 1930), professor at the University of Rochester. Genovese applied Marxist theory to the subject, viewing the slave institution as a remnant of a precapitalist economic system. From this perspective, masters sought to use traditional paternalism to control slaves, and slaves resisted this control through a variety of mechanisms. Like other Marxists, especially Gramscists, he viewed religion as a central mechanism for controlling people, and in this case, Christianity was used to pacify and control slaves. While slavery was brutal, the Civil War brought little relief to the oppressed slave class. Rather than a war of liberation, Genovese saw the Civil War as northern capitalist aggression to seize southern markets. Contrary to earlier historians, Genovese argued that the Emancipation Proclamation and the Reconstruction Amendments to the Constitution, which granted civil rights to former slaves, did not improve the oppressed and economically unjust position of African Americans. While Genovese later repudiated his Marxist theories, his works inspired a generation of historians to apply Marxist ideas to other social phenomena.

Blassingame

As more African Americans became professional historians, they brought their own perspectives to the study of American history. Building upon Stampp's negative assessment of slavery, as well as W. E. B. Du Bois's emphasis on the strength and courage of African Americans, and New Left bottom-up histories, African American historians such as John Blassingame (b. 1940) exposed how so-called objective histories written by white men were actually racist. He undertook the study of slavery from the bottom-up, from the perspective of the actual slaves. In *The Slave Community: Plantation Life in the Antebellum South* (1972), Blassingame observed that despite all of the oppression and violence of the slave system, slaves used whatever means possible to maintain their dignity, family life, culture, and community. He analyzed many aspects of slave culture, such as religion, songs, traditions, and stories as evidence of this black resistance and power. Slaves resisted authority in a multitude of ways and succeeded in creating their own distinctive culture, separate from white culture. In the midst of the Black Power movement of the late 1960s and early 1970s, these conclusions appealed to many in the African American community and challenged historians to include new perspectives in their work.

The Black Power movement, together with the efforts of African American historians, prompted the creation of Black Studies programs at hundreds of universities across the nation. These interdisciplinary programs in turn encouraged more interdisciplinary research on the field of African American history. The 1970s and 1980s witnessed a tremendous outpouring of African American histories on a wide variety of subjects. The authors are too many to list here, but some prominent leaders in the field include John Hope Franklin, Ira Berlin, Leon Litwack, and Herbert Gutman.

Franklin   John Hope Franklin (1915–2009) is one of the most well-known of these historians, having been president of the Organization of American Historians and the American Historical Association, and awarded the Presidential Medal of Freedom. He was born in Oklahoma, graduated from Fisk University, and received his PhD in history from Harvard in 1941. He was a lifelong activist in the African American community and he saw his historical work as an extension of that activism. He was a professor at Howard University, the University of Chicago, and Duke University. His most famous work is *From Slavery to Freedom* (1947), but he has written extensively on subjects related to African American history. Franklin had begun publishing even before the civil rights movement began in the 1950s, but because he continued to write new histories through the 1990s, his publications reflect the changing currents in African American thought. His first histories reflected his desire to bring balance to American history by adding African American history, which had long been neglected by a predominantly white historical profession. In the 1970s, however, his histories reflected the same disillusionment which shaped the Black Power movement, and Franklin grew increasingly critical of the racism which infused all of America's past. By the 1990s, however, Franklin's histories focused more on the efforts of African American activists throughout history to challenge racism and make the nation live up to its promise of equality for all.

A less positive outcome of the Black Power movement's interest in African American history, however, was its insistence that only black historians should write these histories. Arguing that historians inevitably bring their own perspective and understanding to a topic, they asserted that only black historians would truly be able to understand the black people they studied. While African American students and community members led this demand, some black historians, such as Vincent Harding and Julian Lester, made many perspectivalist arguments to support it. They verbally attacked Kenneth Stampp, Herbert Gutman, and other white historians who had committed their lives to helping the black community rewrite its past. This hostility alienated many white historians and aided in a backlash against multiculturalism in the 1980s and 1990s.

Despite this backlash, African American historiography inspired many historians to explore the experiences of other racial and ethnic minorities in the United States. Applying New Left bottom-up and sociological methods, new research on the history of American Indians, Hispanic Americans, Asian Americans, and other social groups emerged in the 1970s and blossomed in the 1980s. While much of this historiography continued to be written by white historians, more minority historians followed the footsteps of Blassingame and Franklin in bringing their own perspectives to the study of American history, dramatically challenging prevailing stereotypes. Considerable new information about these groups emerged as a result of this new inquiry.

The history of American Indians especially witnessed an explosion of new literature in this period. Partly as a result of the American Indian Movement's demand for more accurate histories of indigenous Americans, American Indian historiography in the 1970s sought to dispel historical myths which had been handed down for generations. In the same vein as Helen Hunt Jackson's seminal work in the nineteenth century, these new American Indian histories were much more critical of European American actions. They attempted to understand American history from the perspective of American Indians, or at least give equal weight to European and indigenous American viewpoints. *Thornton* One good example of this new American Indian historiography is Russell Thornton's *American Holocaust and Survival* (1987). Using demographic statistical methods, Thornton demonstrated not only that the population of the Americas was much higher than originally estimated, but that the warfare and disease brought by European conquerors were much more destructive than previously imagined. His controversial use of the word "holocaust" to describe the experience of American Indians expresses the horror and magnitude of the losses they incurred. More accepted among mainstream historians, however, are James Merrell's *The Indians' New World: Catawbas and Their Neighbors from European Contact through the Era of Removal* (1989) and Colin Calloway's *The American Revolution in Indian Country: Crisis and Diversity in Native American Communities* (1995). Both add the complex dimensions of Native American contributions to American history. Hundreds of other American Indian histories have been published since the 1970s, as historians use a wide variety of sources and methods to reconstruct the long neglected past of the nation's first inhabitants.

Gutiérrez New histories of Hispanic Americans and Asian Americans have also proliferated since the 1970s. Ramón Gutiérrez has been a pioneer in writing about the early colonial history of American Indians, Spanish, and Anglo interactions in the borderlands of the Spanish Southwest. He helped to establish an ethnic studies program at the University of California at San Diego, where he was a professor for many years. The most famous *Takaki* historian of Asian American experiences is probably Ronald T. Takaki (1939–2009). He established the first doctoral program in ethnic studies at the University of California at Berkeley and helped to pioneer the field. Born in Hawaii and the grandson of Japanese immigrants, Takaki's *Strangers from a Different Shore: A History of Asian Americans* (1989) became the textbook for this subject in the 1990s. He later expanded his research to include multiple ethnicities in *A Different Mirror: A Multicultural* *Nash* *History of America* (1993). Gary B. Nash (b. 1933) has also been a strong advocate of multicultural histories, expanding his research on marginalized Americans in the American Revolution to include multiple races and ethnicities,[4] and studying racial relations across the Americas in his pioneering *Red, White, and Black: The Peoples of Early America* (1974). Graduating with his PhD from Princeton in 1964, Nash was a professor at UCLA for many years and has had an extremely prolific career. He was

---

[4]Gary B. Nash, *The Unknown American Revolution: The Unruly Birth of Democracy and the Struggle to Create America* (New York: Viking, 2005).

elected president of the Organization of American Historians and has been a leader in advocating multiculturalism in history since the 1970s. Writing from the perspective of racial minorities, these new social histories criticized European American racism and violence, and directly contradicted the nationalist consensus account of American history by exposing the long history of injustices in the United States.

The civil rights movements of the 1960s and 1970s changed the historical profession forever. As a result of their demands for more racial diversity in higher education, many more minorities were accepted into universities and were hired as history professors. Despite the push for increased numbers of minority faculty in the 1970s, the number of minority faculty in the historical discipline remains low. In a 2008 survey of history faculty in the United States, only 1.4 percent were American Indian, 5.4 percent were Asian American, 4.9 percent were African American, and 3 percent were Hispanic, far below their proportions in the last census.[5] These small numbers of minority historians, however, have made a tremendous impact on the writing of American history. Criticized as being overly negative and antiwhite, new social historians proved their case with overwhelming evidence and succeeded in adding the perspectives of racial minorities to U.S. history. American history, as a consequence, is now much more diverse and inclusive than ever before.

Women's History

Another important branch of new social history is women's history, which blossomed as a result of the women's rights movement of the 1960s. Mary Beard had pioneered this field earlier in the century, but since few women were admitted to graduate history programs or were hired as history professors, the historical profession remained male-dominated and historiography reflected their interests. Attention to women's history, however, surged as the civil rights movement and other social movements of the Sixties inspired thousands of young women to explore the historical origins of sex discrimination in their quest to achieve equality and justice for women. Simone de Beauvoir's *The Second Sex* (1949) and Betty Friedan's *The Feminine Mystique* (1963) were extremely influential in the early phases of the new feminist movement, raising new questions about the origins of patriarchal oppression. Feminists in organizations such as Friedan's National Organization for Women and the Women's Equity Action League demanded an end to sex discrimination in higher education, and to quotas and other policies which limited the numbers of women in certain professions. They pushed politicians to support Title IX of the Higher Education Act of 1972, which banned sex discrimination in higher education. By the 1970s, these efforts resulted in larger numbers of women entering male-dominated fields, such as law schools, medical schools, and graduate history programs. Similar to racial minorities, once women won equal access to university education and professional positions, they too began to transform the historical profession.

---

[5]Robert B. Townshend, "The Status of Women and Minorities in the History Profession, 2008," *Perspectives on History*, September 2008, 2.

Lerner   In order to achieve their goal of eliminating sexism, these new women's historians traced the history of patriarchal oppression and of how women had contributed to American history. A leader in this early historiography was Gerda Lerner (1920–). Her search for the origins of patriarchy set the agenda for women's history in the 1960s and 1970s. Lerner and her generation of women's historians, however, focused most of their efforts on writing "compensatory" history: uncovering as much knowledge about women in the past as possible in order to compensate for the centuries of neglect of women's history.[6] Quoted by President Carter in his proclamation of the first National Women's History Week, Lerner proclaimed, "Women's history is women's right—an essential, indispensable heritage from which we can draw pride, comfort, courage, and long range vision."[7] As her career demonstrates, feminism, or the belief in the inherent equality of all people regardless of sex, was foundational to the early women's history movement. Lerner herself was a founding member of the most famous feminist organization of the period, the National Organization for Women. Women's historians thus viewed their search for a usable past as critical to their political goals, and this sense of importance and mission imbued many women's histories of the 1960s and 1970s.

Lerner was also very active in supporting women's history in the profession. She created the first graduate program in women's history at Sarah Lawrence College in the 1970s and was a charter member of the Coordinating Committee of Women in the Historical Profession, which was organized at the AHA in 1969.[8] The Coordinating Committee promoted educational, employment, and publication opportunities for female scholars in a number of historical organizations. As a result of this type of professional activism, the numbers of women receiving doctorates in history and positions in history faculties rose dramatically, as did publications on women's history. In 1970, only twenty-four books on women in U.S. history existed, but between 1998 and 2000 alone, 150 books of the topic were published.[9] While only 13 percent of history PhDs were granted to women prior to 1959, 35 percent of history PhDs went to women in 1992.[10] As of 2008, 42 percent of history PhDs were awarded to women, but only 30 percent of history faculty in American colleges and universities are women.[11] Because of this discrepancy, women continue to work within historical associations and through the Berkshire Conference of Women Historians to achieve gender equity in the profession and support women's history.

---

[6]Gerda Lerner, *The Majority Finds Its Past* (1979) and *The Creation of Patriarchy* (Oxford University Press, 1987).

[7]Gerda Lerner, as quoted by President Carter, on the *National Women's History Museum* Web site http://www.nwhm.org/Education/biography_glerner.html (accessed August 15, 2009).

[8]Townshend, "The Status of Women and Minorities," 2.

[9]Gerda Lerner, "U.S. Women's History: Past, Present, and Future," *Journal of Women's History* 16, no. 4 (2004): 11–12.

[10]Carla Hesse, with the assistance of Katharine Norris and Gail Phillips, "Report on the Hiring of Women and Minority Historians," *American Historical Association Web site* (1992), http://www.historians.org/pubs/Free/WomenMinorityHiring.htm (accessed August 15, 2009).

[11]Townshend, "The Status of Women and Minorities," 1.

Although some American women's historians were influenced by the New Left and saw capitalism as the root of patriarchal oppression, Lerner and many others believed that patriarchal oppression pre-dated capitalism and would continue even if capitalism were overthrown in a socialist revolution. These "radical feminists" looked for other keys to understanding and dismantling sex discrimination and oppression. Some believed that the family structure itself and men's control of women's reproductive power was the root of oppression. Others looked to cultural and religious origins of patriarchy. Joan Kelly, Linda Kerber, Nancy Cott, and Alice Kessler-Harris were all pioneers in the new women's history.[12]

Smith-Rosenberg

While these authors tended to see women as victims of oppression, other women's historians focused upon the strength and accomplishments of women despite their oppression. This manifested itself in a number of ways, including efforts to write great women into the broader history of the United States, and focusing on the accomplishments and contributions of powerful women, as well as attempting to rewrite all of American history with an equal focus on the contributions of men and women. A good example of this approach is the work of Carroll Smith-Rosenberg (b. 1939). She graduated with her PhD in history from Columbia University in 1968 and was a longtime professor at the University of Michigan. Although she has published prolifically, her essay "The Female World of Love and Ritual" (1975) is still her most famous work. It explored the "homosocial" relationships of women in the nineteenth century, which resulted from the separate gender spheres of that era. Instead of viewing women as victims, she argued that in some ways, gender ideology actually empowered women.[13] Her work continued to evolve and reflect changes in feminist historiography since the 1970s, exploring psychological theories and gender constructions in *Disorderly Conduct: Visions of Gender in Victorian America* (1986) and her later works. Another good example of women's history demonstrating the importance and complexity of

Ulrich

women's roles in the past was Laurel Thatcher Ulrich's *A Midwife's Tale* (1991), which won the Pulitzer, Bancroft, and Dunning prizes. This work uncovered the life of an eighteenth-century midwife and placed it within the wider cultural, social, and political history of the period.

Many of these early women's historians focused on European American women's experiences because of the availability of sources, but in the 1980s and 1990s, a new generation of women's historians explored the diversity of women's experiences, especially how race and sexual orientation affected women's lives. The numbers of African American, Hispanic American, Native American, and other ethnic women's histories exploded, and lesbian history established its own historiography. Some good examples of authors in these fields include Deborah Gray White, Jacqueline Jones,

---

[12]Joan Kelly, *Women, History, and Theory* (1986), Linda Kerber, *Women of the Republic: Intellect and Ideology in Revolutionary America* (1980), Nancy Cott, *The Bonds of Womanhood: "Woman's Sphere" in New England, 1780–1835* (1977), Alice Kessler-Harris, *Out to Work: A History of Wage-Earning Women in the United States* (1982).

[13]Caroll Smith-Rosenberg, "The Female World of Love and Ritual: Relations between Women in the Nineteenth Century," *Signs* 1, no. 1 (Autumn 1975): 1–29.

Paula Giddings, Theda Perdue, Vicki Ruiz, Sarah Deutsch, Lillian Faderman, and Estelle Freedman.[14] These works and the hundreds of other women's histories written between the 1970s and 1990s contributed a wealth of new material to American historiography, raising important new questions and demonstrating the importance of women's perspectives in creating a more balanced story of the past.

As new social historians sought to study large groups of people, many of whom had left behind few written records, they drew from the methods of other social sciences, especially those of psychology, sociology, and economics. Braudel's *Annales* methods of studying geographical, economic, social, and cultural factors were especially influential in this endeavor. Out of this merger came new types of history, including psychohistory, historical sociology, and cliometrics.

Psychohistory

Freud

One especially attractive methodology for social historians was that of psychoanalysis. The father of psychoanalysis Sigmund Freud (1856–1939) was a Viennese doctor who specialized in mental health. He developed a theory that individual aberrations from normal psychological development caused mental disorders. He posited that each human brain possesses an "id" which causes individuals to strive toward gratification and freedom. The "ego" attempts to satisfy the id in a realistic way, but the "superego," or the culturally constructed, learned, and internalized aspect of personality, is at war with the id, limiting and controlling its behavior. Each individual varies according to which aspect is stronger, but those who fail to develop through "normal" stages are considered psychological deviants in need of therapy. To understand the psychological development of each individual, Freud analyzed the subconscious of patients who manifested some type of psychological disorder. He questioned his patients about their dreams and childhoods, attempting to discover their particular pathologies in order to correct them.

Freud's theories are too complex and wide ranging to cover fully here, but they did have some relevance for the study of history, which Freud himself recognized. He saw that psychoanalysis could help historians explore the emotional and unconscious motivations of people not only in the present, but also in the past.[15] Freud wrote several works exploring the motivations of individuals in the past, but he eventually

---

[14]Deborah Gray White, *Ar'n't I A Woman: Female Slaves in the Plantation South* (1985), Jacqueline Jones, *A Labor of Love, a Labor of Sorrow: Black Women, Work and the Family from Slavery to the Present* (1985), Paula Giddings, *When and Where I Enter: The Impact of Black Women on Race and Sex in America* (1988), Theda Perdue, *Sifters: Native American Women's Lives* (2001), Sarah Deutsch, *No Separate Refuge: Culture, Class, and Gender on an Anglo-Hispanic Frontier in the American Southwest, 1880–1940* (1987), Vicki Ruiz, *Cannery Women, Cannery Lives: Mexican Women, Unionization, and the California Food Processing Industry, 1930–1950* (1987), Lillian Faderman, *Odd Girls and Twilight Lovers: A History of Lesbian Life in Twentieth-Century America* (1991), Estelle Freedman and John D'Emilio, *Intimate Matters: A History of Sexuality in America* (1988).

[15]Peter Loewenberg, "Psychohistory," in *The Past Before Us: Contemporary Historical Writing in the United States*, ed. Michael Kammen (Ithaca, NY: Cornell University Press, 1980), 408.

broadened his study to include historical events and groups in order to form general-izations about human psychological responses to similar events. For example, in *Totem and Taboo* (1912), he explained the creation of the human social order, moral laws, and religion with an elaborate theory about group psychological interactions of the earliest human beings. All of his history was hypothetical of course, with no empirical evidence to substantiate it, but it gave historians food for thought about the possibili-ties of using psychoanalysis to increase our understanding of the psychological motiva-tions of humans in the past.

Psychoanalytical history gained more acceptance following World War II, when the U.S. Office of Strategic Services (OSS) created a psychobiography of Adolf Hitler. Another major turning point in the use of psychoanalysis in historical research came in 1957, when William L. Langer, president of the American Historical Association and former OSS researcher, called upon professional historians to apply psychoana-lytical methods in their own research.[16] A number of studies of Hitler's personality, psychosis, and appeal, as well as other psychobiographies, followed in the 1960s and 1970s.[17] By the 1970s, two professional journals, *The Journal of Psychohistory* and *The Psychohistory Review*, specialized in psychoanalytical history.

Erikson   Probably the most prominent psychoanalytical historian is Erik Erikson (1902–1994). Erikson was born in Germany, but as a Jew was forced to flee to the United States when the Nazis came to power. Trained in child psychology, he became famous in his own disci-pline for his theories on psychosocial development and ego psychology. While most of his work is in psychology, he published a number of important psychohistories from the 1940s through the 1960s. His famous essay "The Legend of Hitler's Childhood" analyzed why Germans supported Hitler. He argued that Hitler appealed to the psychological disposi-tions of middle-class Germans which were formed by common childhood experiences.[18] His *Young Man Luther* explored the psychological reasons for Martin Luther's rebellion against the Roman Catholic Church.[19] Erikson inspired a generation of psychologists and historians to use psychoanalytical methods in historical practice.

A number of American historians began to add psychoanalytical methods to their repertoire of traditional historical methods to write social and cultural histories in the *Demos* 1970s and 1980s. John Demos's (1937–) *Entertaining Satan: Witchcraft and the Culture of Early New England* (1982) studied the witchcraft trials at Salem in the seventeenth century using psychoanalysis to understand the accusers' psychological motivations and the community's response. Demonstrating the historical profession's acceptance of these methods, Demos was granted the most prestigious award in American history,

---

[16]Ibid., 411.

[17]Walter C. Langer, *The Mind of Adolf Hitler: The Secret Wartime Report* (New York: Basic Books, 1972); Richard A. Koenigsberg, *Hitler's Ideology: A Study in Psychoanalytic Sociology* (New York: Library of Social Science, 1975); and R. G. L. Waite, *The Psychopathic God: Adolf Hitler* (New York: Basic Books, 1977).

[18]Erik H. Erikson, "The Legend of Hitler's Childhood," in *Childhood and Society* (London: Random House, 1950): 294–310.

[19]Erik H. Erikson, *Young Man Luther: A Study in Psychoanalysis and History* (New York: Norton, 1962).

Gay   the Bancroft Prize, for this book. Another prominent psychoanalytical historian is Peter Gay (1923–), who published a number of important psychohistories in the 1980s and 1990s, including *Freud for Historians* (1985). In women's history, Carroll Smith-Rosenberg applied psychoanalytical theories to understand outbreaks of hysteria among nineteenth-century women. Psychoanalysis has also influenced a number of political historians, including David Horowitz's interpretation of the psychological origins of the American Revolution and Richard Hofstadter's investigation of the role of emotion in American politics.[20] As these studies demonstrate, psychoanalytical history may reveal important insights into the subconscious reasons for human behavior by analyzing personalities, lifestyles, slips of speech and writing, and dreams to reveal individual or collective pathologies.[21]

Psychohistory reached a peak in popularity in the 1980s, but has declined in importance since then. While psychohistories reveal interesting insights and have been popular, professional historians have generally criticized this form of history because its analysis of subconscious motivation makes it difficult to prove its assertions. Not only are its subjects usually dead, and therefore unable to respond to psychoanalytical questions, but few people leave enough personal writing or recordings to determine their thoughts accurately, much less diagnose their psychoses. Although they continue to bear much criticism for their general lack of empirical evidence, psychohistories have raised important questions which have stimulated the profession as a whole.

Historical Sociology

Another discipline which has appealed to many social historians is sociology. The academic study of both sociology and history originated in the nineteenth century, and both were heavily influenced by social scientific empirical methods from the beginning. While the two disciplines generally had separate trajectories in the twentieth century, with sociologists focusing more on analyzing contemporary social structures and phenomena, and historians distinguishing themselves by focusing only on past societies, the field of historical sociology united them by bringing sociological perspectives to the practice of history. Both historical sociologists and social historians study past societies and social phenomena, but they differ in that historical sociologists generally focus on models and general patterns of social events and social structures, while social historians pay more attention to causes and effects, as well as individual actions and historical context. The two subdisciplines, however, overlap in so many ways that their studies are sometimes almost identical. Encouraged by the interdisciplinary studies of the *Annalistes* and the New Left's demand for more knowledge about the experiences of the masses of people, historical sociology became very popular in the 1960s and 1970s.

---

[20]David Horowitz, *The First Frontier: The Indian Wars and America's Origins, 1607–1776* (New York: Simon and Schuster, 1978) and Richard Hofstadter, *The Paranoid Style in American Politics* (New York: Knopf, 1965).

[21]Loewenberg, "Psychohistory," 409.

Weber

One of the most influential historical sociologists of the twentieth century was Max Weber (1864–1920). A German professor of economics, Weber studied history, politics, economics, theology, and sociology. This interdisciplinary background informed his most influential work of historical sociology, *The Protestant Ethic and the Spirit of Capitalism* (1904). This history of the origins of modern capitalism explained why industrial capitalism developed first in Europe and the United States by comparing these with other countries in the rest of the world. Going beyond Marx's emphasis on the economic origins of industrial capitalism, Weber asserted that cultural developments in Western Europe, specifically Protestant rationalism, were the distinguishing feature of those countries which developed modern capitalism. He developed complex models categorizing "rationality" and analyzed social stratifications and comparisons, blending these sociological methods with historical analysis of the multiple causes of historical change and examining his subject over time. His work became an inspiration to both historians and sociologists and broke new ground in the subdiscipline of historical sociology.

Tilly

Skocpol

Other historical sociologists in the twentieth century followed in Weber's footsteps by using comparative methods to explore social developments and phenomena. Comparative historical sociology especially focused on the development and structure of modern capitalist societies, revolutions, and social movements. Two of the more famous historical sociologists since the 1960s are Charles Tilly (1929–2008) and Theda Skocpol (b. 1947). Tilly was most noted for his investigations of collective actions in Europe and use of quantitative methods to gather enormous amounts of data to support his conclusions.[22] Skocpol is known for her studies of revolutions using a structuralist approach of comparing the social structures which cause revolutions.[23] These topics are not coincidentally similar to those of Marxist historians, and indeed, many historical sociologists support Marxist interpretations of their subject matter.

Oral History

Another method which especially appealed to new social historians was oral history. This is a method of gathering evidence that is not in the written record. It can be done in a number of different ways, for a number of different purposes, but it typically involves a researcher interviewing a subject and using that interview as the basis for understanding a specific topic. Oral histories have an ancient lineage within the historical profession. Early historians relied upon them heavily, and most mythopoetic narratives originated as oral traditions, often told from generation to generation over centuries. These oral traditions are valued for understanding the inner workings of preliterate peoples' minds and gleaning some idea of their history where no other source exists. In the nineteenth century, however, professional historians rejected oral histories as a basis for their research. They argued that oral history is an unreliable source of information, even for recent history, because it is hopelessly warped by the

---

[22]Charles Tilly, *As Sociology Meets History* (New York: Academic Press, 1981).

[23]Theda Skocpol, *States and Social Revolutions: A Comparative Analysis of France, Russia, and China* (Cambridge: Cambridge University Press, 1979).

memory of the individual being interviewed. Traditional historians preferred instead to gather eyewitness accounts written at the time of the historical event or shortly after to moderate the impact of memory. This method works for historians interested in literate people who are powerful and important enough to have their written records preserved, but for new social historians, attempting to uncover the lives of the illiterate and "unimportant" masses, oral history offered a useful methodology.

Reconstructive   Since the 1960s, new social historians have used oral history in a number of different ways, developing new methods to ensure that their findings are as accurate as possible. Reconstructive oral history uses interviews with eyewitnesses as another type of primary source evidence from which they can reconstruct the actual events of the past. To catch any inaccuracies caused by flawed memory, these interviews are weighed against other interviews and written evidence of the same event. For example, Paul Thompson's analysis of class structures in early twentieth-century Britain included five hundred interviews of a cross-section of British society.[24] In the United States, the best-known oral histories are those of broadcaster and writer Louis "Studs" Terkel (1912–2008). His oral history of World War II, *"The Good War:" An Oral History of World War Two* (1985), won a Pulitzer Prize. A number of oral history projects now exist in the United States to gather and preserve the memories of participants in specific events, such as the Vietnam War and Women's Suffrage Movement. Countering arguments that reconstructive oral history is still fundamentally flawed by memory, its defenders argue that accounts written as events are happening are more biased by those events than oral histories taken down years afterward, which give the eyewitnesses time to think about the event more deeply and make more sense of the event.[25]

Interpretative   Just as controversial and useful is interpretative oral history, which analyzes interviews as evidence not of the actual events, but rather of how people internalize these events and construct their own perspective of the past. This is especially useful for psychohistory, but is also used in a variety of ways for other social histories. Italian historian Luisa Passerini's work has been extremely influential in exploring this type of oral history. In her *Fascism and Popular Memory* (1987), she demonstrated that oral stories reveal deep psychological insights and the process of memory formation. While still controversial, oral history has helped new social historians to uncover the hidden histories of those who left behind few written records.

Cliometrics

Cliometrics   Another important methodology borrowed from the social sciences is quantitative history, or "cliometrics." Cliometrics refers to the statistical use of quantified data to support historical arguments. Historians have always made quantified statements, such

---

[24]Paul Thompson, *The Voice of the Past* (Oxford: Oxford University Press, 1988).

[25]Anna Green and Kathleen Troup, Chapter 9: Oral History, in *The Houses of History: A Critical Reader in Twentieth-century History and Theory* (New York: New York University Press, 1999), 230–237.

as "most people did this," or "the feeling was widespread," or "it resulted in significant change," but quantitative historians want to precisely define "most," "widespread," and "significant." Some Progressive historians, such as Charles Beard, attempted to quantify data to support their arguments, but they ran into problems of incomplete data and the enormously time-consuming nature of collecting data on thousands of people. Since the mid-twentieth century, however, new computer technologies have helped historians to gather and organize the data they need to reveal the experiences of large groups of people and economic trends.

Borrowing statistical techniques from economics and sociology, quantitative history attempts to state precise questions and define relevant variables, build models which help to answer the question, use the evidence to re-create the past exactly, and use counterfactual deduction to test the model.[26] Data can be gathered from censuses, business records, and a variety of other sources. Where information is scarce, the statistical models are meant to extend previous data and patterns to areas where none is available, thus using existing data to hypothesize about missing information. While this method is time-consuming, it helps historians to uncover information about those who left few written records and to identify larger social and economic patterns in history. As one cliometrician put it,

> Instead of looking at cities or rural communities only from the limited points of view of those who left written records, we can follow the life courses of groups of ordinary people, seeking to explain their differing experiences by variations in the areas where they lived, the economic conditions they faced, their ethnic and class positions and so on.[27]

Fogel

For these reasons, quantitative methods grew in popularity after the 1960s as social and economic history came to dominate the profession. The most famous promoter of new economic history is Robert W. Fogel (b. 1926). Fogel was an American communist organizer before he studied statistics at Columbia University. Turning his back on communism and Marxism, Fogel was a positivist who sought to eliminate all bias and allegiance to overarching theories from history. His *Railroads and American Economic Growth* (1964) broke new ground not only in using mathematical models and copious amounts of economic data, but also in counterfactual argument. He tested the hypothesis that railroads were the key to industrialization in America by constructing a model of how the economy would have operated in the absence of railroads. Using hundreds of pages of mathematical models to analyze various sectors of the American economy in the nineteenth century in this scenario, he concluded that the United States would have industrialized without railroads. His book, with Stanley Engerman, *Time on the*

---

[26]Lance Davis, "The New Economic History: II. Professor Fogel and the New Economic History," *Economic History Review* 19 (1966): 657, quoted in Anna Green and Kathleen Troup, eds., *The Houses of History: A Critical Reader in Twentieth-century History and Theory* (New York: New York University Press, 1999), 142.

[27]J. Morgan Kousser, "Quantitative Social-Scientific History," in *The Past Before Us: Contemporary Historical Writing in the United States*, ed. Michael Kammen (Ithaca, NY: Cornell University Press, 1980), 444.

Cross: The Economics of American Negro Slavery (1974) broke even more ground by applying these methods to the question of whether slavery was unprofitable and inefficient. Although they personally felt that slavery was immoral, they used economic data and the records of slaveholders to conclude that slavery was indeed economically successful and that the material experience of slavery was not as bad as previously believed.

While they won a Bancroft Prize for their work, and Fogel won a Nobel Prize for his contributions to economics, these works were severely criticized by a number of historians. Their opponents argued that numbers and models could never encompass human reality or represent a true picture of historical experience. Others argued that new economic history obscured the real story with all of its statistical models and numbers. Herbert Gutman's entire monograph *Slavery and the Numbers Game* (1975) attacked *Time on the Cross* and both books became the center of heated discussions among historians across the nation.[28] His own study of slavery *The Black Family in Slavery and Freedom* (1976) was published the next year and used quantitative methods in a manner which was more acceptable to historians.[29] Nevertheless, Fogel and his counterparts stirred up interest in economic history for over a decade and influenced social and political history with their methods and findings.

Serial History

Gutman and many other historians were also busily using quantitative methods in a myriad of other types of social history, including serial history and historical demography. Social and popular culture histories, which seek to reconstruct the thoughts, experiences, and beliefs of large numbers of people, have turned to these forms of statistical analysis to help them answer their questions. Serial history refers to histories which attempt to track long-term changes in quantifiable phenomenon, such as wages, prices, crimes, and literacy rates. For example, if historians wanted to know whether wages increased, decreased, or stayed the same in a certain place and period, they would gather data, perhaps from tax records, for that place over a series of years and look for an overarching pattern. This data would then become the historical evidence which would be analyzed and interpreted to form conclusions about the subject.

Demographic History

Like serial history, demographic history analyzes series of data over time, but it focuses more narrowly upon questions of population history, such as changes in birth, death, and marriage rates. Census records, and before that parish records, are essential for this type of history. Historical demography is most useful for historical sociologists and new social historians in their attempt to re-create past social structures and better understand the lives of the masses. *Annaliste* Emmanuel Le Roy Ladurie (1929–) was a pioneer in the use of serial and demographic history in the 1960s. His *Peasants of Languedoc* (1966) went beyond Braudel in using rigorous empirical scientific methodology to analyze the relationship between climate, agricultural productivity,

Ladurie

---

[28]Herbert G. Gutman, *Slavery and the Numbers Game: A Critique of 'Time on the Cross'* (Champaign, IL: University of Illinois Press, 2003).

[29]Herbert G. Gutman, *The Black Family in Slavery and Freedom, 1750–1925* (New York: Vintage Books, 1977).

and demographics in the Languedoc region of France over several centuries. Without quantitative methods, *Annales* histories of this scale and scope would be impossible.

Like all quantitative history, however, gathering data for serial and demographic history is extremely time-consuming. Many historians overcome this difficulty by limiting the scope of their study to one specific town and shorter time periods. Others utilize research assistants and centers to help gather the data and computers to process it. In order to provide the resources to collect and process vast amounts of data, a number of important organizations were created in the 1960s. The Mathematical Social Science Board created a History Advisory Committee which organized a number of research conferences to generate publications and train graduate history students in quantitative methods. The Inter-University Consortium for Political and Social Research additionally established a Historical Data Archive to aid in quantitative research projects across the country.[30] Their efforts resulted in a number of journals publishing almost exclusively quantitative histories in the 1960s and 1970s, including the *Journal of Economic History*, *Journal of Social History*, *Historical Methods*, and the *Journal of Interdisciplinary History*. These organizations and publications helped to forge new branches of history, including new economic history and demographic history, and contributed new methods for social and political histories.

In many respects, quantitative history's emphasis on overwhelming empirical data to prove the truth about the past was the apotheosis of positivist and empiricist history. Some historians even believed that history could not be accurate without quantifiable evidence. For example, French sociocultural historian Emmanuel Le Roy Ladurie famously asserted, "History that is not quantifiable cannot claim to be scientific."[31] In spite of its popularity among social scientific historians, many historians have criticized quantitative history on a number of grounds. One important reason for this opposition is that quantitative methods do not conform to traditional approaches which are narrative, historicist, and idealist. Quantitative methods, from this perspective, are too positivist, too analytical and reliant on mathematical models, too much like other social sciences to be counted as "good" history. Revealing the depth of the revulsion some historians feel toward quantitative history, one AHA president even warned historians to never "worship at the shrine of that Bitch-goddess, quantification."[32] While some historians still write purely quantitative history á la Fogel, most now blend quantitative methods within a narrative framework, making their work more readable and satisfying some traditionalist critics.

New social history and social scientific history, while popular among empiricist professional historians, suffer from many of the same flaws and criticism as quantitative

---

[30]Allan G. Bogue, "The New Political History in the 1970s," in *The Past Before Us: Contemporary Historical Writing in the United States*, ed. Michael Kammen (Ithaca, NY: Cornell University Press, 1980), 235.

[31]Quoted in Gordon S. Wood, *The Purpose of the Past: Reflections on the Uses of History* (New York: Penguin, 2008), 43.

[32]Carl Bridenbaugh, quoted in J. Morgan Kousser, "Quantitative Social-Scientific History," in *The Past Before Us: Contemporary Historical Writing in the United States*, ed. Michael Kammen (Ithaca, NY: Cornell University Press, 1980), 434.

history. It may be precise, specific, and accurate, but it often makes for poor reading. Leading political historian Gordon Wood explains, "This new social-science history is not meant for storytelling but for problem solving."[33] Like new social history, social scientific history helped to widen the gap between "what gained applause as popular history…and minutely detailed, methodologically involuted professional monographs that few outside the academy read."[34] Social science history failed to communicate with a wider audience because of its reliance on jargon, quantification, and large trends rather than individual people.[35] What historians gained in information and accuracy, they lost in popularity.

New social history, however, has continued to grow and expand into new fields since 1970. In 1971, Eric Hobsbawm grouped social history into six categories: "demography and kinship, urban studies, classes and social groups, mentalities or culture, the transformation of societies, and social movements."[36] This expansion and change in focus in the historical profession, however, has had little impact on popular history. The general public has remained interested in sensationalized patriotic stories about national heroes and glory in wars. Popular history, as evidenced in numerous blockbuster films—such as *The Patriot* and *Saving Private Ryan*—and in documentaries on *The History Channel* and *PBS*, has continued to focus on great men, heroes and leaders, and military histories which showed the United States as the greatest democracy in the world. Despite these limitations, new social history has transformed the historical profession in the United States, bringing a new emphasis on diversity and critical thinking, explicit ideological perspectives, and new topics to the forefront of the profession.

Robert William Fogel and Stanley L. Engerman, *Time on the Cross*

Punishment, Rewards, and Expropriation

The exploitative nature of slavery is most apparent in its system of punishment and rewards. Whipping was probably the most common punishment meted out against errant slaves. Other forms of punishment included the deprivation of various privileges (such as visits to town), confinement in stocks, incarceration, sale, branding, and the death penalty.

Whipping could be either a mild or a severe punishment, depending on how it was administered. Some whippings were so severe that they resulted in death. Indeed, in cases such as murder, the sentences of slaves who would otherwise have been executed were frequently converted to severe whipping, coupled with exportation

---

[33]Wood, *The Purpose of the Past*, 43.

[34]Peter Charles Hoffer, *Past Imperfect: Facts, Fictions, Fraud—American History from Bancroft and Parkman to Ambrose, Bellesiles, Ellis, and Goodwin* (New York: Public Affairs, 2004), 94.

[35]Evans, "Prologue," 7.

[36]Geoff Eley, "Is All the World a Text," in *Practicing History: New Directions in Historical Writing after the Linguistic Turn*, ed. Gabrielle M. Spiegel (New York: Routledge, 2005), 38.

Source: Robert William Fogel and Stanley L. Engerman, *Time on the Cross: The Economics of American Negro Slavery* (New York: W. W. Norton & Co, 1995): pp. 144–157. Reprinted by permission of W. W. Norton & Company, Inc.

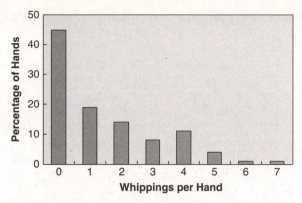

FIGURE 7.1: The Distribution of Whippings on the Bennet H. Barrow Plantation during a Two-Year Period Beginning in December, 1840

to another state or a foreign country. For, by converting the death penalty to whipping and exportation, the state could recover a substantial part of the value of a slave that would have been lost through his execution. In other instances, whipping was as mildly applied as the corporal punishment normally practiced within families today.

Reliable data on the frequency of whipping is extremely sparse. The only systematic record of whipping now available for an extended period comes from the diary of Bennet Barrow, a Louisiana planter who believed that to spare the rod was to spoil the slave. His plantation numbered about 200 slaves, of whom about 120 were in the labor force. The record shows that over the course of two years a total of 160 whippings were administered, an average of 0.7 whippings per hand per year. About half the hands were not whipped at all during the period.

There was nothing exceptional about the use of whipping to enforce discipline among slaves until the beginning of the nineteenth century. It must be remembered that through the centuries whipping was considered a fully acceptable form of punishment, not merely for criminals but also for honest men or women who in some way shirked their duties. Whipping of wives, for example, was even sanctified in some versions of the

Scripture. The Matthew's Bible, which preceded the King James version, told the husband, in a note at I Pet. 3, that if his wife was "not obedient and healpfull unto hym endeuoureth to beate the feare of God into her heade, and that therby she maye be compelled to learne her duitie and do it." During the seventeenth and most of the eighteenth centuries whipping was commonly employed as a punishment in the North as well as in the South. Not until the end of the eighteenth century and the beginning of the nineteenth century did whipping rapidly fall from favor in the free states.

To attribute the continuation of whipping in the South to the maliciousness of masters is naïve. Although some masters were brutal, even sadistic, most were not. The overwhelming majority of the ex-slaves in the W.P.A. narratives who expressed themselves on the issue reported that their masters were good men. Such men worried about the proper role of whipping in a system of punishment and rewards. Some excluded it altogether. Most accepted it, but recognized that to be effective whipping had to be used with restraint and in a coolly calculated manner. Weston, for example, admonished his overseer not to impose punishment of any sort until twenty-four hours after the offense had been discovered. William J. Minor, a sugar planter, instructed his managers "not [to] cut the skin when punishing, nor punish in a passion." Many planters forbade the whipping of slaves except by them or in their presence. Others limited the number of lashes that could be administered without their permission.

The decline of whipping as an instrument of labor discipline outside of the South appears to have been heavily influenced by economic considerations. With the rise of capitalism, impersonal and indirect sanctions were increasingly substituted for direct, personal ones. The hiring of free workers in the marketplace provided managers of labor with a powerful new disciplinary weapon. Workers who were lazy, indifferent, or who otherwise shirked their duties could be fired—left to starve beyond the eyesight or expense of the employer. Interestingly enough, denial of food was rarely used to enforce discipline on slaves. For the illness and lethargy caused by malnutrition reduced the capacity of the slave to labor in the fields. Planters preferred whipping to incarceration because the lash did not generally lead to an extended loss of the slave's labor time. In other words, whipping persisted in the South because the cost of substituting hunger and incarceration for the lash was greater for the slaveowner than for the northern employer of free labor. When the laborer owns his own human capital, forms of punishment which impair or diminish the value of that capital are borne exclusively by him. Under slavery, the master desired forms of punishment which, while they imposed costs on the slave, did so with the minimum impairment to the human capital which the master owned. Whipping generally fulfilled these conditions.

While whipping was an integral part of the system of punishment and rewards, it was not the totality of the system. What planters wanted was not sullen and discontented slaves who did just enough to keep from getting whipped. They wanted devoted, hard-working, responsible slaves who identified their fortunes with the fortunes of their masters. Planters sought to imbue slaves with a "Protestant" work ethic and to transform that ethic from a state of mind into a high level of production. "My negros have their name up in the neighbourhood," wrote Bennet Barrow, "for making more than any one else & they think Whatever they do is better than any body Else." Such an attitude could not be beaten into slaves. It had to be elicited.

Much of the managerial attention of planters was focused on the problem of motivating their hands. To achieve the desired response they developed a wide-ranging system of rewards. Some rewards were directed toward improving short-run performance. Included in this category were prizes for the individual or the gang with the best picking record on a given day or during a given week. The prizes were such items as clothing, tobacco, and whiskey;

sometimes the prize was cash. Good immediate performance was also rewarded with unscheduled holidays or with trips to town on weekends. When slaves worked at times normally set aside for rest, they received extra pay—usually in cash and at the rate prevailing in the region for hired labor. Slaves who were performing well were permitted to work on their own account after normal hours at such tasks as making shingles or weaving baskets, articles which they could sell either to their masters or to farmers in the neighborhood.

Some rewards were directed at influencing behavior over periods of intermediate duration. The rewards in this category were usually paid at the end of the year. Year-end bonuses, given either in goods or cash, were frequently quite substantial. Bennet Barrow, for example, distributed gifts averaging between $15 and $20 per slave family in both 1839 and 1840. The amounts received by particular slaves were proportional to their performance. It should be noted that $20 was about a fifth of national per capita income in 1840. A bonus of the same relative magnitude today would be in the neighborhood of $1,000.

Masters also rewarded slaves who performed well with patches of land ranging up to a few acres for each family. Slaves grew marketable crops on these lands, the proceeds of which accrued to them. On the Texas plantation of Julian S. Devereux, slaves operating such land produced as much as two bales of cotton per patch. Devereux marketed their crop along with his own. In a good year some of the slaves earned in excess of $100 per annum for their families. Devereux set up accounts to which he credited the proceeds of the sales. Slaves drew on these accounts when they wanted cash or when they wanted Devereux to purchase clothing, pots, pans, tobacco, or similar goods for them.

Occasionally planters even devised elaborate schemes for profit sharing with their slaves. William Jemison, an Alabama planter, entered into the following agreement with his bondsmen:

[Y]ou shall have two thirds of the corn and cotton made on the plantation and as much of the wheat as will reward you for the sowing it. I also furnish you with provisions for this year. When your crop is gathered, one third is to be set aside for me. You are then to pay your over-seer his part and pay me what I furnish, clothe yourselves, pay your own taxes and doctor's fee with all expenses of the farm. You are to be no expense to me, but render to me one third of the produce and what I have loaned you. You have the use of the stock and plantation tools. You are to return them as good as they are and the plantation to be kept in good repair, and what clear money you make shall be divided equally amongst you in a fair proportion agreeable to the services rendered by each hand. There will be an account of all lost time kept, and those that earn most shall have most.

There was a third category of rewards. These were of a long-term nature, often requiring the lapse of a decade or more before they paid off. Thus, slaves had the opportunity to rise within the social and economic hierarchy that existed under bondage. Field hands could become arti-sans or drivers. Artisans could be allowed to move from the plantation to town where they would hire themselves out. Drivers could move up to the position of head driver or overseer. Climbing the economic ladder brought not only social status, and sometimes more freedom; it also had significant payoffs in better housing, bet-ter clothing, and cash bonuses.

Little attention has hitherto been paid to the manner in which planters selected the slaves who were to become the artisans and managers. In some cases boys were apprenticed to carpen-ters, blacksmiths, or some similar craftsmen when they were in their early teens, as was typically done with whites. For slaves, this appears to have been the exception rather than the rule. Analysis of occupational data derived from probate and plantation records reveals an unusual distribu-tion of ages among slave artisans. Slaves in their twenties were substantially underrepresented, while slaves in their forties and fifties were overrepresented. This age pattern suggests that the selection of slaves for training in the crafts was frequently delayed until slaves reached their late twenties, or perhaps even into the thirties.

Normally this would be an uneconomical policy, since the earlier an investment is made in occupational training, the more years there are to reap the returns on that investment. Slavery altered this pattern by shifting the authority to determine occupational investments from the parents to the masters. In free societies, kinship is usually the pri-mary basis for determining which members of the new generation are trained in skilled occupations. But the slaveholder lacked the vested interests of a parent. He could, therefore, treat entry into the skilled occupations as a prize that was to be claimed by the most deserving, regardless of family background. The extra effort put forth by young field hands who competed for these jobs appears to have more than offset the loss in returns due to the curtailed period over which the occupational investment was amortized. We do not mean to suggest that kinship played no role in the intergen-erational transfer of skills among slaves. We merely wish to stress that its role was significantly reduced as compared with free society.

Another long-run reward was freedom through manumission. The chance of achieving this reward was, of course, quite low. Census data indicate that in 1850 the manumission rate was just 0.45 per thousand slaves. Manumission could be achieved either through the philanthropy of a master or through an agreement which permit-ted a slave to buy himself out. Sometimes gifts of freedom were bestowed while the master was still alive. More often it was a bequest set forth in a will. Self-purchase involved arrangements under which slaves were permitted to purchase them-selves with money that they earned from work on their own account, or in the case of skilled urban slaves, by increasing the share of income which the artisan paid to his master. Some skilled slaves were able to accumulate enough capital to purchase their freedom within a decade. For oth-ers the period extended to two decades or more. Little information is currently available on the prices at which such transactions were concluded. It is not known whether slaves involved in self-purchase were generally forced to pay a price in excess of their market value.

From the foregoing it is clear that slaves did not all live at a uniform level of income. The elaborate system of rewards erected by planters introduced substantial variation in the slave standard of living. Much work remains to be done before it will be possible to reconstruct with reasonable accuracy the full range of the slave income distribution. It has been possible, however, to estimate the "basic income" of slaves in 1850. This, together with some fragmentary evidence on the higher incomes of slaves, will at least suggest the range of income variation that prevailed.

By "basic income" we mean the value of the food, clothing, shelter, and medical care furnished to slaves. The average value of the expenditure on these items for an adult male in 1850 was about $48.00. The most complete information on the extra earnings of field hands comes from several Texas plantations. The leading hands on these estates frequently earned between $40 and $110 per year above basic income through the sale of cotton and other products raised on their patches. This experience was not unique to Texas. On one Alabama plantation, eight hands produced cotton that earned them an average of $71 each, with the high man collecting $96. On still another plantation the average extra earnings of the thirteen top hands was $77. These scattered cases suggest that the ratio of high earnings to basic earnings among field hands was in the neighborhood of 2.5.

When the incomes of artisans are taken into account, the spread in slave earnings became still wider. The top incomes earned by craftsmen must have been several times basic income. This is implied by the high prices which artisans had to pay to buy themselves out. The average price of a prime-aged blacksmith was about $1,700 in 1850. Thus, a thirty-year-old man who was able to buy himself out in a decade probably earned in the neighborhood of $170 per year over subsistence.

This suggests a ratio of artisan to basic income of about 4.5.

The highest annual figure we have been able to uncover for extra earnings by a field hand in a single year is $309. Aham, the Alabama slave whose sales of peaches, apples, and cotton yielded this sum, had accumulated enough capital over the years so that in 1860 he held notes on loans totaling over $2,400. The ratio of Aham's agricultural income to basic income is 7.4. If we assume that Aham earned 6 percent, or $144, on the loans, the ratio would rise to 10.4. The highest income above maintenance that we have found for an artisan is $500. In this case the ratio of earned to basic income is 11.4.

While the reward structure created much more room for upward mobility within the slave system than is usually supposed, the scope of opportunity should not be exaggerated. The highest levels of attainment were irrevocably foreclosed to slaves. The entrepreneurial talent obviously possessed by bondsmen such as Aham could not be used to catapult them into the stewardship of great businesses as long as they remained slaves. No slave, regardless of his gifts, could aspire to political position. No man of letters—there were slaves who acquired considerable erudition—could ever hold an appointment in the faculty of a southern university as long as he was a bondsman. The entrepreneurial genius had to settle for lingering in the shadow of the master on whose protection he was dependent. The man of letters could go no further than the position of tutor to the children of a benevolent and enlightened planter. It was on the talented, the upper crust of slave society, that deprivations of the peculiar institution hung most heavy. This, perhaps, explains why it was that the first to flee to northern lines as Yankee advances corroded the Rebel positions were not the ordinary field hands, but the drivers and the artisans.

As previously noted, a part of the income that slaves produced was expropriated from them. Determination of the average annual amount of this expropriation over the life cycle of the entire slave population is an extremely complex matter. For the rate of expropriation differed from slave to slave, as well as from year to year for particular slaves. The issues involved in the computation and the procedures employed are discussed in *Appendix B*. The results of the computation are displayed in figure 7.1. This figure presents the average accumulated value or, in the language of economists, the "expected present value" of the income that was expropriated at each age of the life cycle. Prior to age twenty-six, the accumulated expenditures by planters on slaves were greater than the average accumulated income which they took from them. After that age the reverse was true. Planters broke even early in the twenty-seventh year. Over the balance of the life cycle the accumulated or present value of the expropriation mounted, on average, to a total of $32. This last figure is 12 percent of the average present value of the income earned by slaves over their lifetimes. In other words, on average, 12 percent of the value of the income produced by slaves was expropriated by their masters.

The relatively late age at which planters broke even is of great significance and requires further discussion. Two factors are responsible for this lateness. The first is that the cost of capital was high in the South, and planters had to advance capital to cover the expense of rearing slaves for many years before they received a return from the labor of slaves. Second, because of the high mortality rates which prevailed for both black and white in the antebellum era, less than half the slaves lived to the break-even age. Fully 40 percent of the slaves died before age nineteen. Thus, a substantial part of the income taken from those slaves who survived into the later years was not an act of expropriation, but a payment required to cover the expenses of rearing children who failed to reach later ages. An additional part of the income taken from productive slaves, much smaller than that taken to cover child rearing, was used to sustain unproductive elderly slaves, as well as the incapacitated at all ages.

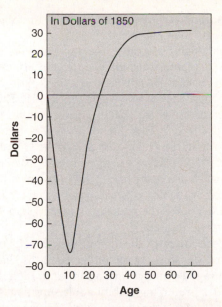

FIGURE 7.2: The Average Accumulated Value (Expected Present Value) of the Income Expropriated from Slaves over the Course of the Life Cycle

These intergenerational transfers of income were not, of course, limited to slave society. They took place among free men as well. For free men must also bear the cost of rearing the young, including those who fail to survive, as well as of supporting the sick and the aged. But among free men, the decision regarding the pattern of intergenerational transfers is made by parents rather than masters. The question thus arises, "How did masters alter the pattern of intergenerational transfers as compared to what it would have been if slaves had been free?" It is much easier to pose the question than to provide an answer. We do not yet have an answer to this question. We would, however, caution against two assumptions. It is not necessarily true that the substitution of planters for parents as decision makers on this issue had a large effect on the pattern of intergenerational transfers. Nor is it necessarily true that readers would consider all changes in the pattern of transfers made by the planters to have been negative. For example, planters spent more (a larger share of earnings) on the medical care of slave children than did the parents of freedmen during the decades following the Civil War.

The high break-even age also helps to explain why U.S. planters encouraged the fertility of slave women, while slaveowners in other parts of the hemisphere appear to have discouraged it. The crux of the matter is that child rearing was profitable only if the expected life of slaves at birth was greater than the break-even age. In the U.S., the life expectation of slaves exceeded the break-even age by more than a half decade. But in colonies such as Jamaica, available evidence suggests that life expectation fell below the break-even age, probably by at least a half decade.

Consequently, during most of the eighteenth century, masters in colonies such as Jamaica discouraged family formation and high fertility rates, preferring to buy adult slaves in Africa rather than to rear them. It was general policy to maintain an imbalance between the sexes with men outnumbering women by a ratio of 4 to 3. To further reduce the basis for stable families, planters encouraged polygamy among slaves by rewarding favored men with second and third wives. Thus, for the remainder of the population, the male-female ratio was about 13 to 8. So large a disproportion between the sexes was bound to encourage sexual activity outside of the family and to reduce fertility. The care given to infants was quite poor compared with the South. Mothers were not encouraged to nurse their children; the southern practice of a 40 to 50 percent reduction of the workload of nursing mothers was not imitated in Jamaica. Further evidence of the neglect of pregnant women is to be found in the high rate of stillbirths. On one of the leading Jamaican plantations, 75 out of 345 births over a four-year period were stillborn. It has also been charged that abortion was both encouraged and widely practiced.

The 12 percent rate of expropriation reported on slave income falls well within the modern tax rate on workers. It has been estimated that about 30 percent of the income of workers at the poverty level is taken from them through sales, real estate, and income taxes. On the other hand such workers, on average, receive payments and various services from the government which more than offset the tax burden. Were there any services received by slaves which offset the income expropriated from them? The answer is yes, but they cannot be quantified reliably at present. Slaves shared in the benefits of large-scale purchases made by the planter. Their clothing, for example, would have been more costly if purchased individually. Perhaps an even more important benefit was the saving on interest charges. Through the intervention of their masters slaves, in effect, were able to borrow at prime rates. Given the high interest charges which black sharecroppers suffered in the post-Civil War era, and the debt-peonage which enmeshed so many of them, the level of interest rates is not a small issue. Pending a more precise measurement of offsetting services, it seems warranted to place the average net rate of the expropriation of slave income at about 10 percent.

Expropriation is not, however, the only form of exploitation…the *economic* burden imposed on slaves by other forms of exploitation probably exceeded that due to expropriation by a considerable margin.

>> Questions for Consideration

1. What evidence is there that this is a quantitative history?
2. What are the strengths and weaknesses of this method of history?
3. What is their argument on whipping? Is it well-proven with evidence? How might their critics have reacted to this argument?

Carroll Smith-Rosenberg, "The Hysterical Woman"

HYSTERIA was one of the classic diseases of the nineteenth century. It was a protean ailment characterized by such varied symptoms as paraplegia, aphonia, hemi-anaesthesia, and violent epileptoid seizures. Under the broad rubric of hysteria, nineteenth-century physicians gathered cases which might today be diagnosed as neurasthenia, hypochondriasis, depression, conversion reaction, and ambulatory schizophrenia. It fascinated and frustrated some of the century's most eminent clinicians; through its redefinition Freud rose to international fame, while towering reputations of Charcot suffered a comparative eclipse. Psychoanalysis can historically be called the child of the hysterical woman.

Not only was hysteria a widespread and—in the intellectual history of medicine—significant disease, it remains to this day a frustrating and ever-changing illness. What was diagnosed as hysteria in the nineteenth century is not necessarily related to the hysterical character as defined in the twentieth century, or again to what the Greeks meant by hysteria when they christened the disease millennia ago. The one constant in this varied history has been the existence in virtually every era of Western culture of some clinical entity called hysteria; an entity which has always been seen as peculiarly relevant to the female experiences, and one which has almost always carried with it a pejorative implication.

For the past half century and longer, American culture has defined hysteria in terms of individual psychodynamics. Physicians and psychologist have seen hysteria as a "neurosis" or a character disorder, the product of an unresolved oedipal complex. Hysterical women, fearful of their own sexual impulses—so the argument went—channeled that energy into psychosomatic illness. Characteristically, they proved unable to form satisfying and stable relationships.[1] More recently psychoanalysts such as Elizabeth Zetzel have refined this Freudian hypothesis, tracing the roots of hysteria to a woman's excessively ambivalent preoedipal relation with her mother and to the resulting complications of oedipal development and resolution.[2] Psychologist David Shapiro has emphasized the hysterical woman's impressionistic thought pattern.[3] All such interpretations focus on exclusive psychodynamics and relations within particular families.

Yet hysteria is also a socially recognized behavior pattern and as such exists within the larger world of cultural values and role relationships. For centuries hysteria has been seen as characteristically female—the hysterical woman the embodiment of a perverse or hyper femininity.[4] Why has this been so? Why did large numbers of women "choose" this character trait of hysteria as their particular mode of expressing

Source: Carroll Smith-Rosenberg, "The Hysterical Woman: Sex Roles and Role Conflict in Nineteenth-Century America," in *Our Selves/Our Past: Psychological Approaches to American History*, ed. Robert J. Brugger (Baltimore: Johns Hopkins University, 1981): pp. 205–227. Reprinted by permission of the New School for Social Research.

[1]For a review of the recent psychiatric literature on hysteria see Aaron Lazare, "The Hysterical Character in Psychoanalytic Theory: Evolution and Confusion," *Archives of General Psychiatry,* XXV (August, 1971), pp. 131–137; Barbara Ruth Easser and S. R. Lesser, "Hysterical Personality: A Reevaluation," *Psychoanalytic Quarterly,* XXXIV (1965), pp. 390–405, and Mare H. Hollander, "Hysterical Personality," *Comments on Contemporary Psychiatry,* I (1971), pp. 17–24.

[2]Elizabeth Zetzel, *The Capacity for Emotional Growth. Theoretical and Clinical Contributions to Psychoanalysis,* 1943-1969 (London: Hogarth Press, 1970), Chap. 1–f, "The So-Called Good Hysteric."

[3]David Shapiro, *Neurotic Style* (New York: Basic Books, 1965).

[4]The argument can be made that hysteria exists among men and therefore is not exclusively related to the female experience; the question is a complete one, and I am presently at work on a

(continued)

malaise, discontent, anger, or pain?[5] To begin to answer this question, we must explore the female role and role socialization. Clearly not all women were hysterics; yet the parallel between the hysteric's behavior and stereotypic femininity is too close to be explained as mere coincidence. To examine hysteria from this social perspective means necessarily to explore the complex relationships that exist between cultural norms and individual behavior, between behavior defined as disease and behavior considered normal.

Using nineteenth-century America as a case study,[6] I propose to explore hysteria on at least two levels of social interaction. The first involves an examination of hysteria as a social role within the nineteenth-century family. This was a period when, it has been argued, social and structural change had created stress within the family and when, in addition, individual domestic role alternatives were few and rigidly defined. From this perspective hysteria can be seen as an alternate role option for particular women incapable of accepting their life situation. Hysteria thus serves as a valuable indicator of both domestic stress and of the tactics through which some individuals sought to resolve that stress. By analyzing the function of hysteria within the family and interaction of the hysteric, her family, and the interceding—yet interacting—physician. I also hope to throw light upon the role of woman and female-male relationships within the larger world of nineteenth-century American society. Secondly, I will attempt to raise some questions concerning female role socialization, female personality options, and the nature of hysterical behavior.[7]

---

parallel study of male hysteria. There are, however, four brief points concerning male hysteria that I would like to make. First, to this day hysteria is still believed to be principally a female "disease" or behavior pattern. Second, the male hysteric is usually seen by physicians as somehow different. Today it is a truism that hysteria is found most frequently among homosexuals; in the nineteenth century men diagnosed as hysterics came almost exclusively from a lower socio-economic status than their physicians—immigrants, especially "new immigrants," miner, railroad workers, blacks. Third, since it was defined by society as a female disease, one may hypothesize that there was some degree of female identification among men who assumed a hysterical role. Lastly, we must recall that a most common form of male hysteria was battle fatigue and shell shock. I should like to thank Erving Goffman for the suggestion that the soldier is in an analogous position to women regarding autonomy and power.

[5]The word choose, even in quotes, is value-laden. I do not mean to imply that hysterical women consciously choose their behavior. I feel that three complex factors interacted to make a woman to arrive at adulthood with significant ego weaknesses; second, certain socialization patters and cultural values which made hysteria a readily available alternative behavior pattern for women, and third, the secondary gains conferred by the hysterical role in terms of enhanced power within the family. Individual case presumably each represented their own peculiar balance of these factors, all of which will be discussed in this paper.

[6]Nineteenth-century hysteria has attracted a good number of students: two of the most important are Henri F. Ellenberger, *The Discovery of the Unconscious* (New York: Basic Books, 1970), and Ilza Veith, *Hysteria: The History of a Disease* (Chicago: University of Chicago Press, 1965). Ellenberger and Veith approach hysteria largely from the framework of intellectual history. For a review of Veith see Charles E. Rosenberg, "Historical Sociology of Medical Thought," *Science*, CL (October 15, 1965), p. 330. For two studies which view nineteenth-century hysteria from a more sociological perspective see Esther Fischer-Homberger, "Hysterie und Misogynie: Ein Aspekt der Hysteriegeschichte," *Gesnerus*, XXVI (1969), pp. 117–127, and Marc H. Hollander, "Conversion Hysteria: A Post-Freudian Reinterpretation of Nineteenth-Century Psychosocial Data," *Archives of General Psychiatry*, XXVI (1972), pp. 311–314.

[7]I would like to thank Renee Fox, Cornelia Friedman, Erving Goffman, Charles E. Rosenberg, and Paul Rosenkrantz for having read and criticized this paper. I would also like to thank my clinical colleagues Philip Mechanick, Henry Bachrach, Ellen Berman, and Carol Wolman of the Psychiatry Department of the University of Pennsylvania for similar assistance. Versions of Society, and initially, in October 1971, at the Psychiatry Department of Hannehmann Medical College, Philadelphia.

It might be best to begin with a brief discussion of three relatively well known areas: first, the role of women in nineteenth-century American society; second, the symptoms which hysterical women presented and which established the definition of the disease, and lastly, the response of male physicians to their hysterical patients.

The ideal female nineteenth-century American was expected to be gentle and refined, sensitive and loving. She was guardian of religion and spokeswoman for morality. Hers was the task of guiding the more worldly and more frequently tempted male past the maelstroms of atheism and uncontrolled sexuality. Her sphere was the hearth and the nursery; within it she was to bestow care and love, peace and joy. The American girl was taught at home, at school, and in the literature of the period, that aggression, independence, self-assertion, and curiosity were male traits, inappropriate for the weaker sex and her limited sphere. Dependent throughout her life, she was to reward her male protectors with affection and submission. At no time was she expected to achieve in any area considered important by men and thus highly valued by society. She was in essence, to remain a child-woman, never developing the strengths and skills of adult autonomy. The stereotype of the middle-class woman as emotional, pious, passive, and nurturant was to become increasingly rigid throughout the nineteenth century.[8]

There were significant discontinuities and inconsistencies between such ideals of female socialization and the real world in which the American woman had to live. The first relates to a dichotomy between the ideal woman and the ideal mother. The ideal woman was emotional, dependent, and gentle—a born follower. The ideal mother, then and now, was expected to be strong, self-reliant, protective, an efficient caretaker in relation to children and home. She was to manage the family's day-to-day finances, prepare food, make clothes, compound drugs, serve as family nurse—and, in rural areas, as physician as well.[9] Especially in the nineteenth-century, with its still primitive obstetrical practices and its high child mortality rates, she was expected to face severe bodily pain, disease, and death—and still serve as the emotional support and strength of her family.[10] As S. Weir Mitchell, the eminent Philadelphia neurologist wrote in the 1880's, "We may be sure that our daughters will be more

---

[8]This summary of women's role and role socialization is drawn from a larger study of male and female gender role socialization in the United State from 1785 to 1895 on which I am presently engaged. This research has been supported by both the Grant Foundation, New York City and the National Institute of Child Health and Human Development, N.I.H. It is difficult to refer succinctly to the wide range of sources on which this paragraph is based. Such a role model appears in virtually every wives and in etiquette books. For a basic secondary source guides to young women and young wives and in etiquette books, see Barbara Welter, "The Cult of True Womanhood," *American Quarterly*, XVIII (1966), pp. 151–174. For an excellent over-all history of women in American see Eleanor Flexner, *Century of Struggle* (Cambridge, Mass.: Harvard University Press, 1959).

[9]For the daily activities of a nineteenth-century American housewife see, for example, *The Maternal Physician: By an American Matron* (New York: Isaac Riley, 1811. Reprinted New York: Arno Press, 1972); Hugh Smith, *Letters to Married Ladies* (New York: Bliss, White and G. & C. Carvill, 1827); John S. C. Abbott, *The Mother at Home* (Boston: Crocker and Brewster, 1833); Lydia H. Sigourney, *Letters to Mothers* (New York: Harper & Brothers, 1841); Mrs. C. A. Hopkinson, *Hints for the Nursery or the Young Mother's Guide* (Boston: Little, Brown & Company, 1836); Catherine Beecher and Harriet Beecher Stowe, *The American Woman's Home* (New York: J. B. Ford & Company, 1869). For an excellent secondary account of the southern woman's domestic life see Anne Firor Scott, *The Southern Lady* (Chicago: University of Chicago Press, 1970).

[10]Nineteenth-century domestic medicine books, gynecological textbooks, and monographs on the diseases of women provide a detailed picture of women's diseases and health expectations.

likely to have to face at some time the grim question of pain than the lads who grow up beside them… To most women…there comes a time when pain is a grim presence in their lives." Yet, as Mitchell pointed out, it was boys whom society taught from early childhood on to bear pain stoically, while girls were encouraged to respond to pain and stress with tears and the expectation of elaborate sympathy.[11]

Contemporaries noted routinely in the 1870's, 1880's, and 1890's that middle-class American girls seemed ill-prepared to assume the responsibilities and trials of marriage, motherhood, and maturation. Frequently women, especially married women with children, complained of isolation, loneliness, and depression. Physicians reported a high incidence of nervous disease and hysteria among women who felt overwhelmed by the burdens of frequent pregnancies, the demands of children, the daily exertion of housekeeping and family management.[12] The realities of adult life no longer permitted them to elaborate and exploit the role of fragile, sensitive, and dependent child.

Not only was the Victorian woman increasingly ill prepared for the trials of childbirth and child-rearing, but changes were also at worth within the larger society which were to make her particular socialization increasingly inappropriate.

Reduced birth and morality rates, growing population concentration in towns, cities, and even in rural areas, a new, highly mobile economy, as well as new patterns of middle-class aspiration—all reached into the family, altering that institution, affecting domestic relations, and increasing the normal quality of intrafamilial stress.[13] Women lived longer; they married later and less often. They spent less and less time in the primary processing of food, cloth and clothing. Increasingly, both middle- and lower-class women took jobs outside the home until their marriages—or permanently if unable to secure a husband.[14] By the post-Civil War years, family limitation—with its necessary implication of altered domestic roles and relationships—had become a real option within the decision-making processes of every family.[15]

Despite such basic social, economic and demographic changes, however, the family and gender role socialization remained relatively inflexible. It is quite possible that many women experienced a significant level of anxiety when forced to confront or adapt in one way or another to these changes. Thus hysteria may have served as one option or tactic offering particular women otherwise unable to respond to these changes a chance to redefine or restructure their place within the family.

---

[11]S. Weir Mitchell, *Doctor and Patient* (Philadelphia: J.B. Lippincott Company, 1887), pp. 84, 92.

[12]See among others Edward H. Dixon, *Woman and Her Diseases* (New York: Charles H. Ping, 1846), pp. 135–136; Alice Stockham, *Tokology: A Book for Every Woman* (Chicago: Sanitary Publishers, 1887), p. 83: Sarah Stevenson, *Physiology of Women*, 2nd ed. (Chicago: Cushing, Thomas & Co., 1881), p. 91; Henry Pye Chavasse, *Advice to a Wife and Counsel to a Mother* (Philadelphia: J. B. Lippincott, 1891), p. 97. A Missouri physician reported the case of a twenty-eight-year-old middle-class woman with two children. Shortly after the birth of her second child, she missed her period, believed herself to be pregnant for a third time and succumbed to hysterical symptoms: depression, headaches, vomiting, and seizures.

[13]For a study of declining nineteenth-century American birth rates see Yasukichi Yasuba, *Birth Rates of the White Population in the United States, 1800-1860* (Baltimore: The Johns Hopkins University Press, 1962) and J. Potter, "American Population in the Early National Period," in *Proceeding of Section V of the Fourth Congress of the International Economic History Association*, Paul Deprez, ed. (Winnipeg, 1970), pp. 55–69.

[14]For a useful general discussion of women's changing roles see Eleanor Flexner, *op. cit.*

[15]For discussion of birth control and its effect on domestic relations see Carroll Smith-Rosenberg and Charles E. Rosenberg, "The Female Animal" Medical and Biological Views of Woman and Her Role in Nineteenth-Century America," *Journal of American History*, LX (September, 1973), pp. 332–56.

So far this discussion of role socialization and stress has emphasized primarily the malaise and dissatisfaction of the middle-class woman. It is only a covert romanticism, however, which permits us to assume that the lower-class or farm woman, because her economic functions within her family were more vital than those of her decorative and economically secure urban sister, escaped their sense of frustration, conflict, or confusion. Normative prescriptions of proper womanly behavior were certainly internalized by many poorer women. The desire to marry and the belief that a woman's social status came not from the exercise of her own talents and efforts but from her ability to attract a competent male protector were as universal among lower-class and farm woman as among middle- and upper-class urban woman. For some of these woman— as for their middle-class sisters—the traditional female role proved functional, bringing material and psychic rewards. But for some it did not. The discontinuity between the child and adult female roles, along with the failure to develop substantial ego strengths, crossed class and geographic barriers—as did hysteria itself. Physicians connected with almshouses, and later in the century with urban hospitals and dispensaries, often reported hysteria among immigrants and tenement house woman.[16] Sex differentiation and class distinctions both play a role in American social history, yet hysteria seems to have followed a psychic fault line corresponding more to distinction of gender than to those of class.

Against this background of possible role conflict and discontinuity, what were the presenting symptoms of the female hysteric in the nineteenth-century America? While physicians agreed that hysteria could afflict persons of both sexes and of all ages and economic classes (the male hysteric was an accepted clinical entity by the late nineteenth century), they reported that hysteria was most frequent among women between the ages of 15 and 40 and of the urban middle and upper middle classes. Symptoms were highly varied. As early as seventeenth century, indeed, Sydenham had remarked that "the frequency of hysteria in no less remarkable than the multiformity of the shapes it puts on. Few maladies are not imitated by it; whatever part of the body it attacks, it will create the proper symptom of the part."[17] The nineteenth-century physician could only concur. There were complaints of nervousness, depression, the tendency to tears and chronic fatigue, or of disabling pain. Not a few women thus afflicted showed a remarkable willingness, to submit to long-term, painful therapy—to electric shock treatment, to blistering, to multiple operations, even to amputations.[18]

---

[16]William A. Hammond, *On Certain Conditions of Nervous Derangement* (New York: G. P. Putnam's Sons, 1881), p. 42; S. Weir Mitchell, *Lectures on the Diseases of the Nervous System, Especially in Women*, 2nd ed. (Philadelphia: Lea Brothers & Co., 1885), pp. 114, 110; Charles K. Mills, "Hysteria," in *A System of Practical Medicine by American Authors*, William Pepper, ed., assisted by Louis Starr, vol. V, "Diseases of the Nervous System" (Philadelphia: Lea Brothers & Co., 1883), p. 213; Charles E. Lockwood, "A Study of Hysteria and Hypochondriasis," *Transactions of the New York State Medical Association*, XII (1895), pp. 340–351. E H. Van Deusen, Superintendent of the Michigan Asylum for Insane, reported that nervousness, hysteria, and neurasthenia were common among farm women and resulted, he felt, from the social and intellectual deprivation of their isolated lives. Van Deusen, "Observations on a Form of Nervous Prostration," *American Journal of Insanity*, XXV (1869), p. 447. Significantly most English and American authorities on hysteria were members of a medical elite who saw the wealthy in their private practices and the very poor in their hospital and dispensary work. Thus the observation that hysteria occurred in different social classes was often made by the very clinicians.

[17]Thomas Sydenham, "Epistolary Dissertation," in *The Works of Thomas Sydenham, M. D. ... with a Life of the Author*, R. G. Lathan, ed. 2 vols. (London: New Sydenham Society, 1850), II, p. 85.

[18]Some women diagnosed as hysterics displayed quite bizarre behavior—including self-mutilation and hallucinations. Clearly a certain percentage of these women would be diagnosed today as

(continued)

The most characteristic and dramatic symptom, however, was the hysterical "fit." Mimicking an epileptic seizure, these fits often occurred with shocking suddenness. At other times they "came on" gradually, announcing their approach with a general feeling of depression, nervousness, crying, or lassitude. Such seizures, physicians generally agreed, were precipitated by a sudden or deeply felt emotion—fear, shock, a sudden death, marital disappointment—or by physical trauma. It began with pain and tension, most frequently in the "uterine area." The sufferer alternatively sobbed and laughed violently, complained of palpitations of the heart, clawed at her throat as if strangling, and, at times, abruptly lost the power of hearing and speech. A death-like trance might follow, lasting hours, even days. At times violent convulsions—sometimes accompanied by hallucinations—seized her body.[19] "Let the reader imagine," New York psychologist E. H. Dixon wrote in the 1840's,

> The patient writhing like a serpent upon the floor, rendering her garments to tatters, plucking out handful of hair, and striking her person with violence—with contorted and swollen countenance and fixed eyes resist every effort of bystanders to control her...[20]

Finally the fit subsided; the patient, exhausted and sore, fell into a restful sleep.

III

The hysterical female emerges from the essentially male medical literature of the nineteenth century as a "child woman," highly impressionable, labile, superficially sexual, exhibitionistic, given to dramatic body language and grand gestures, with strong dependency needs, a masochistic or self-punishing behavior pattern, and decided ego weakness. She resembles in many ways the hysterical personality described in the 1968 *Diagnostic and Statistical Manual of Mental Disorders* of the American Psychiatric Association: a personality characterized, that is, by "excitability, emotional instability, overreactive, self-dramatization, attention seeking, immaturity, vanity, and unusual dependence." Her symptoms correspond closely to those Otto Kernberg describes as an "infantile personality" or Samuel B. Guze as a "hysterical personality."[21] Thus we find the child-woman a person who, filled with self-doubt, constantly needs the reassurance and attention of others. In fact, these characteristics are merely hypertrophied versions of traits and behaviors routinely reinforced throughout the nineteenth century in girls, female adolescents, and adult woman.

In attempting to understand hysteria, then, it might be best not only to look at stress and dysfunction within the hysteric's particular psychic background but also to examine the correspondence between this personality pattern and the

---

schizophrenic. The majority of the women diagnosed as hysterical, however, did not display such symptoms, but rather appear from clinical descriptions to have had a personality similar to that considered hysterical by mid-twentieth-century psychiatrists.

[19]For three typical descriptions of such seizures, see Buel Eastman, *Practical Treatise on Diseases Peculiar to Women and Girls* (Cincinnati: C. Cropper & Son, 1848), p. 40; Samuel Ashwell, *A Practical Treatise on the Disease Peculiar to Women* (London: Samuel Highly, 1844), pp. 210–212; William Campbell, *Introduction to the Study and Practice of Midwifery and the Disease of Children* (London: Longman, Rees, Orme, Brown, Green & Longman, 1833), pp. 440–442.

[20]E. H. Dixon, *op. cit.*, p. 133.

[21]*Diagnostic and Statistical Manual of Mental Disorders*, 2d ed. (Washington, D.C.: American Psychiatric Association, 1968), p. 43. Otto Kernberg, "Borderline Personality Organization," *Journal of the American the Psychoanalytical Association*, XV (July, 1967), pp. 641–85; Samuel B. Guze, "The Diagnosis of Hysteria: What are We Trying to Do?" *American Journal of Psychiatry*, CXXIV (October, 1967), pp. 491–98.

literature to which a young woman was exposed. This method means discussing normative cultural values or prescription rather than actual behavior. Yet what women were supposed to do and be provides the historian with a valuable source. Prescriptive value—most universally accepted in a culture and actively fostered by its authority figures—undoubtly influence the child-rearing practices of mothers and the behavior of children, especially during the early years of life when gender identity is formed. From this perspective, then, the historian is justified in exploring the possible way in which female gender roles socialization affected the development of ego strengths and weaknesses in nineteenth-century women.

At a time when American society accepted egalitarian democracy and free will as transcendent social values, women were routinely socialized to fill a weak, dependent, and severely limited social role. There is evidence from children's books, child-rearing manuals, marriage guides, and books of etiquette that women were sharply discouraged from expressing competition or mastery in such "masculine" areas as physical skill, strength, and courage, or in academic, scientific, or commercial pursuits. Instead they were encouraged to be coquettish, entertaining, nonthreatening, and nurturant. Overt anger and violence were forbidden as unfeminine and vulgar. Women were not rewarded for curiosity, intrusiveness, or exploratory behavior. Indeed when such characteristics conflicted with the higher feminine values of cleanliness, proper deportment, unobtrusiveness, and obedience, women were criticized or punished—yet these same habits of mind are now deemed essential to the development of autonomy and identity in children. Most children's literature asserted that boys were brave, active, lively. Girls, on the other hand, were taught that their greatest happiness lay in an unselfish routine of caring for the needs of others.[22]

Nineteenth-century American society provided but one socially respectable, nondeviant role for women—that of loving wife and mother. Thus women, who presumably came in assorted psychological and intellectual shapes and sizes, had to find adjustments in only one prescribed social role—one that demanded continual self-abnegation and desire to please others. Children's literature and genteel women's magazines in every case required of women an altruistic denial of their own ambitions and a displacement of their wishes and abilities onto the men in their lives. We may assume that for a certain percentage of women such sacrifice led to a form of what Anna Freud and Edward Bibring defined as "altruistic surrender."[23] In other cases training to fit a narrowly defined role must have resulted in significant ego restriction—the ego choosing not to develop in certain directions because the pain of punishment or of being defined as deviant was too costly. "When the ego is young and Plastic," Anna Freud wrote,

> its withdrawal from one field of activity is sometimes compensated for by excellence in another, upon which it concentrates. But, when it has become rigid or has already acquired an intolerance of "pain" and so is obsessionally fixated to the method of flight, such withdrawal is punished by impaired development. By abandoning one position after another it becomes onesided, loses too many interests and can show but a meager achievement.[24]

Significant differences appear to lie as well in the ways in which boys and girls were punished in the nineteenth century. It is true that disciplinary patterns were changing then, and that corporal punishment seems to have decreased in frequency for boys as well as girls. Nevertheless, sociological studies offer evidence that even until fairly recently boys received far more physical

---

[22]These conclusions are based on the analysis of American children's books, 1760–1890, that I am currently completing.

[23]Anna Freud, *The Ego and the Mechanism of Defense*. Revised ed. (New York: International Universities Press, 1966), pp. 122–37.

[24]Ibid., pp. 102–3. See chapter 8 for Freud's discussion of ego restriction.

punishment than did girls, who commonly were punished by being made to feel guilty and by being threatened with withdrawal of love or actually being separated from parents. Social psychologist and sociologists such as Uri Brofenbrenner and Judith Bardwick have argued that while such "love-oriented punishment" produced obedient and docile children, it also made children timid, anxious, dependent, and sensitive to rejection.[25] Other psychologists have recently argued that love-oriented punishment and girls' more socialized behavior in early childhood tend to delay their forming an independent identity until late adolescence—if then—and lead them to be overly dependent upon the approval and support of significant others in their lives.[26] To put it differently, women in nineteenth-century society necessarily restricted their ego functions to love-prestige areas, remaining dependent on others and altruistically wishing worldly success not for themselves but for their husbands, fathers, or brothers. The effect of this socialization may well have been to impede ego development significantly in many women and—if there is an aggressive drive in the id—to repress it. The behavioral result appears to have been to limit opportunities for conflict-free ego growth, or to neglect that form of the ego development.

Thus one finds suggestive parallels between the "hysterical" woman of the nineteenth century and the "masochistic" female personality that Karen Horney described in *New Ways to Psychoanalysis* (1949). The masochistic woman, argued Horney, suffered from "free floating anxiety," a deep-rooted sense of inferiority, and an absence of adequate aggression, by which Horney meant that ability to take initiative, to make efforts, to carry things through to completion, and to form and express autonomous views.

Insecure, afflicted with anxieties, she demanded constant attention and expressions of affection, which she sought to secure by appealing to pity and displaying inferiority feelings, weakness, and suffering. Such a self-image and pattern of object relations necessarily "generated hostile feelings, but feelings which the masochistic woman was unable to express directly because they would have jeopardized her dependency relationships." Weakness and suffering, Horney continued, "already serving many functions, now also act as a vehicle for the indirect expression of hostility." While both men and women develop masochistic personalities, Horney hypothesized that far larger numbers of women and men would do so in cultures in which women more than men (1) "manifest[ed]…inhibitions in the direct expression of demands and aggressions; (2) regard[ed]…themselves as weak, helpless, or inferior and implicitly or explicitly demand[ed] considerations and advantages on this basis; (3) [became] emotionally dependent on the other sex; (4) show[ed]…tendencies to be self-sacrificing, to be submissive, to feel used or to be exploited, to put responsibility on the other sex; (5) us[ed]…weakness and helplessness as a means of wooing and subduing the other sex."[27]

In short, many nineteenth-century women reach maturity with major ego weaknesses and narrowly limited compensatory ego strengths, all of which implies a relationship between this pattern of socialization and one's adoption of hysterical behavior. The reasons why each individual displayed the pattern of behavior that nineteenth-century physicians called "hysteria" must remain moot. It seems plausible to suggest that a certain percentage of nineteenth-century women, faced the stress developing out of their own peculiar personality needs or out of

---

[25]Judith Bardwick and Elizabeth Douvan, "Ambivalence: the Socialization of Women," in Vivian Gornick and Barbara K. Moran, eds., *Women in a Sexiest Society* (New York: Basic Books, 1971).

[26]Elizabeth Douvan, "Sex Differences in Adolescent Character Processes," *Merrill-Palmer Quarterly*, VI (1958), pp. 203–11.

[27]Karen Horney, "The Problem of Female Masochism," in *Feminine Psychology* (New York: W. W. Norton and Co., 1967), pp. 214–33 and especially pp. 228–29.

situational anxieties, might well have defended themselves against such stress by regressing towards the childish hyperfemininity of the hysteric. The discontinuity between the roles of courted young woman and pain-bearing, self-sacrificing wife and mother, the realities of an unhappy marriage, the loneliness and chagrin of spinsterhood may all have made the petulant infantilism and narcissistic self-assertion of the hysteric a necessary alternative to women who felt unfairly deprived of their promised social role and who had few strengths with which to adapt to a more trying one. Society had indeed structured this regression by consistently reinforcing those very emotional traits characterized in the stereotype of the female and caricatured in the symptomatology of the hysteric. At the same time, the nineteenth-century female hysteric also exhibited a significant level of hostility and aggression-rage—which may have led in turn to her depression and to her self-punishing psychosomatic illness. In all these ways, then, the hysterical woman was both product and indictment of her culture. This paper has sought to suggest why certain symptoms were available and why women, in particular, tended to resort to them. It has sought as well to use the reactions of contemporaries to illuminate the realities of female-male and intrafamilial role. As such it has dealt with hysteria as a psychological role produced by the functional within a specific set of social circumstances.

>> Questions for Consideration

1. How does Smith-Rosenberg blend the methods of psychohistory and women's history in the excerpt?
2. How does this history reflect the influence of the women's rights movement?
3. Does this seem like a radically different kind of history? Why or why not?

John Hope Franklin, "The Moral Legacy of the Founding Fathers"

The Moral Legacy of the Founding Fathers

As we approach the bicentennial of the independence of the United States, it may not be inappropriate to take advantage of the perspective afforded by these last two centuries. Such a perspective should enable us to understand the distance we have traveled and where we are today.

This stock-taking, as it were, seems unusually desirable, thanks to the recent crises in leadership, in confidence in our political institutions, and in the standards of public morality to which we have paid only a "nodding acquaintance" over the years. As we do so, it is well to remember that criticism does not necessarily imply hostility, and, indeed, the recognition of human weakness suggests no alienation. One thing that becomes painfully clear as we look today at the shattered careers of so many public servants, with their confusion of public service with personal gain, is that we cannot always be certain of the validity or the defensibility of the positions taken by those who claim to be out leaders.

Source: John Hope Franklin, "The Moral Legacy of the Founding Fathers," *University of Chicago Magazine* XLVII: 4 (Spring 1975). Reprinted by permission of the University of Chicago Magazine.

To be sure, we ally ourselves with one political party or another—as we have done since the time of Jefferson and Hamilton—and we have railed against the politics of one party or, now and then, the conduct of party leaders.

On the whole, however, our criticisms have been superficial and the glass houses we have occupied have, for obvious reasons, prevented our engaging in all-out strictures against our adversaries. The result has been that we have usually engaged in the most gentle rapping of the knuckles of those who have betrayed their public trust, and seldom have we called our public servants to account in a really serious way.

In the effort to create an "instant history" with which we could live and prosper, our early historians intentionally placed our early national heroes and leaders beyond the pale of criticism. From the time that Benjamin Franklin created his own hero in "Poor Richard" and Mason L. Weems created the cherry tree story about George Washington, it has been virtually impossible to regard our founding fathers as normal, fallible human beings. And this distorted image of them has not only created a gross historical fallacy, but it has also rendered it utterly impossible to deal with our past in terms of the realities that existed at the time. To put it another way, our romanticizing about the history of the late eighteenth century has prevented our recognizing the fact that the founding fathers made serious mistakes that have greatly affected the course of our national history from that time to the present.

In 1974 we observed the bicentennial of the first Continental Congress, called to protest the new trade measures invoked against the colonies of Great Britain and to protest the political and economic measures directed particularly against the colony of Massachusetts. In a sense these measures were, indeed, intolerable as the colonists were forced to house British soldiers stationed in their midst, and Quebec was given political and economic privileges that appeared to be clearly discriminatory against the thirteen colonies.

But were these measures imposed by the British more intolerable than those imposed or, at least, sanctioned by the colonists against their own slaves? And yet, the colonists were outraged that the mother country was denying them their own freedom—the freedom to conduct their trade as they pleased.

It was not that the colonists were unaware of the problem of a much more basic freedom than that for which they were fighting in London. First of all, they knew of the 1772 decision of Lord Mansfield in the Somerset case, in which slavery was outlawed in Britain on the compelling ground that human bondage was "too odious" in England without specific legislation authorizing it. Although the colonists did have the authorization to establish and maintain slavery, Lord Mansfield's strictures against slavery could not have been lost on them altogether.

Secondly, and even more important, the slaves themselves were already pleading for their own freedom even before the first Continental Congress met. In the first six months of 1773 several slaves in Massachusetts submitted petitions to the general court, "praying to be liberated from a State of slavery." In the following years scores of others slaves, denying that they had ever forfeited the blessings of freedom by any compact or agreement to become slaves, asked for their freedom and for some land on which each of them "could sit down quietly under his own fig tree." The legislature of Massachusetts colony debated the subject of slavery in 1774 and 1775, but voted simply that "the matter now subside."

But the matter would neither die nor subside. As the colonists plunged into war with Great Britain, they were faced with the problem of what to do about Negro slavery. The problem presented itself in the form of urgent questions.

First, should they continue to import slaves? This was a matter of some importance to British slave-trading interests who had built fortunes out of the traffic in human beings and to colonist who feared that new, raw recruits from the West Indies and Africa would be more of a problem than a blessing. Most of the colonies opposed any new importations, and the Continental Congress affirmed the prohibition in April, 1776.

Secondly, should the colonists use black soldiers in their fight against Britain? Although a few were used in the early skirmishes of the war, a pattern of exclusion of blacks had developed by the time that independence was declared. In July 1775, the policy had been set forth that recruiters were not to enlist any deserter from the British army, "nor any stroller, negro, or vagabond."

Then, late in the year the British welcomed all Negroes willing to join His Majesty's troops, and promised to set them free in return. The colonists were terrified, especially with the prospect of a servile insurrection. And so the Continental Congress shortly reversed its policy and grudgingly admitted blacks into the Continental Army.

The final consideration, as the colonists fought for their own freedom from Britain, was what would be the effect of their revolutionary philosophy on their own slaves. The colonists argued in the Declaration of Independence that they were oppressed, and they wanted their freedom. Thomas Jefferson, in an early draft, went so far as to accuse the king of England of imposing slavery on them, but more "practical" heads prevailed, and that provision was stricken from the Declaration.

Even so, the Declaration said "all men are created equal." "Black men as well as white men?" some wondered. Every man had an inalienable right to "life, liberty, and the pursuit of happiness." Every black man as well as every white man?" some could well have asked.

How could the colonists make distinctions in their revolutionary philosophy? They either meant that *all* men were created equal or they did not mean it at all. They either meant that *every* man was entitled to life, liberty, and the pursuit of happiness, or they did not mean it at all.

To be sure, some patriots were apparently troubled by the contradictions between their revolutionary philosophy of political freedom and the holding of human beings in bondage. Abigail Adams, the wife of John Adams, admitted that there was something strange about their fighting to achieve and enjoy a status that they daily denied to others. Patrick Henry, who had

cried "Give me liberty or give me death," admitted that slavery was "repugnant to humanity", but it must not have seemed terribly repugnant, for he continued to hold blacks in bondage. So did George Washington and Thomas Jefferson and George Mason and Edmund Randolph and many others who signed the Declaration of Independence or the federal Constitution. They simply would not or could not see how ridiculous their position was.

And where the movement to emancipate the slaves took hold, as in New England and in some of the Middle Atlantic states, slavery was not economically profitable anyway. Consequently, if the patriots in those states were genuinely opposed to slavery, they could afford the luxury of speaking against it. But in both of the Continental Congresses and in the Declaration of Independence the founding fathers failed to take an unequivocal, categorical stand against slavery. Obviously, human bondage and human dignity were not as important to them as their own political and economic independence.

The founding fathers were not only compelled to live with their own inconsistency but they also had to stand convicted before they very humble group which they excluded from their political and social fellowship. In 1777 a group of Massachusetts blacks told the whiles of that state that every principle that impelled America to break with England "plead stronger than a thousand arguments" against slavery. In 1779 a group of Connecticut slaves petitioned the state of their liberty, declaring that they "groaned" under the burdens and indignities they were required to bear.

In 1781, Paul Cuffe and his brother, two young enterprising blacks, asked Massachusetts to excuse them from the duty of paying taxes, since they "had no influence in the election of those who tax us." And when they refused to pay their taxes, those who had shouted that England's taxation without representation was tyranny, slapped the Cuffe brothers in jail.

Thus, when the colonists emerged victorious from their war with England, they had both their independence *and* their slaves. It seemed to matter so little to most of the patriots that the slaves themselves had eloquently pointed out their inconsistencies or that not a few of the patriots themselves saw and pointed out their own fallacious position. It made no difference that five thousand blacks had joined in the fight for independence, only to discover that *real* freedom did not apply to them. The agencies that forged a national policy against England—the Continental Congresses and the government under the Articles of Confederation—were incapable of forging—or unwilling to forge—a national policy in favor of human freedom.

It was not a propitious way to start a new nation, especially since its professions were so different from its practices and since it presumed to be the model for other new world colonies that would, in time, seek their independence from the tyranny of Europe.

Having achieved their own independence, the patriots exhibited no great anxiety to extend the blessings of liberty to those among them who did not enjoy it. They could not altogether ignore the implications of the revolutionary philosophy, however. As early as 1777 the Massachusetts legislature had under consideration a measure to prohibit "the practice of holding persons in Slavery." Three years later the new constitution of that state declared that "all men are born free and equal." Some doubtless hoped that those high sounding words would mean more in the constitution of Massachusetts than they had meant in the Declaration of Independence.

Her neighbors, however, were more equivocal, with New Hampshire, Connecticut, and Rhode Island vacillating, for one reason or another, until another decade had passed. Although Pennsylvania did abolish slavery in 1780, New York and New Jersey did no better than prepare the groundwork for gradual emancipation at a later date.

One may well be greatly saddened by the thought that the author of the Declaration of Independence and the commander of the Revolutionary army and so many heroes of the Revolution were slaveholders. Even more disheartening, if such is possible, is that those *same* leaders and heroes were not greatly affected by the philosophy of freedom which they espoused. At least they gave no evidence of having been greatly affected by it.

Nor did they show any great magnanimity of spirit, once the war was over and political independence was assured. While northerners debated the questions of how and when they would free their slaves, the institution of human bondage remained as deeply entrenched as ever—from Delaware to Georgia. The only area on which there was national agreement that slavery should be prohibited was the area east of the Mississippi River and north of the Ohio River—the Northwest Territory. The agreement to prohibit slavery in that area, where it did not really exist and where relatively few white settlers lived, posed no great problem and surely it did not reflect a ground swell for liberty.

Meanwhile the prohibition, it should be noted, did not apply to the area south of the Ohio River, where slaveholders were more likely to settle anyway! This clearly shows that the founding fathers were willing to "play" with the serious question of freedom, thus evincing a cynicism that was itself unworthy of statesmanship.

Nor is one uplifted or inspired by the attitude of the founding fathers towards the slave trade, once their independence was secured. In the decade following independence the importation of slaves into the United States actually increased over the previous decade as well as over the decade before the War of Independence began. Far from languishing, the institution of slavery was prospering and growing. In its deliberations between 1781 and 1789 the Congress of the Confederation barely touched on the question of slavery or the slave trade. There was, to be sure, some concern over the capture of slaves, and the Congress gave some attention to the Quaker petition against the trade, but it took no action.

On the whole the nation did not raise a hand against it. The flurry of activity in the states, which led to the prohibition of slave importations in some of them and a temporary cessation of the trade in others, had the effect of misleading many people into thinking that slavery's hold on the nation was weakening.

That this was far from the actual situation became painfully clear when the delegates gathered in Philadelphia in 1787 to write a new constitution. In the discussion over the slave trade only practical and economic considerations held sway. Humane considerations simply were not present. Maryland and Virginia tended to oppose the slave trade simply because they were overstocked and were not anxious to have any large importations into their midst. South Carolina and Georgia, where the death rate in the rice swamps was high and where slaveholders needed new recruits to develop new areas, demanded an open door for slave dealers.

And who rushed to the rescue when South Carolina demanded concessions on the question of the slave trade? It was Oliver Ellsworth of Connecticut, who observed that a provision in the Constitution against the slave trade would be "unjust towards South Carolina and Georgia. Let us not intermeddle," he said. "As population increases, poor laborers will be so plenty as to render slaves useless." It is impossible to conceive that such temporizing on the part of a leading colonist would have been tolerated in the late dispute with England.

Could the new national government that was designed to be strong have *anything* to say regarding slavery and the slave trade in the states? Elbridge Gerry of Massachusetts answered that it could not. It only had to refrain from giving direct sanction to the system.

Perhaps this is the view that seemed to silence the venerable Benjamin Franklin. The oldest and easily one of the most respected members of the Constitutional Convention, Franklin brought with him a strong resolution against the slave trade that had been entrusted to him by the Pennsylvania Abolition Society. Although he was one of the most frequent speakers at the convention, he never introduced the resolution. With faint hearts such as Gerry's and Franklin's there is little wonder that South Carolina and Georgia

were able to have their own way in wording the provision that declared that the slave trade could not be prohibited for another twenty years. One need only to look at the slave importation figures between 1788 and 1808 to appreciate how much advantage was taken of this generous reprieve.

The founding fathers did no better when it came to counting slaves for purposes of representation and taxation. Northerners, who regarded slaves as property, insisted that for the purpose of representation they could not be counted as people. Southern slaveholders, while cheerfully admitting that slaves were property, insisted that they were also people and should be counted as such. It is one of the remarkable ironies of the early history of this democracy that the very men who had shouted so loudly that all men were created equal could not agree on whether or not person of African descent were men at all.

The irony was compounded when, in the so-called major compromise of the Constitution, the delegates agreed that a slave was three-fifth of a man, meaning that five slaves were to be counted as three persons. The magic of racism can work magic with the human mind. One wonders whether Catherine Drinker Bowen had this in mind when she called her history of the Constitutional Convention *The Miracle at Philadelphia*.

At the outset it was observed that we tend to shy away from making criticisms or judgments of those who occupy the seats of the mighty. This is not good either for ourselves or the institutions and way of life we seek to foster. If we would deal with our past in terms of the realities that existed at the time, it becomes necessary for us to deal with our early leaders in their own terms, namely, as frail, fallible human beings, and—at times—utterly indifferent to the great cause they claimed to serve...

We are concerned here not so much for the harm that the founding fathers did to the cause they claimed to serve as for the harm that the moral legacy has done to every generation of their progeny. Having created a tragically flawed revolutionary doctrine and a constitution that did not bestow the blessings of liberty on its posterity, the founding fathers set the stage for every succeeding generation of American to apologize, compromise, and temporize on those principles of liberty that were supposed to be the very foundation of our system of government and way of life.

Racial segregation, discrimination, and degradation are not unanticipated accidents in this nation's history. They stem logically and correctly from the legacy that the founding fathers bestowed upon contemporary America. The denial of equality in the year of independence led directly to the denial of equality in the era of the bicentennial independence. The so-called compromises in the Constitution of 1776 led directly to arguments in our own time that we can compromise equality with impunity and somehow use the Constitution as an instrument to preserve privilege and to foster inequality. It has then become easy to invoke the spirit of the founding fathers whenever we seek ideological support for the social, political, and economic inequities that have become a part of the America way.

It would be perverse indeed to derive satisfaction from calling attention to the flaws in the character and conduct of the founding fathers. And it would be irresponsible to do so merely to indulge in whimsical iconoclasm. But it would be equally irresponsible in the era of a bicentennial independence not to use the occasion to examine our past with a view to improving the human condition.

An appropriate beginning, it would seem, would be to celebrate our origins for what they were—to honor the principles of independence for which so many patriots fought and died. It is equally appropriate to be outraged over the manner in which the principles of human freedom and human dignity were denied and debased by those same patriots. Their legacy to us in this regard cannot, under any circumstance, be cherished or celebrated. Rather, this legacy represents a continuing and dismaying problem that requires us all to put forth as much effort to overcome it as the founding fathers did in handing it down to us.

>> Questions for Consideration

1. In what ways might this essay be called "perspectival"?
2. How did Watergate, the civil rights movement, and the Black Power movement shape Franklin's perspective of the Revolution?
3. Compare Franklin's history of the American Revolution to that of George Bancroft. What explains the differences?

Chapter 8

The Linguistic Turn, Postmodernism, and New Cultural History

Michel Foucault (CORBIS-*NY*).

At the same time scholars turned to new social scientific methods to study history from the bottom-up, others borrowed new theories and methods from the fields of linguistics, literary analysis, and cultural anthropology. Similar to historicists in the nineteenth century, who sought to understand the past societies in their own terms and context, these new historicists closely analyzed literary and nonliterary texts to reconstruct the mental world of their authors. Inspired by E. P. Thompson and the *Annalistes*, these historians were especially interested in cultural and intellectual history. Some new historicists, however, rejected empiricism, preferring the more constructivist philosophy advocated by postmodernists.[1] Reflecting a general disillusionment with science following its extensive use in World War II to exterminate masses of people, many intellectuals began to

---

[1]Constructivists believe truth and reality are constructed by individuals and all observations are consequently subjective, whereas empiricists believe that truth and reality exist independently of individuals and consequently may be objectively observed.

question scientific claims to objectivity and even reject the Modern worldview created after the Scientific Revolution. Questioning all claims to universal truths and objectivity, they searched for new perspectives on knowledge and asked new questions. Called "postmodernism," this intellectual trend crossed many different disciplines and claimed to have moved beyond the Modern definition of truth and knowledge. Emerging during the cultural revolution of the 1960s, postmodernism appeared to many as a theoretical manifestation of radical cultural movements. In history, this new search for knowledge and meaning affected many different branches of study, but none so much as that of cultural history. As a consequence, some of the most revolutionary and controversial histories of the past thirty years have been in new cultural history.

The Turn Toward Relativism

It is difficult to determine a precise date for the shift away from empiricism which marks the postmodern turn in history, but a starting point is the nineteenth century with its questioning of the Enlightenment's master narrative of modernity and historical progress, and especially its claims to objectivity and universal truth. Karl Marx challenged the Enlightenment master narrative by positing that the superstructures of capitalism created and controlled literature and knowledge to support class hierarchy.[2] Marxist historians in the twentieth century, such as Antonio Gramsci and Louis Althusser, further explored this idea, tracing exactly how ruling elites controlled the superstructure of knowledge and culture in support of their own class interests, establishing "cultural hegemony." Although Marxists offered their own alternative master narrative of history, their theories implied that even scientific or historical literature was constructed by individuals and thus relative and subjective.

Nietzsche   For some theorists, the contradiction between Modernist and Marxist master narratives undermined the entire notion of any universal master narrative. Prussian philosopher Friedrich Nietzsche (1844–1900) took Marxism to the next level, arguing that all forms of truth and knowledge are created by human beings in order to obtain and maintain their power. In this view, history, like all forms of knowledge, is never objective and does not accurately represent reality. Nietzsche argued that all historical patterns and meanings were artificially constructed by historians and that the past is actually a series of disjunctures and disruptions, with no rational pattern or cause and effect. Historians merely impose order on facts to create truth. Many of Nietzsche's ideas were taken up by existentialists in the twentieth century. Like Nietzsche, existentialists Jean-Paul Sartre and Albert Camus rejected rationalism and empiricism. Instead, they argued that in the absence of universal laws of morality or ethics, individuals are free to create their own laws, ethics, and meanings in life. As these theories

Existentialism

---

[2]Christoph Reinfandt, "Reading Texts after the Linguistic Turn: Approaches from Literary Studies and their Implications," in *Reading Primary Sources: The Interpretation of texts from 19th and 20th Century History*, ed. Miriam Dobson and Benjamin Ziemann (New York: Routledge, 2009), 41.

became more widespread in the twentieth century, so too did the questioning of positivist empiricism.

Even as professional historians used objectivity to support their claims to scientific legitimacy, relativism and subjectivism emerged as topics of debate in the early twentieth century. Many Progressive historians, and indeed most professional historians since then, noted the role of subjectivity in historical interpretation, admitting that their own perspective informed their interpretations of the facts. The historical context of the mid-twentieth century greatly aided in the popularity of these relativist ideas. Following World Wars I and II, more Europeans and Americans began to question the objective benevolence of modern science. Science had contributed to the increased killing efficiency of weapons, the effective execution of Jews in the Holocaust, and the shocking devastation of Hiroshima and Nagasaki. This disillusionment with science and established worldviews eventually led to a flowering of a countercultural movement in Europe and the United States in the 1960s and 1970s, preparing the way for alternative versions of reality and truth.

Kuhn Many scientists attempted to defend the legitimacy and objectivity of their disciplines against this onslaught. Attempting to support scientific claims to objectivity and truth, Thomas Kuhn's *The Structure of Scientific Revolutions* (1962) argued that all of the sciences were organized around paradigms, or collections of truths, assumptions, theories, and ideas, which are supported by evidence and accepted by other scientists. Over the course of history, anomalies cause shifts in these paradigms, and paradigm shifts cause scientific revolutions, when scientists agree that overwhelming evidence points to a new paradigm. One of the most well-known examples of a paradigm shift is the Copernican revolution which overthrew the Ptolemaic view of the universe. Rather than support scientific objectivity, however, Kuhn's argument was easily turned to support the relativists' argument. If scientific paradigms changed over time, scientific truth also changed, implying that even scientific truth is relative.

The Linguistic Turn

While relativism remained in the background of historical discourse, linguistic and literary scholars in Europe developed powerful new theories which would further undermine Modernism. In the first decades of the twentieth century, French and Russian literary theorists began to move away from viewing texts as having static meaning and value based on unchanging standards of form and function toward a more structuralist theory of texts, which saw the meaning of texts and all of reality as constructed by societies, and consequently changing over time. The theories of French linguist Ferdinand de Saussure (1857–1913) led the way in this move toward *Structuralism* structuralism. While positivists saw the meaning of words as inherent, unchangeable, and closed, de Saussure saw the meaning of words and texts as fluid and changeable, *de Saussure* since they are internally created by society and their own structure. For example, binary oppositions, such as man–woman or light–dark, are common structures of language. The meanings of these words are created by their opposites. For example, a woman is the opposite of a man, and the meaning of woman is everything opposite of man. The meaning of words, therefore, is relative to other words, not just to the physical objects to which they refer.

Saussure and other linguists expanded on these theories by analyzing the relationship of words to the physical object to which they referred (the referent). Since the sound and appearance of a word is merely a symbol for an object, rather than the object or idea itself, the meanings of words and symbols are not fixed, natural, or universal, but rather are created by human beings and may reflect their brain structures. This idea created a new field of study within linguistics called semiotics, which studies the signs and symbols of a culture to uncover the deeper mental structures which give meaning to its communications. Cultures teach individuals the meanings of words through dictionaries, *Semiotics*   language classes, and other tools, but each individual uses words in their own unique way to signify reality. Since the meanings of language structures are culturally and individually determined, all meaning must be relative to the specific culture in which it is understood and reflexive[3] to the writer and reader of the text in which it is expressed.

In addition to individuals shaping the meaning of words, words and language shape the knowledge and realities of individuals. De Saussure argued that one could not imagine a thing for which one had no words. The words in a given language, therefore, limit the expressive ability of individuals and shape their worldview. Despite his belief in language's power to shape reality, de Saussure and the structuralists who followed him did not completely reject empiricism's attempt to scientifically understand reality and find truth. Structural linguistics and semiotics did, however, strongly suggest the relativism of meaning and truth in language, and since language is the root of all knowledge and it is used to convey information in academic subjects, their theories profoundly affected other disciplines in the following decades.

Postmodernism

Existentialist and structural linguistic theories took the French philosophical world by storm in the 1960s, where it developed into what some call "postmodernism." One of the first books to define postmodernism, Jean Lyotard's *The Postmodern Condition* (1984) explained it as "a disbelief in metanarratives."[4] A metanarrative is an overarching story or belief held by a society as a universal truth.[5] While postmodernists are varied in the topics they study and their methodology, they all question the objectivity of

---

[3]Reflexivity is a literary concept frequently adopted by historical philosophers to refer to the idea that reality reflects and is created by one's own identity, assumptions, and worldview. Every individual, therefore, has its own unique reality. Reality is relative to the individual, it is argued, not to any outside, natural referent.

[4]Michael Bentley, "Introduction: Approaches to Modernity: Western Historiography since the Enlightenment," in *Companion to Historiography*, ed. Michael Bentley (New York: Routledge, 1997), 491.

[5]An example of a metanarrative is the Enlightenment belief that human reason and science would lead to progress.

modern Western knowledge, particularly human sciences such as history. They argue that historical reality is constructed by historians and the written documents they study, that historical truth is shaped by and reflects the perspective of the historian and the society in which he or she writes, and is thus relative and reflexive, making all conclusions at least somewhat subjective, and true objectivity an impossibility.

Barthes   One of the first French theorists to build upon de Saussure's structuralism and apply it to cultural studies was Roland Barthes (1915–1980). Barthes argued that popular culture, including sign systems in everyday life, such as in advertisements, tourist attractions, sporting events, and films, created knowledge systems which controlled society and normalized oppressive ideologies. His popular magazine articles deconstructing the signs of cultural manifestations, ranging from the preaching of Billy Graham to professional wrestling, brought semiotics and structuralist theory to a wider audience and paved the way for cultural studies and popular culture history.[6]

Foucault   French philosopher and historian Michel Foucault (1926–1984) was perhaps the most famous and influential of a new generation of historians who applied these theories to historical study. Foucault was born in Poitiers, France, the son of a prominent surgeon. He encountered new relativist theories as he worked toward degrees in Philosophy, Psychology, and Psychopathology at top French universities in the 1940s and 1950s. During this time, he became familiar with Marxist theory, studying with famous structuralist Marxist Louis Althusser, and briefly joining the French Communist Party. He held positions at a number of prestigious universities in France, Tunisia, and the United States throughout the 1960s and 1970s. He was very active in the left-wing protests rocking France in that period. He was especially active in defending the rights of prisoners as well as homosexuals. He was open with his long-term homosexual relationship with Daniel Defert and was one of the first famous homosexuals to die of AIDS in France in 1984.

Well versed in the theories of Nietzsche and de Saussure, Foucault extended their theories and explicitly applied them to his historical studies. Similar to Marx and Nietzsche, Foucault believed that political and economic forces, such as governments and the bourgeoisie, shaped knowledge production for their own political and economic interests, what he called a "political economy of truth." He believed *Discourse*   that by studying the production of knowledge through discourses, or the words, phrases, ideas, and symbols associated with a specific topic, historians could better understand the past. He argued that various cultural groups, such as political, economic, or social groups, create and add to discourses to shape knowledge about a *épistémès*   particular subject. Discourses then create *épistémè*s, mental structures which organize knowledge and prioritize new information as important/unimportant, true/false, or scientific/unscientific. These *épistémè*s then shape the identity of individuals and create the mental world in which individuals live. Individuals, therefore, were products of discourses in their lives, rather than historical agents with their own free will.

---

[6]Callum Brown, *Postmodernism for Historians* (Edinburgh Gate: Pearson Education, 2005), 37–39.

Foucault, however, was not just a theorist; he was also a practitioner. He developed his own method for studying history, which he called an "archeology of knowledge." He argued that, like an archeologist, the historian must painstakingly uncover the inner workings and structure of past societies. Because all texts are relative and reflexive, historians cannot just simply interpret them and claim to have reconstructed *Deconstruction* the truth about what happened in the past and why. Historians must deconstruct texts, closely analyzing them as if they were archeological fragments of the worldviews from which they were created. Like Nietzsche, Foucault believed cause-and-effect relationships were only fictive creations of historians, but suggested that historians could seek to understand how and why discourse changed by looking for beginnings of new discourses, differences in existing discourses, and ruptures and disjunctions in *épistémè*s. Because these changes and ruptures reveal the power and forces which shaped the discourse at that particular moment in time, they help us to reconstruct the history of knowledge.

Rather than study historical subjects from the perspective of the dominant power that shaped the discourse, Foucault sought to "decenter" the subject under study, examining the past from unexpected perspectives, from "the other": the outsider, the oppressed, the marginalized, and the anomalous.[7] These alternative perspectives may reveal a rupture which had been covered up by conventional sources. For this reason, Foucault studied taboo subjects, such as sexuality, madness, disorder, disease, and imprisonment.[8] His works caused quite a stir in the historical community in France in the 1960s and in the English-speaking world when they were translated into English in the 1970s.

Since Barthes and Foucault had built upon structuralism, their new theories *Poststructuralism* became known as poststructuralism. Poststructuralism in history refers to new cultural theories in the 1960s and 1970s which studied linguistic and social structures in order to uncover the way knowledge and truths are constructed. It emerged alongside and contributed significantly to the social movements exploding in Europe and the United States in the 1960s. The student protest, gay and women's liberation, Black Power, counterculture, and anticolonialism movements of this era all shared with poststructuralism a questioning of authority, traditional structures, and prejudicial language, and they fed off of each other through the 1970s. Many poststructuralist academics participated in these movements and became identified with them, so that they are often seen as identical movements. When these social movements ended in the 1970s, however, poststructuralism continued to spread through academia in the 1980s and 1990s.

Poststructural theories were initially the most popular in France, where philosophers and historians alike discussed, debated, and applied them to their own works *Derrida* and theories. A friend and student of Foucault, Jacques Derrida (1930–2004) claimed

---

[7]Anomalous refers to an anomaly, something unusual or out of the ordinary.

[8]Some of his most famous works include *Madness and Civilization* (1961), *The Order of Things: An Archaeology of the Human Sciences* (1966), *The Archaeology of Knowledge* (1969), *Discipline and Punish: The Birth of the Prison* (1975), and his three volumes, *The History of Sexuality* (1976–1984).

that as revolutionary as Foucault was, he was still trapped in the cultural categories which he had exposed. Derrida asserted that by continuing to analyze and interpret texts from his own viewpoint, and believing that he could actually understand and explain the meaning of the past, Foucault was deluding himself. Derrida asserted that meaning cannot be determined or evaluated by reference to facts, and that truth and reality are impossible to discern because they can only be represented by texts, which cannot reconstruct reality. His famous statement, "there is nothing outside of the text," summarizes this belief that while reality exists, human beings do not have the ability to reconstruct it, except by using texts, which are themselves created by human beings, not by the reality itself. He argued that to truly understand reality, intellectuals must get outside of the trap of society's limitations on knowledge, question everything, create new words and language structures to explain new ideas, and deconstruct all texts. In many ways, Derrida was much more radical than Foucault, moving beyond poststructuralism to a much more relativistic form of postmodernism.

De Certeau   In response to the criticisms of the defenders of empiricism, Derrida and other French philosophers went even further in their critique of empirical history. French theorist Michel de Certeau (1925–1986) asserted in *The Writing of History* (1975) that "The past is the fiction of the present."[9] Critiquing Foucault and most other poststructuralists, de Certeau argued that all histories were manufactured by historians and served to manipulate people in the present. In the 1980s, French philosopher and literary theorist *Lyotard*   Jean-Francois Lyotard (1924–1998) argued that sets of discourses created metanarratives, or overarching stories and explanations of reality, such as the story of historical progress. These metanarratives, while entirely fictional and not grounded in reality, limited the creativity and freedom of individuals, and imposed a false consensus in societies. He argued that in reality, dissensus prevailed, and multiple values and truths competed with each other. With de Certeau and Lyotard, postmodernism reached an extreme of radical skepticism and relativism, questioning the validity of historical practice itself.

Yet most postmodernist and poststructuralist historians do not completely reject empiricist methods. In fact, postmodernist historian Callum Brown argues that "the postmodernist needs empiricist method for the essential skills, and any student of History *must* learn and deploy them."[10] He, however, differentiates historical events from historical facts. While the events actually happened, facts are records explaining the events and are "laden with problems of accuracy, bias, editing…and the sheer restrictions of human description."[11] Since reality is too complex, being made up of "an infinity of events," postmodernists believe that historians can never completely replicate it or reconstruct it, and this is what separates them from nonpostmodernists.[12] Brown argues that histories which claim to be merely presenting the fixed facts or the

---

[9]Michel de Certeau, *The Writing of History*, trans. Tom Conley (New York: Columbia University Press, 1988), 10.

[10]Brown, *Postmodernism for Historians*, 25.

[11]Ibid., 27.

[12]Ibid., 47.

unchanging truth tend to also present morality as fact-based and history-based. Thus, they use their version of history as a powerful weapon to support their own values, making their histories undemocratic and dangerous. Postmodernism, as a philosophy which encourages suspicion of hierarchy and claims to essential universal truths, is in his view not only a superior historical philosophy, but a superior moral philosophy.[13]

The Literary Turn

White

As French theorists spent time in American universities and as their works were translated into English, their theories took the American academy by storm in the 1970s and 1980s. While there were no identifiable leaders of this trend, Hayden White (b. 1928), professor of Historical Studies at the University of California–Santa Cruz, became the exemplar for the literary turn in American historiography. In his most famous work *Metahistory: The Historical Imagination in Nineteenth-century Europe* (1973), White challenged empirical history's claims to objectivity and narrative history's claims of being distinct from fictional literature. White's primary argument was that history and literature had more in common than not. Both were imaginative representations of reality: Historians used their imaginations, just as all novelists and poets did, to select information, organize it, and interpret it, in order to make a coherent, plausible story out of it. Historians were driven by the same desire to make their reconstructions of reality readable and believable, and operated under the same linguistic constraints as did all writers.

Tropes

White developed a theory of tropes to explain how all of narrative history was shaped by underlying linguistic structures, used by all discourse and literature. He posited that all historical accounts use one of four literary tropes, which are tools or ways of telling a story to explain reality. These tropes are metaphor, metonymy, synecdoche, and irony. For example, a metaphoric history would explain the civil rights movement as a wave, which rose, crested, and crashed over time. Metonymy uses one concept to refer to a related concept, so that "the Crown" refers to the monarchy. Synecdoche is related to metonymy, but uses a part to refer to its larger whole or vice versa. "The press," for example, refers to journalists. Irony is using a term to refer to its opposite, such as "this test is just wonderful!" White further categorized historical narratives into three more literary categories of explanation: emplotment, formal argument, and ideological implication. Like all authors, historians consciously, or more likely unconsciously, choose a trope and a method of explanation as they write their histories. While literary jargon infuses White's theories, his point about how all history is at least in part fictional stirred debate in the historical profession. Empiricists hotly defended their objectivity and nonfictional history, while a new generation of historians, influenced by other postmodern theories, supported White's perspective of history as fictive.[14]

---

[13]Ibid., 29–30.

[14]Hayden White, "The Fictions of Factual Representation," in Anna Green and Kathleen Troup, eds. *The Houses of History* (New York: New York University Press, 1999).

Schama   Although the radical skeptical theories of Derrida and Certeau influenced philosophers and academic theorists like White, these discussions were far too philosophical and theoretical to interest more than a small minority of historians. It took popular Harvard historian Simon Schama (b. 1945) to bring postmodern relativism to a wider audience. His best-selling *Dead Certainties: Unwarranted Speculations* (1991) was a collection of several essays on different, but connected subjects, including the Battle of Quebec in 1759, nineteenth-century historian Francis Parkman, and his uncle, George Parkman, who was murdered in 1849.[15] The murder trial revealed how selective fragments of evidence are used in the courts to reconstruct what happened, just as historians like Francis Parkman subjectively selected fragments of evidence to reconstruct what happened during the Battle of Quebec. While many historians could appreciate this insight into the fragmentary nature of history, Schama's invention of fictional material in his story was more controversial. Schama freely admitted his own imaginative work to prove his point about the highly imaginative and subjective nature of history, but some historians felt that this went too far.

The Anthropological Turn

Lévi-Strauss   Somewhat less controversial was the impact of linguistic theory on the field of anthropology, and new cultural anthropology in turn had a tremendous impact on history. Cultural anthropologist and specialist in Native American cultures, Claude Lévi-Strauss (1908–2009) used linguistic theories to challenge the then-dominant anthropological paradigm, which viewed Western Civilization as superior to all other civilizations. He considered all human cultures to be systems of symbolic communication and argued that to understand how each culture constructed reality, the scholar must study symbols. Each culture has its own way of communicating reality and meaning, and since we as the judges are limited by our own view of reality, there is no objective way of determining which view of reality is more true or accurate than another. Lévi-Strauss's application of linguistic theories and cultural relativism revolutionized the field of anthropology in the 1950s and 1960s.

Geertz   Lévi-Strauss's theories inspired a new generation of cultural anthropologists led by Clifford Geertz (1926–2006). In the 1960s and 1970s, Geertz adopted Lévi-Strauss's ideas and linguistic theory as he created a new symbolic anthropology built upon the foundation of cultural relativism. Like Lévi-Strauss, Geertz believed that all human cultures are equally important, and that values and behaviors should be understood only within the culture from which they originate. Influenced by poststructuralists, however, Geertz pioneered "thick description," a method of deconstructing and analyzing cultural symbols to decipher how different cultures constructed truth and reality in their own metanarratives. Because no one can be completely objective in their analysis or know for certain which is the most accurate analysis, Geertz believed that cultural anthropologists must guess at meanings,

---

[15]Simon Schama, *Dead Certainties (Unwarranted Speculations)* (London: Penguin, 1991).

assess the guesses, and draw conclusions from the better guesses.[16] These theories and methods not only transformed anthropology, but inspired many social and cultural historians.

The Cultural Turn

Since the 1970s, elements of cultural anthropology, literary analysis, and poststructuralism have found their way into every field of history, but they have caused the most profound transformations in the fields of cultural and ideological history. Cultural history has been practiced ever since Herodotus, but since the nineteenth century, it had focused on intellectual leaders and high culture, such as famous painters, thinkers, and writers. Geertz's symbolic anthropology, however, has led cultural historians to view culture more broadly as an "interworked system of construable signs" and as "the whole body of practices, beliefs, institutions, customs, habits, myths, and so on built up by humans and passed on from generation to generation."[17] Cultural historians now seek to understand how past cultures shaped identity and created knowledge and reality.

Viewing all groups in society as equally important, cultural histories now study a myriad of different events and peoples, connecting all of them to the production of discourse and knowledge. Rather than looking for cause and effect, new cultural histories decipher meaning from the discourses of the past. Historian Richard J. Evans asserts that while cultural historians differ widely, they share:

> the belief that historical writing can enhance our appreciation of the human condition by bringing to life and explaining beliefs and cultures that are very different from our own, and so perhaps adding to the richness of human experience and understanding, and fostering tolerance of different cultures and belief systems in our time.[18]

Because this sort of analysis is extremely difficult for large, diverse groups of people or broad periods of time, microhistories are an especially popular form of new cultural history. Rather than studying institutions and large-scale socioeconomic structures, microhistories focus on specific people, cases, and cultural phenomena. Historiographer John Burrow explains this genre:

Microhistories   …micro-history takes a small area, a narrow time band, perhaps a protagonist, though one with varying degrees of dominance, and a small community. It illuminates something more general than itself, but it is not necessarily to be thought of exactly as "evidence" of a given type.…Sometimes its subject is a single central event, or a sequence of them,

---

[16]Clifford Geertz, *The Interpretation of Cultures* (New York: Basic Books, 1973), 20.

[17]Gabrielle M. Spiegel, *Practicing History: New Directions in Historical Writing after the Linguistic Turn*, ed. Gabrielle M. Spiegel (New York: Routledge, 2005), 8 and 80.

[18]Richard J. Evans, "Prologue," in *What Is History Now?* ed. David Cannadine (London: Palgrave Macmillan, 2002), 9.

understanding whose meaning requires painstaking scholarship, and perhaps some resort to available generalizations from elsewhere....[19]

Some of the most fascinating cultural histories produced in the past thirty years illustrate this microhistorical approach. Much of this work began in European history. Emmanuel Le Roy Ladurie's *Montaillou* (1975) used inquisition records to re-create the mental world of a village in thirteenth-century Languedoc.[20] Professor of Renaissance Studies, *Ginzburg* Carlo Ginzburg (b. 1939) likewise examined inquisition records in his exploration of the trial of a self-educated miller in sixteenth-century Italy in his famous *The Cheese and* *Davis* *the Worms: The Cosmos of a Sixteenth Century Miller* (1980).[21] Natalie Zemon Davis's (b. 1928–) *The Return of Martin Guerre* (1983) was based on the sixteenth-century court case of an imposter, who posed as Martin Guerre, a peasant in the Pyrenees. She used this court case to carefully reconstruct the world and culture of this particular time and place.

Darnton   Robert Darnton's *The Great Cat Massacre* (1989) is an especially fascinating example of this approach. Darnton (b. 1939) was born in New York and earned his bachelor's degree from Harvard and his PhD in early modern European history from Oxford University in 1964. He has had a prestigious career at Princeton and Harvard and was elected president of the American Historical Association in 1999. *The Great Cat Massacre* investigates a working-class massacre of cats which took place in Paris in the 1730s. Darnton chose this particular episode because it was so odd, or as Foucault put it, *anomalous*. Why would the workers find this grotesque act so funny? By deconstructing the cultural symbols and discourse surrounding this specific incident, Darnton unearthed the class hostility and cultural values which gave it meaning. Darnton later explained how he was inspired by Geertz's theories. He had taught a class with him at Princeton and became convinced of the benefits of this approach.[22] Cultural microhistories of this sort have become very popular and added much to our understanding of the mental worlds of past societies.

While most new cultural histories focused on early modern European history in the 1970s and 1980s, American historians began to apply their methods to American history topics in the 1980s and cultural history swept the American historical profession off its feet in the 1990s. One of the first histories of the American Revolution to apply culturalist approaches is Rhys Isaac's Pulitzer Prize-winning *The Transformation of Virginia* (1982). This applied insights from symbolic anthropology to explain the simultaneous shift in political and religious worldviews in eighteenth-century America.[23]

---

[19]John Burrow, *A History of Histories: Epics, Chronicles, Romances and Inquiries from Herodotus and Thucydides to the Twentieth Century* (New York: Alfred A Knopf, 2008), 477.

[20]Emmanuel Le Roy Ladurie, *Montaillou* (New York: Vintage Books, 1979).

[21]Carlo Ginzburg, *The Cheese and the Worms: The Cosmos of a Sixteenth Century Miller* (Baltimore: Johns Hopkins University Press, 1980).

[22]Burrow, *A History of Histories*, 477.

[23]Christopher Grasso and Karin Wulf, "Nothing Says 'Democracy' Like a Visit from the Queen: Reflections on Empire and Nation in Early American Histories," *Journal of American History* 95, no. 3 (December 2008), 769.

More recently, historians of the American Revolution have studied the construction of the meanings of liberty and republicanism in this period, exploring these constructions from the perspective of differing classes, races, genders, and locales. In intellectual history, cultural historians have closely analyzed texts to re-create the mental worlds of the Puritans and other specific groups in American history. Popular culture in American history has also grown in importance and popularity in recent decades, with historians exploring everything from charivaris to tavern cultures, and everything in between. All of this has led to a remarkable diversity in historical topics, many of which are extremely popular even outside of academia.

Gender and Identity Histories

Poststructuralism, literary analysis, cultural anthropology, and new cultural history have dramatically affected social history since the 1980s. Following Geertz's example, many social historians have moved away from studying behavior and material status toward analyzing meaning and symbolic representation through discourse.[24] Foucault's ideas about how discourse constructs identity especially appeals to those who seek to understand how racial and gender categories were constructed in the past and changed over time. If concepts such as masculine and feminine and black and white were not based on essentialist unchanging biological definitions, but were instead historically and discursively constructed and changing, these categories, with their inherent political implications, could be constructed differently in the present and future.[25] As a consequence, much sociocultural history since the 1980s has focused on how language and discourse have historically constructed and set limits for people of different genders, races, and ethnicities.

Many feminist historians were especially attracted to the idea that knowledge about gender and sexuality was socially and historically constructed. Their own experience and research had revealed the extent to which male dominance in academia had excluded or shaped knowledge about women and gender roles. As such, feminist historians applied poststructuralist theories to their research on how knowledge about women, femininity, and masculinity had been constructed in the past, and how these gender constructions had shaped the lives of men and women in different societies all over the world. In the 1980s, American historian Joan Scott famously applied Foucault's theories in her support for using gender as a "useful category of historical analysis."[26] In all her work since then, Scott has developed and demonstrated the methods of gender history by deconstructing gendered discourses

Scott

---

[24]Ernst Breisach, *Historiography: Ancient, Medieval, and Modern*, 2nd ed. (Chicago, IL: University of Chicago Press, 1994), 599.

[25]Gabrielle M. Spiegel, "Introduction," in *Practicing History: New Directions in Historical Writing after the Linguistic Turn*, ed. Gabrielle M. Spiegel (New York: Routledge, 2005), 25.

[26]Joan W. Scott, "Gender: A Useful Category of Historical Analysis," *American Historical Review* 91, no. 5 (December 1986): 1053–1075.

and uncovering how these have shaped identity, social institutions, and social relations.

Gender history has become enormously influential since that time and is arguably one of the fastest growing and most innovative areas in historical research. Indeed, gender history has replaced women's history to a large extent. Many women's historians realized that studying women in isolation from men tended to ghettoize women's history, making it a small segment of the larger discipline, instead of fully integrating women into the larger historical narrative. Women's history was also intimately related to men's history, and neither could be fully understood without reference to the other. In a widely read article entitled "Women's History in Transition" (1976), Natalie Zemon Davis called for the integrated historical analysis of both sexes and since then has been a leader in doing this in her own work.[27] Many other women's historians, such as Carroll Smith-Rosenberg, Lynn Hunt, Judith Butler, and Kathryn Kish Sklar, have found this methodology and theory useful in studying the history of women in relation to the wider cultural history of societies.[28]

Bloch   A good example of a gendered approach to American history is the work of Ruth Bloch (b. 1949). She was born in Palo Alto, California, to parents who had immigrated to the United States in the 1930s to escape the Nazis and were physics professors. She attended Radcliffe College, the former women's college within Harvard University, in the late 1960s, in the midst of the student movement against the Vietnam War and the beginnings of the women's movement. The radical idealism of the period made her more curious about the history of social change, so she chose an interdisciplinary major that enabled her to combine readings in social theory, American literature, and history. She then attended graduate school in History at the University of California at Berkeley, where she took courses with Natalie Zemon Davis. Her PhD thesis and later works reflect these interests in religious, cultural, and gender history. She has been a member of the faculty of the Department of History at UCLA since 1982.[29] In *Gender and Morality in Anglo-American Culture, 1650–1800* (2003), she explored the gendered meanings of the American Revolution, including discourse on virtue, morality, and privacy. She has revealed how concepts of masculinity and femininity not only shaped revolutionary ideas, but how revolutionary ideas affected men and women differently. These gendered meanings were at the heart of her reconstruction of American cultures in the eighteenth and nineteenth centuries.

The histories of racial and ethnic social groups have also been transformed by poststructuralist theories on how all identity is shaped by discourse. By studying race and ethnicity as historical constructs, historians have uncovered the ways in which

---

[27]Natalie Zemon Davis, "'Women's History' in Transition: The European Case," *Feminist Studies* 3 (1976): 83–103.

[28]See, for example, Joan Wallach Scott, *Gender and the Politics of History* (New York: Columbia University Press, 1988), Lynn Hunt, *The New Cultural History* (Berkeley, CA: University of California Press, 1989), and Judith Butler, *Gender Trouble: Feminism and the Subversion of Identity* (New York: Routledge, 1990), and Carroll Smith-Rosenberg, *Disorderly Conduct: Visions of Gender in Victorian America* (New York: A.A. Knopf, 1985).

[29]Email from Ruth Bloch to Carrie Hoefferle (September 27, 2009).

these discourses signified power in specific historical contexts. Indeed, many histories since the 1980s have explored the ways in which race, class, and gender discourses shaped historical events and experiences, and revealed power relationships inherent in all societies. Since the 1990s, these identity histories have moved on to exploring the construction of masculinity, heterosexuality, homosexuality, and whiteness, as well as adding new perspectives on imperialism, diasporas, and all aspects of historical study.

At the beginning of the third millennium, new sociocultural history became the most popular historical approach in the United States. Of the ten best articles in American history selected by the Organization of American Historians in 2006, seven dealt with either race or gender. Many historians, who have little interest in theory or knowledge of postmodernism or the literary turn, have adopted race and gender for their historical analyses simply because of interest and publishability. In fact, some now argue that "being a student of history in the early twenty-first century requires an informed knowledge of the postmodernist position."[30] The literary turn and the evolution of postmodernism in history presented some radical new ideas and injected history with a stronger sense of theory than ever before. It faces, however, tremendous opposition from traditionalist historians who are especially offended by the relativism and subjectivism of postmodern extremists, and want a return to objectivist, empirical history. The linguistic turn and postmodernism have indeed muddied the waters of the profession, but they have led to some remarkable new understandings of past cultures and a wealth of intriguing insights.

Michel Foucault, *Discipline and Punish*

The following, according to an order published at the end of the seventeenth century, were the measures to be taken when the plague appeared in a town.[1]

First, a strict spatial partitioning: the closing of the town and its outlying districts, a prohibition to leave the town on pain of death, the killing of all stray animals; the division of the town into distinct quarters, each governed by an intendant. Each street is placed under the authority of a syndic, who keeps it under surveillance; if he leaves the street, he will be condemned to death. On the appointed day, everyone is ordered to stay indoors: it is forbidden to leave on pain of death. The syndic himself comes to lock the door of each house from the outside; he takes the key with him and hands it over to the intendant of the quarter; the intendant keeps it until the end of the quarantine. Each family will have made its own provisions; but, for bread and wine, small wooden canals are set up between the street and the interior of the houses, thus allowing each person to receive his ration without communicating with the suppliers and other residents; meat, fish and herbs will be hoisted up into the houses with pulleys and baskets. If it is absolutely necessary to leave

---

[30]Brown, *Postmodernism for Historians*, 1.

Source: Michel Foucault, "Panopticism" in *Discipline & Punish* by Michel Foucault. English translation copyright © 1977 by Alan Sheridan (New York: Pantheon). Originally published in French as *Surveiller et Punir.* Copyright © 1975 by Editions Gallimard. Reprinted by permission of Georges Borchardt Inc., for Editions Gallimard.

[1]Archives militaires de Vincennes, A 1,516 91 sc. Piece. This regulation is broadly similar to a whole series of others that date from the same period and earlier.

the house, it will be done in turn, avoiding any meeting. Only the intendants, syndics and guards will move about the streets and also, between the infected houses, from one corpse to another, the "crows", who can be left to die: these are "people of little substance who carry the sick, bury the dead, clean and do many vile and abject offices". It is a segmented, immobile, frozen space. Each individual is fixed in his place. And, if he moves, he does so at the risk of his life, contagion or punishment.

Inspection functions ceaselessly. The gaze is alert everywhere: "A considerable body of militia, commanded by good officers and men of substance", guards at the gates, at the town hall and in every quarter to ensure the prompt obedience of the people and the most absolute authority of the magistrates, "as also to observe all disorder, theft and extortion". At each of the town gates there will be an observation post; at the end of each street sentinels. Every day, the intendant visits the quarter in his charge, inquires whether the syndics have carried out their tasks, whether the inhabitants have anything to complain of; they "observe their actions". Every day, too, the syndic goes into the street for which he is responsible; stops before each house: gets all the inhabitants to appear at the windows (those who live overlooking the courtyard will be allocated a window looking onto the street at which no one but they may show themselves); he calls each of them by name; informs himself as to the state of each and every one of them—"in which respect the inhabitants will be compelled to speak the truth under pain of death"; if someone does not appear at the window, the syndic must ask why: "In this way he will find out easily enough whether dead or sick are being concealed." Everyone locked up in his cage, everyone at his window, answering to his name and showing himself when asked—it is the great review of the living and the dead.

This surveillance is based on a system of permanent registration: reports from the syndics to the intendants, from the intendants to the magistrates or mayor At the beginning of the "lock up", the role of each of the inhabitants present in the town is laid down, one by one; this document bears "the name, age, sex of everyone, notwithstanding his condition": a copy is sent to the intendant of the quarter, another to the office of the town hall, another to enable the syndic to make his daily roll call. Everything that may be observed during the course of the visits—deaths, illnesses, complaints, irregularities—is noted down and transmitted to the intendants and magistrates. The magistrates have complete control over medical treatment; they have appointed a physician in charge; no other practitioner may treat, no apothecary prepare medicine, no confessor visit a sick person without having received from him a written note "to prevent anyone from concealing and dealing with those sick of the contagion, unknown to the magistrates". The registration of the pathological must be constantly centralized. The relation of each individual to his disease and to his death passes through the representatives of power, the registration they make of it, the decisions they take on it.

Five or six days after the beginning of the quarantine, the process of purifying the houses one by one is begun. All the inhabitants are made to leave; in each room "the furniture and goods" are raised from the ground or suspended from the air; perfume is poured around the room; after carefully sealing the windows, doors and even the keyholes with wax, the perfume is set alight. Finally, the entire house is closed while the perfume is consumed; those who have carried out the work are searched, as they were on entry, "in the presence of the residents of the house, to see that they did not have something on their persons as they left that they did not have on entering". Four hours later, the residents are allowed to re-enter their homes.

This enclosed, segmented space, observed at every point, in which the individuals are inserted in a fixed place, in which the slightest movements are supervised, in which all events are recorded, in which an uninterrupted work of writing links the centre and periphery, in which power is exercised without division, according to a continuous hierarchical figure, in which each individual is constantly located, examined and distributed among the living beings, the sick and the dead—all this constitutes a compact model of the disciplinary mechanism. The plague is met by order; its function is to sort out every possible confusion: that of the disease, which is transmitted when bodies are mixed together; that of the evil, which is increased when fear and death overcome prohibitions. It lays down for each individual his place, his body, his disease and his death, his well-being, by means of an omnipresent and omniscient power that subdivides itself in a regular, uninterrupted way even to the ultimate determination of the individual, of what characterizes him, of what belongs to him, of what happens to him. Against the plague, which is a mixture, discipline brings into play its power, which is one of analysis. A whole literary fiction of the festival grew up around the plague: suspended laws, lifted prohibitions, the frenzy of passing time, bodies mingling together without respect, individuals unmasked, abandoning their statutory identity and the figure under which they had been recognized, allowing a quite different truth to appear. But there was also a political dream of the plague, which was exactly its reverse: not the collective festival, "but strict divisions; not laws transgressed, but the penetration of regulation into even the smallest details of everyday life through the mediation of the complete hierarchy that assured the capillary functioning of power; not masks that were put on and taken off, but the assignment to each individual of his 'true' name, his 'true' place, his 'true' body, his 'true' disease". The plague as a form, at once real and imaginary, of disorder had as its medical and political correlative discipline. Behind the disciplinary mechanisms can be read the haunting memory of "contagions", of the plague, of rebellions, crimes, vagabondage, desertions, people who appear and disappear, live and die in disorder.

If it is true that the leper gave rise to rituals of exclusion, which to a certain extent provided the model for and general form of the great Confinement, then the plague gave rise to disciplinary projects. Rather than the massive, binary division between one set of people and another, it called for multiple separations, individualizing

distributions, an organization in depth of surveillance and control, an intensification and a ramification of power. The leper was caught up in a practice of rejection, of exile-enclosure; he was left to his doom in a mass among which it was useless to differentiate; those sick of the plague were caught up in a meticulous tactical partitioning in which individual differentiations were the constricting effects of a power that multiplied, articulated and subdivided itself; the great confinement on the one hand; the correct training on the other. The leper and his separation; the plague and its segmentations. The first is marked; the second analyzed and distributed. The exile of the leper and the arrest of the plague do not bring with them the same political dream. The first is that of a pure community, the second that of a disciplined society. Two ways of exercising power over men, of controlling their relations, of separating out their dangerous mixtures. The plague-stricken town, traversed throughout with hierarchy, surveillance, observation, writing; the town immobilized by the functioning of an extensive power that bears in a distinct way over all individual bodies—this is the utopia of the perfectly governed city. The plague (envisaged as a possibility at least) is the trial in the course of which one may define ideally the exercise of disciplinary power. In order to make rights and laws function according to pure theory, the jurists place themselves in imagination in the state of nature; in order to see perfect disciplines functioning, rulers dreamt of the state of plague. Underlying disciplinary projects the image of the plague stands for all forms of confusion and disorder; just as the image of the leper, cut off from all human contact, underlies projects of exclusion.

They are different projects, then, but not incompatible ones. We see them coming slowly together, and it is the peculiarity of the nineteenth century that it applied to the space of exclusion of which the leper was the symbolic inhabitant (beggars, vagabonds, madmen and the disorderly formed the real population) the technique of power proper to disciplinary partitioning. Treat "lepers" as "plague victims", project the subtle segmentations of discipline onto the confused space of internment, combine it with the methods of analytical distribution proper to power, individualize the excluded, but use procedures of individualization to mark exclusion—this is what was operated regularly by disciplinary power from the beginning of the nineteenth century in the psychiatric asylum, the penitentiary, the reformatory, the approved school and, to some extent, the hospital. Generally speaking, all the authorities exercising individual control function according to a double mode; that of binary division and branding (mad/sane; dangerous/harmless; normal/abnormal); and that of coercive assignment of differential distribution (who he is; where he must be; how he is to be characterized; how he is to be recognized; how a constant surveillance is to be exercised over him in an individual way, etc.). On the one hand, the lepers are treated as plague victims; the tactics of individualizing disciplines are imposed on the excluded; and, on the other hand, the universality of disciplinary controls makes it possible to brand the "leper" and to bring into play against him the dualistic mechanisms of exclusion. The constant division between the normal and the abnormal, to which every individual is subjected, brings us back to our own time, by applying the binary branding and exile of the leper to quite different objects; the existence of a whole set of techniques and institutions for measuring, supervising and correcting the abnormal brings into play the disciplinary mechanisms to which the fear of the plague gave rise. All the mechanisms of power which, even today, are disposed around the abnormal individual, to brand him and to alter him, are composed of those two forms from which they distantly derive.

Bentham's *Panopticon* is the architectural figure of this composition. We know the principle on which it was based: at the periphery, an annular building; at the centre, a tower; this tower is pierced with wide windows that open onto the inner side of the ring; the peripheric building is divided into cells, each of which extends the whole width of the building; they have two windows, one on the inside, corresponding to the windows of the tower; the other, on the outside, allows the light to cross the cell from one end to the other. All that is needed, then, is to place a supervisor in a central tower and to shut up in each cell a madman, a patient, a condemned man, a worker or a schoolboy. By the effect of backlighting, one can observe from the tower, standing out precisely against the light, the small captive shadows in the cells of the periphery. They are like so many cages, so many small theatres, in which each actor is alone, perfectly individualized and constantly visible. The panoptic mechanism arranges spatial unities that make it possible to see constantly and to recognize immediately. In short, it reverses the principle of the dungeon; or rather of its three functions—to enclose, to deprive of light and to hide—it preserves only the first and eliminates the other two. Full lighting and the eye of a supervisor capture better than darkness, which ultimately protected. Visibility is a trap.

To begin with, this made it possible—as a negative effect—to avoid those compact, swarming, howling masses that were to be found in places of confinement, those painted by Goya or described by Howard. Each individual, in his place, is securely confined to a cell from which he is seen from the front by the supervisor; but the side walls prevent him from coming into contact with his companions. He is seen, but he does not see; he is the object of information, never a subject in communication. The arrangement of his room, opposite the central tower, imposes on him an axial visibility; but the divisions of the ring, those separated cells, imply a lateral invisibility. And this invisibility is a guarantee of order. If the inmates are convicts, there is no danger of a plot, an attempt at collective escape, the planning of new crimes for the future, bad reciprocal influences; if they are patients, there is no danger of contagion; if they are madmen there is no risk of their committing violence upon one another; if they are schoolchildren, there is no copying, no noise, no chatter, no waste of time; if they are workers, there are no disorders, no theft, no coalitions, none of those distractions that slow down the rate of work, make it less perfect or cause accidents. The crowd,

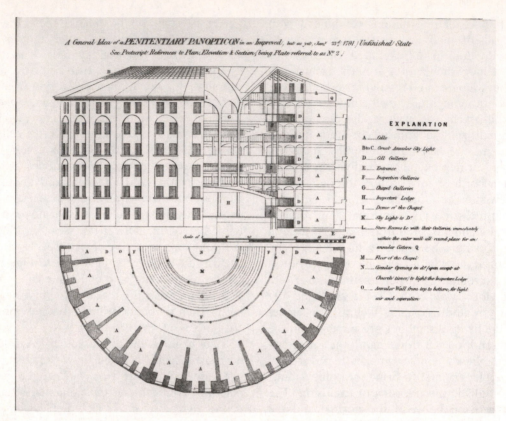

FIGURE 8.1: Jeremy Bentham's Plan of the Penitentiary Panopticon between pages 38–39 from *The Works of Jeremy Bentham*, volume 4, 1838–43. Reference (shelfmark) 265 i.228. Bodleian Library, University of Oxford.

a compact mass, a locus of multiple exchanges, individualities merging together, a collective effect, is abolished and replaced by a collection of separated individualities. From the point of view of the guardian, it is replaced by a multiplicity that can be numbered and supervised; from the point of view of the inmates, by a sequestered and observed solitude (Bentham, 60–64).

Hence the major effect of the Panopticon: to induce in the inmate a state of conscious and permanent visibility that assures the automatic functioning of power. So to arrange things that the surveillance is permanent in its effects, even if it is discontinuous in its action; that the perfection of power should tend to render its actual exercise unnecessary; that this architectural

apparatus should be a machine for creating and sustaining a power relation independent of the person who exercises it; in short, that the inmates should be caught up in a power situation of which they are themselves the bearers. To achieve this, it is at once too much and too little that the prisoner should be constantly observed by an inspector: too little, for what matters is that he knows himself to be observed; too much, because he has no need in fact of being so. In view of this, Bentham laid down the principle that power should be visible and unverifiable. Visible: the inmate will constantly have before his eyes the tall outline of the central tower from which he is spied upon. Unverifiable: the inmate must never know whether he is being looked at at any one moment; but he must be sure that he may always be so. In order to make the presence or absence of the inspector unverifiable, so that the prisoners, in their cells, cannot even see a shadow, Bentham envisaged not only venetian blinds on the windows of the central observation hall, but, on the inside, partitions that intersected the hall at right angles and, in order to pass from one quarter to the other, not doors but zig-zag openings; for the slightest noise, a gleam of light, a brightness in a half-opened door would betray the presence of the guardian. The Panopticon is a machine for dissociating the see/being seen dyad: in the peripheric ring, one is totally seen, without ever seeing; in the central tower, one sees everything without ever being seen.

It is an important mechanism, for it automatizes and disindividualizes power. Power has its principle not so much in a person as in a certain concerted distribution of bodies, surfaces, lights, gazes; in an arrangement whose internal mechanisms produce the relation in which individuals are caught up. The ceremonies, the rituals, the marks by which the sovereign's surplus power was manifested are useless. There is a machinery that assures dissymmetry, disequilibrium, difference. Consequently, it does not matter who exercises power. Any individual, taken almost at random, can operate the machine: in the absence of the director, his family, his friends, his visitors, even his servants (Bentham, 45). Similarly, it does not matter what motive animates him: the curiosity of the indiscreet, the malice of a child, the thirst for knowledge of a philosopher who wishes to visit this museum of human nature, or the perversity of those who take pleasure in spying and punishing. The more numerous those anonymous and temporary observers are, the greater the risk for the inmate of being surprised and the greater his anxious awareness of being observed. The Panopticon is a marvelous machine which, whatever use one may wish to put it to, produces homogeneous effects of power.

A real subjection is born mechanically from a fictitious relation. So it is not necessary to use force to constrain the convict to good behavior, the madman to calm, the worker to work, the schoolboy to application, the patient to the observation of the regulations. Bentham was surprised that panoptic institutions could be so light: there were no more bars, no more chains, no more heavy locks; all that was needed was that the separations should be clear and the openings well arranged. The heaviness of the old "houses of security", with their fortress-like architecture, could be replaced by the simple, economic geometry of a "house of certainty". The efficiency of power, its constraining force have, in a sense, passed over to the other side—to the side of its surface of application. He who is subjected to a field of visibility, and who knows it, assumes responsibility for the constraints of power; he makes them play spontaneously upon himself; he inscribes in himself the power relation in which he simultaneously plays both roles; he becomes the principle of his own subjection. By this very fact, the external power may throw off its physical weight; it tends to the non-corporal; and, the more it approaches this limit, the more constant, profound and permanent are its effects: it is a perpetual victory that avoids any physical confrontation and which is always decided in advance.

....the Panopticon was also a laboratory; it could be used as a machine to carry out experiments, to alter behavior, to train or correct individuals. To experiment with medicines and monitor their effects. To try out different punishments on prisoners, according to their crimes and character, and to seek the most effective ones. To teach different techniques simultaneously to the workers, to decide which is the best. To try out pedagogical experiments—and in particular to take up once again the well-debated problem of secluded education, by using orphans. One would see what would happen when, in their sixteenth or eighteenth year, they were presented with other boys or girls; one could verify whether, as Helvetius thought, anyone could learn anything; one would follow "the genealogy of every observable idea"; one could bring up different children according to different systems of thought, making certain children believe that two and two do not make four or that the moon is a cheese, then put them together when they are twenty or twenty-five years old; one would then have discussions that would be worth a great deal more than the sermons or lectures on which so much money is spent; one would have at least an opportunity of making discoveries in the domain of metaphysics. The Panopticon is a privileged place for experiments on men, and for analysing with complete certainty the transformations that may be obtained from them. The Panopticon may even provide an apparatus for supervising its own mechanisms. In this central tower, the director may spy on all the employees that he has under his orders: nurses, doctors, foremen, teachers, warders; he will be able to judge them continuously, alter their behavior, impose upon them the methods he thinks best; and it will even be possible to observe the director himself. An inspector arriving unexpectedly at the centre of the Panopticon will be able to judge at a glance, without anything being concealed from him, how the entire establishment is functioning. And, in any case, enclosed as he is in the middle of this architectural mechanism, is not the director's own fate entirely bound up with it? The incompetent physician who has allowed contagion to spread, the incompetent prison governor or workshop manager will be the first victims of an epidemic or a revolt. "'By every tie I could devise", said the master of the Panopticon, 'my own fate had been bound up by me with theirs'" (Bentham, 177). The Panopticon functions as a kind of laboratory of power. Thanks to its mechanisms of observation, it gains in efficiency and in the ability to penetrate into men's behavior; knowledge follows the advances of power, discovering new objects of knowledge over all the surfaces on which power is exercised.

....the Panopticon presents a cruel, ingenious cage. The fact that it should have given rise, even in our own time, to so many variations, projected or realized, is evidence of the imaginary intensity that it has possessed for almost two hundred years. But the Panopticon must not be understood as a dream building: it is the diagram of a mechanism of power reduced to its ideal form; its functioning, abstracted from any obstacle, resistance or friction, must be represented as a pure architectural and optical system: it is in fact a figure of political technology that may and must be detached from any specific use.

It is polyvalent in its applications; it serves to reform prisoners, but also to treat patients, to instruct schoolchildren, to confine the insane, to supervise workers, to put beggars and idlers to work. It is a type of location of bodies in space, of distribution of individuals in relation to one another, of hierarchical organization, of disposition of centres and channels of power, of definition of the instruments and modes of intervention of power, which can be implemented in hospitals, workshops, schools, prisons. Whenever one is dealing with a multiplicity of individuals on whom a task or a particular form of behavior must be imposed, the panoptic schema may be used. It is—necessary modifications apart—applicable "to all establishments whatsoever, in which, within a space not too large to be covered or commanded by buildings, a number of persons are meant to be kept under inspection" (Bentham, 40; although Bentham takes the penitentiary house as his prime example, it is because it has many different functions to fulfill—safe custody, confinement, solitude, forced labor and instruction).

In each of its applications, it makes it possible to perfect the exercise of power. It does this in several ways: because it can reduce the number of those who exercise it, while increasing the number of those on whom it is exercised. Because it is possible to intervene at any moment and because the constant pressure acts even before the offences, mistakes or crimes have been committed. Because, in these conditions, its strength is that it never intervenes, it is exercised spontaneously and without noise, it constitutes a mechanism whose effects follow from one another. Because, without any physical instrument other than architecture and geometry, it acts directly on individuals; it gives "power of mind over mind". The panoptic schema makes any apparatus of power more intense: it assures its economy (in material, in personnel, in time); it assures its efficacity by its preventative character, its continuous functioning and its automatic mechanisms. It is a way of obtaining from power "in hitherto unexampled quantity", "a great and new instrument of government…; its great excellence consists in the great strength it is capable of giving to *any* institution it may be thought proper to apply it to" (Bentham, 66).

It's a case of "it's easy once you've thought of it" in the political sphere. It can in fact be integrated into any function (education, medical treatment, production, punishment); it can increase the effect of this function, by being linked closely with it; it can constitute a mixed mechanism in which relations of power (and of knowledge) may be precisely adjusted, in the smallest detail, to the processes that are to be supervised; it can establish a direct proportion between "surplus power" and "surplus production". In short, it arranges things in such a way that the exercise of power is not added on from the outside, like a rigid, heavy constraint, to the functions it invests, but is so subtly present in them as to increase their efficiency by itself increasing its own points of contact. The panoptic mechanism is not simply a hinge, a point of exchange between a mechanism of power and a function; it is a way of making power relations function in a function, and of making a function function through these power relations. Bentham's Preface to *Panopticon* opens with a list of the benefits to be obtained from his "inspection-house": "*Morals reformed—health preserved— industry invigorated— instruction diffused—public burthens lightened*—Economy seated, as it were, upon a rock—the gordian knot of the Poor-Laws not cut, but untied—all by a simple idea in architecture!" (Bentham, 39)

Furthermore, the arrangement of this machine is such that its enclosed nature does not preclude a permanent presence from the outside: we have seen that anyone may come and exercise in the central tower the functions of surveillance, and that, this being the case, he can gain a clear idea of the way in which the surveillance is practised. In fact, any panoptic institution, even if it is as rigorously closed as a penitentiary, may without difficulty be subjected to such irregular and constant inspections: and not only by the appointed inspectors, but also by the public; any member of society will have the right to come and see with his own eyes how the schools, hospitals, factories, prisons function. There is no risk, therefore, that the increase of power created by the panoptic machine may degenerate into tyranny; the disciplinary mechanism will be democratically controlled, since it will be constantly accessible "to the great tribunal committee of the world". This Panopticon, subtly arranged so that an observer may observe, at a glance, so many different individuals, also enables everyone to come and observe any of the observers. The seeing machine was once a sort of dark room into which individuals spied; it has become a transparent building in which the exercise of power may be supervised by society as a whole.

The panoptic schema, without disappearing as such or losing any of its properties, was destined to spread throughout the social body; its vocation was to become a generalized function. The plague-stricken town provided an exceptional disciplinary model: perfect, but absolutely violent; to the disease that brought death, power opposed its perpetual threat of death; life inside it was reduced to its simplest expression; it was, against the power of death, the meticulous exercise of the right of the sword. The Panopticon, on the other hand, has a role of amplification; although it arranges power, although it is intended to make it more economic and more effective, it does so not for power itself, nor for the immediate salvation of a threatened society: its aim is to strengthen the social forces—to increase production, to develop the economy, spread education, raise the level of public morality; to increase and multiply.

How is power to be strengthened in such a way that, far from impeding progress, far from weighing upon it with its rules and regulations, it actually facilitates such progress? What intensificator of power will be able at the same time to be a multiplicator of production? How will power, by increasing its forces, be able to increase those of society instead of confiscating them or impeding them? The Panopticon's solution to this problem is that the productive increase of power can be assured only if, on the one hand, it can be exercised continuously in the very foundations of society, in the subtlest possible way, and if, on the other hand, it functions outside these sudden, violent, discontinuous forms that are bound up with the exercise of sovereignty. The body of the king, with its strange material and physical presence, with the force that he himself deploys or transmits to some few others, is at the opposite extreme of this new physics of power represented by panopticism; the domain of panopticism is, on the contrary, that whole lower region, that region of irregular bodies, with their details, their multiple movements, their heterogeneous forces, their spatial relations; what are required are mechanisms that analyze distributions, gaps, series, combinations, and which use instruments that render visible, record, differentiate and compare: a physics of a relational and multiple power, which has its maximum intensity not in the person of the king, but in the bodies that can be individualized by these relations. At the theoretical level, Bentham defines another way of analyzing the social body and the power relations that traverse it; in terms of practice, he defines a procedure of subordination of bodies and forces that must increase the utility of power while practicing the economy of the prince. Panopticism is the general principle of a new "political anatomy" whose object and end are not the relations of sovereignty but the relations of discipline. The celebrated, transparent, circular cage, with its high towers powerful and knowing, may have been for Bentham a project of perfect disciplinary institution; but he also set out to show how one may "unlock" the disciplines and get them to function in a diffused, multiple, polyvalent way throughout the whole social body. These disciplines, which the classical age had elaborated in specific, relatively enclosed places—barracks, schools, workshops—and whose total implementation had been imagined only at the limited and temporary scale of a plague-stricken town, Bentham dreamt of transforming into a network of mechanisms that would be everywhere and always alert, running through society without interruption in space or in time. The panoptic arrangement provides the formula for this generalization. It programs, at the level of an elementary and easily transferable mechanism, the basic functioning of a society penetrated through and through with disciplinary mechanisms.

"Discipline" may be identified neither with an institution nor with an apparatus; it is a type of power, a modality for its exercise, comprising a whole set of instruments, techniques, procedures, levels of application, targets; it is a "physics" or an "anatomy" of power, a technology. And it may be taken over either by "specialized" institutions (the penitentiaries or "houses of correction" of the nineteenth century), or by institutions that use it as an essential instrument for a particular end (schools, hospitals), or by pre-existing authorities that find in it a means of reinforcing or reorganizing their internal mechanisms of power (one day we should show how intra-familial relations, essentially in the parents-children cell, have become "disciplined", absorbing since the classical age external schemata, first educational and military, then medical, psychiatric, psychological, which have made the family the privileged locus of emergence for the disciplinary question of the normal and the abnormal); or by apparatuses that have made discipline their principle of internal functioning (the disciplinarization of the administrative apparatus from the Napoleonic period), or finally by state apparatuses whose major, if not exclusive, function is to assure that discipline reigns over society as a whole (the police).

The panoptic modality of power—at the elementary, technical, merely physical level at which it is situated—is not under the immediate dependence or a direct extension of the great juridico-political structures of a society;

it is nonetheless not absolutely independent. Historically, the process by which the bourgeoisie became in the course of the eighteenth century the politically dominant class was masked by the establishment of an explicit, coded and formally egalitarian juridical framework, made possible by the organization of a parliamentary, representative regime. But the development and generalization of disciplinary mechanisms constituted the other, dark side of these processes. The general juridical form that guaranteed a system of rights that were egalitarian in principle was supported by these tiny, everyday, physical mechanisms, by all those systems of micro-power that are essentially non-egalitarian and asymmetrical that we call the disciplines. And although, in a formal way, the representative regime makes it possible, directly or indirectly, with or without relays, for the will of all to form the fundamental authority of sovereignty, the disciplines provide, at the base, a guarantee of the submission of forces and bodies. The real, corporal disciplines constituted the foundation of the formal, juridical liberties. The contract may have been regarded as the ideal foundation of law and political power; panopticism constituted the technique, universally widespread, of coercion. It continued to work in depth on the juridical structures of society, in order to make the effective mechanisms of power function in opposition to the formal framework that it had acquired. The "Enlightenment", which discovered the liberties, also invented the disciplines.

>> Questions for Consideration

1. What exactly is Panopticism and what is its purpose? What historical role does it play? What examples of Panopticism in our current society can you think of?

2. How does this compare to the histories in Chapter 7?

3. Where does Foucault's poststructuralist method and assumptions about discourse and power appear in this excerpt?

Robert Darnton, "Workers Revolt"

THE FUNNIEST THING that ever happened in the printing shop of Jacques Vincent, according to a worker who witnessed it, was a riotous massacre of cats. The worker, Nicolas Contat, told the story in an account of his apprenticeship in the shop, rue Saint-Séverin, Paris, during the late 1730s.[1] Life as an apprentice was hard, he explained. There were two of them: Jerome, the some-what fictionalized version of Contat himself, and Léveillé. They slept in a filthy, freezing room, rose before

---

Source: Robert Darnton, "Workers Revolt: The Great Cat Massacre of the Rue Saint-Séverin," in *The Great Cat Massacre and Other Episodes in French Cultural History*. New York: Basic Books, 1984, pp. 75–101 (omitting visuals). Copyright © 2009 Robert Darnton. Reprinted by permission of Basic Books, a member of the Perseus Books Group. The notes are Darnton's, but have been transferred from endnotes to footnotes.

[1]Nicolas Contat, *Anecdotes typographiques où l'on voit la description des coutumes, moeurs et usages singuliers des compagnons imprimeurs*, ed. Giles Barber (Oxford, 1980). The original manuscript is dated 1762. Barber provides a thorough description of its background and of Contat's career in his introduction. The account of the cat massacre occurs on pp. 48–56.

dawn, ran errands all day while dodging insults from the journeymen and abuse from the master, and received nothing but slops to eat. They found the food especially galling. Instead of dining at the master's table, they had to eat scraps from his plate in the kitchen. Worse still, the cook secretly sold the leftovers and gave the boys cat food, old, rotten bits of meat that they could not stomach and so passed on to the cats, who refused it.

This last injustice brought Contat to the theme of cats. They occupied a special place in his narrative and in the household of the rue Saint-Séverin. The master's wife adored them, especially *la grise* (the gray), her favorite. A passion for cats seemed to have swept through the printing trade, at least at the level of the masters, or *bourgeois* as the workers called them. One bourgeois kept twenty-five cats. He had their portraits painted and fed them on roast fowl. Meanwhile, the apprentices were trying to cope with a profusion of alley cats who also thrived in the printing district and made the boys' lives miserable. The cats howled all night on the roof over the apprentices' dingy bedroom, making it impossible to get a full night's sleep. As Jerome and Léveillé had to stagger out of bed at four or five in the morning to open the gate for the earliest arrivals among the journeymen, they began the day in a state of exhaustion while the bourgeois slept late. The master did not even work with the men, just as he did not eat with them. He let the foreman run the shop and rarely appeared in it, except to vent his violent temper, usually at the expense of the apprentices.

One night the boys resolved to right this inequitable state of affairs. Léveillé, who had an extraordinary talent for mimicry, crawled along the roof until he reached a section near the master's bedroom, and then he took to howling and meowing so horribly that the bourgeois and his wife did not sleep a wink. After several nights of this treatment, they decided they were being bewitched. But instead of calling the curé—the master was exceptionally devout and the mistress

exceptionally attached to her confessor—they commanded the apprentices to get rid of the cats. The mistress gave the order, enjoining the boys above all to avoid frightening her *grise*.

Gleefully Jerome and Léveillé set to work, aided by the journeymen. Armed with broom handles, bars of the press, and other tools of their trade, they went after every cat they could find, beginning with *la grise*. Leveillé smashed its spine with an iron bar and Jerome finished it off. Then they stashed it in a gutter while the journeymen drove the other cats across the rooftops, bludgeoning everyone within reach and trapping those who tried to escape in strategically placed sacks. They dumped sackloads of half-dead cats in the courtyard. Then the entire workshop gathered round and staged a mock trial, complete with guards, a confessor, and a public executioner. After pronouncing the animals guilty and administering last rites, they strung them up on an improvised gallows. Roused by gales of laughter, the mistress arrived. She let out a shriek as soon as she saw a bloody cat dangling from a noose. Then she realized it might be *la grise*. Certainly not, the men assured her: they had too much respect for the house to do such a thing. At this point the master appeared. He flew into a rage at the general stoppage of work, though his wife tried to explain that they were threatened by a more serious kind of insubordination. Then master and mistress withdrew, leaving the men delirious with "joy," "disorder," and "laughter".[2]

The laughter did not end there. Léveillé reenacted the entire scene in mime at least twenty times during subsequent days when the printers wanted to knock off for some hilarity. Burlesque reenactments of incidents in the life of the shop, known as *copies* in printers' slang, provided a major form of entertainment for the men. The idea was to humiliate someone in the shop by satirizing his peculiarities. A successful copy would make the butt of the joke fume with rage—*prendre la chèvre* (take the goat) in the shop slang—while

---

[2]Contat, *Anecdotes typographiques*, p. 53.

his mates razzed him with "rough music." They would run their composing sticks across the tops of the cases, beat their mallets against the chases, pound on cupboards, and bleat like goats. The bleating (*bats* in the slang) stood for the humiliation heaped on the victims, as in English when someone "gets your goat." Contat emphasized that Léveillé produced the funniest *copies* anyone had ever known and elicited the greatest choruses of rough music. The whole episode, cat massacre compounded by *copies*, stood out as the most hilarious experience in Jerome's entire career.

Yet it strikes the modern reader as unfunny, if not downright repulsive. Where is the humor in a group of grown men bleating like goats and banging with their tools while an adolescent re-enacts the ritual slaughter of a defenseless animal? Our own inability to get the joke is an indication of the distance that separates us from the workers of pre-industrial Europe. The perception of that distance may serve as the starting point of an investigation, for anthropologists have found that the best points of entry in an attempt to penetrate an alien culture can be those where it seems to be most opaque. When you realize that you are not getting something—a joke, a proverb, a ceremony—that is particularly meaningful to the natives, you can see where to grasp a foreign system of meaning in order to unravel it. By getting the joke of the great cat massacre, it may be possible to "get" a basic ingredient of artisan culture under the Old Regime.

It should be explained at the outset that we cannot observe the killing of the cats at firsthand. We can study it only through Contat's narrative, written about twenty years after the event. There can be no doubt about the authenticity of Contat's quasi-fictional autobiography, as Giles Barber has demonstrated in his masterful edition of the text. It belongs to the line of autobiographical writing by printers that stretches from Thomas Platter to Thomas Gent, Benjamin Franklin, Nicolas Restif de la Bretonne, and Charles Manby Smith. Because printers, or at least compositors, had to be reasonably literate in order to do their work, they were among the few artisans who could give their own accounts of life in the working classes two, three, and four centuries ago. With all its misspellings and grammatical flaws, Contat's is perhaps the richest of these accounts. But it cannot be regarded as a mirror image of what actually happened. It should be read as Contat's version of a happening, as his attempt to tell a story. Like all story telling, it sets the action in a frame of reference; it assumes a certain repertory of associations and responses on the part of its audience; and it provides meaningful shape to the raw stuff of experience. But since we are attempting to get at its meaning in the first place, we should not be put off by its fabricated character. On the contrary, by treating the narrative as fiction or meaningful fabrication we can use it to develop an ethnological *explication de texte*.

The first explanation that probably would occur to most readers of Contat's story is that the cat massacre served as an oblique attack on the master and his wife. Contat set the event in the context of remarks about the disparity between the lot of workers and the bourgeois—a matter of the basic elements in life: work, food, and sleep. The injustice seemed especially flagrant in the case of the apprentices, who were treated like animals while the animals were promoted over their heads to the position the boys should have occupied, the place at the master's table. Although the apprentices seem most abused, the text makes it clear that the killing of the cats expressed a hatred for the bourgeois that had spread among all the workers: "The masters love cats; consequently [the workers] hate them." After masterminding the massacre, Léveillé became the hero of the shop, because "all the workers are in league against the masters. It is enough to speak badly of them [the masters] to be esteemed by the whole assembly of typographers."[3]

---

[3]Ibid., pp. 52 and 53

Historians have tended to treat the era of artisan manufacturing as an idyllic period before the onset of industrialization. Some even portray the workshop as a kind of extended family in which master and journeymen labored at the same tasks, ate at the same table, and sometimes slept under the same roof.[4] Had anything happened to poison the atmosphere of the printing shops in Paris by 1740?

During the second half of the seventeenth century, the large printing houses, backed by the government, eliminated most of the smaller shops, and an oligarchy of masters seized control of the industry.[5] At the same time, the situation of the journeymen deteriorated. Although estimates vary and statistics cannot be trusted, it seems that their number remained stable: approximately 335 in 1666, 339 in 1701, and 340 in 1721. Meanwhile the number of masters declined by more than half, from eighty-three to thirty-six, the limit fixed by an edict of 1686. That meant fewer shops with larger work forces, as one can see from statistics on the density of presses: in 1644 Paris had seventy-five printing shops with a total of 180 presses; in 1701 it had fifty-one shops with 195 presses. This trend made it virtually impossible for journeymen to rise into the ranks of the masters. About the only way for a worker to get ahead in the craft was to marry a master's widow, for masterships had become hereditary privileges, passed on from husband to wife and from father to son.

The journeymen also felt threatened from below because the masters tended increasingly to hire *alloués*, or under-qualified printers, who had not undergone the apprenticeship that made a journeyman eligible, in principle, to advance to a mastership. The *alloués* were merely a source of cheap labor, excluded from the upper ranks of the trade and fixed, in their inferior status, by an edict of 1723. Their degradation stood out in their name: they were *à louer* (for hire), not *compagnons (journeymen)* of the master. They personified the tendency of labor to become a commodity instead of a partnership. Thus Contat served his apprenticeship and wrote his memoirs when times were hard for journeymen printers, when the men in the shop in the rue Saint-Séverin stood in danger of being cut off from the top of the trade and swamped from the bottom....

Journeymen and masters may have lived together as members of a happy family at some time somewhere in Europe, but not in the printing houses of eighteenth-century France and Switzerland.

Contat himself believed that such a state had once existed. He began his description of Jerome's apprenticeship by invoking a golden age when printing was first invented and printers lived as free and equal members of a "republic," governed by its own laws and traditions in a spirit of fraternal "union and friendship."[6] He claimed that the republic still survived in the form of the *chapelle* or workers association in each shop. But the government had broken up general associations; the ranks had been thinned by *alloués*; the journeymen had been excluded from masterships; and the masters had withdrawn into a separate world of *haute cuisine* and *grasses matinées*. The master in the rue Saint-Séverin ate different food, kept different hours, and talked a different language. His wife and daughters dallied with worldly abbes. They kept pets. Clearly, the bourgeois belonged to a different subculture—one which meant above all

---

[4]See, for example, Albert Soboul, *La France à la veille de la Révolution* (Paris, 1966), p. 140; and Edward Shorter, "The History of Work in the West: An Overview" in *Word and Community in the West*, ed. Edward Shorter (New York, 1973).

[5]The following discussion is derived from Henri-Jean Martin, *Livre, pouvoirs et société à Paris au XVII siècle* (1598–1701) (Geneva, 1969); and Paul Chauvet, *Les Ouvriers du livre en France, des origines à la Révolution de 1789* (Paris, 1959). The statistics come from investigations by the authorities of the Old Regime as reported by Martin (II, 699–700) and Chauvet (pp. 126 and 154).

[6]Contat, *Anecdotes typographiques*, pp. 30–31

that he did not work. In introducing his account of the cat massacre, Contat made explicit the contrast between the worlds of worker and master that ran throughout the narrative: "Workers, apprentices, everyone works. Only the masters and mistresses enjoy the sweetness of sleep. That makes Jerome and Léveillé resentful. They resolve not to be the only wretched ones. They want their master and mistress as associates (associes)."[7] That is, the boys wanted to restore a mythical past when masters and men worked in friendly association. They also may have had in mind the more recent extinction of the smaller printing shops. So they killed the cats.

But why cats? And why was the killing so funny? Those questions take us beyond the consideration of early modern labor relations and into the obscure subject of popular ceremonies and symbolism. Folklorists have made historians familiar with the ceremonial cycles that marked off the calendar year for early modern man.[8] The most important of these was the cycle of carnival and Lent, a period of revelry followed by a period of abstinence. During carnival the common people suspended the normal rules of behavior and ceremoniously reversed the social order or turned it upside down in riotous procession. Carnival was a time for cutting up by youth groups, particularly apprentices, who organized themselves in "abbeys" ruled by a mock abbot or king and who staged charivaris or burlesque processions with rough music in order to humiliate cuckolds, husbands who had been beaten by their wives, brides who had married below their

age group, or someone else who personified the infringement of traditional norms. Carnival was high season for hilarity, sexuality, and youth run riot—a time when young people tested social boundaries by limited outbursts of deviance, before being re-assimilated in the world of order, submission, and Lentine seriousness. It came to an end on Shrove Tuesday or Mardi Gras, when a straw mannequin, King Carnival or Caramantran, was given a ritual trial and execution. Cats played an important part in some charivaris. In Burgundy, the crowd incorporated cat torture into its rough music. While mocking a cuckold or some other victim, the youths passed around a cat, tearing its fur to make it howl. *Faire le chat*, they called it. The Germans called charivaris *Katzenmusik*, a term that may have been derived from the howls of tortured cats.[9]

Cats also figured in the cycle of Saint John the Baptist, which took place on June 24, at the time of the summer solstice. Crowds made bonfires, jumped over them, danced around them, and threw into them objects with magical power, hoping to avoid disaster and obtain good fortune during the rest of the year. A favorite object was cats—cats tied up in bags, cats suspended from ropes, or cats burned at the stake. Parisians liked to incinerate cats by the sackful, while the Courimauds (*cour à mioud* or cat chasers) of Saint Chamond preferred to chase a flaming cat through the streets. In parts of Burgundy and Lorraine they danced around a kind of burning May pole with a cat tied to it. In the Metz region they burned a dozen cats at a time in a basket on

---

[7]Ibid., p. 52.

[8]For a recent overview of the vast literature o folklore and French history and bibliographic references, see Nicole Belmont, *Mythes et croyances dans l'ancienne France* (Paris, 1973). The following discussion is based primarily on the material collected in Eugène Rolland, *Faune populaire de la France* (Paris, 1881), IV; Paul Sébillot, *Le Folk-lore de France* (Paris, 1904–7), 4 vols., especially III, 72–155 and IV, 90–98; and to a lesser extent Arnold Van Gennep, *Manuel de folklore français contemporain* (Paris, 1937–58), 9 vols.

[9]In Germany and Switzerland, *Katzenmusik* sometimes included mock trials and executions. The etymology of the term is not clear. See E. Hoffmann-Krayer and Hans Bächtold-Stäubli, *Handwörterbuch des deutschen Aberglaubens* (Berlin and Leipzig, 1931–32), IV, 1125–32 and Paul Grebe et al., *Duden Etymologie: Herkunftsworterbuch der deutschen Sprache* (Mannheim, 1963), p. 317.

top of a bonfire. The ceremony took place with great pomp in Metz itself, until it was abolished in 1765. The town dignitaries arrived in procession at the Place du Grand-Saulcy, lit the pyre, and a ring of riflemen from the garrison fired off volleys while the cats disappeared screaming in the flames. Although the practice varied from place to place, the ingredients were everywhere the same: *afeu de joie* (bonfire), cats, and an aura of hilarious witchhunting.[10]

It should be said at the outset that there is an indefinable *je ne sais quoi* about cats, a mysterious something that has fascinated mankind since the time of the ancient Egyptians. One can sense a quasi-human intelligence behind a cat's eyes. One can mistake a cat's howl at night for a human scream, torn from some deep, visceral part of man's animal nature. Cats appealed to poets like Baudelaire and painters like Manet, who wanted to express the humanity in animals along with the animality of men—and especially of women.[11]

This ambiguous ontological position, a straddling of conceptual categories, gives certain animals—pigs, dogs, and cassowaries as well as cats—in certain cultures an occult power

associated with the taboo. That is why Jews do not eat pigs, according to Mary Douglas, and why Englishmen can insult one another by saying "son-of-a-bitch" rather than "son-of-a-cow," according to Edmund Leach.[12] Certain animals are good for swearing, just as they are "good for thinking" in Lévi-Strauss's famous formula. I would add that others—cats in particular—are good for staging ceremonies. They have ritual value. You cannot make a charivari with a cow. You do it with cats: you decide to *faire le chat*, to make *Katzenmusik*. The torture of animals, especially cats, was a popular amusement throughout early modern Europe. You have only to look at Hogarth's *Stages of Cruelty* to see its importance, and once you start looking you see people torturing animals everywhere. Cat killings provided a common theme in literature, from *Don Quixote* in early seventeenth-century Spain to *Germinal* in late nineteenth-century France.[13] Far from being a sadistic fantasy on the part of a few half-crazed authors, the literary versions of cruelty to animals expressed a deep current of popular culture, as Mikhail Bakhtin has shown in his study of Rabelais.[14] All sorts of

---

[10]Information on the cat burning in Saint Chamond comes from a letter kindly sent to me by Elinor Accampo of Colorado College. The Metz ceremony is described in A. Benoist, "Traditions et anciennes coutumes du pays messin," *Revue des traditions populaires, XV (1900), 14.*

[11]The black cat in Manet's *Olympia* represents a common motif, the animal "familiar" of a nude. On Baudelaire's cats, see Roman Jakobson and Claude Lévi-Strauss, "*Les Chats* de Charles Baudelaire," *L'Homme,* II (1962), 5–21; and Michel Riffaterre, "Describing Poetic Structures: Two Approaches to Baudelaire's *Les Chats,*" in *Structuralism,* ed. Jacques Ehrmann (New Haven, 1966).

[12]Mary Douglas, *Purify and Danger: An Analysis of Concepts of Pollution and Taboo* (London, 1966); and E.R. Leach, "Anthropological Aspects of Language: Animal Categories and Verbal Abuse, "in *New Directions in the Study of Language,* ed. E.H. Lenneberg (Cambridge, Mass., 1964).

[13]Cervantes and Zola adapted traditional cat lore to the themes of their novel. In *Don Quixote* (part II, chap. 46), a sack full of howling cats interrupts the hero's serenade to Altisidora. Taking them for devils, he tries to mow them down with his sword, only to be bested by one of them in single combat. In *Germinal* (part V, chap. 6), the symbolism works in the opposite way. A mob of workers pursues Maigrat, their class enemy, as if he were a cat trying to escape across the rooftops. Screaming "Get the cat! Get the cat!" they castrate his body "like a tomcat" after he falls from the roof. For an example of cat killing as a satire on French legalism, see Friar John's plan to massacre the Furry Lawcats in Rabelais' *Gargantua and Pantagruel,* book V, chap. 15.

[14]Mikhail Bahktin, *Rabelais and His World,* trans. Helene Iswolsky (Cambridge, Mass., 1968). The most important literary version of cat lore to appear in Contat's time was *Les Chats* (Rotterdam, 1728) by Francois Augustin Paradis de Moncrif. Although it was a mock treatise aimed at a sophisticated audience, it drew on a vast array of popular superstitions and proverbs, many of which appeared in the collections of folklorists a century and a half later.

ethnographic reports confirm that view. On the *dimanche les brandons* in Semur, for example, children used to attach cats to poles and roast them over bonfires. In the *jeu du chat* at the Fete-Dieu in Aix-en-Provence, they threw cats high in the air and smashed them on the ground. They used expressions like "patient as a cat whose claws are being pulled out" or "patient as a cat whose paws are being grilled." The English were just as cruel. During the Reformation in London, a Protestant crowd shaved a cat to look like a priest, dressed it in mock vestments, and hanged it on the gallows at Cheapside.[15] It would be possible to string out many other examples, but the point should be clear: there was nothing unusual about the ritual killing of cats. On the contrary, when Jerome and his fellow workers tried and hanged all the cats they could find in the rue Saint-Séverin, they drew on a common element in their culture. But what significance did that culture attribute to cats?

To get a grip on that question, one must rummage through collections of folktales, superstitions, proverbs, and popular medicine. The material is rich, varied, and vast but extremely hard to handle. Although much of it goes back to the Middle Ages, little can be dated. It was gathered for the most part by folklorists in the late nineteenth and early twentieth centuries, when sturdy strains of folklore still resisted the influence of the printed word. But the collections do not make it possible to claim that this or that practice existed in the printing houses of mid-eighteenth-century Paris. One can only assert that printers lived and breathed in an atmosphere of traditional customs and beliefs which permeated everything. It was not everywhere the same—France remained a patchwork of *pays* rather than a unified nation until late in the nineteenth century—but everywhere some common motifs could be found. The commonest were attached to cats. Early modern Frenchmen probably made more symbolic use of cats than of any other animal, and they used them in distinct ways, which can be grouped together for the purposes of discussion, despite the regional peculiarities.

First and foremost, cats suggested witchcraft. To cross one at night in virtually any corner of France was to risk running into the devil or one of his agents or a witch abroad on an evil errand. White cats could be as satanic as the black, in the daytime as well as at night. In a typical encounter, a peasant woman of Bigorre met a pretty white house cat who had strayed in the fields. She carried it back to the village in her apron, and just as they came to the house of a woman suspected of witchcraft, the cat jumped out, saying "Merci, Jeanne."[16] Witches transformed themselves into cats in order to cast spell on their victims. Sometimes, especially on Mardi Gras, they gathered for hideous sabbaths at night. They howled, fought, and copulated horribly under the direction of the devil himself in the form of a huge tomcat. To protect yourself from sorcery by cats there was one, classic remedy: maim it. Cut its tail, clip its ears, smash one of its legs, tear or burn its fur, and you would break its malevolent power. A maimed cat could not attend a sabbath or wander abroad to cast spells. Peasants frequently cudgeled cats who crossed their paths at night and discovered the next day that bruises had appeared on women believed to be witches—or so it was said in the lore of their village. Villagers also told stories of farmers who found strange cats in barns and broke their limbs to save the cattle. Invariably a broken limb would appear on a suspicious woman the following morning.

---

[15]C.S.L. Davies, *Peace, Print, and Protestantism* (St. Albans, Herts, 1977). The other references come from the sources cited in note 14. Among the many dictionaries of proverbs and slangs, see André-Joseph Panckoucke, *Dictionnaire des proverbs françois et des facons de parler comiques, burlesques, et familières* (Paris, 1748) and Gaston Esnault, *Dictionnaire historique des argots francais* (Paris, 1965).

[16]Rolland, *Faune populaire*, p. 118. See note 14 for the other sources on which this account is based.

Cats possessed occult power independently of their association with witchcraft and deviltry. They could prevent the bread from rising if they entered bakeries in Anjou. They could spoil the catch if they crossed the path of fishermen in Brittany. If buried alive in Bearn, they could clear a field of weeds. They figured as staple ingredients in all kinds of folk medicine aside from witches' brews. To recover from a bad fall, you sucked the blood out of a freshly amputated tail of a tomcat. To cure yourself from pneumonia, you drank blood from a cat's ear in red wine. To get over colic, you mixed your wine with cat excrement. You could even make yourself invisible, at least in Brittany, by eating the brain of a newly killed cat, provided it was still hot.

There was a specific field for the exercise of cat power: the household and particularly the person of the master or mistress of the house. Folktales like "Puss 'n Boots" emphasized the identification of master and cat, and so did superstitions such as the practice of tying a black ribbon around the neck of a cat whose mistress had died. To kill a cat was to bring misfortune upon its owner or its house. If a cat left a house or stopped jumping on the sickbed of its master or mistress, the person was likely to die. But a cat lying on the bed of a dying man might be the devil, waiting to carry his soul off to hell. According to a sixteenth-century tale, a girl from Quintin sold her soul to the devil in exchange for some pretty clothes. When she died, the pallbearers could not lift her coffin; they opened the lid, and a black cat jumped out. Cats could harm a house. They often smothered babies. They understood gossip and would repeat it out of doors. But their power could be contained or turned to your advantage if you followed the right procedures, such as greasing their paws with butter or maiming them when they first arrived.

To protect a new house, Frenchmen enclosed live cats within its walls—a very old rite, judging from cat skeletons that have been exhumed from the walls of medieval buildings.

Finally the power of cats was concentrated on the most intimate aspect of domestic life: sex. *Le chat, la chaste, le minet* mean the same thing in French slang as "pussy" does in English, and they have served as obscenities for centuries.[17] French folklore attaches special importance to the cat as a sexual metaphor or metonym. As far back as the fifteenth century, the petting of cats was recommended for success in courting women. Proverbial wisdom identified women with cats: "He who takes good care of cats will have a pretty wife." If a man loved cats, he would love women; and vice versa: "As he loves his cat, he loves his wife," went another proverb. If he did not care for his wife, you could say of him, "He has other cats to whip." A woman who wanted to get a man should avoid treading on a cat's tail. She might postpone marriage for a year—or for seven years in Quimper and for as many years as the cat meowed in parts of the Loire Valley. Cats connoted fertility and female sexuality everywhere. Girls were commonly said to be "in love like a cat"; and if they became pregnant, they had "let the cat go to the cheese." Eating cats could bring on pregnancy in itself. Girls who consumed them in stews gave birth to kittens in several folktales. Cats could even make diseased apple trees bear fruit, if buried in the correct manner in upper Brittany.

It was an easy jump from the sexuality of women to the cuckolding of men. Caterwauling could come from a satanic orgy, but it might just as well be toms howling defiance at each other when their mates were in heat. They did not call as cats, however. They issued challenges in their masters' names, along with sexual taunts about their mistresses: "Reno! Francois!" "Où al ezvous?—Voir

---

[17]Emile Chautard, *La Vie étrange de l'argot* (Paris, 1931), pp. 367–68. The following expressions come from Panckoucke, *Dictionnaire des proverbes françois;* Esnault, *Dictionnaire historique des argots francais;* and *Dictionnaire de l'Académie française* (Paris, 1762), which contains a surprising amount of polite cat lore. The impolite lore was transmitted in large measure by children's games and rhymes, some of them dating from the sixteenth century: Claude Gaignebet, *Le Folklore obscene des enfants* (Paris, 1980), p. 260.

la femme à vous.—Voir la femme à mod! Rouah!" (Where are you going?—To see your wife.—To see my wife! Ha!) Then the toms would fly at each other like the cats of Kilkenny, and their sabbath would end in a massacre. The dialogue differed according to the imaginations of the listeners and the onomatopoetic power of their dialect, but it usually emphasized predatory sexuality.[18] "At night all cats are gray," went the proverb, and the gloss in an eighteenth-century proverb collection made the sexual hint explicit: "That is to say that all women are beautiful enough at night."[19] Enough for what? Seduction, rape, and murder echoed in the air when the cats howled at night in early modern France. Cat calls summoned up *Katzenmusik*, for charivaris often took the form of howling under a cuckold's window on the eve of Mardi Gras, the favorite time for cat sabbaths.

Witchcraft, orgy, cuckoldry, charivari, and massacre, the men of the Old Regime could hear a great deal in the wail of a cat. What the men of the Rue Saint Séverin actually heard is impossible to say. One can only assert that cats bore enormous symbolic weight in the folklore of France and that the lore was rich, ancient, and widespread enough to have penetrated the printing shop. In order to determine whether the printers actually drew on the ceremonial and symbolic themes available to them, it is necessary to take another look at Contat's text.

The text made the theme of sorcery explicit from the beginning. Jerome and Léveillé could not sleep because "some bedeviled cats make a sabbath all night long."[20] After Léveillé added his cat calls to the general caterwauling, "the whole neighborhood is alarmed. It is decided that the cats must

be agents of someone casting a spell." The master and mistress considered summoning the curé to exorcise the place. In deciding instead to commission the cat hunt, they fell back on the classic remedy for witchcraft: maiming. The bourgeois—a superstitious, priest-ridden fool took the whole business seriously. To the apprentices it was a joke. Léveillé in particular functioned as a joker, a mock "sorcerer" staging a fake "sabbath," according to the terms chosen by Contat. Not only did the apprentices exploit their master's superstition in order to run riot at his expense, but they also turned their rioting against their mistress. By bludgeoning her familiar, *la grise*, they in effect accused her of being the witch. The double joke would not be lost on anyone who could read the traditional language of gesture.

The theme of charivari provided an additional dimension to the fun. Although it never says so explicitly, the text indicates that the mistress was having an affair with her priest, a "lascivious youth," who had memorized obscene passages from the classics of pornography—Aretino and *L'Academie des dames*—and quoted them to her, while her husband droned on about his favorite subjects, money and religion. During a lavish dinner with the family, the priest defended the thesis "that it is a feat of wit to cuckold one's husband and that cuckolding is not a vice." Later, he and the wife spent the night together in a country house. They fit perfectly into the typical triangle of printing shops: a doddering old master, a middle-aged mistress, and her youthful lover.[21] The intrigue cast the master in the role of a stock comic figure: the cuckold. So the revelry of the workers took the form of a

---

[18]Sébillot, *Le Folk-lore de France*, III, 93–94.

[19]Panckoucke, *Dictionnaire des proverbs françois*, p. 66.

[20]This and the following quotations come from Contat's account of the cat massacre, *Anecdotes typographiques*, pp. 48–56.

[21]According to Giles Barber (ibid., pp. 7 and 60), the actual Jacques Vincent for whom Contat worked began his own apprenticeship in 1690; so he probably was born about 1675. His wife was born in 1684. Thus when Contat entered the shop, the master was about 62, the mistress about 53, and the bawdy young priest in his twenties. That pattern was common enough in the printing

(continued)

charivari. The apprentices managed it, operating within the liminal area where novitiates traditionally mocked their superiors, and the journeymen responded to their antics in the traditional way, with rough music. A riotous, festival atmosphere runs through the whole episode, which Contat described as a *fête*: "Léveillé and his comrade Jerome preside over the *fête*," he wrote, as if they were kings of a carnival and the cat bashing corresponded to the torturing of cats on Mardi Gras or the *fête* of Saint John the Baptist. As in many Mardi Gras, the carnival ended in a mock trial and execution. The burlesque legalism came naturally to the printers because they staged their own mock trials every year at the *fête* of Saint Martin, when the chapel squared accounts with its boss and succeeded spectacularly in getting his goat. The chapel could not condemn him explicitly without moving into open insubordination and risking dismissal. (All the sources…indicate that masters often fired workers for insolence and misbehavior. Indeed, Léveillé was later fired for a prank that attacked the bourgeois more openly.) So the workers tried the bourgeois in absentia, using a symbol that would let their meaning show through without being explicit enough to justify retaliation. They tried and hanged the cats. It would be going too far to hang *la grise* under the master's nose after being ordered to spare it; but they made the favorite pet of the house their first victim, and in doing so they knew they were attacking the house itself, in accordance with the traditions of cat lore. When the mistress accused them of killing *la grise*, they replied with mock deference that "nobody would be capable of such an outrage and that they have too much respect for that house." By executing the cats with such elaborate ceremony, they condemned the house and declared the bourgeois guilty—guilty of overworking and underfeeding his apprentices, guilty of living in luxury while his journeymen did all the work, guilty of withdrawing from the shop and swamping it with *alloués* instead of laboring and eating with the men, as masters were said to have done a generation or two earlier, or in the primitive "republic" that existed at the beginning of the printing industry. The guilt extended from the boss to the house to the whole system. Perhaps in trying, confessing, and hanging a collection of half-dead cats, the workers meant to ridicule the entire legal and social order.

They certainly felt debased and had accumulated enough resentment to explode in an orgy of killing. A half century later, the artisans of Paris would run riot in a similar manner, combining indiscriminate slaughter with improvised popular tribunals.[22] It would be absurd to view the cat massacre as a dress rehearsal for the September Massacres of the French Revolution, but the earlier outburst of violence did suggest a popular rebellion, though it remained restricted to the level of symbolism.

Cats as symbols conjured up sex as well as violence, a combination perfectly suited for an attack on the mistress. The narrative identified her with *la grise*, her *chatte favorite*. In killing it, the boys struck at her: "It was a matter of consequence, a murder, which had to be hidden." The mistress reacted as if she had been assaulted: "They ravished from her a cat without an equal, a cat that she loved to madness." The text described her as lascivious and "impassioned for cats" as if she were a shecat in heat during a wild cat's sabbath of howling, killing, and rape. An explicit reference to rape would violate the proprieties that were generally observed in eighteenth-century writing. Indeed, the symbolism would work only if it remained veiled—ambivalent enough to dupe the master and sharp enough

industry, where old masters often left their business to younger wives, who in turn took up with still younger journeyman. It was a classic pattern for charivaris, which often mocked disparities in age among newlyweds as well as humiliating cuckolds.

[22]Pierre Caron, *Les Massacres de septembre* (Paris, 1935).

to hit the mistress in the quick. But Contat used strong language. As soon as the mistress saw the cat execution she let out a scream. Then the scream was smothered in the realization that she had lost her *grise*. The workers assured her with feigned sincerity of their respect and the master arrived. "'Ah! the scoundrels,' he says. 'Instead of working they are killing cats.' Madame to Monsieur: 'These wicked men can't kill the masters; they have killed my cat.'…It seems to her that all the blood of the workers would not be sufficient to redeem the insult."

It was metonymic insult, the eighteenth-century equivalent of the modern schoolboy's taunt: "Ah, your mother's girdle!" But it was stronger, and more obscene. By assaulting her pet, the workers ravished the mistress symbolically. At the same time, they delivered the supreme insult to their master. His wife was his most precious possession, just as her *chatte* was hers. In killing the cat, the men violated the most intimate treasure of the bourgeois household and escaped unharmed. That was the beauty of it. The symbolism disguised the insult well enough for them to get away with it. While the bourgeois fumed over the loss of work, his wife, less obtuse, virtually told him that the workers had attacked her sexually and would like to murder him. Then both left the scene in humiliation and defeat. "Monsieur and Madame retire, leaving the workers in liberty. The printers, who love disorder, are in a state of great joy. Here is an ample subject for their laughter, a beautiful *copie*, which will keep them amused for a long time."

This was Rabelaisian laughter. The text insists upon its importance: "The printers know how to laugh, it is their sole occupation." Mikhail Bakhtin has shown how the laughter of Rabelais expressed a strain of popular culture in which the riotously funny could turn to riot, a carnival culture of sexuality and sedition in which the revolutionary element might be contained within symbols and metaphors or might explode in a general uprising, as in 1789. The question remains, however, what precisely was so funny about the cat massacre? There is no better way

to ruin a joke than to analyze it or to overload it with social comment. But this joke cries out for commentary—not because one can use it to prove that artisans hated their bosses (a truism that may apply to all periods of labor history, although it has not been appreciated adequately by eighteenth-century historians), but because it can help one to see how workers made their experience meaningful by playing with themes of their culture.

….it seems clear that the workers found the massacre funny because it gave them a way to turn the tables on the bourgeois. By goading him with cat calls, they provoked him to authorize the massacre of cats, then they used the massacre to put him symbolically on trial for unjust management of the shop. They also used it as a witch hunt, which provided an excuse to kill his wife's familiar and to insinuate that she herself was the witch. Finally, they transformed it into a charivari, which served as a means to insult her sexually while mocking him as a cuckold. The bourgeois made an excellent butt of the joke. Not only did he become the victim of a procedure he himself had set in motion, he did not understand how badly he had been had. The men had subjected his wife to symbolic aggression of the most intimate kind, but he did not get it. He was too thick-headed, a classic cuckold. The printers ridiculed him in splendid Boccaccian style and got off scot-free.

The joke worked so well because the workers played so skillfully with a repertory of ceremonies and symbols. Cats suited their purposes perfectly. By smashing the spine of *la grise* they called the master's wife a witch and a slut, while at the same time making the master into a cuckold and a fool. It was metonymic insult, delivered by actions, not words, and it struck home because cats occupied a soft spot in the bourgeois way of life. Keeping pets was as alien to the workers as torturing animals was to the bourgeois. Trapped between incompatible sensitivities, the cats had the worst of both worlds….

Insubstantial as it may seem today, this joking was a risky business in the eighteenth century. The risk was part of the joke, as in many forms of humor, which toy with violence and tease repressed passions. The workers pushed their symbolic horseplay to the brink of reification, the point at which the killing of cats would turn into an open rebellion. They played on ambiguities, using symbols that would hide their full meaning while letting enough of it show through to make a fool of the bourgeois without giving him a pretext to fire them. They tweaked his nose and prevented him from protesting against it. To pull off such a feat required great dexterity. It showed that workers could manipulate symbols in their idiom as effectively as poets did in print.

The boundaries within which this jesting had to be contained suggest the limits to working-class militancy under the Old Regime. The printers identified with their craft rather than their class. Although they organized in chapels, staged strikes, and sometimes forced up wages, they remained subordinate to the bourgeois. The master hired and fired men as casually as he ordered paper, and he turned them out into the road when he sniffed insubordination. So until the onset of proletarianization in the late nineteenth century, they generally kept their protests on a symbolic level. A *copie*, like a carnival, helped to let off steam; but it also produced laughter, a vital ingredient in early artisanal culture and one that has been lost in labor history. By seeing the way a joke worked in the horseplay of a printing shop two centuries ago, we may be able to recapture that missing element—laughter, sheer laughter, the thigh-slapping, rib-cracking Rabelaisian kind, rather than the Voltairian smirk with which we are familiar.

>> Questions for Consideration

1. What does the cat massacre reveal about class relations in preindustrial France?
2. Why did workers find the cat massacre funny?
3. What specific evidence is there of Foucault's and Geertz's influence in this excerpt?
4. Compare this excerpt to Thompson's. Which do you prefer and why?

Ruth H. Bloch, "The Construction of Gender in a Republican World"

References to gender continuously intruded into American revolutionary discourse, for notions of civic morality were repeatedly encoded in language describing ideal masculine and feminine traits. Between the 1760s and 1790s, moreover, dominant ideals of masculinity and femininity were subtly transformed. What had earlier been an essentially male standard of public virtue gradually gave way to a conception of social morality as largely depending on female influence. Ideas about the proper arena in which to perform civic obligations concurrently shifted away from the military and government towards the private institutions of the church and the family. A new view of appropriate relationships within the family served to elevate the status

Source: Ruth H. Bloch, "The construction of gender in a republican world," in *A Companion to the American Revolution*, ed. Jack P. Greene and J.R. Pole (Malden, MA: Blackwell, 2000): pp. 605–609. Reprinted by permission of Wiley-Blackwell. Bloch's original reference note format has been retained.

of wives and mothers, whose very femininity was now often perceived as indispensable to the maintenance of republican virtue.

How much these underlying changes in conceptions of gender were specifically due to the events of the Revolution is a debatable question. A similar upgrading of the roles of wife and mother occurred, for example, among the English bourgeoisie during the same general period. In the broadest sense, this reconstruction of gender relations can be associated with the long-term development of commercial economy and the ascendency of a pre-Romantic cultural of sentimentalism as much as with the American Revolution itself. Across the Atlantic world the ascendant commercial middle classes increasingly celebrated the value of private domestic life, and the emotionalism previously held against women came to be viewed in a positive light.

In America, however, the Revolution did cast these general, transatlantic changes in a specifically republican and national framework. Both the history of female participation in the patriot cause and the growth of female education in the early republic pushed towards a more generous assessment of women's capabilities. Since gender symbolism permeated revolutionary debate, moreover, critical changes in republican ideology hinged in part on the revision of gender definitions. The shift from a masculine to a feminine conception of virtue simultaneously reflected a new understanding of gender relations and a new understanding of republicanism itself.

Unlike other concepts associated with America revolutionary ideology—such as liberty, equality, property, happiness—gender was not, however, considered by eighteenth-century Americans themselves to be revolutionary issue. Republican ideology contained no explicit call for reconstruction of popular understanding of masculine and femininity. Whatever tensions and changes occurred in gender relations during the American Revolution were barely noticed by contemporaries. For the most part even those who commented explicitly on such matters as

marriage and female education assumed the continuance of a legal and political system that institutionalized female subordination and relegated men and women to fundamentally different social roles.

1. The Masculine Concept of Power

The main intellectual sources of early revolutionary ideology, Lockean liberalism and classical republicanism, both assumed the dependency and invisibility of women. According to each of these traditions, citizenship was based on a combination of property-holding and military service. For both, the fundamental contest for power within states was a male drama including in its cast of characters free propertyholders, noblemen, and kings. Opposition to absolute despotism was justified in the interest of preserving the liberty and independence of a citizenry that was composed of self-reliant, rights-holding, and arms-bearing men.

Frequently such a conflict between tyrant and subject was described in familial terms. Royalists had long employed the metaphor of paternal authority to legitimate monarchical rule. A king, argued James I, can be compared with "Fathers of families; for King is trewly *Parens patriae*, the politique father of his people" (McIlwain, 1918, p. 307). In his anti-patriarchal argument against Filmer, Locke had redefined citizenship as a contractual agreement analogous to marriage. Yet both marriage and the subordination of women still remained, in his view, outside politics. The invention of the state was an exclusively masculine act.

In the early revolutionary movement, American patriot ideology drew heavily from both liberal and classical republican thought in its formulations of the imperial conflict. The metaphor of England as the "mother country" has in traditional royalist fashion long pointed to the familial obligations and loyalties inherent in the imperial system. Initially American patriots expressed themselves in these conventional terms in the hopes of achieving peaceful reconciliation. As James Otis phrased his appeal in response to the Revenue Act of 1764, "few if any instance can be given where colonies have been disposed to forsake or disobey a tender mother" (Otis, [1764] 1965, p. 448). As the struggle with Britain intensified, however, the image of the imperial mother quickly turned from tender to cruel. In 1765 John Adams likened mother Britain to the monstrous Lady Macbeth, who would have "plucked her nipple from the [infant's] boneless gums, /And dashed the brains out" (Adams, 1850–6, 3: p. 464). The tyrannical lust for power represented a violation of the feminine maternal principle earlier associated with benign imperial rule. Power itself was typically symbolized as aggressively masculine, embodied above all in the supposedly ruthless and self-interested machinations of the King's notorious ministers.

The King himself was usually spared such negative characterization until the mid-1770s. Until then, protestations of loyalty still typically sought to distance expressions of loyalty of filial love for the father from the outrage expressed towards his ministers. Yet after the battles of Concord and Lexington, the image of George III as a heartless father emerged with a vengeance. "We swore allegiance to him as a *King,* not as a *Tyrant,*" as patriot newspaper angrily declared in 1775, "as a *Father,* not as a *Murderer*" (*Boston Gazette,* July 17, 1775). Crystallizing this growing anti-patriarchal sentiment, Thomas Paine's *Common Sense* characterized George III as "the royal Brute of Britain." As Paine elaborated the familiar familial analogy, America was best understood not as a dependent child but as an adolescent son coming of age. King George figured in this pamphlet as a "wretch, that with the pretended title FATHER OF HIS PEOPLE can unfeelingly hear of their slaughter, and composedly sleep with their blood upon his soul" (Paine, [1776] 1976, p. 92).

2. The Feminine Concept of Liberty

If the image of tyrannical power was aggressively male, the image of its symbolic opposite, liberty, was passively female. Particularly in the early years of the revolutionary movement, liberty was commonly depicted as delicate and vulnerable, susceptible, to brutal acts of violence suggestive of rape. Cartoons and other graphic portrayals of the imperial struggle often presented America as a chaste virgin. The portrait of America as an Amerindian princess uncorrupted by European civilization was a common variation on this theme. Another popular feminine image of America was drawn from the Book of Revelation—that of unprotected women in the wilderness encountering the wrath of the anti-Christian dragon. Taken together, these various patriotic representations of women highlighted the fragility of American liberty in the face of British power.

3. The Militant Ideal of Masculine Virtue

The symbolic dualism of active male power and passive female virtue was particularly pronounced during the period of resistance in the 1760s and early 1770s. As the patriot movement progressed from resistance to rebellion, however, an alternative masculine ideal of virtue rose to the fore. Paine's influential view of America as an adolescent boy chafing against unjust parental restrictions merged in the mid-1770s with a patriotic ideal of youthful male heroism. In accord with fundamental assumption of classical republicanism, the language of republicanism in the opening years of the war glorified the physical courage and valiant self-sacrifice of male citizen-soldiers. Military service offered young men the promise of public glory and fame. At the height of the military vogue, a toast on the first anniversary of American Independence made the underlying exclusion of women from this militant conception of citizenship particular clear, declaring, "May only those Americans enjoy freedom who are ready to die for its defense" (Royster, 1979, p. 32).

Ironically, women were in fact present in the American Army as camp followers. Far from being valorized for their participation, however, they only embarrassed the military leadership. A suggestive woodcut of a woman posed with a gun occasionally appeared in publications of the 1770s, but the image of female militancy predated the conflict with Britain and the stories it was chosen to illustrate had no connection to the American Revolutionary War. Only later would the disguised woman soldier Deborah Sampson Gannett become the popular heroine of American folklore. The term "manly" became itself nearly synonymous with public virtue in revolutionary discourse. "Effeminacy," on the contrary, signified laziness, cowardliness, and corruption. "Idleness is the mother or nurse of almost every vice," explained the college president John Witherspoon in a patriotic sermon predicting the victory of American troops over "those effeminate and delicate soldiers, who are nursed in the lap of self-indulgence" (Witherspoon, 1776, pp. 56–7).

This ideological association of femininity with laziness and luxury left little room for a republican ideal of woman analogous to that of the militant republican man. Women received recognition as patriots only rarely in the 1760s and 1770s, and then primarily for acts of stoic self-denial in support of the cause. They were praised for abstaining from extravagant imported goods and for laboring to produce homespun yarn, both as individuals and occasionally as "Daughters of Liberty." Women who worked hard and spurned luxury could thus be perceived as renouncing "effeminacy" and as conforming in a limited way to the essentially masculine ideal of republican virtue. A patriotic speech delivered by a young college graduate in 1780 praised the "ladies" for "their generous contributions to relieve the wants of the defenders of their country" (Kerber, 1980, p. 106). Women are similarly valorized in revolutionary propaganda for eagerly sending their men into battle. Young single women ostensibly favored the amorous attentions of courageous soldiers, for, in the words of a patriotic poem of 1778, "*Love hates a coward's impotent embrace*" (Royster, 1979, p. 30). One Philadelphia newspaper publicized the fighting words of a New Jersey matron to her soldier grandson, "Let me beg of you…that if you fall, it may be like men" (Kerber, 1989, p. 21).

At the height of the military fervor, the feminine conception of liberty as passive and in need of protection thus merged with the otherwise masculine version of heroic republican virtue.

4. A Less Combative Ideal: Family Life

The symbolic elevation of the male soldier proved, however, short-lived. In the face of growing anxieties about corruption and social disorder both during and after the war, American revolutionaries needed to establish a less combative ideal of republican citizenship consistent with peace and stability. Widespread political disillusionment in the 1780s undercut earlier millennial expectation of social perfection. American lost their earlier confidence that liberty would be preserved if it depended for its survival on the self-sacrificial virtue of the people.

The ideological transformation that underlay the United States Constitution redefined the relationship of men to the state. No longer urged into direct public service, ordinary citizens could, argued the authors of the *Federalist Papers*, indirectly contribute to the greater public good by exercising their freedom to pursue separate and competing interests. The state would protect itself against the destructive forces of selfish factionalism through an election system designed to filter out the most local and particular interests and a structure of government based on the institutional mechanisms of checks and balances. The active display of public virtue, still expected among civic leaders, was no longer required of the majority of republican men.

Not that the revolutionary generation altogether abandoned its hopes for a virtuous society. The virtue that had earlier been associated with the collective, public life gradually became redefined as a private, individual characteristic. Instead of being demonstrated in political activism and public service, it became chiefly manifest in the personal relationships of friendship and family.

This shift away from the earlier valorization of public virtue corresponded to a change in the representation of gender within republican ideology. The increased emphasis on the virtues of private life focused greater amounts of attention on emotional relationships between women and men. Just as the patriarchal family had long stood for royalists as a natural justification of monarchial government, so American revolutionaries devised their own republican understandings of courtship and marriage. Novels and magazines of the 1780s and 1790s excoriated parents for arranging mercenary marriages detrimental to their children's happiness. Couples were to marry out of neither self-interest nor lust but affectionate friendship. The marital relationship was idealized as voluntary and equal, a metaphor for the relationship between citizens in a republic. And the future of the nation depended on the capacity for mutual love that was best learned in marriage. "That MAN who resolves to live without WOMAN, or that WOMAN who resolves to live without MAN, are ENEMIES TO THE COMMUNITY in which they dwell," pronounced a piece on the "Genius of Liberty" printed in 1798 (Lewis, 1987, p. 709).

5. The New Civic Role of Women

Yet the egalitarian values expressed in this republican conception of marriage reflected no commitment to the political or social equality of women and men. Unlike French revolutionary women, who insisted on bearing arms and forming their own republican societies, American women never claimed universal rights for themselves. Instead of appealing to the ideal of universal equality, the primary justification for female self-assertion was made on the grounds of gender difference. The feminine qualities of sympathy, delicacy, and piety would, according to this view, soften the sensibilities of otherwise overly aggressive and self-interested man. One anonymous tract of 1787 entitled *Woman Invited to War* called American women to a collective religious crusade against postwar corruption and greed. Women were increasingly accorded recognition for a new civic role, that of requiring proper republican behavior of male suitors,

husbands, and sons. As a Columbia College orator expounded upon the public importance of this private influence, "Yes, ye fair the reformation of the world is in your power" (*New York Magazine*, May 1795, p. 298).

These new ideas of femininity found repeated expression in the growing body of literature in the early republic devoted to female education. Male leaders such as Benjamin Rush began to insist that American women needed greater knowledge in order to inculcate proper republican manners and morals in their husbands and children. Not only men but educated and articulate women, ranging from the sentimental novelist Hannah Foster to the political polemicist and historian Mercy Otis Warren, contributed to the delineation of the roles of republican wife and mother. Even Judith Sargent Murray, who came the closest to anticipating Mary Wollstonecraft in her insistence upon women's innate rational capacities, never rejected the centrality of marriage and motherhood.

While differing from the modern idea of social and political equality, a feminine principle thus entered into conceptions of the relationship between civil society and the republican polity. This was a new development in the history of American political thought, one anticipated by neither classical republican nor classical liberal theory. Women were now increasingly represented as a crucial part of the republican moral order even as they remained outside the institutions of government. The expanded definition of female civil obligations also enhanced women's domestic status, challenging, if by no means eliminating, older hierarchies within the family. In the course of reformulating this analogy, gender relations had been significantly redefined.

These ideological changes never overcame strict limitations in the appropriate roles for republican women, however. The more elevated notion of the civic value of personal domestic relationships gave rise to a still more deeply gendered definition of public and private spheres. The Revolution provided no impetus to re-evaluate the context of male economic and political power that rendered women ultimately dependent for all their newfound authority within the home. The idealization of domestic relationships encouraged the privatization of morality, a process which indirectly sanctioned men's pursuit of self-interest in the public domain. The republican construction of gender—built on the premise that female virtue could counteract male selfishness—at once increased the public value attributed to women and widened the symbolic polarity between feminine dependency and masculine autonomy within subsequent American culture.

>> Questions for Consideration

1. How does Bloch use gender as a category of historical analysis?

2. What evidence can you find of the influence of cultural anthropology and poststructuralist discourse analysis in this excerpt?

3. Explain Bloch's argument on the impact of the American Revolution. How does this compare to Franklin's argument? What might explain the differences?

Chapter 9

World Histories

(Aziz Khan © Dorling Kindersley/Media Library)

Over the course of the twentieth century, the American historical profession witnessed not only philosophical and methodological revolutions, but also a gradual shifting away from its national history focus toward a global perspective. This trend reflected the nation's transition from an isolationist stance toward other countries to an interventionist and international worldview during and after World War II. The creation of international agencies such as the United Nations and the North Atlantic Treaty Organization following World War II encouraged scholars to move beyond national histories to explore international connections in the past. Anticolonial revolutions following the war led to renewed interest in the histories of imperialism and colonialism. Lastly, increasing globalization in the last decades of the twentieth century has led to a dramatic rise in the demand for global history courses which explore the origins of this controversial trend. Global history, consequently, has recently become an exploding area of research.

As global perspectives have become more popular in the historical profession, historians are increasingly aware of the fact that no historical event or process exists in isolation. Since the histories of the world's peoples have always been intertwined, local, national, and regional histories just cannot fully encompass the extent of these interconnections. A global perspective, therefore, improves our ability to understand historical phenomena and processes across boundaries and broadens our historical vision.[1] As American historian Jerry H. Bentley asserts,

> ...world history is one of the big intellectual issues of our times. It draws attention to the mind-boggling processes of change, development, and transformation that human beings have generated and driven through time... It forces us to confront the phenomenon of globalization and situate it in historical context by conceiving and explaining the largest patterns in the experience of human beings on planet earth. As the field of study that deals most directly with the whole record of human achievements, world history is essential as the enterprise that enables human beings to understand themselves and their place in the world.[2]

Because world history is so big, it demands different research methods and theoretical approaches, and so has emerged as a distinct branch of history in the past decade.

Regional and World Histories prior to 1960

Although national histories dominated nineteenth- and twentieth-century Western historiography, regional and world histories date back to the ancient Greeks and initially were more common than national histories. Herodotus' *Histories*, for example, was actually a regional history of all the peoples involved in the Greco-Persian wars and Enlightenment thinkers, such as Voltaire and Condorcet, were interested in universal histories, or histories of humankind. National histories began to dominate historiography only in the nineteenth century, as modern nation-states developed and shaped the emerging historical profession. Nineteenth-century historians, consequently, conceived of the nation-state as the most important historical object of study, and their histories reflected this national framework. A few historians in the nineteenth and early twentieth century continued to look for universal patterns in the history of mankind, but national histories remained dominant through the 1960s.

Spengler   One of the most popular world historians prior to 1945 was Oswald Spengler (1880–1936). Spengler was born into a middle-class family in Central Germany. He completed doctoral dissertations on ancient Greek history and biological evolution in the animal kingdom. Although he was primarily interested in German history, the international crises of the early twentieth century, including World War I, convinced him to broaden the scope of his study. In his most famous work *The Decline of the West* (1918), Spengler determined that eight "high cultures" had dominated world history: Indian, Babylonian, Egyptian, Chinese, Mexican, Arabian, Greco-Roman, and European-Western. Spengler termed his approach to history as "physiogmatic."[3]

---

[1] Arif Dirlik, "Performing the World: Reality and Representation in the Making of World Histor (ies)," *Journal of World History* 16, no. 4 (2005): 392.

[2] Jerry J. Bentley, "Why Study World History?" *World History Connected* 5, no. 1 http://worldhistoryconnected.press.illinois.edu/5.1/bentley.html (accessed 18 April, 2009).

[3] Keith Stimely, "Oswald Spengler: An Introduction to His Life and Ideas," *The Journal for Historical Review* 17, no. 2 (March/April 1998): 2.

Organicist

Rather than looking at specific facts and details, Spengler sought to see the forest through the trees, to see the essence or heart of the overarching or universal pattern of history. He argued that this pattern was organic and cyclical, rather than progressive and linear. Each culture passed through one thousand-year organic cycles of birth, development, fulfillment, decay, and death. While many professional historians criticized his work for its lack of evidence, its simplicity made it enormously popular with European and American readers.

Toynbee

A famous contemporary of Spengler was Arnold J. Toynbee (1889–1975), English professor of Greek history. Like Spengler, Toynbee studied civilizations rather than nations and looked for some universal pattern to explain all of world history. He argued that national history was unintelligible without putting it into its wider global context. He too saw a primarily cyclical view of the rise and fall of civilizations, but his approach was less deterministic and more empirical than Spengler's. His theories were best expressed in his twelve-volume *A Study of History* (1934–1961). By comparing twenty-three civilizations throughout the world, Toynbee found that each civilization rose to greatness and progressed by responding creatively to challenges or obstacles. Civilizations stagnated when they lacked challenges and creativity, and declined when they failed to meet challenges. Leaders were the key historical agents in this theory, as it was up to the leaders of each civilization to invent solutions to obstacles and move their people forward or backward. He argued that "I do not believe that civilizations have to die because civilization is not an organism. It is a product of wills."[4] Toynbee's work was especially popular in the 1940s and 1950s, but many historians criticized him for manipulating the evidence to fit his theory.

Modernization Theory

While Spengler and Toynbee were influential in the United States, equally as powerful were new modernization theories which were built upon Enlightenment ideas of progress and adjusted them to the changing political order of the twentieth century. Modernization theorists argued that nations and cultures progressed through universal stages of development. In this view, the wealthiest and most powerful nations in Europe and America were the most highly developed and modern of all nations. Poorer, less-powerful nations in Africa, Asia, the Middle East, and Latin America, therefore, were less developed and less modern. Reasons for development and lack thereof varied from place to place, but modernization theorists asserted that all nations could become developed, wealthy, and powerful if they passed through the various stages of modernization experienced by the United States, Britain, and other powerful countries.

Rostow

The most famous modernization theorist was undoubtedly economist Walt Whitman Rostow (1916–2003), who greatly influenced U.S. and global economic policies throughout the 1950s and 1960s. Rostow graduated with his PhD in economic history from Yale University and was a professor at Columbia University and Massachusetts Institute of Technology (MIT) He later worked in high-level positions for Eisenhower, Kennedy, and Johnson administrations. Rostow's seminal

---

[4]Recalled on his death, *Time*, November 3, 1975.

work *The Stages of Economic Growth: A Non-Communist Manifesto* (1960) used the economic history of Britain and the United States as the role models for how countries developed. He argued that preindustrial, "traditional" economies would need to develop certain preconditions, such as technology, markets for raw materials and other mechanisms before their economies could achieve industrial "takeoff." After industrialization occurred, an economy would mature and eventually advance to a consumer-based "modern" economy. While this model has largely been discredited for ignoring historical factors differentiating various countries and the role of imperialism, it was very influential in shaping world historiography in the 1950s and 1960s.

Despite these important steps toward global history, most American historiography remained national or regional in focus through the 1960s, with the history of Western civilizations as the nearest relative to global history. Western Civilization history emerged in the United States following World War I as historians sought to grasp the origins of the conflict. As an American reaction to the war, the first Western Civilization courses consequently defined "the West" as the Allied nations of Western Europe and the United States, often excluding Germany, Austro-Hungary, Russia, and Eastern Europe. Following World War II, Western Civilization history and courses became much more popular as part of the anticommunist struggle to unite the opponents of communism. In the 1950s, these histories typically stressed the importance of liberal capitalism, freedom, and democracy, which supposedly united the West in a common heritage. While anticommunism provided a justification for requiring these courses for all students, in practice, most history professors had the freedom to teach them in less ideological terms. By the 1970s, Western Civilization history included the Middle East as the birthplace of Western cultural institutions, and Russia, to explain how it had diverged from the path of the West. Despite the narrowness of this approach, Western Civilization courses continue to be taught at many universities.

Postcolonial Histories

Like Rostow, most Europeans and European Americans had ignored the negative impact of imperialism and colonialism on colonized peoples. Writing from a Eurocentric perspective, European and American historians wrote about imperialism's modernizing and "civilizing" effects upon colonized peoples, and its contribution to global progress. Colonized peoples, however, had long witnessed and recorded the negative effects of imperialism and challenged Eurocentric histories of it. For example, *Chunder Dutt* nineteenth-century Indian nationalist Romesh Chunder Dutt (1848–1909) wrote a history of how British colonization had negatively affected India.[5] His history and the historical perspectives of other colonized peoples, however, were largely ignored in

---

[5]Romesh Dutt, *The Economic History of India Under Early British Rule* (London: Routledge and Kegan Paul; 1950, orig. 1904) and *The Economic History of India in the Victorian Age* (London: Routledge and Kegan Paul, 1950, orig. 1904).

Europe and America until the mid-twentieth century, when a number of movements converged to challenge the Eurocentric view of world history.

Most importantly, one by one former colonies around the world fought wars of independence from their European masters. In the process of fighting and winning these wars, they cultivated their own theories and histories challenging the European perspective of world history. Postcolonial history refers primarily to these histories, written during and after the mid–twentieth century wars of independence. Driven by the needs of these nationalist movements, postcolonial historians were overtly political in their intent and focus: They rejected Eurocentric histories and focused instead on telling history from the perspective of the colonized. Postcolonial history from the bottom-up went hand-in-hand with new social history. In fact, they overlap in many ways: both study economic, political, social, and cultural forces which oppress certain groups of people, focus on the oppressed rather than the oppressors, and have the political goal of solving the social and economic problems created by historical inequalities. Postcolonial history, however, differs from new social history primarily in that it is directly influenced by colonial independence movements, and therefore focuses explicitly on colonized nations and global systems, rather than on segments of society within a nation.

Fanon   Frantz Fanon (1925–1961) is probably the most famous and important of the first generation of postcolonial theorists. An educated, middle-class black man, born in the French colony of Martinique, Fanon fought against French imperialism in the Algerian war of independence in the 1950s. His book *The Wretched of the Earth* (1961) challenged imperialist ideology and offered a new view of race relations in which he urged colonized peoples to rewrite history and create a new world, totally throwing off the yoke of imperialism.[6] Many historians who considered themselves to be colonized peoples, including African American and American Indian historians, put his ideas into practice by rewriting American history from the perspective of oppressed racial minorities. Some argued that this new postcolonial history must be written by the colonized, and no one else, because only these historians could truly represent the perspective of the colonized. While Fanon wrote little history and died in 1961, his works remained enormously influential among historians, both in the former colonies of the world and in Europe and the United States.

Wallerstein   The ideas of Fanon and other revolutionaries coincided with and inspired the New Left in Europe and the United States in the 1960s. Influenced by postcolonialism and New Left critiques of imperialism as the cause of global economic inequalities, as well as Fernand Braudel's analysis of European economic networks, American historical sociology professor Immanual Wallerstein (b. 1930) sought to understand the origins of the problems facing postcolonial societies in the 1960s and 1970s. His most important work *The Modern World-System* (1974) divided the world into three regions: the capitalist core, the semi-periphery, and the periphery. He asserted that after the fifteenth century, northwestern European countries in the core exploited raw materials from

---

[6]Frantz Fanon, *The Wretched of the Earth*, trans. Richard Philcox (New York: Grove Press, 1963).

peripheral countries in order to develop their own capitalist systems. Arguing that Western capitalism required the economic exploitation and political domination of the non-Western world, Wallerstein concluded that this global imperialist capitalist system generated wealth for core countries, while political and economic chaos for the periph-

World Systems   ery for centuries to come. This World Systems theory of global history challenged impe-rialist histories which had viewed European expansion as a function of natural progress. It still, however, exhibited some Eurocentrism in its assumption that European coun-tries were at the core of the system and the primary agents of change, thus allowing little room for independent historical developments in other areas of the world.

Other historians in the 1960s joined Wallerstein in challenging the Eurocentric approach to world history and exploring imperialism from the eyes of the colonized. One

Subaltern   important branch of postcolonial history is subaltern studies, associated with the journal
Studies   *Subaltern Studies: Writings on South Asian History and Society,* founded in 1982. Ranajit Guha (1923–), an Indian historian working at the University of Sussex in England, was

Guha   a founding editor of this journal and has been a leader in this field. Guha borrowed the term "subaltern" from Gramsci's categorization of peoples of inferior rank (e.g., class, race, caste, age, or gender).[7] Guha explicitly criticized earlier "elitist" histories, those written from the perspective of the colonial elite and the nationalist indigenous elite, for ignoring the contributions of the people, or the lower castes, who made up the masses of the Indian population.[8] Borrowing ideas from neo-Marxists and New Leftists such as E. P. Thompson, he specialized in reconstructing the histories of peasant insurgencies in India.

Most of the other subaltern historians also focus on some aspect of Indian history from the bottom-up. In more recent years, many of the subaltern studies' historians have begun to adopt the methods of poststructuralism, using literary analysis and anthropo-logical "reading against the grain" to deconstruct colonial discourse. Unlike some earlier nationalist postcolonial historians, subaltern historians reject the idea that only indige-nous peoples should write their own histories. While they value indigenous accounts, they argue that historians, regardless of ethnicity or race, can study the history of subjugated peoples. As a consequence, many subaltern historians are Europeans or Americans.

Other postcolonial historians have been even more strongly influenced by the literary turn and poststructuralism. An important pioneer in this branch of postcolo-

Said   nial studies was Edward Said (1935–2003). He was born in Palestine and eventually immigrated to the United States, where he received a PhD in comparative literature from Harvard University. From the 1970s until his death in 2003, he was one of the most well-known critics of European imperialism in the world. Said adopted post-structuralist linguistic and postcolonial theories as he explored how imperialism shaped European ideas and discourse. In one of his most famous works, *Orientalism: Western Conceptions of the Orient* (1978), he uncovered the European construction of

---

[7]Anna Green and Kathleen Troup, *Houses of History: A Critical Reader in History and Theory* (Manchester: Manchester University Press, 1999), 283. See Chapter 6 for more on Gramsci.

[8]Ranajit Guha, "On Some Aspects of the Historiography of Colonial India," in *Selected Subaltern Studies*, ed. Ranajit Guha and Gayatri Chakravorty Spivak (New York: Oxford University Press, 1988), 37–39.

knowledge about the Orient, and how this knowledge served to justify European colonization of the Middle East and Asia.[9] Through close textual analysis, Said traced how European scholars in history, ethnology, and comparative anatomy created knowledge about the "Oriental Other" as the opposite of the "West."[10] By analyzing European texts about Egypt and other colonies, Said demonstrated how this knowledge was clearly biased by European prejudices, yet continued to dominate European discussion of these regions through the early twentieth century.

Said influenced a whole generation of postcolonial historians, who critiqued imperialism and colonization by reconstructing the damage they did to colonized peoples, and by deconstructing colonial discourse to uncover the deep intellectual roots of imperialism and how it shaped world history. Re-writing history from the perspective of the colonized, however, raises its own problems. Relatively few primary sources written by the colonized survive to give their perspective of events. Many postcolonial historians, therefore, use the techniques of anthropologists, archeologists, and oral historians to reconstruct events from a non-European perspective. Adapting the anthropological method of "reading against the grain," postcolonial historians closely read European primary sources, looking for shreds of evidence about those people they conquered and unintentionally wrote about.[11]

Comparative History

The comparative method is one method of writing postcolonial and international history. While comparative histories have been around for centuries, new social science methods renewed interest in comparative history in the 1960s, 1970s, and 1980s. Sociologists have long used comparative studies which systematically analyzed structural similarities and differences between societies, and historical sociologists often use the comparative method to understand past societies. This method helps to clarify unique characteristics of specific societies, as well as expose general patterns among multiple societies. Because of their interest in change over time, comparative historians typically compare two or more societies as they changed over time to determine the cause and meaning of these changes and draw more historical conclusions from their comparisons. A good example of this approach applied to the American Revolution is Patrice Higonnet's *Sister Republics* (1988), comparing the American and French revolutions. This argued that the French Revolution involved more class conflict, while the American Revolution had more class consensus but African American inequality.

Comparative history has many benefits, especially its ability to go beyond national borders and create regional and global historical analyses, but it has a number of

---

[9]The literal meaning of "orient" is East, while "occident" refers to West.

[10]Edward W. Said, *Orientalism* (New York: Pantheon, 1978), 31–42.

[11]See Bart Moore-Gilbert, *Postcolonial Theory: Contexts, Practices, Policies* (1997); Robert Young, *White Mythologies: Writing History and the West* (1990); and Patrick Williams and Laura Chrisman (eds.), *Colonial Discourse and Post-Colonial Theory: A Reader* (1992).

serious problems as well. One important obstacle to comparing multiple societies is the need to know multiple languages to read primary sources in their original language. This difficulty leads many historians to compare only societies which speak the same language, or to rely heavily on secondary sources which have already been translated. The comparative approach also assumes that the societies or units of comparison are independent of each other and can be separated from each other in order to explore their similarities and differences. But as the world becomes increasingly globalized, with media, corporations, and organizations blurring national boundaries, no country is completely independent from another, especially when one discusses cultures. As new cultural history becomes more pervasive, it has made national boundaries less significant. Cultures do not conform to national boundaries: they overlap and interact with each other so much so that their histories can hardly be disentangled. They share trade, warfare, technology, ideas, religions, languages, and a host of other things. As cultural historian William Sewell puts it, "Systems of meaning do not correspond in any neat way with national or societal boundaries—which themselves are not nearly as neat as we sometimes imagine."[12] So while comparative history does explore the international and national dimensions of historical phenomena, it is limited as a method for global history.

Regional History since 1960

On an even wider scope than national and comparative histories are regional histories. Closely linked to geographical and interdisciplinary studies, regional histories attempt to study broad sections of the globe, such as Asia, Africa, or Latin America as a whole, similar to Braudel's *Annales* approach earlier in the century. In the United States, Atlantic history as a regional study has made a considerable impact on American history. Rather than studying the nation in isolation as most historians have done for over one hundred years, many Americanists now place American history in the broader context of all the cultures surrounding the Atlantic basin, thus challenging long-held assumptions about American exceptionalism and revealing its true place in the broader history of the world. Wallerstein's World Systems theory seemed uniquely applicable to the Atlantic world and encouraged the growth of new Atlantic studies, but all historians of empire and slavery could recognize the intrinsic value of transatlantic history. These tendencies, together with the political climate of the Cold War and the international institutions created by it, encouraged more American historians to view Atlantic history as the natural scope of their studies.

Atlantic Turn   This trend toward studying American history in the context of the Atlantic world has been termed "the Atlantic turn." It got an important institutional start in academia in Johns Hopkins University's seminar in Atlantic history in 1967 and its

---

[12]William H. Sewell, Jr., "The Concept (s) of Culture," in *Practicing History: New Directions in Historical Writing after the Linguistic Turn*, ed. Gabrielle M. Spiegel (New York: Routledge, 2005), 90–91.

interdisciplinary program, which developed a few years later.[13] Reflecting colonial historians' interests in transatlantic slavery, commerce, and cultural exchange, American historians increasingly compared the North American experience with that of other regions in the Atlantic. *Curtin* Philip D. Curtin put Atlantic studies on the map with his path-breaking quantitative history of the transatlantic slave trade, *The Atlantic Slave Trade: A Census* (1969). *Crosby* Historian Alfred Crosby's (1931–) *The Columbian Exchange: Biological and Cultural Consequences of 1492* (1973) was also a foundational contribution to Atlantic history. He used ecological, biological, and archeological insights to explore how the European colonization of the Americas created an exchange of plants, animals, diseases, and ideas, unprecedented in world history.[14] Since then, his conclusions have been included in many American history textbooks.

Many prominent historians of the United States have also come to the conclusion that the American Revolution must be understood within a wider framework. Bernard *Bailyn* Bailyn (b. 1922) is one of the most prominent historians of the American Revolution and has also been a leading advocate of Atlantic histories. His most important early work *The Ideological Origins of the American Revolution* (1967) argued that the roots of the American Revolution lay in English republicanism. Since 1995, his Atlantic History Seminar at Harvard has become the focal point of most Atlanticist history. Other prominent historians of the American Revolution have extended Bailyn's Atlanticist argument. *Wood* Gordon S. Wood (b. 1933) agreed with the European origins of American thought, but argued that American revolutionaries made a radical departure from past traditions by synthesizing different strands of republican thought and placing them within a new *Pocock* American context.[15] J. G. A. Pocock's (b. 1924) *The Machiavellian Moment* (1975) traced American republican ideology all the way back to the Italian Renaissance. In recent *Langley* years, Lester D. Langley has studied the American Revolution in relation to the Haitian Revolution and Latin American wars for independence. He indicates that the American Revolution inspired the other revolutions, but differed from them considerably in many ways.[16] His follow-up book *The Americas in the Modern Age* (2003) extended this analysis from the 1800s through the 1990s. Partly as a result of these important studies and of "globalization fever" in the 1990s, Atlantic history has "moved from novelty to establishment" in the American historical profession and at least some Atlantic perspectives are now included in most American history textbooks.[17]

---

[13]Christopher Grasso and Karin Wulf, "Nothing Says 'Democracy' Like a Visit from the Queen: Reflections on Empire and Nation in Early American Histories," *Journal of American History* 95, no. 3 (December 2008): 772.

[14]Alfred W. Crosby, Jr., *The Columbian Exchange: Biological and Cultural Consequences of 1492* (Westport, CT: Greenwood, 1973).

[15]Gordon S. Wood, *The Creation of the American Republic, 1776–1787* (Chapel Hill, NC: University of North Carolina Press, 1969).

[16]Lester D. Langley, *The Americas in the Age of Revolution, 1750–1850* (New Haven: Yale University Press, 1996).

[17]Alison Games, "Atlantic History: Definitions, Challenges, and Opportunities," *American Historical Review* 111, no. 3 (June 2006): 745.

Global Histories

Histoire Croisée

In the wake of insights from new cultural history and of accelerated sharing between cultures, sometimes termed "internationationalization" or "globalization," historians have become more interested in transnational approaches, as opposed to comparative or regional approaches. Some historians label this new approach to world history as *histoire croisée* (entangled history).[18] As opposed to treating national histories as independent and self-contained, *histoire croisée* refers to histories which are inter-crossing, intersecting, interconnected, and entangled on many levels. This approach, therefore, is much less interested in comparing similarities and differences than in studying interconnecting global processes. As historical theorist Jurgen Kocka explains it, "One speaks of entanglements; is interested in traveling ideas, migrating people, and transnational commerce; mutually held images of 'the other'; one talks about mental mapping, including aspects of power, subordination, and dominance."[19] This new transnational trend is more complex than comparative history, but ultimately may better represent the reality of global history.

McNeill

Diamond

A persistent question in global history has been how the West (Europe and the United States) came to be the most powerful and wealthy region in the world, and the long history of wealth and poverty in general. Canadian American historian William McNeill (b. 1917) spent ten years writing *The Rise of the West: A History of the Human Community* (1963) in an attempt to answer this question. He challenged Spengler's and Toynbee's assumption of separate histories of distinct civilizations, finding extensive interconnections between the world's civilizations throughout the ages. Biologist and historical geographer Jared Diamond's (b. 1937) Pulitzer Prize-winning *Guns, Germs, and Steel: The Fates of Human Societies* (1997) used biology, geography, ecology, and demography to argue that diseases, geography, and technology led to the rise of the West. He asserted that "History followed different courses for different peoples because of differences among peoples' environments, not because of biological differences among people themselves."[20] Other historians have addressed this question through economic histories. Kenneth Pomeranz and Steven Topik's *The World that Trade Created* (2006) proved that the global integration of markets and indeed globalization itself is nothing new. It traced a variety of economic phenomena across the globe, connecting the impact of corporate decisions on large populations, thus explaining the long history of how the rich get richer, and the poor get poorer.[21]

Crosby, McNeill, Diamond, and a number of other world historians have also been influenced by the modern environmental movement which began in the 1960s.

---

[18]Jurgen Kocka, "Comparison and Beyond," *History and Theory* 42 (February 2003): 42.

[19]Ibid., 42–43.

[20]Jared Diamond, *Guns, Germs, and Steel: The Fates of Human Societies* (New York: W. W. Norton, 1999), 25.

[21]Kenneth Pomeranz and Steven Topik's *The World that Trade Created: Society, Culture, and the World Economy, 1400 to the Present*, 2nd ed. (Armonk, NY: M.E. Sharpe, 2006).

Alarmed by the pollution and destruction of ecosystems in contemporary civilizations, environmentalists seek government intervention to stop the degradation of the world's environment. As American society has become increasingly aware of global environmental problems, there has been an increased demand in histories which explore the origins of environmental problems.

Environmental History

Indeed, Alfred Crosby's *Columbian Exchange* was partly a response to this movement and one of the pacesetters for environmental history. He was involved in a number of social movements in the 1960s, including the environmental movement, and his history reflected the same desire to use history to change the future, shared by new social historians. Since the 1970s, he has written other histories, more specifically about the environment, such as *Children of the Sun: A History of Humanity's Unappeasable Appetite for Energy* (2006) and *Germs, Seeds, and Animals: Studies in Ecological History* (1994). Both McNeill and Diamond have also written histories focusing specifically on environmental factors.[22] Most recently, Anthony Penna's *The Human Footprint: A Global Environmental History* (2009) synthesizes global environmental history from the Paleolithic era to the present day using interdisciplinary methods. As concern over environmental collapse continues to rise, environmental history promises to expand in coming years.

Big History

Other historians have taken an even broader scope in attempting to address the meaning of human existence in "Big History." Big History refers to a kind of world history which starts at the beginning of the universe, putting human history in the much broader context of the history of the universe and the planet. With this wide lens, historians can see large patterns that smaller-scale histories may not. Innovations in science have greatly aided in this type of history. Since the 1960s, the discovery of plate tectonics, genetic mapping, and more accurate dating of the universe have helped historians to better understand not only the human past, but the history of the universe and all it contains. Because 90 percent of human history occurred before writing was invented, and the universe existed long before that, Big History requires new methodology.

Christian

Historian David Christian (1946–) has been a pioneer in combining geology, biology, paleontology, archeology, physics, astronomy, and history to write Big History. Christian is a citizen of the world himself: he was born in Brooklyn, New York, grew up in Africa and England, received his PhD from Oxford University, and has taught in Australia and the United States. His *Maps of Time* (2004) has pioneered the field of Big History, arguing that historians need the widest lens possible to capture the larger patterns in human history and understand its place in the grand scheme of the universe.[23] Big History has taken the historical profession by storm, but is remarkably difficult to write and teach because of its interdisciplinary nature as well as its gargantuan breadth.

---

[22]William McNeill, *Plagues and Peoples* (New York: Bantam Doubleday Dell, 1976); *The Human Condition: An Ecological and Historical View* (Princeton, NJ: Princeton University Press, 1980); Jared Diamond, *Collapse: How Societies Choose to Fail or Succeed* (New York: Viking, 2005).

[23]David Christian, *Maps of Time* (Berkeley, CA: University of California Press, 2004).

Bender   While most U.S. historians continue to specialize in national history on very specific topics, world history has considerably broadened the scope of American history since the 1990s. Thomas Bender (b. 1944), professor of history and humanities at New York University, has been a leader in encouraging the study of U.S. history within a global context. Bender graduated with his PhD in history from the University of California, Davis, in 1971. Like most other world historians, he specialized in national history at first, specifically American urban and cultural history. By the 1990s, however, Bender had begun to place his research within a broader regional and global framework. *A Nation Among Nations: America's Place in World History* (2006) is the culmination of these efforts. In a relatively short book, he explores major themes in American history from its beginning to the modern day, placing them within a global context and exploring the limits of American exceptionalism.

While global history has greatly broadened historians' perspectives on their specific research, it also presents many challenges. One of the most important questions in creating a truly global history is what to include and what to leave out. Similar to *Annalistes*, world history seeks to be a totalizing history, but with so much information on so many cultures in so many time periods, how does one determine what is important enough to include? This dilemma is of course present in all historical research, but it is multiplied many times over because of the scope of global history. Some world historians overcome this dilemma by taking a social scientific approach and focusing on patterns and themes which universally affect the world's peoples. These themes are typically changes in technology, economies, political structures, or social organizations. Focusing on large-scale universal patterns, however, frequently downplays or ignores individuals, human agency, and cultural diversity.

Another important obstacle to creating truly global histories is access to documents written in many languages and housed in archives around the world. Few historians know more than two or three languages, and few have the time and resources to visit archives in all of the countries required for world history research. While this continues to be a major hindrance to the research of global history, an important tool in overcoming this obstacle has been the Internet. Many archives, especially in more developed countries, have begun to digitize their documents and post them on Web sites. Many online archives now exist, some even independently of physical archives. Researchers may also have documents translated online for free. These translations may not always be as precise and accurate as historians require, but they may give some idea of the content and thus aid in the selection of relevant documents. Online archives have been a boon to overcoming the cost and time of travel to distant archives, but have their own pitfalls. The quality of the digital copy may be poor and taken out of its context and other details about authors, dates, and locations may be omitted from Web sites. Another problem is that digital archives are even more selective than physical archives, so that many documents may not be available to researchers, forcing them to travel to the archives anyway. Despite these issues, the Internet has become an extremely useful tool for historians of all subjects.

World history has come a long way since the middle of the twentieth century. Rather than a Eurocentric Western Civilization course taught at universities, it has grown into a research field in its own right. Spurred on by new social history, colonial independence movements, globalization, and technological advances, world history has become truly global. World history teachers and researchers have forged new ways of writing about their subject and new theories about the relationships of the world's peoples. Some continue to look for universal themes or patterns in history, while others emphasize local diversity. World history also helps us to understand national histories within their global context, and as a consequence, better appreciate local, national, and transnational dimensions of the past. Although it is still one of the most difficult subjects to master because of its large scale, it has added much to our understanding of national boundaries, identities, and the interconnections between all peoples. These new developments in world history as well as the recent American fascination with "globalization" have made global history much more popular at the beginning of the twenty-first century than ever before.

Edward W. Said, *Orientalism*

On a visit to Beirut during the terrible civil war of 1975–1976 a French journalist wrote regretfully of the gutted downtown area that "it had once seemed to belong to...the Orient of Chateaubriand and Nerval."[1] He was right about the place, of course, especially so far as a European was concerned. The Orient was almost a European invention, and had been since antiquity a place of romance, exotic beings, haunting memories and landscapes, remarkable experiences. Now it was disappearing; in a sense it had happened, its time was over. Perhaps it seemed irrelevant that Orientals themselves had something at stake in the process, that even in the time of Chateaubriand and Nerval Orientals had lived there, and that now it was they who were suffering; the main thing for the European visitor was a European representation of the Orient and its contemporary fate, both of which had a privileged communal significance for the journalist and his French readers.

Americans will not feel quite the same about the Orient, which for them is much more likely to be associated very differently with the Far East (China and Japan, mainly). Unlike the Americans, the French and the British—less so the Germans, Russians, Spanish, Portuguese, Italians, and Swiss—have had a long tradition of what I shall be calling Orientalism, a way of coming to terms with the Orient that is based on the Orient's special place in European Western experience. The Orient is not only adjacent to Europe; it is also the place of Europe's greatest and richest and oldest colonies, the source of its civilizations and languages, its cultural contestant, and one of its deepest and most recurring images of the Other. In addition, the Orient has helped to define Europe (or the West) as its contrasting image, idea, personality, experience. Yet none of this Orient is merely imaginative. The Orient is an integral part of European material civilization

[1]Thierry Desjardins, *Le Martyre du Liban* (Paris: Plon, 1976), p. 14.

and culture. Orientalism expresses and represents that part culturally and even ideologically as a mode of discourse with supporting institutions, vocabulary, scholarship, imagery, doctrines, even colonial bureaucracies and colonial styles. In contrast, the American understanding of the Orient will seem considerably less dense, although our recent Japanese, Korean, and Indochinese adventures ought now to be creating a more sober, more realistic "Oriental" awareness. Moreover, the vastly expanded American political and economic role in the Near East (the Middle East) makes great claims on our understanding of that Orient.

It will be clear to the reader (and will become clearer still throughout the many pages that follow) that by Orientalism I mean several things, all of them, in my opinion, interdependent. The most readily accepted designation for Orientalism is an academic one, and indeed the label still serves in a number of academic institutions. Anyone who teaches, writes about, or researches the Orient—and this applies whether the person is an anthropologist, sociologist, historian, or philologist—either in its specific or its general aspects, is an Orientalist, and what he or she does is Orientalism. Compared with Oriental studies or area studies, it is true that the term Orientalism is less preferred by specialists today, both because it is too vague and general and because it connotes the high-handed executive attitude of nineteenth-century and early-twentieth-century European colonialism. Nevertheless books are written and congresses held with "the Orient" as their main focus, with the Orientalist in his new or old guise as their main authority. The point is that even if it does not survive as it once did, Orientalism lives on academically through its doctrines and theses about the Orient and the Oriental.

Related to this academic tradition, whose fortunes, transmigrations, specializations, and transmissions are in part the subject of this study, is a more general meaning for Orientalism. Orientalism is a style of thought based upon an ontological and epistemological distinction made between "the Orient" and (most of the time) "the Occident." Thus a very large mass of writers, among whom are poets, novelists, philosophers, political theorists, economists, and imperial administrators, have accepted the basic distinction between East and West as the starting point for elaborate theories, epics, novels, social descriptions, and political accounts concerning the Orient, its people, customs, "mind," destiny, and so on. This Orientalism can accommodate Aeschylus, say, and Victor Hugo, Dante and Karl Marx. A little later in this introduction I shall deal with the methodological problems one encounters in so broadly construed a "field" as this.

The interchange between the academic and the more or less imaginative meanings of Orientalism is a constant one, and since the late eighteenth century there has been a considerable, quite disciplined—perhaps even regulated—traffic between the two. Here I come to the third meaning of Orientalism, which is something more historically and materially defined than either of the other two. Taking the late eighteenth century as a very roughly defined starting point Orientalism can be discussed and analyzed as the corporate institution for dealing with the Orient—dealing with it by making statements about it, authorizing views of it, describing it, by teaching it, settling it, ruling over it: in short, Orientalism as a Western style for dominating, restructuring, and having authority over the Orient. I have found it useful here to employ Michel Foucault's notion of a discourse, as described by him in *The Archaeology of Knowledge* and in *Discipline and Punish*, to identify Orientalism. My contention is that without examining Orientalism as a discourse one cannot possibly understand the enormously systematic discipline by which European culture was able to manage—and even produce—the Orient politically, sociologically, militarily, ideologically, scientifically, and imaginatively during the post-Enlightenment period. Moreover, so authoritative a position did Orientalism have that I believe no one writing, thinking, or acting on the Orient could do so without taking account of the limitations on thought and action imposed by Orientalism. In brief, because of Orientalism the Orient was not (and is not) a free subject of thought or action. This is not to say that Orientalism unilaterally determines what can be said about the Orient, but that it is the whole network of interests inevitably brought to bear on (and therefore always involved in) any occasion when that peculiar entity "the Orient" is in question. How this happens is what this book tries to demonstrate. It also tries to show that European culture gained in strength and identity by setting itself off against the Orient as a sort of surrogate and even underground self.

Historically and culturally there is a quantitative as well as a qualitative difference between the Franco-British involvement in the Orient and—until the period of American ascendancy after World War II—the involvement of every other European and Atlantic power. To speak of Orientalism therefore is to speak mainly, although not exclusively, of a British and French cultural enterprise, a project whose dimensions take in such disparate realms as the imagination itself, the whole of India and the Levant, the Biblical texts and the Biblical lands, the spice trade, colonial armies and a long tradition of colonial administrators, a formidable scholarly corpus, innumerable Oriental "experts" and "hands," an Oriental professorate, a complex array of "Oriental" ideas (Oriental despotism, Oriental splendor, cruelty, sensuality), many Eastern sects, philosophies, and wisdoms domesticated for local European use—the list can be extended more or less indefinitely. My point is that Orientalism derives from a particular closeness experienced between Britain and France and the Orient, which until the early nineteenth century had really meant only India and the Bible lands. From the beginning of the nineteenth century until the end of World War II France and Britain dominated the Orient and Orientalism; since World War II America has dominated the Orient, and approaches it as France and Britain once did. Out of that closeness, whose dynamic is enormously productive even if it always demonstrates the comparatively greater strength of the

Occident (British, French, or American), comes the large body of texts I call Orientalist. It should be said at once that even with the generous number of books and authors that I examine, there is a much larger number that I simply have had to leave out. My argument, however, depends neither upon an exhaustive catalogue of texts dealing with the Orient nor upon a clearly delimited set of texts, authors, and ideas that together make up the Orientalist canon. I have depended instead upon a different methodological alternative—whose backbone in a sense is the set of historical generalizations I have so far been making in this Introduction—and it is these I want now to discuss in more analytical detail.

....Orientalism is not a mere political subject matter or field that is reflected passively by culture, scholarship, or institutions; nor is it a large and diffuse collection of texts about the Orient; nor is it representative and expressive of some nefarious "Western" imperialist plot to hold down the "Oriental" world. It is rather a distribution of geopolitical awareness into aesthetic, scholarly, economic, sociological, historical, and philological texts; it is an elaboration not only of a basic geographical distinction (the world is made up of two unequal halves, Orient and Occident) but also of a whole series of "interests" which, by such means as scholarly discovery, philological reconstruction, psychological analysis, landscape and sociological description, it not only creates but also maintains; it is, rather than expresses, a certain will or intention to understand, in some cases to control, manipulate, even to incorporate, what is a manifestly different (or alternative and novel) world; it is, above all, a discourse that is by no means in direct, corresponding relationship with political power in the raw, but rather is produced and exists in an uneven exchange with various kinds of power, shaped to a degree by the exchange with power political (as with a colonial or imperial establishment), power intellectual (as with reigning sciences like comparative linguistics or anatomy, or any of the modern policy sciences), power cultural (as with orthodoxies and canons of taste, texts, values), power moral (as with ideas about what "we" do and what "they" cannot do or understand as "we" do). Indeed, my real argument is that Orientalism is—and does not simply represent—a considerable dimension of modern political-intellectual culture, and as such has less to do with the Orient than it does with "our" world....

Knowing the Oriental

On June 13, 1910, Arthur James Balfour lectured the House of Commons on "the problems with which we have to deal in Egypt." These, he said, "belong to a wholly different category" than those "affecting the Isle of Wight or the West Riding of Yorkshire." He spoke with the authority of a long-time member of Parliament, former private secretary to Lord Salisbury, former chief secretary for Ireland, former secretary for Scotland, former prime minister, veteran of numerous overseas crises, achievements, and changes. During his involvement in imperial affairs Balfour served a monarch who in 1876 had been declared Empress of India; he had been especially well placed in positions of uncommon influence to follow the Afghan and Zulu wars, the British occupation of Egypt in 1882, the death of General Gordon in the Sudan, the Fashoda Incident, the battle of Omdurman, the Boer War, the Russo-Japanese War. In addition his remarkable social eminence, the breadth of his learning and wit—he could write on such varied subjects as Bergson, Handel, theism, and golf—his education at Eton and Trinity College, Cambridge, and his apparent command over imperial affairs all gave considerable authority to what he told the Commons in June 1910. But there was still more to Balfour's speech, or at least to his need for giving it so didactically and moralistically. Some members were questioning the necessity for "England in Egypt," the subject of Alfred Milner's enthusiastic book of 1892, but here designating a once-profitable occupation that had become a source of trouble now that Egyptian nationalism was on the rise and the continuing British presence in Egypt no longer so easy to defend. Balfour, then, to inform and explain.

Recalling the challenge of J. M. Robertson, the member of Tyneside, Balfour himself put Robertson's question again: "What right have you to take up these airs of superiority with regard to people whom you choose to call Oriental?" The choice of "Oriental" was canonical; it had been employed by Chaucer and Mandeville, by Shakespeare, Dryden, Pope, and Byron. It designated Asia or the East, geographically, morally, culturally. One could speak in Europe of an Oriental personality, an Oriental atmosphere, an Oriental tale, Oriental despotism, or an Oriental mode of production, and be understood. Marx had used the word, and now Balfour was using it; his choice was understandable and called for no comment whatever.

> I take up no attitude of superiority. But I ask [Robertson and anyone else] who has even the most superficial knowledge of history, if they will look in the face the facts with which a British statesman has to deal when he is put in a position of supremacy over great races like the inhabitants of Egypt and countries in the East. We know the civilization of Egypt better than we know the civilization of any other country. We know it further back; we know it more intimately; we know more about it. It goes far beyond the petty span of the history of our race, which is lost in the prehistoric period at a time when the Egyptian civilisation had already passed its prime. Look at all the Oriental countries. Do not talk about superiority or inferiority.

Two great themes dominate his remarks here and in what will follow: knowledge and power, the Baconian themes. As Balfour justifies the necessity for British occupation of Egypt, supremacy in his mind is associated with "our" knowledge of Egypt and not principally with military or economic power. Knowledge to Balfour means surveying a civilization from its origins to its prime to its decline—and of course, it means being able to do that. Knowledge means rising above immediacy, beyond self, into the foreign and distant. The object of such knowledge is inherently vulnerable to scrutiny; this object is a "fact" which, if it develops, changes, or otherwise transforms itself in the way that civilizations frequently do, nevertheless is fundamentally, even ontologically stable. To have such knowledge of such a thing is to dominate it, to have authority over it. And authority here means for "us" to deny autonomy to "it"—the Oriental country—since we know it and it exists, in a sense, as we know it. British knowledge of Egypt is Egypt for Balfour, and the burdens of knowledge make such questions as inferiority and superiority seem petty ones. Balfour nowhere denies British superiority and Egyptian inferiority; he takes them for granted as he describes the consequences of knowledge.

> First of all, look at the facts of the case. Western nations as soon as they emerge into history show the beginnings of those capacities for self-government…having merits of their own…You may look through the whole history of the Orientals in what is called, broadly speaking, the East, and you never find traces of self- government. All their great centuries—and they have been very great—have been passed under despotisms, under absolute government. All their great contributions to civilisation—and they have been great—have been made under that form of government. Conqueror has succeeded conqueror; one domination has followed another; but never in all the revolutions of fate and fortune have you seen one of those nations of its own motion establish what we, from a Western point of view, call self-government. That is the fact. It is not a question of superiority and inferiority. I suppose a true Eastern sage would say that the working government which we have taken upon ourselves in Egypt and elsewhere is not a work worthy of a philosopher—that it is the dirty work, the inferior work, of carrying on the necessary labour.

Since these facts are facts, Balfour must then go on to the next part of his argument.

> Is it a good thing for these great nations—I admit their greatness—that this absolute government should be exercised by us? I think it is a good thing. I think that experience shows that they have got under it far better government

> than in the whole history of the world they ever had before, and which not only is a benefit to them, but is undoubtedly a benefit to the whole of the civilised West…. We are in Egypt not merely for the sake of the Egyptians, though we are there for their sake; we are there also for the sake of Europe at large.

Balfour produces no evidence that Egyptians and "the races with whom we deal" appreciate or even understand the good that is being done them by colonial occupation. It does not occur to Balfour, however, to let the Egyptian speak for himself, since presumably any Egyptian who would speak out is more likely to be "the agitator [who] wishes to raise difficulties" than the good native who overlooks the "difficulties" of foreign domination. And so, having settled the ethical problems, Balfour turns at last to the practical ones. "If it is our business to govern, with or without gratitude, with or without the real and genuine memory of all the loss of which we have relieved the population [Balfour by no means implies, as part of that loss, the loss or at least the indefinite postponement of Egyptian independence] and no vivid imagination of all the benefits which we have given to them; if that is our duty, how is it to be performed?" England exports "our very best to these countries." These selfless administrators do their work "amidst tens of thousands of persons belonging to a different creed, a different race, a different discipline, different conditions of life." What makes their work of governing possible is their sense of being supported at home by a government that endorses what they do. Yet

> directly the native populations have that instinctive feeling that those with whom they have got to deal have not behind them the might, the authority, the sympathy, the full and ungrudging support of the country which sent them there, those populations lose all that sense of order which is the very basis of their civilisation, just as our officers lose all that sense of power and authority, which is the very basis of everything they can do for the benefit of those among whom they have been sent.

Balfour's logic here is interesting, not least for being completely consistent with the premises of his entire speech. England knows Egypt; Egypt is what England knows; England knows that Egypt cannot have self-government; England confirms that by occupying Egypt; for the Egyptians, Egypt is what England has occupied and now governs; foreign occupation therefore becomes "the very basis" of contemporary Egyptian civilization; Egypt requires, indeed insists upon, British occupation. But if the special intimacy between governor and governed in Egypt is disturbed by Parliament's doubts at home, then "the authority of what…is the dominant race— and as I think ought to remain the dominant race—has been undermined." Not only does English prestige suffer; "it is vain for a handful of British officials— endow them how you like, give them all the qualities of character and genius you can imagine—it is impossible for them to carry out the great task which in Egypt, not we only, but the civilised world have imposed upon them."[2]

As a rhetorical performance Balfour's speech is significant for the way in which he plays the part of, and represents, a variety of characters. There are of course "the English," for whom the pronoun "we" is used with the full weight of a distinguished, powerful man who feels himself to be representative of all that is best in his nation's history. Balfour can also speak for the civilized world, the West, and the relatively small corps of colonial officials in Egypt. If he does not speak directly for the Orientals, it is because they after all speak another language; yet he knows how they feel since he knows their history, their reliance upon such as he, and their expectations. Still, he does speak for them in the sense that what they might have to say, were they to be asked and

might they be able to answer, would somewhat uselessly confirm what is already evident: that they are a subject race, dominated by a race that knows them and what is good for them better than they could possibly know themselves. Their great moments were in the past; they are useful in the modern world only because the powerful and up-to-date empires have effectively brought them out of the wretchedness of their decline and turned them into rehabilitated residents of productive colonies.

Egypt in particular was an excellent case in point, and Balfour was perfectly aware of how much right he had to speak as a member of his country's parliament on behalf of England, the West, Western Civilization, about modern Egypt. For Egypt was not just another colony: it was the vindication of Western imperialism; it was, until its annexation by England, an almost academic example of Oriental backwardness; it was to become the triumph of English knowledge and power. Between 1882, the year in which England occupied Egypt and put an end to the nationalist rebellion of Colonel Arabi, and 1907, England's representative in Egypt, Egypt's master, was Evelyn Baring (also known as "Over-baring"), Lord Cromer. On July 30, 1907, it was Balfour in the Commons who had supported the project to give Cromer a retirement prize of fifty thousand pounds as a reward for what he had done in Egypt. Cromer made Egypt, said Balfour:

Everything he has touched he has succeeded in…. Lord Cromer's services during the past quarter of a century have raised Egypt from the lowest pitch of social and economic degradation until it now stands among Oriental nations, I believe, absolutely alone in its prosperity, financial and moral.[3]

---

[2]This and the preceding quotations from Arthur James Balfour's speech to the House of Commons are from Great Britain, *Parliamentary Debates* (Commons), 5th ser., 17 (1910): 1140–46. See also A. P. Thornton, *The Imperial Idea and Its Enemies: A Study in British Power* (London: MacMillan & Co., 1959), pp. 357–60. Balfour's speech was a defense of Eldon Gorst's policy in Egypt; for a discussion of that see Peter John Dreyfus Mellini, "Sir Eldon Gorst and British Imperial Policy in Egypt," unpublished Ph.D. dissertation, Stanford University, 1971.

[3]Denis Judd, *Balfour and the British Empire: A Study in Imperial Evolution, 1874–1932* (London: MacMillan & Co., 1968), p. 286. See also p. 292: as late as 1926 Balfour spoke—without irony—of Egypt as an "independent nation."

How Egypt's moral prosperity was measured, Balfour did not venture to say. British exports to Egypt equaled those to the whole of Africa; that certainly indicated a sort of financial prosperity, for Egypt and England (somewhat unevenly) together. But what really mattered was the unbroken, all-embracing Western tutelage of an Oriental country, from the scholars, missionaries, businessmen, soldiers, and teachers who prepared and then implemented the occupation to the high functionaries like Cromer and Balfour who saw themselves as providing for, directing, and sometimes even forcing Egypt's rise from Oriental neglect to its present lonely eminence.

If British success in Egypt was as exceptional as Balfour said, it was by no means an inexplicable or irrational success. Egyptian affairs had been controlled according to a general theory expressed both by Balfour in his notions about Oriental civilization and by Cromer in his management of everyday business in Egypt. The most important thing about the theory during the first decade of the twentieth century was that it worked, and worked staggeringly well. The argument, when reduced to its simplest form, was clear, it was precise, it was easy to grasp. There are Westerners, and there are Orientals. The former dominate; the latter must be dominated, which usually means having their land occupied, their internal affairs rigidly controlled, their blood and treasure put at the disposal of one or another Western power. That Balfour and Cromer, as we shall soon see, could strip humanity down to such ruthless cultural and racial essences was not at all an indication of their particular viciousness. Rather it was an indication of how streamlined a general doctrine had become by the time they put it to use—how streamlined and effective.

>> Questions for Consideration

1. How does Said define "Orientalism?"
2. How does Said use Balfour's speeches to support his theory of Orientalism?
3. In what way does this excerpt show the influence of Michel Foucault?

David Christian, *"World History in Context"*

History is all about context. As Joyce Appleby, Lynn Hunt, and Margaret Jacob have written, "what historians do best is to make present and the potential of the future."[1] That is why historians so often complain about fields such as international relations that focus almost exclusively on current events and issues. However, historians haven't always been so good at putting their own discipline in context. Oddly enough, this applies even to world history. One of the

Source: David Christian, "World History in Context," *Journal of World History* 14: 4 (2003): pp. 437–438 & 446–458. Reprinted by permission of the University of Hawaii Press. Reference notes are Christian's. This essay is based, in part, on a paper given to the Royal Holland Society of Science and Humanities at their 250th anniversary symposium in Haarlem in May 2002: "Maps of Time: Human History and Terrestrial History," in *Symposium ter Gelegenheid van het 250-jarig Jubileum*, Koninklijke Hollandsche Maatschappij der Wetenschappen: Haarlem, 2002.

[1]Joyce Appleby, Lynn Hunt, and Margaret Jacob, *Telling the Truth about History* (New York and London: W.W. Norton, 1995), p. 9.

virtues of world history is that it can help us see more specialized historical scholarship in its global context. But what is the context of world history itself? This is a question that has not been sufficiently explored by world historians.[2] Yet it should be, for all the reasons that historians understand so well when we criticize other disciplines for neglecting context.

One of the aims of world history is to see the history of human beings as a single, coherent story, rather than as a collection of the particular stories of different communities. It is as much concerned with nonliterate communities (whether they lived in the Paleolithic era or today) as with the literature communities that gathered the written documents on which most historical research has been based. World history tries to describe the historical trajectory that is shared by all humans, simply because they are humans. Understood in this sense, world history is about a particular species of animal, a species that is both strange and immensely influential on this earth. So, to ask about the context of world history is to ask about the place of our particular type of animal, Homo sapiens, in the larger scheme of things. This question encourages us to see world history as a natural bridge between the history discipline and other disciplines that study changes in time, from biology to cosmology....

It is collective learning that distinguishes human history from natural history. Collective learning ensures that human history, unlike that of other species, is a process of accumulation and acceleration, and it is this process of cumulative and accelerating adaptation to the natural environment that is traced in world history. All in all, collective learning is so powerful an adaptive mechanism that there is a case for arguing that it plays an analogous role in human history to that of natural selection in the histories of other organisms. If so, perhaps collective learning should be a central theme in any attempt to weave a coherent account of world history.

The acceleration in human ecological power made possible by this new adaptive mechanism is already apparent in the archeological record of the Paleolithic era. Before modern humans appeared, technological change occurred, but it was extremely slow. The Acheulian stone tools characteristic of Homo erectus changed little in a million years. However, as an important recent survey of African prehistory shows, there are hints that the pace of technological change began to accelerate from about 250,000 years ago.[3] That acceleration may date the first appearance of modern humans equipped with symbolic language and capable of collective learning. For perhaps one hundred thousand years or more, modern humans were confined to the African continent, but innovation is apparent in new types of stone tools, in the appearance of new technologies such as the use of shellfish, and in evidence of long-distance exchanges. Then, from about one hundred thousand years ago the evidence becomes clearer. Further innovations allowed groups of humans to migrate to new environments, both within Africa (where humans began to settle regions of desert and equatorial forests) and beyond. Whereas our closest relatives, chimpanzees, remained in the ecological niche within which they had evolved, humans learned how to exploit an increasing variety of niches throughout

---

[2]Exceptions include William H. McNeil, whose article "History and the Scientific Worldview," in *History and Theory*, 37, no. ▢ (1998): 1–13, places world history within the context of other historical sciences, including biology and cosmology; and Fred Spier, *The Structure of Big History: From the Big Bang until Today* (Amsterdam University Press, 1996). There have also been some remarkable books by scientists that set human history in its cosmological context; they include Nigel Calder's remarkable chronology *Time-scale: An Atlas of the Fourth Dimension* (London: Chatto and Windus, 1983) and John Gribbin, *Genesis: The Origins of Man and the Universe* (New York: Delta, 1981), both of which are now slightly dated. Fred Spier has compiled a fuller bibliography of such works by historians and scientists. It can be found at http://www.120.uva.nl/inhoud/engels/bighistorybooks.htm.

[3]Sally McBrearty and Alison S. Brooks, "The Revolution That Wasn't: A New Interpretation of the Origin of Modern Human Behaviour," *Journal of Human Evolution* 39 (2000): 453–563.

the world, despite the fact that each niche required new skills and new knowledge. By one hundred thousand years ago, some modern humans had migrated out of Africa. This in itself was not particularly significant. The environments they found in the southern parts of the Eurasian landmass were not that different from those of their African homelands, and many other primate and mammal species (including some of our own hominid ancestors) had made similar migrations. The first migration that provides clear evidence of a significant increase in human adaptive skills is probably the migration to Sahul (the ice-age continent of Australia and Papua New Guinea). This took place between sixty thousand and forty thousand years ago. No earlier mammal had made this migration; the sea crossing alone suggests remarkable seafaring skills, while learning to exploit the unfamiliar plants and animals of Sahul must have demanded great ecological suppleness. The second migration that demonstrates our species's growing ecological virtuosity is the migration into ice-age Siberia that began perhaps forty thousand years ago. To survive in these cold lands, our ancestors had to learn new survival skills, including improved control of fire and new forms of tailoring, as well as new hunting skills. These migrations continued with the entry of humans into the Americas (perhaps thirteen thousand years ago), by which time humans could be found in most parts of the world. The process was completed by the migrations that populated the many islands of the Pacific in recent millennia.[4]

Then, a mere ten thousand years ago, humans began to exploit their environments intensively.[5] They found ways of extracting more energy from a given area, by diverting more of the energy flowing through the biosphere to their own uses. They did this by manipulating their surroundings so as to reduce the production of species they did not need ("weeds" and "pests" are the generic terms we use today for such organisms) and to increase the production of species they found useful. Eventually, such manipulation began to modify the generic structure of the most favored species in the Neolithic version of generic engineering that we call "domestication." In these ways, agriculture increased human control over local energy flows, allowing our ancestors to live in larger and more densely settled communities. Humans began not just to adapt to new niches, but to create new niches in the villages and cities of the Neolithic era. As populations grew, interactions between individuals and communities multiplied, and the process of collective learning itself intensified. In recent centuries, the rate of change has accelerated once more. The web of human interactions has thickened and stretched out until in the last five hundred years it has linked all societies on earth. Within the global networks of the modern era, information can be exchanged faster and more effectively than before and processes of collective learning can generate entirely new levels of synergy.[6]

As humans settled in denser communities they became more inter-dependent and their social networks became more complex. State formation, from about five thousand years ago, is one of the most striking measures of the increasing complexity of human societies, as individuals and communities found themselves incorporated into larger and more complex social machines

---

[4]Useful surveys of these migrations include Clive Gamble, *Timewalkers* (Harmondsworth: Penguin, 1995); John Mulvaney and Johan Kamminga, *Prehistory of Australia* (Sydney: Allen and Unwin, 1999); Brian M. Fagan, *The Journey from Eden: The Peopling of Our World* (London: Thames and Hudson, 1990); Ben Finney, "The Other One-Third of the Globe," *Journal of World History* 5, no.2 (1994): 273–297; J.R. McNeill, "Of Rats and Men: A Synoptic Environmental History of the Island Pacific," *Journal of World History* 5, no. 2 (1994): 299–349.

[5]B.D. Smith, *The Emergence of Agriculture* (New York: Scientific American Library, 1995), is a good summary of the transition to agriculture.

[6]The growth of networks or "webs" of exchange and communication is the central theme of J.R. McNeill and William H. McNeill, *The Human Web: A Bird's-Eye view of World History* (New York: W.W. Norton, 2003).

than ever before. Given Chaisson's notion of the link between energy use and complexity, we should expect to find that these changes correlate with increasing use of energy, and they do. Population growth is itself a powerful measure of the increasing ecological power of our species, as it implies the capacity to control more and more of the energy available to the biosphere. Just to keep their bodies functioning, humans need about three thousand calories of energy a day. Ten thousand years ago, there may have been six million humans, each consuming at least this much energy, but not much more. Today, there are one thousand times as many humans (more than six billion), so we can be sure that our species now consumes at least one thousand times as much energy as we did ten thousand years ago. At the same time, as Table 9.1 and Chart 9.1 suggest, each modern human consumes on average about fifty times as much energy as our ancestors did ten thousand years ago. If these figures are correct, they suggest that, as a species, we now consume about fifty thousand times as much energy as our ancestors once did (Chart 9.2).

They demonstrate a control over energy that no other species can match. The equivalent graph for chimpanzees (or, for that matter, for any other nonhuman animals) would show no

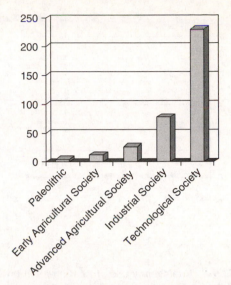

CHART 9.1   Energy Consumption per Capita in Different Eras (measured in 1,000 calories per person per day)
Data from Table 9.1

significant change in either total or per capita energy consumption over the last one hundred thousand years or more.

The accelerating ecological power of humans shows up in many other ways as well. One of the most powerful measures of human ecological power is summarized in Table 9.2.

TABLE 9.1   Average Daily per Capita Energy Consumption in Different Historical Era (units of energy = 1,000 calories per day)

	Food (incl. animal Feed)	Home and commerce	Industry and agriculture	Transportation	Total per capita	World population (millions)	Total energy consumption
Technological society (now)	10	66	91	63	230	6,000	1,380,000
Industrial society (100 B.P.)	7	32	24	14	77	1,600	123,200
Advanced agricultural society (1000 B.P.)	6	12	7	1	26	250	6,500
Early agricultural society (5000 B.P.)	4	4	4		12	50	600
Hunting society (10,000 B.P.)	3	2			5	6	30
Protohumans	2				2		

Based on I. G. Simmons, *Changing the Face of the Earth: Culture, Environment, History*, 2nd ed. (Oxford: Blackwell, 1996), p. 27.

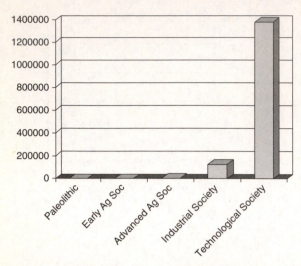

CHART 9.2   Total Energy Use of All Humans in Different Eras Total Human Energy Use over 100,000 Years (1,000 calories per Day)
Source: Data from Table 9.1

TABLE 9.2   Quartiles of Human-induced Environmental Change from 10,000 B.C. to mid-1980s

Form of transformation	Dates of quartiles		
	25%	50%	75%
Deforested area	1700	1850	1915
Terrestrial vertebrate diversity	1790	1880	1910
Water withdrawals	1925	1955	1975
Population size	1850	1950	1970
Carbon releases	1815	1920	1960
Sulfur releases	1940	1960	1970
Phosphorus releases	1955	1975	1980
Nitrogen releases	1970	1975	1980
Lead releases	1920	1950	1965
Carbon tetrachloride production	1950	1960	1970

From R. W. Kates, B. L. Turner, and W. About Clark, "The Great Transformation," in B. L. Turner, W. About Clark, R. W. Kates, J. F. Richards, J. T. Mathews, W. B. Meyer, eds., *The Earth as Transformed by Human Action: Global and Regional Changes in the Biosphere over the Past 300 Years* (Cambridge: Cambridge University Press, 1990), p. 7. Reprinted with the permission of Cambridge University Press.

The table gives the dates by which 25%, then 50%, then 75% of several different types of ecological impact had been reached. For example, the date 1950 in the population row and the 50% column implies that half of all human population growth occurred after that date (within the lifetime of many people alive today). The table shows clearly how human impacts on the environment have accelerated in the last two centuries.[7]

On What Scales Are Humans Significant?

Clearly, human history marks something new in the history of our planet. How significant is the appearance of our species? Can we measure our impact? In rough and ready ways we can, and these measures offer an important way of appreciating the wider significance of the history of our species.

Most of the energy that supports life on earth arrives in the form of sunlight. Living organisms need a lot of energy. So it is no accident that we live near a very hot object, the sun. At its center, our sun is at least ten million degrees, the temperature needed for fusion reactions to begin. Yet the average temperature of the universe is about three degrees above absolute zero. Like campers around a campfire, we live in a cold universe, near a source of heat, and it is this colossal energy differential that sustains complexity on earth. The torrent of energy that pours from the sun into the icy surroundings of space provides most of the energy needed to support our biosphere. Through photosynthesis, plants tap some of the energy of sunlight and store it in the cells of their own bodies. Other organisms capture their share of that energy by eating plants, or other animals that have eaten

---

[7]This acceleration has been explored superbly in John McNeill's recent environmental history of the twentieth-century, *Something New under the Sun: An Environmental History of the twentieth-Century World* (New York and London: W. W. Norton, 2000); see also Andrew Goudie, *The Human Impact on the Natural Environment*, 5th ed. (Oxford: Blackwell, 2000).

plants. In this way, like water flowing through irrigation canals, the energy of sunlight is distributed throughout the food chains of the biosphere. However, in a powerful demonstration of the effects of the second law of thermodynamics, much of that energy (often more than 90%) is dissipated at each step in its flow through the food chain, so that less and less is available to do the hard work of nourishing complex organisms. This is why food chains normally have fewer than four or five links, and why we normally find fewer organisms in the later links of the food chain. This is why wolves are less numerous than sheep.

However, the new adaptive mechanism of collective learning has helped our own species to overcome many of the ecological constraints that check the growth of all other species on earth. By diverting to their own use the energy channeled through many different food webs, humans have multiplied despite their position at the top of many food chains. The Russian physicist and demographer Sergey Kapitza has argued that "the human species now numbers at least one hundred thousand times more members than any other mammal of similar size and with a similar position in the food chain."[8] Today, humans may be controlling anything from 25% to 40% of the energy derived from photosynthesis and distributed through land-based food chains.[9] In addition, in the last two centuries, humans have learned to tap the huge stores of energy buried millions of years ago in the fossilized bodies of ancient plants and microorganisms, and available today in coal, oil, and natural gas. These statistics indicate the astonishing ecological power acquired by our species in the course of its history.

Increasing human control over the energy and resources of the biosphere has measurable consequences for the entire biosphere. If one organism hogs so much of the energy needed to sustain the biosphere, less will be available for other organisms. So it is no surprise that as humans have flourished other species have withered. (The exceptions are those plants and animals that have been invited or have barged their way onto the human ecological team, from cows and corn to rats and rabbits.[10]) This means that rates of extinction provide a rough measure of our impact on the biosphere. Currently, about 1,096 of 4,629 mammal species (24%) are thought to be "threatened"; 1,107 of 9,627 bird species (11%); 253 of 6,900 reptile species (4%); 124 of 4,522 amphibian species (3%); 734 of 25,000 fish species (3%); 25,971 of 270,000 higher plant species (10%).[11] The pace of extinctions appears to be accelerating, so we can expect a lot more in the near future.

But even current rates of extinction are shockingly high. Some paleontologists have concluded that they are approaching the rates of extinction during the five or six most drastic extinction episodes of the last billion years.[12] If so, human activity, and particularly human activity in recent centuries, will be visible on the

[8]Cited in Johan Goudsblom, "Introductory Overview: The Expanding Anthroposphere," in B. DeVries and J. Goudsblom, eds., *Mappae Mundi: Humans and Their Habitats in a Long-Term Socio-Ecological Perspective* (Amsterdam: Amsterdam University Press, 2002), pp. 21–46, from p. 26.

[9]I.G. Simmons, *Changing the Face of the Earth: Culture, Environment, History,* 2nd ed. (Oxford: Blackwell, 1996), p. 361, adapted from J.M. Diamond, "Human Use of World Resources," *Nature* 328 (1987): 479–480.

[10]Alfred W. Crosby, *Ecological Imperialism: The Biological Expansion of Europe, 900–1900* (Cambridge: Cambridge University Press, 1986), is all about the impact of this sort of teamwork in the last 500 years.

[11]*World Resources 2000–2001: People and Ecosystems: The Fraying Web of Life* (Washington, D.C.: World Resources Institute, 2000), pp. 246, 248.

[12]See, for example, Richard Leaky and Roger Lewin, *The Sixth Extinction: Patterns of Life and the Future of Humankind* (New York: Doubleday, 1995).

scale of a billion years. If paleontologists visit this planet in one billion years' time and try to decipher the history of this planet using the tools of contemporary human paleontology, they will identify a major extinction event at about the period we live in, and they will notice it was quite sudden. They will find it comparable to five or six other events of similar magnitude that occurred during the previous billion years, and they may be tempted to think of it as the equivalent of a meteoritic impact, such as the impact or impacts that appear to have driven most species of dinosaurs to extinction about sixty-seven million years ago. Our impact will certainly be detectable on a scale of six hundred million years (that of multicelled organisms) and probably on the scale of planetary history (4.5 billion years). This means that the history of our species is a matter of planetary significance. To say this of a group of species, such as the dinosaurs, might not be so remarkable; to say it of a single species really is odd.

There are tentative arguments suggesting that the level of complexity represented by human societies may be rare, not just on a planetary scale, but even on a galactic scale. Simple life forms, analogous, perhaps, to earthly bacteria, may turn out to be very common in the universe. At present, we simply don't know if this is true. However, as we come to understand how common planetary systems are, how rugged simple organisms can be, and how fast life evolved on our own earth, it appears more and more likely that there are millions, if not billions of life-friendly planets just within our own galaxy, and life may have evolved on many of them.[13]

However, intelligent, networked species like ourselves that can adapt through collective learning may be much rarer, because collective learning depends on the existence of more complex structures than those that power the other familiar adaptive mechanisms of natural selection and individual learning. On this planet, the vehicle for collective learning is symbolic language. Symbolic language depends on the evolution of unusually large and powerful brains....

If the evolution of creatures capable of collective learning was unlikely within the frame of planetary history, it may also have been unlikely on much larger scales.[14] After all, if such creatures were common, they should have evolved somewhere else, perhaps even within our own galaxy with its hundred billion stars, and some of them should have appeared millions, even billions, of years ago. In principle, they could have appeared within a few billion years of the first supernovae, which began scattering through the universe the chemical elements that are the raw material of chemical and biochemical evolution. If species capable of collective learning had evolved several billion years ago, some would surely have achieved the level of technological sophistication of modern humans and passed well beyond it. Eventually, some would surely have created technologies vastly superior to those we have created on Earth, including superior technologies of transportation and communication. By this logic, there ought to be creatures such as ourselves. Yet we have not a shred of evidence that this is so. As the physicist Fermi once asked, "Where are they?"[15] In the

---

[13] Paul Davies, *The Fifth Miracle: The Search for the Origin of Life* (Harmondsworth: Penguin, 1999) (particularly chapter 10, "A Bio-friendly Universe?"), and Malcolm Walter, *The Search for Life on Mars* (Sydney: Allen and Unwin, 1999), discuss how common life may be in the universe.

[14] There is a good discussion in Nikos Prantzos, *Our Cosmic Future: Humanity's fate in the Universe* (Cambridge University Press, 2000), pp. 162–169.

[15] Nikos Prantzos, *Our Cosmic Future*, pp. 162–169. As Prantzos points out (p. 164), Fermi's question had already been raised by Fontenelle in the eighteenth century. For a more optimistic assessment of the chances of finding intelligent life, see Armand Delsemme, *Our Cosmic Origins: From the Big Bang to the Emergence of Life and Intelligence* (Cambridge University Press, 1998), pp. 236–244.

twentieth century, humans managed to leave their own planet for the first time. If we do not destroy ourselves, it is likely that in the next few centuries we will travel to nearby planets and in a millennium or two we will travel to nearby star systems. (If it takes us a hundred thousand instead of just a thousand years, the argument still stands.) As we travel beyond our solar system, we will broadcast our presence in signals that will travel far ahead of us. At present, we have no reason to believe that intelligent beings anywhere else in the galaxy have achieved as much. The absence of clear evidence for extraterrestrials capable of collective learning suggests that human beings may be unique on a galactic, even perhaps a cosmological scale. So, while the evidence is growing that *life* in general may be common in the universe, *intelligent, networked* life-forms such as ourselves that can adapt through collective learning may be extraordinarily rare. Perhaps entities as complex as modern human societies arise close to the limit of our universe's capacity to generate complexity.

These arguments may or may not work. All they are intended to suggest is that the modern creation story does not necessarily deprive human history of meaning and significance. From some points of view, the modern creation story suggests that humans are remarkable, unusual, and profoundly important. In the distant future, many billions of years after we are gone, the universe will run down. It will continue to expand, but, under the harsh rule of the second law of thermodynamics, the energy differentials that support life today will diminish. Stars will flicker out and die, the universe will get colder and colder as it ages, and it will gradually lose the ability to fashion complex objects such as a fly or a polar bear or a human being. In retrospect, it will seem that we were among the most complex entities created by the universe in the youthful period when it had the energy to conjure up such miracles. On the modern map of complexity, humans are as central as they were within most traditional cosmologies.

For world historians, this conclusion is full of significance. It suggests, first, that world history—the discipline that studies the history of human beings—has significance across many scales and well beyond the conventional boundaries of the history discipline. It also suggests why compiling world history is so extraordinarily difficult. Constructing a coherent history of a species as complex as ours is a challenge as daunting as any in modern science. It will require many different types of historical research and scholarship, on many different scales. Fortunately, the field is already characterized by a remarkable openness to different approaches, styles, and methodologies. Yet the argument of this essay suggests that writing world history well may also require a serious attempt to see the history of our species in the context of other stories, including those of our planet and our universe. That will mean making more use than we normally do of the insights of specialists in neighboring fields, from biology to cosmology.[16] Just as the early pictures of earth taken from the Apollo missions made it easier to appreciate our own planet, so the view from outside world history may make it easier to understand the uniqueness and importance of world history, to identify the themes and problems that set it apart from neighboring disciplines, and to appreciate its underlying cohesion.

---

[16]Recent works by Jared Diamond have shown how fruitful and provocative the insights of a biologist can be for world historians. See, in particular, *Guns, Germs, and Steel* (New York: W.W. Norton, 1997).

>> Questions for Consideration

1. In what specific ways might this history be called "interdisciplinary"? In what ways might it be called "quantitative" history?

2. Compare Christian's approach to that of Condorcet?

3. Can you detect the influence of globalization and environmentalism in this monograph? What trends influenced Christian the most?

Thomas Bender, *A Nation Among Nations*

The "Great War" and the American Revolution

The Declaration of Independence promulgated by the thirteen colonies was the first time a people had formally and successfully claimed "independence" from the imperial power that had ruled them.[1] Since 1500, history seemed to work in the other direction, toward the accumulation of new territories or concessions. The ocean world invited global contests for more territory, trade, and power, but the struggles also created the conditions for and accounted for the success of the audacious claim by British Americans to a "separate and equal Station". And it was this proposition that the revolutionaries "submitted to a candid World" on July 4, 1776.

Carl Becker famously observed in 1909 that the American Revolution was a double contest: about home rule and about who would rule at home.[2] In fact, it was a triple contest. It was part of a global war between European great powers, it was a struggle for American independence, and it was a social conflict within its

colonies. Here I shall emphasize the first and largest of these three, for it was too little known and quite important, as no less a contemporary than James Madison recognized. Speaking behind the closed doors of the Constitutional Convention in Philadelphia, Madison observed that throughout history great powers tended to seek the destruction of each other, often to the advantage of the weaker nations:

> Carthage & Rome tore one another to pieces instead of uniting their forces to devour weaker nations of the earth. The Houses of Austria & France were hostile as long as they remained the great powers of Europe. England and France have succeeded to the preeminence & to the enmity. *To this principle we owe perhaps our liberty.*[3]

Madison's point, if we take it seriously, invited us to reframe the story of the Revolution, extending both the chronology and the geography of the explanatory context.

The struggle between England and France for hegemony in Europe and the riches of the empire was played out on a global scale between 1689

Source: Thomas Bender, *A Nation Among Nations: America's Place in World History* (New York: Hill and Wang, 2006): pp. 61–70. Copyright © 2006. Reprinted by permission of Farrar, Straus & Giroux. The reference notes are Bender's.

[1]On the novelty of the word in the lexicon of European diplomacy, see Richard B. Morris, *The Peacemakers: The Great Powers and American Independence* (New York, 1965), p. 147.

[2]Carl Becker, *History of Political Parties in the Province of New York, 1760–1776* (Madison, WI, 1909).

[3]Max Farrand, ed., *The Records of the Federal Convention of 1787,* rev.ed., 4 vols. (New Haven, CT, 1966), June 28, 1787, vol. 1, p. 448. Emphasis mine.

and 1815. The prolonged cycle of wars between them was known as the "Great War" until what Americans call World War I made the earlier one the *first* "Great War." The British colonies in North America were mostly on the periphery of these wars, but they reaped rewards from that larger conflict, the most important of which was independence. The global conflicts brought troubles as well: trade regulations were imposed by the global empires; changing alliances and naval strategies made the oceanic commerce that was the principal source of income both dangerous and uncertain. When the French withdrew from Canada as a result of the Seven Years' war (1756–63), the colonists welcomed the new security, but there were new sources of instability, too: it emboldened the Americans, and the English became concerned about the administration and cost of their dramatically expanding empire.

After its independence was secured by the Treaty of Paris (1783), the United States, with its large merchant marine, hoped for international recognition as a neutral power in the oceanic world. The profits from global trade could be and at times were considerable, but so were the risks. Too often the American desire for commerce with all nations was denied by either Britain or France or both. The difficulties were evident in the new American republic's first two wars, both fought to protect American commerce, the first against the Barbary States of Algiers, Morocco, Tripoli, and Tunis (1801–1805), the second and more dangerous against Great Britain itself (1812–15). Without British protection in the eastern Mediterranean, which they had lost with independence, American ships were prey in waters patrolled by pirates based in North Africa.[4] The second war came

after decades of difficulty in an oceanic world dominated by the great powers; the situation became intolerable when the Napoleonic wars reached their climax. The continual presence of Franco-British rivalry in the domestic and foreign affairs of the new nation restricted its practical independence, and American reactions to foreign presences and entanglements shaped and misshaped U.S. politics and economy. Great power rivalries had helped the Americans win their independence and their freedom, and now they threatened the very survival of the vulnerable republic.

Most historians of the Revolution and new nation have largely ignored this international context. For example, when, in his widely and long admired volume The *Birth of the Republic* (1956, 1977, 1992), Edmund Morgan, one of the most distinguished historians of colonial America, sets the scene with a description of Lexington Green, where the "shot heard round the world" was fired on April 19, 1775, the largest context he describes is "the history of the American's search for principles." Gordon Wood, another leading historian of the era, introduces the crisis of the 1750s as a sudden English intrusion into a colonial venture sustained by "benign neglect." "Great Britain thrust its imperial power" into a society that had become distinctive in its social practices and values, and this "precipitated a crisis within a loosely organized empire."[5]

There is nothing wrong with these framings, but the narrative is so tightly focused, with the English and imperial constitution at the center of the story, that it obscured the larger context that, among other things, encouraged the colonists to expand their rhetorical claims from the "rights of Englishmen" to the "rights of man."[6] Only by

---

[4]Robert J. Allison, *The Crescent Obscured: The United States and the Muslim World, 1776–1815* (New York, 1995), pp. xv, 17.

[5]Edmund S. Morgan, *The Birth of the Republic* (Chicago, 1992), pp. 1–3; Gordon Wood, *The American Revolution* (New York, 2002), p. 3.

[6]See R. Ernest Dupuy, Gay Hammerman, and Grace P. Hayes, *The American Revolution: A Global War* (New York, 1977), p. 18. See also T.H. Breen, "Ideology and Nationalism on the Eve of the American Revolution," *Journal of American History* 84, no. 1 (1997), pp. 13–39, where he shows that a vigorous English nationalism also weakened colonial claims of the "rights of Englishmen." Of course, these putatively universal rights were denied to women, to black slaves, to Indians.

claiming these rights and, declaring independence could they expect the foreign help necessary for success.[7] Nor can one grasp what seems obvious to a European, that, as the French historians Jacques Godechot has written, a civil war quickly transformed into an international one with global implications, fought on a global scale, from Lake Champlain to the West Indies, from southern England to the Cape of Good Hope and the Coromandel coast of India.[8]

Americans at the time were aware of these international implications more so than historians have been since. In 1777, before the colonists sealed their alliance with France, some Americans asked themselves whether it was reasonable, or even morally right, to draw France into what would surely expand into a war among the European powers.[9] They need not have worried. France had its reasons, as Madison knew: revenge for the British victory in the Seven Years' War was crucial, but also, France feared that if the English and Americans settled their differences they might mount a joint assault on France's West Indian possessions.

For contemporaries elsewhere, it was clear that the American Revolution was embedded in a longer sequence of global wars between France and England.[10] The battles fought between 1778, when France allied itself with the North American rebels, and 1783 touched every continent, and the major French objectives were not in America but elsewhere. In the 1770s, the average Frenchman probably had a clearer idea of Turkey and India than of the British American colonies.[11] The French wanted to reverse their losses in the Seven Years' War, which, in their view, had given Britain too much power within the European balance of powers, and they wanted to regain influence in India and the slave-trading depots at Gorée and the Senegal River.

These French ambitions explain the logic of their support for the Americans, and account for the secret aid for the Americans managed by the dramatist Pierre-Augustin Caron de Beaumarchais. While he was staging his new play *The Barber of Seville* and before was any formal French alliance, he was already funneling substantial funds from the French king to the Americans. He seems to have been moved to act partly out of sympathy with the Americans' republicanism, but he mainly undertook this work to avenge earlier French losses to the English. The Marquis de Lafayette initially joined the American cause for the glory of it and "hatred of the British."[12]

But British North America was not the main theater of this war. In 1779, for example, the French army that crowded onto five hundred Spanish ships in a joint effort to invade England was vastly larger than any army commanded by Washington in North America. (His

---

[7]Octavius Pickering, *The Life of Timothy Pickering, by His Son,* ed. Charles Upham, 4 vols. (Boston, 1867–73), vol. 4, p. 464.

[8]Jacques Godechot, *France and the Atlantic Revolution of the Eighteenth Century, 1770–1799,* trans. Herbert H. Rowen (New York, 1965), p. 3; Morris, *Peacemakers,* p. 386.

[9]See Robert Morris to John Jay, Sept. 23, 1776. Henry P. Johnston, ed., *The Correspondence and Public Papers of John Jay,* 4 vols. (New York, 1890–93), vol. 1, p. 85. I am indebted to Stacy Schiff for bringing this letter to my attention.

[10]Louis Gottschalk, "The Place of the American Revolution in the Causal Pattern of the French Revolution," in Esmond Wright, ed. *Causes and Consequences of the American Revolution* (Chicago, 1966), p. 296. For another measure of the place of the American Revolution in European politics, see Paul W. Schroeder, *The Transformation of European Politics, 1763–1848* (Oxford, 1994), an excellent international history of the era from 1763 to 1848 from a European perspective. There are twenty times more references in the index to the Ottoman Empire (eighty) than to the United States (four), and four times more to India (fifteen).

[11]Stacy Schiff, *The Great Improvisation: Franklin, France, and the Birth of America* (New York, 2005), p. 4.

[12]Gottschalk, "Place of the American Revolution," p. 294.

largest command was of sixteen thousand troops at Yorktown, half of whom were French.) Spain, an ally of France but not formally an ally of the Americans, was focused on Gibraltar, which it had lost to Britain in 1704. The massive invasion plan, something of a comedy of errors, was aborted.[13] When the war ended in 1783 in a series of separate treaties, the French "rejoiced not so much because the United States was independent as because England had been humbled."[14] But this was true only in North America. Overall, the British were anything but humbled, and it was this larger truth, not simply the American victory at Yorktown, that determined the shape of the peace. Neither France nor Spain had achieved its initial war aims, and Britain came out of the war in command of the sea and more powerful than before.[15]

One can say that global trade implies global wars, yet this seeming truism became practically true only when the rules of war and statecraft were transformed between the seventeenth and the eighteenth centuries. In 1559, Spain and France had agreed that conflicts "beyond the line" that for both of them marked the limit of Europe (which extended to the Azores) would not be taken as a basis or a reason for hostilities in Europe. When the Treaty of Westphalia (1648) had legitimated national boundaries and protected them from violation, much of the rivalry among European states for land or territory played out in relation of their colonial possessions. By the eighteenth century, however, the old phrase "peace beyond the line" ceased to have meaning. The Dutch were the first to consider colonies integral to a war with other European powers: the Treaty of Breda (1667), which concluded a war involving England, the Dutch Republic, France, and Denmark, was the first multilateral peace settlement that had as much concern for extra-European as for European affairs. Indeed, it was in this agreement that the Dutch let the English keep New Amsterdam or, as it had been renamed, New York, while they held the former English possession of Surinam. Then, in 1739, two European powers went to war over a non-European issue for the first time, when Britain challenged Spain's claim to search ships in the Caribbean—a war known in England as the War of Jenkins' Ear.[16] Global empires now implied global wars—and global politics.

Jacques Turgot, Louis XVI's minister of finance, recognized that the boundaries of the political world became "identical with those of the physical world."[17] Balance-of-power politics was similarly extended globally. "The balance of commerce of the nations in America," a French diplomat had observed in 1757, "is like the balance of power in Europe. One must add that these two balances are actually one." When France entered the Seven Years' war, Foreign Minister Choiseul declared that "the true balance of power really resides in commerce and in America." To weaken Britain in America, he concluded, would shift "considerable weight in the balance of power."[18] By 1776, it was widely understood that conflict in any part of an empire

[13]Richard Morris describes it as "hobbled not alone by senescent leadership but by inept civilian direction as well." Morris, *Peacemakers*, p. 29.

[14]Gottschalk, "Place of the American Revolution," pp. 294, 296–97. See also Alexander Deconde, "The French Alliance in Historical Speculation," in Ronald Hoffman and Peter Albert, eds., *Diplomacy and Revolution: The Franco-American Alliance of 1778* (Charlottesville, VA, 1981), pp. 1–37.

[15]The best accounts of the peace are Morris, *Peacemakers*; and Vincent T. Harlow, *The Founding of the Second British Empire*, 2 vols. (London, 1952–64).

[16]J.M. Roberts, *History of the World*, 3rd ed. (London, 1997), pp. 634, 636, 637. See also Felix Gilbert, *To the Farewell Address: Ideas of Early American Foreign Policy* (Princeton, NJ, 1961), p. 104.

[17]Quoted in Gilbert, *To the Farewell Address*, p. 57.

[18]Quoted in ibid., p. 106.

was not contained, nor was it exempt from global power considerations. That is why and how the American Revolution became part of a world war of more than a century's duration.

Global Empires

In the Atlantic and Indian oceans, dominance in the two linked enterprises of commerce and naval power passed from the Portuguese to the Dutch and then, by the end of the seventeenth century, to the English. Spain and France were land-base powers with territorial empires—Spain's much more extensive one distributed across the globe. But Spain made less of it, and the Iberian monarchy lost its initial advantage and had become a secondary power. The armies of Louis XIV, by contrast, rose to dominance on the Continent. Though France was slow to develop a maritime empire, by the mid-eighteenth century *outre-mer* France was considerable, with outposts in India, most importantly at Pondicherry; in Madagascar, off the east African coast; and in West Africa, with small trading posts at Gorée and along the Senegal River. In the Americas, France laid claim to the great expanse of what is now Canada, of value for its fur trade and fisheries. And ever since 1697, when Spain had ceded the western half of the island of Hispaniola to France, in St. Domingue (today's Haiti) it had the jewel of the Caribbean sugar islands, as well as several other small island colonies there.

By nineteenth-century British standards England's colonial empire was still modest. But the secret of British imperial and commercial success lay in the Royal Navy, not in the amount of colonized territory. At the outset, Sir Walter Raleigh had articulated the rule that would undergird British power. "Whosoever commands the sea," he observed, "commands the trade of the world; whosoever commands the trade of the world, commands the riches of the world, and consequently the world itself."[19]

Earlier types of naval power relied on a combination of fortified ports in key locations, as well as convoys protecting ships with valuable cargoes; this was the case with the Spanish galleons. But after the War of the Spanish Succession (1702–13) Britain initiated a more ambitious strategy to ensure the safety of all sea-lanes necessary for British commerce; this policy required massive, continuing investment in the Royal Navy.[20] The British therefore dramatically increased both taxes and debt, and created the bank of England. This state formation, which the historian John Brewer has called the "military-fiscal" state, was both the foundation and the product of a century of war that enabled an island to become a world power. It was extraordinarily successful, but it placed heavy burdens on the imperial structure. Between 1680 and 1780 the British military establishment (mostly the navy) trebled in size and expenditures. These fiscal and administrative challenges were handled with remarkable political consensus, skill, and efficiency.[21] But when the Seven Years' war vastly increased the empire and the cost of maintaining it, the British tried to shift some of the costs of their new military-fiscal state to their colonies. That was when tensions rose. Conflicts in India and North America threatened the empire at the very moment of its apparent success. Likewise in France and Spain military investments increased, and the imperial bureaucracies were reformed. And here, too, the debts, taxes, and administrative reorganizations produced instability. Domestic

---

[19]Quoted in Lawrence Stone, introduction to Lawrence Stone, ed., *An Imperial State at War: Britain from 1689 to 1815* (New York, 1994), p. 25.

[20]John Robert McNeill, *Atlantic Empires of France and Spain: Louisbourg and Havana, 1700–1763* (Chapel Hill, NC, 1985), pp. 76–78.

[21]John Brewer, "The Eighteenth-Century British State," in Stone, ed., *Imperial State at War*, pp. 57–61. See also John Brewer, *The Sinews of Power: War, Money, and the English State, 1688–1783* (London, 1989).

and colonial tensions led to revolution in France in 1789 and in St. Domingue two years later, while new fiscal demands and regulations triggered rebellions and insurgencies in Spanish and Portuguese America.

So this growing fiscal crisis was global, driven by the increasing military expenditures due to greater global integration and to developments in military technology; conflict and preparing for it became more expensive. The first signs of strain actually appeared in the Ottoman Empire, beginning in the 1690s. Within a century the pressure on its state finances had reached a crisis point, the result of war with the Russian Empire on the north shores of the Black Sea and the Crimean region, of conflict with the Habsburg Empire in Europe, and of the challenges of the French occupation of Egypt in 1798. In addition, demographic growth caused inflation that further reduced tax revenues that were already in decline because of the shift of trade out onto the oceans. Once the British drove Napoleon's army out of Egypt, its governor, Mehmet Ali, began acting independently, though maintaining allegiance to the sultan, while Serbia in 1804 and Greece in 1821 (having already revolted over land distribution in the 1770s) claimed independence.[22]

Britain's victory in the Seven Years' War greatly expanded its empire, and colonial issues became more present in the minds of political and administrative leaders in London. The empire seemed newly comprehensive, with the metropole and colonies together constructing a single global entity.[23] Arthur Young, writing in 1772, explained, "British dominions consist of Great Britain, Ireland, and diverse colonies and settlements in all parts of the world."[24] Yet a distinction was often made between the "empire" in the Americas and the "establishments" in Africa and Asia.[25] That said, it was undeniable that Bengal was considered an integral part of the British Empire, even if its administration was delegated to the east India Company, which presumed sovereignty there. Thus Edmund Burke in 1777 declared that "the native of Hindustan and those of Virginia" were each equally part of the "comprehensive dominion which the divine Providence has put in our hands."[26]

This increase in the size, wealth, and power of the British Empire worried Spain and Portugal. To protect themselves, they would need to enact similar reforms. José de Gálvez, visitor general of New Spain (1765–72) and minister of the Indies (1775–85), brought the empire closer to the metropole and increased trade within it through a policy of *comercio libre*, which offered economic stimuli and an increase in tax revenues without challenging the political status quo by taxing at home. These commercial and administrative reforms not surprisingly caused instability in the colonies during the 1780s. And in Portugal, Sebastião José de Carvalho e Mello, who became the Marqués de Pombal in 1769, was an authoritarian administrator who, having energetically directed the rebuilding of Lisbon after it had been destroyed in the great earthquake of 1775,

---

[22]Molly Green, "The Ottoman Experience," *Daedalus* 134 (Spring 2005), p. 96; Jack A. Goldstone, *Revolution and Rebellion in the Early Modern World* (Berkeley, CA, 1991), pp. 324–93; C.A. Bayly, *The Birth of the Modern World, 1780–1914: Global Connections and Comparisons* (Oxford, 2004), p. 90; William H. McNeill, "The Ottoman Empire in World History," in Kemal H. Karpat, ed., *The Ottoman State and Its Place in World History* (Leiden, 1974), p. 44.

[23]P.J. Marshall, introduction to P.J. Marshall, ed., *The Eighteenth Century,* vol.2 of *The Oxford History of the British Empire* (Oxford, 1998), p. 3.

[24]Quoted in ibid., p. 8.

[25]P.J. Marshall, "Britain and the World in the Eighteenth Century: I, Reshaping the Empire," *Transactions of the Royal Historical Society,* 6th ser., 8 (1998), pp. 10–11.

[26]Quoted in ibid., p. 11.

then turned to strengthening the Portuguese Empire. Here, too, there were rebellions, notably in Pernambuco and Rio de Janeiro, both of which resisted centralizing reforms.[27]

The tensions within each empire easily developed into revolt, for the colonial system depended on the cooperation of local elites, which typically expected a significant degree of autonomy, more often customary than official. The empires' local officials tended to soften the edge of imperial rule, making pragmatic adjustments that often increased their own power more than the crown's. With great variations among the empires and among different colonies in the same empire, it is fair to say that local populations helped to shape the imperial systems that ruled over them.

After the Seven Years' War, when new fiscal and administrative policies disrupted these established and comfortable patterns, protest and rebellion followed. More was usually involved than administration and taxation. The growth in world trade was putting new pressures on local social life. The merchants at the nodes of global trade were becoming very rich, and this made for a double problem: changing power relations among local elites, and their efforts to assert authority within the empire commensurate with their new high status. Even at the periphery of an empire, people were developing a sense of their communities' identity, perhaps even a proto-nationalist feeling, and they were often committed to preserving their traditions and privileges and to loosening their ties to the metropole. In some cases these new political cultures were simply the precipitate of social experiences over time, but in others, as with Mehmet Ali's satrapy in Egypt after 1805, the greater administrative and political autonomy prompted stronger attachments to the colony at the expense of the empire.[28]

Historians writing on the American Revolution have recently been paying attention to the sense of difference, distance, and distinction that developed in British North America; it might fairly be considered an emergent form of nationalism.[29] But one sees the same phenomenon within the older empires of the Middle East and South Asia. Similar tensions weakened the Safavid Empire in Iran; Mughal authority in India began to fragment as early as the 1720s. Often the new local movements were restorative in spirit, sometimes associated with religious revitalization, as one sees with the Sikhs, who resisted efforts of the Mughal elites to exact greater taxes from them. Followers of Muhammad ibn Abd al-Wahhab in Arabia resisted both the religious and the secular authority of the Ottomans throughout the late eighteenth century, and the Wahhabi sect sought autonomy in order to preserve what they claimed was a purer Islam.[30] The Incas' rebellion in Peru in 1780 was another indigenous effort to restore an older politics. In North America, "Pontiac's Rebellion," coming after the defeat of the French in the Seven Years' War aimed to push the British out of the Ohio valley, but Pontiac's military campaign was partly sustained by a widely held restorative impulse among Native Americans of the region to strengthen and confirm their own identity. He often deployed the language of the "Delaware Prophet," an Indian visionary who exhorted tribes to stay away from European trade and goods and held out the dream that the whites would go away.

---

[27]Here, as in the following paragraph, for the cases of Spain and Portugal, I rely on Jeremy Adelman, *Sovereignty and Revolution in the Iberian Atlantic* (Princeton, NJ, 2006).

[28]Khaled Fahmy, *All the Pasha's Men: Mehmet Ali, His Army, and the Making of Modern Egypt* (Cambridge, UK, 1997).

[29]See Breen, "Ideology and Nationalism," pp. 13–39.

[30]Bayly, *Birth of the Modern World*, pp. 88–89.

Empires in the eighteenth century were filled with uncontrolled, even unmapped areas, and even in places under formal organizational control, constant negotiations were required to sustain them. Though one should not exaggerate the agency or power of the colonized, one must acknowledge that empire depends on the tacit consent and cooperation of local elites. British imperial power collapsed in North America when the colonists withdrew their cooperation; at the same time in India, there were tensions yet local leaders found power and profit by remaining within the empire. It is doubtful that the British could have maintained their authority had the populace refused to go along, even though the governor-general in India had plenty of political and administrative power, as well as military support, more than any North American royal official. Coercive power was real in the eighteenth-century empires, but it was not the whole story.

>> Questions for Consideration

1. How does Bender "internationalize" the history of the American Revolution? What new insights does this method add to your understanding of the conflict?

2. What kind of evidence does Bender use? Why do you think he uses this kind of evidence?

3. Compare Bender's history of the American Revolution to those of Boorstin and the Beards. How do you explain the similarities and differences?

4. How does this type of history challenge the myth of American exceptionalism?

Recent Trends in the Historical Profession

The growth of global histories is only one dimension of the ongoing changes in the historical profession in the twenty-first century. Another more controversial dimension of contemporary historiography has been the ongoing debate between nationalist consensus historians and those who advocate more pluralist and/or relativist approaches to the discipline. Beginning with New Left history, the American historical profession has increasingly moved away from top–down national consensus history toward bottom–up histories of the poor, the marginalized, the oppressed, and the silent.[1] These academic histories have become more and more theoretical and focused on cultural aspects, such as class, gender, and race. Historians have borrowed heavily from the social sciences, including anthropology, ethnography, sociology, and psychology, as well as literary criticism, making the pursuit of history more interdisciplinary than ever before. Yet there has been a strong reaction against this historiographical revolution by conservatives inside and outside of academia. Out of this debate, however, a synthesis has begun to emerge. This synthesis adopts some elements of the new histories, but retains some elements of empirical history.

The Traditionalist–Postmodernist Debate

At the heart of this recent debate is postmodernism's critique of empirical truth, especially extremists' claims that all history is subjective and fictional. Many historians have deep misgivings, if not downright fear and opposition to these ideas. Viewing these theories as chaotic, irrational, nihilistic,[2] and contrary to the scientific foundations of history, they argue that postmodernism represents a dire threat to the future of historical study. To them, postmodernism seems to reject all truth and all reality, and worst of all, to imply that, since no truth exists and all writing is fictional, lies and distortions are valid forms of history. Pulitzer Prize-winning historian Gordon S. Wood reacted strongly against relativistic postmodern history in the 1990s arguing,

> What is called "New historicism" is now infecting everything from scientific thinking and law to philosophy and women's studies. We are being told to abandon all universal values and standards and to recognize that everything is relative—or that everything is, in other words, a product of specific historical circumstances. Scholars in a number of disciplines are urging us to understand the peculiar historicity of every person, event, value, or ideal, to acknowledge once and for all that there are no truths outside of that historicity… One can accept the view that the historical record is fragmentary and incomplete, that recovery of the past is partial and difficult, and that historians will never finally agree in their interpretations, and yet can still believe intelligibly and not naively in an objective truth about the past that can be observed and empirically verified. Historians may never see and represent

---

[1]Gordon S. Wood, *The Purpose of the Past: Reflections on the Uses of History* (New York: Penguin, 2008), 2.

[2]Nihilism is the belief that there is no purpose or meaning in life, no morality or ethical code, and no truth.

that truth wholly and finally, but some of them will come closer than others, be more nearly complete, more objective, more honest, in their written history, and we will know it, and have known it, when we see it.[3]

Other historians who advocate a return to objectivist consensus history conflate postmodern relativists with new social historians, and link them all to the moral decline and chaos they associate with the anti-intellectual student movement, ghetto rioting, and counterculture of the 1960s and 1970s. In 1997, Australian historian Keith Windschuttle asserted that postmodernist "dissidents" and "radicals" had taken over academia in English-speaking countries, especially in America, warning that "if historians allow themselves to be prodded all the way to this theoretical abyss, they will be rendering themselves and their discipline extinct."[4] He links postmodernism to feminism, Marxism, and even Nazism to support his argument on the dangers of this ideology. Many new social historians, on the other hand, were extremely critical of the linguistic turn, and many New Leftists argued that postmodernism was in fact a conservative reaction against their histories.

All forms of "revisionism" (a term used by consensus historians to describe all histories which "revise" the consensus interpretation in some way) came under attack in the 1980s. Traditionalists (those advocating a return to narrative, political, nationalist, and/or consensus history) blamed revisionists for fragmenting the profession into narrow fields of specialization, introducing technical jargon which made their histories unintelligible to those outside their field, and introducing questionable methods and theories to the discipline. The relativism and perspectivalism of revisionists especially alarmed traditionalists, who argued that these trends would lead to blatant distortions and falsifications being accepted as historical truths and overall lower professional history standards. Historiographer Ernst Breisach asserts that "The matter-of-fact, anti-theoretical and anti-philosophical objectivist empiricism which had always been the dominant stance of American historians continued to be enormously powerful. For those in this group it remained taken for granted that truth was 'out there'; something found, rather than made; unitary, not perspectival."[5] The historical profession, as a consequence, was sharply divided into two hostile camps.

One important issue raised by this debate was whether there are in fact any universal standards or methods that should be required of historians. Historian Peter Hoffer studied this controversy in-depth in *Past Imperfect* (2004), which traced the debate back to its origins in nineteenth-century historiography. At the heart of this debate is the role of historians' own opinions and perspectives on the evidence they interpret. He agrees with revisionists in asserting that the nature of inference, interpretation, and organization of evidence is inherently subjective, shaped in large part by the preferences and imagination of the historian. According to Hoffer, "Today, most professional historians would agree that historical facts are not stones one finds lying about. They are instead little arguments constructed from evidence."[6] Given the nature of historical imagination, however, how much subjectivity and imagination are too much? When does history cross the line from a scientifically driven quest for truth to a completely fictional representation of the past? This point has been debated since the creation of the profession in the nineteenth

---

[3]Wood, *The Purpose of the Past*, 85 and 108.

[4]Keith Windschuttle, *The Killing of History: How Literary Critics and Social Theorists Are Murdering Our Past* (New York: The Free Press, 1997), 9 and 36.

[5]Ernst Breisach, *Historiography: Ancient, Medieval, and Modern*, 2nd ed. (Chicago: University of Chicago Press, 1994), 593–594.

[6]Peter Charles Hoffer, *Past Imperfect: Facts, Fictions, Fraud—American History from Bancroft and Parkman to Ambrose, Bellesiles, Ellis, and Goodwin* (New York: Public Affairs, 2004), 20.

century. Hoffer argues that revisionism remained in the background of professional discussions, as long as historians gave each other the benefit of the doubt and politely agreed to disagree on the topic. After the 1970s, however, as professional historians became increasingly critical of each other's work and as their work became increasingly theoretical and different from popular history, the public began to lose faith in professional historians' ability and willingness to tell the truth. In the 1990s and first years of the twenty-first century, this crisis manifested itself in a number of public plagiarism and fraud cases, an international trial, and even in mainstream politics and media.

Plagiarism Cases

Ambrose   The most well-known plagiarism cases involved popular historians Stephen Ambrose and Doris Kearns Goodwin in 2002. Ambrose was especially prolific in publishing his work. His *Band of Brothers* (1992) and *Undaunted Courage* (1996) were very popular among the general public, and his books sold in the millions. He himself did not believe in historical relativism, stating in 2000 that: "Nothing is relative. What happened, happened. What didn't happen, didn't…"[7] He cited his primary sources but sometimes lifted them from other historians' work or borrowed heavily from other historians, using identical phrasing and wording without giving due credit. Ambrose defended his work, saying that he wrote for a popular audience and that getting the story right was more important than getting the citations right. He also used so many research assistants and published so prolifically; he admitted that some small percentage of his work may have been inadvertently plagiarized, but that it was never intentional. While Ambrose died in the midst of the controversy, Hoffer indicates that his plagiarism was indeed much more widespread and intentional than Ambrose had let on. In that same year, the *Weekly Standard* accused Pulitzer-Prize *Kearns* winning Doris Kearns Goodwin of appropriating "whole sentences from other scholars' work in *Goodwin* her *The Fitzgeralds and the Kennedys*" (1987).[8] Goodwin's publishers, Simon & Schuster, paid the author of the plagiarized work in 1989 to stop the matter from going further, but Goodwin never admitted to the fraud.[9] While these accusations led to no court trials and, for the most part, public admiration of their work never dimmed, they did tarnish the history profession's credibility.

The Irving–Lipstadt Trial

One important case of historical falsification that did indeed come before a court of justice was the Irving–Lipstadt Trial of 2000. David Irving was a British historian who claimed that the dominant Holocaust interpretation was invented by Jews to gain world sympathy and power. He spoke about his theories to a number of neo-Nazi groups in the 1990s. A Jewish American history professor, Deborah Lipstadt, accused him of fabrication of evidence motivated by his anti-Semitism. Irving then sued her for libel in the British courts. The case was widely publicized in Europe and America, and NOVA made a documentary of it called *Holocaust on Trial*. In the trial, Irving argued that he was a revisionist, legitimately challenging the traditional anti-Nazi interpretation of the Holocaust. He argued that previous historians of the Nazis (Jews and dupes of the Jews) had selectively

---

[7]Stephen Ambrose, "Old Soldiers Never Lie," http://www.forbes.com/asap/2000/1002/11.html quoted in Hoffer, *Past Imperfect*, 177.

[8]Hoffer, *Past Imperfect*, 198.

[9]Ibid., 203.

mistranslated Nazi documents. Like all good historians, he was merely offering an alternative interpretation of the topic. Lipstadt's lawyers countered with overwhelming evidence that the traditional anti-Nazi interpretation of the Holocaust was in fact correct. They showed how Irving had fabricated and distorted evidence to conform to his anti-Semitic interpretation of the event.

To many historians, this case demonstrated the dangers of revisionism and historical relativism: If there is no truth, or all truths are equal, it follows that lies and omissions are acceptable. Relativists, however, argued that while no history is truly objective and free of ideological bias, Irving was wrong not to admit his bias or work to limit its influence on his work. Although Irving lost his case, historians were left with no clear resolution of the issues it raised.

The Multiculturalism Debate

Cases like these exposed revisionist and postmodernist theory to criticism from outside the profession as well. In *The Closing of the American Mind* (1987), American philosopher Allan Bloom argued that postmodernism had led to the abandonment of objectivity and truth in the humanities and social science departments of our universities.[10] Bloom and other critics asserted that literary critics and postmodernists were really "ideologically motivated assaults on the intellectual and moral substance of our culture."[11] Conservative theorists saw cultural relativism and the critique of Enlightenment rationalism as "logically vacuous and politically irresponsible."[12] In 1996, even the Christian Broadcasting Network's *700 Club* weighed in "denouncing postmodernism as an amoral pseudo-religion."[13] Conservative politicians responded to these allegations by trying to promote traditionalist history instead. In 2005, the U.S. Congress voted to spend millions of dollars to support the teaching of "traditional American history," specifying political, intellectual, economic, constitutional, and diplomatic history, blatantly leaving out social history.[14] In 2006, Florida passed legislation requiring that "American history shall be viewed as factual, not as constructed…"[15] The politicization of this historiographical debate has profoundly affected the teaching of history in public schools as a consequence.

Conservatives have also attacked the multiculturalism of new social and cultural history in recent years. The public debate over historical multiculturalism centers on the country's twin desires to recognize and appreciate diversity, and to emphasize patriotism, pride, and consensus. While new social and cultural historians sought to emphasize diversity, expose injustices in America's past, and treat all cultures with equal respect, conservative educators in The Heritage Foundation and their political allies in the American Enterprise Institute and Republican Party sought a return to nationalist consensus history, insisting that "schoolchildren must be taught a certain core of key facts, because these facts proved the superiority of American history over all others."[16] Fed by the wave of patriotism sweeping the United

---

[10]Windschuttle, *The Killing of History*, 10.

[11]Roger Kimball, *Tenured Radicals* (1990) in Windschuttle, *The Killing of History*, 11.

[12]Windschuttle, *The Killing of History*, 11.

[13]Fred Leebron, et al., *The Norton Anthology of Postmodern Fiction* (New York: WW Norton, 1997), x.

[14]Gary J. Kornblith and Carol Lasser, "A Century of Scholarship on American Social History," *OAH Magazine of History*, October 2006, 8.

[15]Ibid., 12.

[16]Hoffer, *Past Imperfect*, 99.

States following the terrorist attacks of September 11, 2001, conservative politicians felt that Americans needed to know more about how their forefathers had fought to preserve freedom and how the United States was different from and better than its enemies. The American Enterprise Institute for Public Policy Research, a conservative group, argued in 2003 that the social history trend in textbooks had led to the current situation of American schoolchildren knowing little "about our nation's founding principles, how the government functions or what our forebears had to overcome the past two centuries to establish and preserve freedom."[17] In 2004, Senator Lamar Alexander (R-TN) argued that history should focus on "American exceptionalism" and teach students "what it means to be an American."[18] To bring the nation's schools up to the challenge of this agenda, Congress spent millions of dollars on history education through the National Endowment for the Humanities (NEH) and the Department of Education's *Teaching American History* project.[19] While these programs do not explicitly promote an ideological agenda, their choice of historical topics reveals the ideological justifications for their funding.

National History Standards Controversy

The multiculturalism debate came to a head during the national history standards and the Enola Gay controversies of the 1990s. The national history standards controversy began in the late 1980s with concern over students' lack of knowledge about history. Educators have been concerned about the lack of historical knowledge since the beginning of the century, but in the late 1980s, the head of the NEH Lynne Cheney began a project to develop models for teaching history nationwide. In 1990, President George H. W. Bush endorsed this goal to enhance student understanding of the nation's "diverse cultural heritage."[20] Out of this effort, the National Council for Humanities in the Schools (NCHS) was formed and it set about the task of creating national history standards for the schools. With new social historian Gary B. Nash at its helm, the Council consulted and gained approval from "more than thirty national organizations of teachers, administrators, curriculum specialists, librarians, parents, and historians."[21]

The final product the National Standards for United States History (1994) reflected the most recent research on history and pedagogy, but its new social history perspective offended conservatives like Cheney and leading Republicans. Even before the standards were published, Cheney published an article in the *Wall Street Journal*, entitled "The End of History," in which she argued that the standards were driven by political revisionism, replacing America's heroes with minor figures.[22] She and conservatives across the country labeled the standards and all new social histories as "politically correct," a derogatory term coined in the 1980s to attack liberals who sought racial and gender inclusiveness, and respect in speech and behavior.[23] Republican Congressman Newt Gingrich argued that the national history standards reflected professional historians' conspiracy to "Take the west down a peg, romanticize 'the Other' (non-whites), treat all cultures as equal, refrain from criticizing non-white cultures."[24] Gingrich and conservative

---

[17]Bruce Craig and Tim Nolan, *NCH Washington Update* 10:40 (October 8, 2004).

[18]Ibid.

[19]Ibid.

[20]Hoffer, *Past Imperfect*, 102.

[21]Gary B. Nash, "The History Wars of the 1990s," *The Lawrence F. Brewster Lecture in History XV* (Greenville, NC: East Carolina University, November 1996), 1.

[22]Lynne Cheney, "The End of History," *Wall Street Journal*, October 20, 1994, A22.

[23]Hoffer, *Past Imperfect*, 110.

[24]Newt Gingrich, "History Standards Are Bunk," *Congressional Record*, 104th Cong., 1st sess., February 8, 1995, E301, quoted in Hoffer, *Past Imperfect*, 110.

commentators such as Rush Limbaugh argued for a return to fact-centered, objective, consensus history. Nash worked to gain support for the standards, but a large Republican majority in Congress rejected the standards. In January 1995, they resolved by a vote of 99-1 that "the voluntary National History Standards were offensive, harmful to young minds, and disrespectful to Western values and achievements."[25] Many school districts have used the standards as their guide, but no national history standards have been attempted since then.

Enola Gay Controversy   The Enola Gay controversy of 1993–1994 likewise reflected this debate between conservatives, who supported a nationalistic consensus interpretation of the past, and new social historians, who sought to include multiple perspectives. In 1993, Martin Harwit, the director of the Smithsonian Air and Space Museum, decided to exhibit the *Enola Gay*, the plane which carried the atomic weapon that destroyed Hiroshima. Harwit wanted the exhibit to tell the story of the event and tried to include multiple versions of the story in order to please all those who supported the different interpretations of the event. New Left historians and Japanese Americans wanted the exhibit to show the inhumanity of the act, while the Air Force and its veterans wanted the exhibit to be a memorial to the efforts of American servicemen and show how the bombing saved the lives of many troops who would have otherwise had to invade Japan. As various organizations and members of Congress demanded revisions to the exhibit and Harwit attempted to please them, the Organization of American Historians (OAH) condemned the political pressure placed upon him to revise his interpretation. In the end, the Senate unanimously resolved that the Enola Gay script was "revisionist, unbalanced, and offensive."[26] Under considerable pressure, Harwit resigned and his successor Michael Heyman presented a much less controversial version of the exhibit. Since that time, a number of online resources have been created to study this important historiographical controversy. A good example of these is Lehigh University's Web site walking the reader through five "rounds" of documents detailing the debates. This Web site and the Enola Gay controversy prove that "history is, in fact, fighting matter."[27]

American history continues to be heavily politicized and the U.S. government has made repeated efforts to get historians to focus less on sociocultural history, and more on consensus political history. Public historians and school teachers have been under enormous pressure to present popular interpretations of controversial subjects. For example, OAH President James Horton reported on a number of school teachers and museum directors in the South being pressured to portray the South and Confederacy more positively and make no reference to slavery in discussions of the Civil War.[28] While political pressure on historians is nothing new, what is new is criticism of historians for their theories and approaches.

A Way Forward?

A positive outcome of the conservative backlash has been to force professional historians to think more carefully about their relationship to the wider public, defend their methods and profession, and seek a path forward. The American Historical Association (AHA) has attempted

---

[25]Nash, "The History Wars of the 1990s," 1.

[26]Ibid., 2.

[27]Edward J. Gallagher, *The Enola Gay Controversy* (Spring 2000), http://digital.lib.lehigh.edu/trial/enola/ (accessed October 4, 2009).

[28]James Horton, "History Matters: Organizing for Mutual Support," *OAH Newsletter* 32 (November 2004).

to address these issues through its Professional Division. This branch of the AHA was originally created in 1974 to deal with ethical concerns such as the position of minorities and women in the historical profession.[29] In 1987, it published a *Statement on Standards of Professional Conduct*, which established basic professional guidelines for all American historians:

> All historians believe in honoring the integrity of the historical record. They do not fabricate evidence. Forgery and fraud violate the most basic foundations on which historians construct their interpretations of the past. Those who invent, alter, remove, or destroy evidence make it difficult for any serious historian ever wholly to trust their work again…. Knowing that trust is ultimately more important than winning a debate for the wrong reasons, professional historians are as interested in defining the limits and uncertainties of their own arguments as they are in persuading others that those arguments are correct.[30]

The statement went on to set guidelines for professional conduct on a number of issues. The AHA, however, has no legal power to enforce its standards. From time to time, the AHA has formed committees to investigate charges of misconduct among its members, but it can do little more than verbally condemn the perpetrators.

Other historians are busily working out a way forward from the revisionist–traditionalist debate, synthesizing linguistic and postmodern history with more traditional approaches, attempting to create a practical program which most historians can accept. All historians, whether postmodernist or traditionalist, still strive to understand the past and still need to somehow use evidence to help them in that endeavor. While highly critical of postmodern extremists, Joyce Appleby, Lynn Hunt, and Margaret Jacob concede some points to postmodernists and suggest a middle ground between postmodernism and traditionalist history.[31] They agree that absolute objectivity is indeed impossible and that all historians' perceptions are shaped by personal and cultural factors, but argue that historians can still create an accurate portrayal of the

Practical Realism

past and uncover its truths. They posit a new theory of objectivity called "Practical Realism" in which historians strive for a limited objectivity, admitting their own philosophy and perspective and their role in shaping historical interpretation, testing the validity and accuracy of sources, and including multiple perspectives in their research. Other historians have joined them in blending moderate relativism with scientific methods, narrative with analysis, and discourse analysis with causal analysis.

The World Wide Web has aided in the quest to bring historians together, to set professional standards, and to share knowledge in new ways. As noted in Chapter 9, many Web sites house digital archives of primary and secondary sources, thus allowing most historians access to these documents. Many other Web sites exist to help historians to communicate with each other and improve their teaching and research. One important Web site is the Humanities and Social Sciences Network (H-Net) created by historians and other scholars in 1993. Housed at Michigan State University, it freely provides discussion networks for many different scholarly

H-Net

interests. In H-Net's discussion lists, historians can share reviews of books, teaching techniques, theoretical ideas, and any other professional inquiry they wish.[32] All of the major historical organizations also have their own Web sites, sharing their professional standards and guidance

[29]Hoffer, *Past Imperfect*, 135.

[30]AHA, "Statement of Professional Standards" (1987, revised 2005), http://www.historians.org/pubs/Free/ProfessionalStandards.cfm (accessed October 3, 2009).

[31]Joyce Appleby et al., *Telling the Truth About History* (New York: WW Norton, 1994), 247–262.

[32]*Humanities and Social Sciences Online*, http://www.h-net.org/ (accessed October 3, 2009).

for any historian to read. In many ways, the Internet has connected historians, exposing them to ideas from other disciplines, historical specialties, and countries. Using new technology and synthesizing theories, historians continue to take historiography in new directions in the twenty-first century.

Conclusion

The American historical profession has come a long way since its birth in the nineteenth century. With distant origins in the ancient Greeks, it has upheld the tradition of making meaning of the past as accurately as possible. Roman and European historians followed the Greeks in this endeavor, bringing their own unique imprint to bear on historiography. In the centuries following the Renaissance, European and American historians wrote increasingly secular stories of the past. This trend continued through the centuries, and with the Enlightenment, historians added new empirical methods to their study of the past, attempting to make it more scientific, more objective, and thus more professional. As new nation-states arose in the eighteenth and nineteenth centuries, historians wrote stories of the past framed around the needs of nation-states and nationalism.

American historiography soon distinguished itself with its own unique schools of thought and approaches. In the twentieth century, nationalist consensus historians vied with Progressive historians for dominance. Neoconsensus and New Left schools, and more recently, new socio-cultural and conservative schools have perpetuated this ongoing division within the American historical profession. Over the years, both sides have profited from new interdisciplinary methods and global perspectives. Through it all, historians have struggled to add to our understanding of the past and left us with an enormous body of historical knowledge to build upon.

These various struggles and approaches are especially reflected in the historiography of the American Revolution. One can detect the underlying theories, assumptions, and methods used by each historian by reading the excerpts included in this reader. Many historians have studied the historiography of the American Revolution and written historiographical review essays to illustrate their understanding of how the history of this subject has changed over the years. An example of a historiographical review of the American Revolution is included in Appendix B to help readers understand how the study of historiography can be applied to a specific topic. This reveals how historians have disagreed on many aspects the American Revolution and greatly varied in their interpretations of the meaning of this important event.

Historiography is so diverse because we historians are so diverse. Influenced by our own personalities and historical context, we choose the topics which we feel are most important, we apply methods and theories which we feel are most appropriate, and we form our own conclusions as best we can. Some of us believe that individuals make history, while others believe that other historical forces make history. Some believe that we can achieve at least limited objectivity in our work, while others maintain that we cannot escape our own perspectives no matter how hard we try. New theories, methods, and topics have emerged and added to our historical knowledge, but these have always caused controversy and resistance. Despite our disagreements and controversies, perhaps history is still a noble profession. What higher goal can one have than to help create meaning and truly understand the world and its past, to think through problems and find answers, and perhaps even to seek truth?

Appendix A

The Critical Analysis of Historical Monographs

1. **Historical context of the author**
   a. Who is the author?
   b. What is the author's gender, race, ethnicity, place of birth, religion, and occupation?
   c. When and where did he or she write?
   d. For what audience is the author writing? Why did the author write this?
   e. What political, social, or economic events might have influenced the author's life and therefore his or her philosophy?

2. **Topic**
   a. What is the topic of the monograph?
   b. How might the topic choice be related to the author's historical context?
   c. What does the topic choice tell us about what the author valued and thought was important?
   d. Does the topic choice tell us anything about the author's perspective on historical agency?

3. **Method**
   a. What evidence does the author use and how does the author use it?
   b. Does the author logically interpret and apply the evidence to support the thesis?
   c. Is there any evidence of bias or outside influences in the interpretation of the evidence?
   d. What does the author's choice of evidence tell us about historical agency and/or philosophy or methodology?

4. **Thesis**
   a. What is the thesis (main argument or conclusion) of the monograph?
   b. What are the most important supporting arguments in the monograph?
   c. Does the thesis and conclusion tell us anything about the author's historical philosophy?

5. **Theory**
   a. What theory or philosophy is at the heart of this monograph?
   b. How do steps one through four determine the historical philosophy of the author as demonstrated in this monograph?
   c. What is the primary agent of historical change here?
   d. Is there an overarching pattern of history at work here (either implied or explicitly referenced)?

Appendix B

Sample Historiographical Review

The American Revolution: Moderate or Radical

The American Revolution is the single most significant event in this country's history. Within twenty years—1763 to 1783—Americans declared their independence, waged a war of liberation, transformed colonies into states, and created a new nation. But scholars disagree about using the term revolutionary to describe how new or different these developments were. Some historians argue that the Revolution was solely aimed at achieving the limited goal of independence from Britain. Colonial society, they say, was democratic, and there was a consensus among Americans about keeping things as they were once the break with Britain had been accomplished. Others claim that the Revolution was accompanied by a violent social upheaval—a class conflict—as the radical lower classes sought to gain a greater degree of democracy in what had been a basically undemocratic society in the colonial era. The question is, then, was the Revolution revolutionary, or was it not?

Throughout most of the nineteenth century, scholars reflected one of the underlying assumptions of that era—that the main theme of American history was the quest for liberty. Within this context, the Revolution was inevitably viewed as a struggle of liberty versus tyranny between America and Britain.

George Bancroft, one of the outstanding exponents of this point of view, set forth his thesis in his ten-volume *History of the United States*, published between the 1830s. To Bancroft, the Revolution represented one phase of a master plan by God for the march of all mankind toward a golden age of greater human freedom. The Revolution was "radical in its character," according to Bancroft, because it hastened the advance of human beings toward a millennium of "everlasting peace" and "universal brotherhood."[1]

In the nineteenth century, Americans desired a national historian who would narrate the Revolution as patriotic epic, and Bancroft fulfilled this longing. In addition, in a turbulent period divided by the bitter politics of Jacksonian era and the brutality of the Civil War, Bancroft reminded Americans that they had once fought as a united people for beliefs they held in common.[2]

Around the turn of the twentieth century, a reaction set in against Bancroft's ultrapatriotic interpretation. With the growing rapprochement between Britain and America, there was a tendency to view past relations between the two countries in a more favorable light. Populism and progressivism, popular reactions against the concentration of power and wealth in the hands of a relatively small number of leaders in industrialized America, influenced some historians to view the Revolution as an uprising by the lower classes against the control of the upper classes....

Source: Excerpt from "The American Revolution: Moderate or Radical?" From Francis G. Couvares, Martha Saxton, Gerald N. Grob, George Athan Billias, *Interpretations of American History: Patterns and Perspectives*, 8th Edition, Vol. 1 Through Reconstruction. Copyright © 2009 by Bedford/St. Martin's. Reprinted by permission of Bedford/St. Martin's.

[1]George Bancroft, *History of the United States of America.* 10 vols. (Boston, 1852), Vol. 4, pp. 12–13.

[2]Wesley F. Craven, "The Revolutionary Era," in *The Reconstruction of American History*, John Higham, ed. (New York, 1962), pp. 46–47.

Progressive historians emphasized the growing economic split caused by the competition between the colonies and mother country. Progressive historians such as Carl L. Becker, Charles A. Beard, Arthur M. Schlesinger Sr., and J. Franklin Jameson stressed class conflict in colonial America in part because they saw their own era in terms of a struggle by the people to free themselves from the shackles of the large corporate monopolies and trusts. They insisted that political or constitutional ideas had an underlying economic basis.

Carl L. Becker, one the first and most effective of the Progressive historians, took the position that the American Revolution should be considered not as one revolution but as two. The first was an external revolution—the colonial rebellion against Britain—caused by a clash of economic interests between the colonies and mother country. The second was an internal revolution—a conflict among America's social classes—to determine who would rule once the British departed. In his first major study of the Revolution, *The History of Political Parties in the Province of New York, 1760–1776*, published in 1909, Becker summed up his thesis of a dual revolution in a memorable phrase. New York politics prior to the Revolution, he wrote, revolved around two questions—the "question of home rule" and the "question...of who should rule at home."[3]

Arthur M. Schlesinger's *The Colonial Merchants and the American Revolution, 1763–1776* (1918) continued in the vein of Charles A. Beard's famous *An Economic Interpretation of the Constitution.* Schlesinger noted that the usually conservative merchant class played a leading role in bringing on the Revolution. Why? Disenchantment of the merchants with British rule, said Schlesinger, arose from the economic reserves they suffered as a result of the strict policy of imperial control enacted by the mother country after the French and Indian war. Merchants' resistance against the mother country grew less intense after 1770, he noted, for fear of [what] might happen to their position and property if the more radical lower classes—"their natural enemies in society"—should gain the upper hand. The merchant class later became, in Schlesinger's words, "a potent factor in the conservative counterrevolution that led to the establishment of the United States Constitution."[4] To Schlesinger, the Constitution was the antithesis of the Revolution.

After World War II, however, a new group of scholars—the consensus historians—challenged the Progressives. The consensus historians, unlike the Progressives, believed that American society was essentially democratic in the colonial period. Most colonists possessed enough land to meet the necessary qualifications for voting. Colonial society was characterized by a high degree of social mobility. Thus the common man in the colonial era was satisfied with his lot in society and felt no urge to participate in class conflict in order to achieve a greater degree of democracy. Consensus scholars argued that Americans fought the Revolution to preserve a social order that was already democratic. When British reforms after 1763 threatened to upset the existing democratic social order in America, the colonists rose up in rebellion. In the struggle between the colonies and mother country, the Americans emerged as the "conservatives" because they were trying to keep matters as they were before 1763.

The consensus interpretation of the Revolution that arose after 1945 reflected the conservative climate of opinion that pervaded the Unites States after World War II. The Cold War made some Americans increasingly preoccupied with the problem of national security. Consensus historians led by Robert E. Brown and Daniel J. Boorstin played down any past differences among Americans in order to present an image of a strong and united nation.

Daniel J. Boorstin argued that the Revolution was conservative on the imperial as well as the local level because Americans were fighting to retain traditional rights and liberties granted

[3]Carl L. Becker, *The History of Political Parties in the Province of New York, 1760–1776* (Madison, Wisc., 1909), p. 22.

[4]Arthur M. Schlesinger, *The Colonial Merchants and the American Revolution, 1763–1776* (New York, 1918), p. 606.

to them under the British constitution. In *The Genius of American Politics*, he argued that Americans resisted British changes after the Seven Years' war because they were contrary to the British constitution. In refusing to accept the principle of no taxation without representation, Boorstin wrote, the patriots were insisting upon an old liberty, not a new right.[5]...

In the 1960s, three groups challenged the consensus school. Certain intellectual historians saw the Revolution as a radical rather than a conservative movement. Neo-Progressive and New Left historians used different approaches to search for the social and economic origins of the revolutionary movement. And an interest in studies of the Loyalists provided a third perspective.

The trend toward greater emphasis upon intellectual history was in part a reaction against the Progressive scholars who had generally shown a profound distrust of ideas as determining forces in history. Strongly influenced by the thought of Freud and Marx, the Progressive historians looked upon ideas as emerging from material conditions or psychological predispositions that motivated human behavior. They thought historians should pursue the material basis for ideas rather than disembodied ideas themselves.

Bernard Bailyn was the foremost among post World War II scholars who rejected this view and saw the Revolution as a radical intellectual movement. In *The Ideological Origins of the American Revolution*, Bailyn took the position that ideas expressed in pamphlet literature before the Revolution constituted its major determinants.[6] Bailyn argued that an elaborate theory of politics lay at the heart of the American revolutionary ideology—an ideology that came to be called republicanism and whose roots could be traced back to the antiauthoritarian or opposition Whig party tradition in England. Man had a natural lust for power, this theory held, and power by its very nature was a corrupting force and could be attained only by depriving others of their liberty. To protect liberty against the corruption force of power, all elements of the body politic had to be balanced off against each other in order to prevent one from gaining dominance over the others. The best solution was a balanced constitution, but the malignant influence of power was such that no system of government whatsoever could be safe or stable for very long.

The colonists, according to Bailyn, were convinced that there was a sinister plot against liberty in both England and America. In England, it was the king's ministers who were conspiring against liberty. They usurped the prerogatives of the crown, systematically encroached upon the independence of the Commons, and upset the balance of the British constitution in their corrupt drive for power, wealth, and luxuries. Americans believed the conspiracy had succeeded in England and that America represented the last bastion for the defense of English liberties and the freedom of all mankind.

...Gordon S. Wood extended this argument in *The Creation of the American Republic, 1776–1787*, which explained how the colonists' antiauthoritarian tradition was transformed after independence into a distinctive American republican ideology. His and Bailyn's works, written in the 1960s, gave rise to what came to be called the "republican synthesis" and coupled with J.G.A. Pocock's *The Machiavellian Moment*, published in the 1970s, claimed that this republican ideology dominated the political culture throughout the whole sweep of American history from the 1760s to the Civil war. The republican synthesis moved John Locke's thought on natural rights from the center of revolutionary thought and replaced it with the republican ideas of citizens acting with disinterested virtue for the common good. Those upholding the republican synthesis relied heavily on the classical republican tradition, which emphasized citizenship and public participation and had roots stretching back to antiquity and the Renaissance. Pocock, in fact, declared the Revolution to be "the last great act of the Renaissance." Ideas of

---

[5]Daniel J. Boorstin, "The American Revolution: Revolution without Dogma," in *The Genius of American Politics* (Chicago, 1953), 66–98.

[6]Bernard Bailyn, *The Ideological Origins of the American Revolution* (Cambridge, Mass., 1967).

republicanism proved to be the most widely accepted interpretation in the voluminous literature written from the mid-1960s to the mid-1980s.[7]

...Meanwhile, a reaction to the republican synthesis was setting in in the 1970s and
1980s from a variety of groups. Bailyn, who had revised the neoconservatives by making the
Revolution seem radical again, was subjected to revisionist assaults, as were Wood and Pocock.
Bailyn was criticized because he seemed to suggest that there was an ideological consensus
among American Whigs and that they all held the same republican ideas in common. Other
scholars quickly pointed out there were other ideologies at work—evangelical Protestantism,
class-based perspectives, or different political orientations—and that America's political culture
was diverse. Supporters of the republican synthesis were criticized, moreover, for omitting a
discussion of the various theories of political economy, including Lockean liberalism, that were
so important to those of the Revolutionary generation.[8]

Rhys Isaac, for example, undermined the idea of an ideological consensus by analyzing different powerful religious ideologies at work before, during, and after the Revolution. Focusing
on pre-Revolutionary Virginia as a case study, Isaac showed that deep ideological differences
existed between the Anglicans and Baptists. Deploying the imaginative techniques of cultural
anthropologists, Isaac identified two contrasting religious subcultures: the tradition-oriented
Anglican gentry who represented the established order and the humble evangelical Baptists
who challenged the ruling Anglican establishment. His work did more than destroy the idea of
a possible ideological consensus; it showed that by omitting much serious discussion of religious
beliefs, Bailyn and Wood had overlooked the important role religion played in the formation of
political beliefs during the Revolution.[9]

...A group of New Left historians emerging in the 1960s blended with the neo-progressive
historians and challenged the ideological interpretation of the Revolution. The neo-Progressive
and New Left historians were influenced not only by the earlier Progressive historians, but also
by the social and political concerns of the times in which they lived. These scholars brought to the
study of the Revolution a renewed awareness of the existence on minorities and the disadvantaged in American history. The protest movements in the 1960s and 1970s made these scholars
sensitive to the claims of social groups who historically had been oppressed. The chief sources of
the revolutionary movement, they argued, were to be found in the profound economic and social
dislocations within eighteenth-century America. The tensions generated by such changes led to
social unrest and protest on the part of the lower social orders during the Revolution. The neo-
Progressive historians portrayed the Revolution as a democratic movement stimulated in part by
these growing social inequalities and aimed at broadening participation in American political life.

...Gary B. Nash, a historian in the neo-Progressive/New Left tradition, discussed in his
Urban Crucible an ideology found among laboring class and artisan groups on the eve of the

---

[7]Gordon S. Wood, *The Creation of the American Republic, 1776–1787* (Chapel Hill, N.C.,
1969), and J.G.A. Pocock, *The Machiavellian Moment: Florentine Political Thought and the
Atlantic Republican Tradition* (Princeton, N.J., 1975). For the Pocock quotation, see "Virtue and
Commerce in the Eighteenth Century," *Journal of Interdisciplinary History* 3 (1972): 12.

[8]For an attack on the idea of an ideological consensus, see some of the essays in Alfred A. Young,
ed., *The American Revolution: Explorations in the History of American Radicalism* (De Kalb, Ill.,
1976). For two books that take up the issue of whether liberalism or republicanism was dominant
in the revolutionary era, see Joyce Appleby, *Capitalism and a New Social Order* (New York,
1984), and Lance Banning, *The Jeffersonian Persuasion: Evolution of a Party Ideology* (Ithaca,
N.Y., 1978). For discussions of the important role of political economy in the revolutionary and
post-Revolutionary period, see the Appleby book and Drew R. McCoy, *The Elusive Republic:
Political Economy in Jeffersonian America* (chapel Hill, NC, 1980).

[9]Rhys Isaac, *Transformation of Virginia, 1740–1790* (Chapel Hill, N.C., 1982).

Revolution that had not been treated by either Bailyn or Wood. Viewing the lives of urban dwellers in Boston, New York, and Philadelphia from the 1680s to the Revolution, Nash concluded that social changes had turned these seaport communities into "crucibles of revolutionary agitation." The increasing poverty and the narrowing of economic opportunities resulted in resentment and rising class consciousness among segments of the artisan class.[10]

…Innovative historians in the 1970s and 1980s brought several major new approaches to the study of the Revolution. The new social historians included among their ranks those who saw the Revolution through community studies or the eyes of forgotten Americans. Others explored the Revolution from a psychological point of view. And yet another group of new military historians studied the dynamics between it and the civilian world.

The new social historians were united loosely by their desire to examine America's social structure and its changes over time. They often directed their attention to small communities. Their work in many instances was characterized by quantitative techniques and research in nontraditional sources like wills, deeds, and tax lists to get at the lives of the inarticulate masses who left few personal memoirs. By employing such records, they hoped to re-create the universe in which ordinary citizens lived. Like the New Left historians, they sometimes were interested in specific socially or politically disadvantaged groups: the poor, blacks, and women. And like the new intellectual historians, they followed changes in the attitudes and behavior in groups over long periods of time.

…The new social historians, among many others, paid more attention to certain social and racial groups such as blacks, women, and Indians to examine how they were affected by the Revolution…. The study of slavery and the Revolution has expanded rapidly. More and more scholars agree that it was central to the colonial experience and explanatory of much that followed. Sylvia Frey in *Water from the Rock* recreated the experiences of slaves during the Revolution and the ways in which both sides used them for their own political and military ends. Simon Schama in the gripping *Rough Crossings* (2006) argued that seeing the Revolution from the standpoint of slaves makes the British the more revolutionary of the two opponents. While ambivalent and very imperfect allies to enslaved people, the British did offer some opportunities for liberation, and the growing British abolitionist movement worked for the welfare of slaves and former slaves.[11]

Gary B. Nash's *Race and Revolution* looked at northerners' responsibility for failing to secure the abolition of slavery nationwide at the time of the Revolution. And recently, his *Forgotten Fifth*, analyzing the writings of disappointed free blacks in the postrevolutionary era, details the ways in which their condition as citizens dramatically worsened after the war to which they had contributed so much.[12]

…Mary Beth Norton and Linda K. Kerber looked at women in the Revolution and postrevolutionary period, finding the outlines of a role for them in the early republic as "republican mothers" or mothers of the virtuous citizens the new nation needed to maintain its purity in a corrupt world. This interpretation has been useful in linking women to the national body politic. Joan Hoff Wilson, on the other hand, found that the Revolution itself meant no change in the lives of women.[13] While the Revolution's positive political results for women are generally

---

[10]Gary B. Nash, *Urban Crucible: The Northern Seaports and the Origins of the American Revolution* (Cambridge, 1979).

[11]Sylvia Frey, *Water from the Rock* (Princeton, NJ, 1991); Simon Schama, *Rough Crossings: Britain, the Slaves, and the American Revolution* (New York, 2006).

[12]Nash, *Race and Revolution* and *The Forgotten Fifth: African Americans in the Age of Revolution* (Cambridge, Mass, 2007).

[13]Linda Kerber, *Women of the Republic: Intellect and Ideology in Revolutionary America* (Chapel Hill, NC, 1980); Mary Beth Norton, *Liberty's Daughters: The Revolutionary Experience of American Women, 1750–1800* (Boston, 1980); Joan Hoff Wilson, "The Illusion of Change: Women and the Revolution," in Young, ed., *The American Revolution*.

agreed not to have developed before the mid-nineteenth century, historians have researched and described women's participation in the Revolution as spinners of homespun, boycotters of English goods, and food rioters seeking a moral economy.[14]

Carol Berkin's *Revolutionary Mothers* synthesizes much material on women's various roles in the conflict, giving a brisk overview of the experiences of African Americans, Native Americans, elite Whigs, camp followers, and Loyalists. The book reminds readers that this was no quaint conflict, but a long, violent war with all that entails, including devastated farms and countrysides, rapes, family separations, death, and pervasive fear. Alfred Young offered perhaps the most unusual angle on women's participation in *Masquerade*, the biography of Deborah Sampson, who served undetected for eighteen months as a man in the Continental army. She spent most of her time in the dangerous Hudson Valley after the fall of Yorktown but before peace came officially. Through Sampson's experiences, Young offered a view of Revolutionary-era religious and social turmoil as well as a close look at the duties, risks, and living conditions of average soldiers. His haunting portrait of Sampson's postwar ill health and poverty and decades of appeals for veterans' benefits make this simultaneously a remarkable work of biography and community study.[15]

The new social history, which later merged with the new political history as it tried to connect social and cultural phenomena with politics, encouraged studies of Indians and the Revolution. Barbara Graymont's *The Iroquois in the American Revolution* was among the first full-scale ethnohistories of Indian participation in the war.[16] Gregory Evans Dowd, Richard White, and James Merrell have discussed the Revolution's effects on certain Indian groups, and in 1995 Colin Calloway published *The American Revolution in Indian Country*, a broad and ambitious look at the Revolution as it played out in various Indian communities...[17]

Some of the new social historians working in the tumultuous 1970s and extending into the 1990s explored the nature of the Revolution in psychological terms. These scholars made use of psychohistory—a subdiscipline that had recently come into prominence. They suggested the Americans may have been caught up in a serous identity crisis as a people on the eve of the Revolution. Such historians saw Americans as profoundly conflicted toward the mother country. Colonial society underwent a process of Anglicization in the eighteenth century, and according to this hypothesis, Americans became more self-consciously English. On the other hand, they admired the mother country so much that they imitated British ways. On the other, they resented the idea of emulating the British because they were seeking to establish a separate

---

[14]Ronald Hoffman and Peter J. Albert, eds., *Women in the Age of the American Revolution* (Charlottesville, VA, 1989); Barbara Clark Smith, "Food Rioters and the American Revolution," *William and Mary Quarterly,* 3rd Ser., LI (1994): 3–38; for two historians who find the Revolution more influential earlier, see Susan Branson, *These Fiery Frenchified Dames: Women and Politics in Early National Philadelphia* (Philadelphia, 2001), and Catherine Allgor, *Parlor Politics: In Which the Ladies of Washington Help Build a City and a Government* (Charlottesville, VA, 2000).

[15]Carol Berkin, *Revolutionary Mothers: Women in the Struggle for America's Independence* (New York, 2005); Alfred F. Young, *Masquerade: The Life and Times of Deborah Sampson, Continental Soldier* (New York, 2004).

[16]Barbara Graymont, *The Iroquois in the American Revolution* (Syracuse, NY, 1972).

[17]Gregory Evans Dowd, *A Spirited Resistance: The North American Indian Struggle for Unity, 1745–1815* (Baltimore, 1992); Richard White, *The Middle Ground: Indians, Empire and Republics in the Great Lakes Region, 1640–1815* (Cambridge, 1991); James Merrell, *The Indians' New World: Catawbas and their Neighbors from European Contact through the Era of Removal* (Chapel Hill, NC, 1989); and Colin Calloway, *The American Revolution in Indian Country: Crisis and Diversity in Native American Communities* (New York, 1995).

sense of American identity. Jack P. Greene, John M. Murrin, and Robert M. Weir, among others, treated the theme of an identity crisis.[18]

...Another innovation that social historians brought about in historiography of the Revolution was recasting military history as social history. The new narrative historians broke away from the old-fashioned drum-and-trumpet narrative approach to war and wedded military and social history. They removed military history from the narrow confines of the battlefield and placed it within a much broader context—that of the relationship between warfare and society as a whole.

Many new military historians believed that the way a nation waged war shed important light on the values held by its people. John Shy, in a book of brilliant essays, maintained that the pattern of military events during the Revolutionary War helped shape the way the American people came to view themselves and their relationship to the rest of the world. To Shy, the war was not an instrument of policy or a sequence of military operations solely, but rather a social process of education.[19]

...While the New Left and the new social historians, including the new military historians and the psychohistorians, had provided insightful case studies and insights into the Revolution, the problem of a general synthesis remained. In 1991, Gordon Wood picked up the challenge and published *The Radicalism of the American Revolution*, in which he argued, as the title suggests, that the Revolution ushered in a new American no longer hampered by habits of deference, feelings of inferiority, or hesitations about economic advancement. This new man (and he was male) felt himself to be anyone's equal and quickly exchanged his republican insistence on suppressing his self-interest for the common good for a more liberal focus on his individual rights and economic well-being.[20]

....comparative work on the Revolutionary era...has continued. In 1988, Patrice Higonnet, a historian of France, published *Sister Republics*, which compared the intellectual and ideological trajectories deriving from the American and French revolutions, finding more political consensus and continuity in the United States despite greater levels of inequality. In France, on the other hand, he contended that there had been less stability and more open conflict over class than in the United States. Nevertheless, Higonnet added, the French worker, while not necessarily benefiting greatly from France's politicized class struggles, has never been as invisible or as despairing of inclusion as African American members of the American working class have been.[21]

Lester D. Langley took a hemisphere approach in 1996, studying the American Revolution, the Haitian Revolution, and the Latin American wars for independence in the late eighteenth and early nineteenth centuries. He found that the American Revolution produced an inspiring ideology on which to base nationalism and further democratic change, although the Revolution itself resulted only in political rights for free white men. For this reason, he described it as a

---

[18]Jack P. Greene, "Search of Identity: An Interpretation of the Meaning of Selected Patterns of Social Response in Eighteenth-Century America," *Journal of Social History* 3 (1980): 189–220; John M. Murrin, "The Legal Transformation: The Bench and Bar of Eighteenth-Century Massachusetts," in Stanley N. Katz, ed., *Colonial America: Essays in Politics and Development* (Boston, 1971); and Robert M. Weir, "Who Shall Rule at Home: The American Revolution as a Crisis of Legitimacy for the Colonial Elite," *Journal of Interdisciplinary History* 6 (1976): 679–700.

[19]John Shy, *A People Numerous and Armed: Reflections on the Military Struggle for American Independence* (New York, 1976), 224. For the British army in America before the Revolution and the colonists' reaction to its presence, see Shy's *Toward Lexington: The Role of the British Army in the American Revolution* (Princeton, NJ, 1965).

[20]Gordon S. Wood, *The Radicalism of the American Revolution* (New York, 1991).

[21]Patrice Higonnet, *Sister Republics: The Origins of French and American Republicanism* (Cambridge, MA, 1988).

revolution from above. The Haitian Revolution instead freed the island from French control and simultaneously slavery, and newly freed men created a state for the first time. Langley called this a revolution from below. The Latin American rebellions, instead, were revolutions denied as they aimed to change government without changing the social and economic structures that supported the ruling class. In his analysis, Langley emphasizes the chaos of revolutionary violence, the "infuriating complications generated by" the conflict between "liberating ideas and traditional customs," and the social exclusivity of meanings of race. Revolutions in the New World had an added charge of unpredictability that Langley argued historians have neglected.[22]

In summary it should be noted that historians who have addressed themselves to the question of whether the Revolution was revolutionary or not must answer a number of related questions. Was American society truly democratic during the colonial period? Or was American society undemocratic during the colonial era, thus resulting in a dual revolution: a struggle to see who would rule at home as well as a fight for home rule? What was the true nature of the Revolution? Was there a radical ideological change in the ideas that most Americans held regarding their image of themselves and of their institutions? Or did most of the changes take place within the political and social sphere rather than in the world of ideas? Was the "republican synthesis," with its emphasis on republican ideology, a convincing interpretation of this cataclysmic event? What were the results of the Revolution for women? For slavery? For Native Americans? For the poor? What motivated men to go off to fight in the Revolutionary war—was it materialism or idealism? The answers to these questions will determine the answer to the broader question of just how revolutionary was the American Revolution.

---

[22]Lester D. Langley, *The Americas in the Age of Revolution: 1750–1850* (New Haven, CT, 1996), 1–10.

Appendix C

Selected Bibliography

General Historiography

Appleby, Joyce, et al. *Telling the Truth About History*. New York: W. W. Norton, 1994.

Bentley, Michael. *Companion to Historiography*. New York: Routledge, 1997.

Breisach, Ernst. *Historiography: Ancient, Medieval, and Modern*, 2nd ed. Chicago, IL: University of Chicago Press, 1994.

Burke, Peter, ed. *New Perspectives in Historical Writing*, 2nd ed. Cambridge: Polity, 2001.

Burns, Robert M. *Philosophies of History: From Enlightenment to Postmodernity*. Malden, MA: Blackwell, 2000.

Burrow John. *A History of Histories: Epics, Chronicles, Romances and Inquiries from Herodotus and Thucydides to the Twentieth Century*. New York: Alfred A. Knopf, 2008.

Collingwood, R. G. *The Idea of History*. Oxford: Oxford University Press, 1946.

Couvares, Francis G., et al. *Interpretations of American History*. Vols. I and II, 8th ed. New York: Bedford/St. Martins, 2009.

Foner, Eric, ed. *The New American History*. Philadelphia: Temple University Press, 1997.

Higham, John. *History: Professional Scholarship in America*. Baltimore, MD: Johns Hopkins University Press, 1983.

Hine, Darlene Clark, ed. *The State of Afro-American History: Past, Present, and Future*. Baton Rouge, LA: Louisiana State University Press, 1986.

Hoffer, Peter Charles. *Past Imperfect: Facts, Fictions, Fraud—American History from Bancroft and Parkman to Ambrose, Bellesiles, Ellis, and Goodwin*. New York: Public Affairs, 2004.

Hughes, Stuart. *History as Art and as Science: Twin Vistas on the Past*. New York: Harper and Row, 1964.

Hughes-Warrington, Marnie. *Fifty Key Thinkers on History*. London: Routledge, 2000.

Iggers, Georg G. *Historiography in the Twentieth Century: From Scientific Objectivity to the Postmodern Challenge*. Hanover, NH: Weslyan University Press, 2005.

Lang, Sean. *The Pursuit of History: Aims, Methods, and New Directions in the Study of Modern History*, 4th ed. New York: Pearson Longman, 2006.

Lemon, M. C. *Philosophy of History: A Guide for Students*. New York: Routledge, 2003.

Meier, August and Elliot Rudwick. *Black History and the Historical Profession 1915–1980.* Urbana, IL: University of Illinois, 1986.

Novick, Peter. *That Noble Dream: The Objectivity Question and the American Historical Profession.* Cambridge: Cambridge University Press, 1988.

Smith, Bonnie G. *The Gender of History: Men, Women, and Historical Practice.* Cambridge, MA: Harvard University Press, 1998.

Stokes, Melvyn, ed. *The State of U.S. History.* New York: Oxford, 2002.

Wang, Q. Edward and Georg G. Iggers. *Turning Points in Historiography: A Cross-Cultural Perspective.* Rochester, New York: University of Rochester Press, 2002.

Wang, Q. Edward and Franz L. Fillafer, eds. *The Many Faces of Clio: Cross-Cultural Approaches to History, Essays in Honor of Georg G. Iggers.* New York: Berghahn Books, 2007.

Wollstonecraft, Mary. *A Vindication of the Rights of Woman.* New York: Penguin, 1992.

Wood, Gordon S. *The Purpose of the Past: Reflections on the Uses of History.* New York: Penguin, 2008.

Chapter 1: Early Histories

Barker, John. *The Superhistorians: Makers of the Past.* New York: Charles Scribner's Sons, 1982.

Bede. *A History of the English Church and People.* Translated by A. M. Sellar. London: George Bell and Sons, 1907.

Breebaart, A. B. *Clio and Antiquity: History and Historiography of the Greek and Roman World.* Hilversum: Verloren, 1987.

Butterfield, Herbert. *The Origins of History.* New York: Basic Books, 1981.

Hartog, Francois. "The Invention of History: From Homer to Herodotus," *History and Theory* 39 (2000): 384–395.

Herodotus. *The Histories* (5th century B.C.E.). Translated by Aubrey de Selincourt, revised with introduction and notes by John Marincola. London: Penguin, 2003.

Hunter, V. *Past and Process in Herodotus and Thucydides.* Princeton, NJ: Princeton University Press, 1982.

Thucydides. *History of the Peloponnesian War.* Translated by Rex Warner. New York: Viking Penguin, 1972.

Chapter 2: The Evolution of Modern History

Anderson, M. S. *Historians and Eighteenth-Century Europe, 1715–1789.* New York: Oxford University Press, 1979.

Baker, Keith M. *Condorcet.* Chicago, IL: University of Chicago Press, 1975.

Berlin, Isaiah. *Vico and Herder: Two Studies in the History of Ideas.* New York: Chatto and Windus, 1976.

Bodin, Jean. *Method for the Easy Comprehension of History* (1566). Translated by B. Reynolds. New York: Columbia University Press, 1945.

Cochrane, Eric W. *Historians and Historiography in the Italian Renaissance.* Chicago, IL: University of Chicago Press, 1981.

De Condorcet, Antoine-Nicolas. *Sketch for a Historical Picture of the Progress of the Human Mind.* Translated by June Barraclough. New York: Noonday Press, 1955, reprinted by Hyperion Press, 1994.

Herder, Johann Gottfried. *Reflections on the Philosophy of History of Mankind.* Chicago: University of Chicago Press, 1968.

Lilla, Mark. *G.B. Vico: The Making of an Anti-Modern.* Cambridge, MA: Harvard University Press, 1993.

Machiavelli, Niccolo. *The Prince.* Translated by Ninian Hill Thomson. London: Kegan Paul, Trench, 1882.

Vico, Giambattista. *The New Science I and III.* Translated by Leon Pompa. New York: Cambridge University Press, 1982.

Ramsay, David. *The History of the American Revolution in Two Volumes (1789).* Edited by Lester H. Cohen. Indianapolis, IN: Liberty Fund, 1990.

Warren, Mercy Otis. *History of the Rise Progress and Termination of the American Revolution interspersed with Biographical, Political and Moral Observations (1805).* Edited by Lester H. Cohen. Indianapolis, IN: Liberty Fund, 1994.

Chapter 3: Nineteenth-Century European Historiography

Bann, Stephen. *The Clothing of Clio: A Study of the Representation of History in Nineteenth Century Britain and France.* New York: Cambridge University Press, 1984.

Clive, John. *Macaulay: The Shaping of the Historian.* New York: Alfred A. Knopf, 1973.

Droysen, Johann Gustav. *Outlines of the Principles of History.* New York: H. Fertig, 1893.

Gooch, George Peabody. *History and Historians in the Nineteenth Century.* London: Longmans, Green & Co., 1913.

Hegel, Georg Wilhelm Friedrich. *Lectures on the Philosophy of World History.* Cambridge: Cambridge University Press, 1975.

Krieger, Leonard. *Ranke: The Meaning of History.* Chicago, IL: University of Chicago Press, 1977.

Macaulay, Thomas Babington. "The History of England (1849)," in *Little Masterpieces: Lord Macaulay.* Edited by Bliss Perry. New York: Doubleday, Page, and Co., 1906.

Marx, Karl. *The Eighteenth Brumaire of Louis Bonaparte.* Translated by Daniel De Leon Chicago, IL: Charles H. Kerr, 1907.

Von Ranke, Leopold. *History of the Reformation in Germany.* Vol. I. Edited by Robert A. Johnson. Translated by Sarah Austin. New York: Frederick Ungar, 1905.

Chapter 4: American History in the Nineteenth Century

Bancroft, George. *History of the United States of American from the Discovery of the Continent.* Vol. IV. New York: D. Appleton, 1889.

Billington, Ray A. *Frederick Jackson Turner: Historian, Scholar, Teacher.* New York: ACLS Humanities, 2008.

Hofstadter, Richard. *Social Darwinism in American Thought, 1860–1915.* Philadelphia, PA: University of Pennsylvania Press, 1944.

Turner, Frederick Jackson. *The Frontier in American History.* New York: Henry Holt, 1920.

Vitzthum, R. C. *The American Compromise: Theme and Method in the Histories of Bancroft, Parkman, and Adams.* Norman, OK: Oklahoma University Press, 1974.

Chapter 5: Conflict and Consensus: The Progressive Challenge to American History

Beard, Charles. *An Economic Interpretation of the Constitution of the United States.* New York: The Macmillan Co, 1913.

Beard, Charles A., and Beard, Mary R. *The Rise of American Civilization.* Vol. I. New York: Macmillan, 1927.

Beard, Mary. *Woman as Force in History: A Study in Traditions and Realities.* New York: Macmillan, 1946.

Breisach, Ernst. *American Progressive History: An Experiment in Modernization.* Chicago, IL: University of Chicago Press, 1993.

Boorstin, Daniel J. *The Genius of American Politics.* Chicago, IL: University of Chicago Press, 1953.

Boorstin, Daniel. *The Americans.* Harmondsworth: Penguin, 1965.

Breisach, E. *American Progressive History: An Experiment in Modernization.* Chicago, IL: University of Chicago Press, 1993.

Du Bois, W. E. B. *Souls of Black Folk.* Chicago, IL: A. C. McClurg & Co., 1903.

Hartz, Louis. *The Liberal Tradition in America: An Interpretation of American Political Thought since the Revolution.* New York: Harcourt Brace, 1955.

Hofstadter, Richard. *The Progressive Historians: Turner, Beard, Parrington.* New York: Alfred A. Knopf, 1968.

Kloppenberg, James T. "Pragmatism and the Practice of History: From Turner and Du Bois to Today," *Metaphilosophy* 35:1/2 (January 2004): 202–225.

Lewis, David Levering. *W.E.B. Du Bois: Biography of a Race, 1868–1919.* New York: Henry Holt, 1993.

Sternsher, Bernard. *Consensus, Conflict, and American Historians.* Bloomington, IN: Indiana University Press, 1975.

Chapter 6: Marxism, *Annales,* and the New Left

Bernstein, Barton J., ed. *Towards a New Past: Dissenting Essays in American History.* New York: Random House, 1969.

Bloch, Marc. *The Historians Craft.* New York: Knopf, 1957.

Braudel, Fernand. *The Mediterranean and the Mediterranean World in the Age of Philip II.* Vol. I. (1949). Translated by Sian Reynolds. New York: Harper and Row, 1972.

Eley, Geoff. *A Crooked Line: From Cultural History to the History of Society.* Ann Arbor, MI: University of Michigan Press, 2005.

Febvre, Lucien. *A New Kind of History and Other Essays.* New York, 1975.

Kolko, Joyce and Kolko Gabriel. *The Limits of Power: The World and United States Foreign Policy, 1945–1954.* New York: Harper and Row, 1972.

Lemisch, Jesse. "Jack Tar in the Streets: Merchant Seamen in the Politics of Revolutionary America," *William and Mary Quarterly, Third Series* 25:3 (July 1968).

Hobsbawm, Eric. *Labouring Men: Studies in the History of Labour.* London: Weidenfeld and Nicolson, 1964.

———. *The Age of Extremes: The Short Twentieth Century, 1914–1994.* London: Michael Joseph, 1994.

Thompson, E. P. *The Making of the English Working Class.* Harmondsworth: Pelican/Penguin Books, 1974.

Williams, William A. *The Tragedy of American Diplomacy.* New York: The World Publishing Company, 1959

Chapter 7: New Social History

Barzun, Jacques. *Clio and the Doctors: PsychoHistory, Quanto-History and History.* Chicago, IL: University of Chicago Press, 1974.

Blassingame, John. *The Slave Community: Plantation Life in the Antebellum South.* (1972); rev. ed. New York: Oxford University Press, 1979.

Burke, Peter. *The French Historical Revolution: The Annales School, 1929–1989.* Palo Alto, CA: Stanford University Press, 1990.

Cannadine, David, ed. *What is History Now.* London: Palgrave Macmillan, 2002.

Calloway, Colin. *The American Revolution in Indian Country: Crisis and Diversity in Native American Communities.* Cambridge, UK: Cambridge University Press, 1995.

Carr, E. H. *What is History?* New York: Knopf, 1962.

Cott, Nancy. *The Bonds of Womanhood: "Woman's Sphere" in New England, 1780–1835.* Princeton, NJ: Yale University Press, 1977.

Demos, John Putnam. *Entertaining Satan: Witchcraft and the Culture of Early New England.* New York: Oxford University Press, 1982.

———. *A Little Commonwealth: Family Life in Plymouth Colony.* New York: Oxford University Press, 1980.

Deutsch, Sarah. *No Separate Refuge: Culture, Class, and Gender on an Anglo-Hispanic Frontier in the American Southwest, 1880–1940.* New York: Oxford University Press, 1987.

Erikson, Erik H. *Young Man Luther: A Study in Psychoanalysis and History.* New York: Norton, 1962.

Faderman, Lillian. *Odd Girls and Twilight Lovers: A History of Lesbian Life in Twentieth-Century America.* New York: Columbia University Press, 1991.

Fogel, Robert William. *Railroads and American Economic Growth: Essays in Econometric Studies.* Boston, MA: Johns Hopkins University, 1964.

Fogel, Robert William and Engerman, Stanley L. *Time on the Cross: The Economics of American Negro Slavery.* Boston, MA: Little, Brown, and Co., 1974.

Franklin, John Hope. *From Slavery to Freedom: A History of African Americans.* New York: Alfred A. Knopf, 1947.

Freedman, Estelle and D'Emilio, John. *Intimate Matters: A History of Sexuality in America.* New York: Harper, 1988.

Gay, Peter. *Freud for Historians.* New York: Oxford University Press, 1985.

Genovese, Eugene. *Roll, Jordan, Roll: The World the Slaves Made.* New York: Pantheon, 1974.

Giddings, Paula. *When and Where I Enter: The Impact of Black Women on Race and Sex in America.* New York: Bantam, 1988.

Gutierrez, Ramon A. *When Jesus Came, the Corn Mothers Went Away: Marriage, Sexuality, and Power in New Mexico, 1500–1846.* Stanford, CA: Stanford University Press, 1991.

Gutman, Herbert. *Slavery and the Numbers Game: A Critique of "Time on the Cross."* Champaign, IL: University of Illinois Press, 2003.

———. *The Black Family in Slavery and Freedom, 1750–1925.* New York: Vintage Books, 1977.

Kelly, Joan. *Women, History, and Theory.* Chicago, IL: University of Chicago Press, 1986.

Kerber, Linda. *Women of the Republic: Intellect and Ideology in Revolutionary America*. Chapel Hill, NC: University of North Carolina Press, 1980.

Kessler-Harris, Alice. *Out to Work: A History of Wage-Earning Women in the United States*. New York: Oxford University Press, 1982.

Lerner, Gerda. *The Creation of Patriarchy*. New York: Oxford University Press, 1987.

Merrell, James. *The Indians' New World: Catawbas and Their Neighbors from European Contact through the Era of Removal*. Chapel Hill, NC: University of North Carolina Press, 1989.

Nash, Gary B. *Red, White, and Black: The Peoples of Early America*. Englewood Cliffs, NJ: Prentice Hall, 1982.

———. *The Urban Crucible: Social Change, Political Consciousness, and the Origins of the American Revolution*. Cambridge, MA: Harvard University Press, 1979.

Perdue, Theda. *Cherokee Women: Gender and Culture Change, 1700–1835*. Lincoln: University of Nebraska Press, 1998.

Ruiz, Vicki. *Cannery Women, Cannery Lives: Mexican Women, Unionization, and the California Food Processing Industry, 1930–1950*. Albuquerque, NM: University of New Mexico Press, 1987.

Skocpol, Theda. *States and Social Revolutions: A Comparative Analysis of France, Russia, and China*. Cambridge: Cambridge University Press, 1979.

Takaki, Ronald. *Strangers from a Different Shore: A History of Asian Americans*. Boston, MA: Little Brown, 1989.

———. *A Different Mirror: A Multicultural History of America*. Boston, MA: Little, Brown, 1993.

Thompson, Paul. *The Voice of the Past*. Oxford: Oxford University Press, 1988.

Tilly, Charles. *As Sociology Meets History*. New York: Academic Press, 1981.

Thornton, Russell. *American Holocaust and Survival: A Population History since 1492*. Norman, OK: University of Oklahoma Press, 1987.

White, Deborah Gray. *Ar'n't I A Woman: Female Slaves in the Plantation South*. New York: Norton, 1985.

Chapter 8: The Linguistic Turn, Postmodernism, and New Cultural History

Appignanesi, Richard and Garratt, Chris. *Postmodernism for Beginners*. Cambridge: Icon, 1995.

Barthes, Roland. *Mythologies*. London: Vintage, 1993.

Bloch, Ruth H. *Gender and Morality in Anglo-American Culture, 1650–1800*. Berkeley, CA: University of California Press, 2003.

Bonnell, Victoria and Hunt, Lynn, eds. *Beyond the Cultural Turn: New Directions in the Study of Society and Culture*. Berkeley, CA: University of California Press, 1999.

Brown, Callum. *Postmodernism for Historians*. Edinburgh Gate: Pearson Education, 2005.

Burke, Peter. *What is Cultural History?* Cambridge: Polity, 2004.

Butler, Judith. *Gender Trouble: Feminism and the Subversion of Identity*. London: Routledge, 1990.

Clark, Elizabeth A. *History, Theory, Text: Historians and the Linguistic Turn*. Cambridge: Harvard University Press, 2004.

Chartier, Roger. *Cultural History: Between Practices and Representations*. Cambridge: Polity, 1988.

De Certeau, Michel. *The Writing of History*. Translated by Tom Conley. New York: Columbia University Press, 1988.

Foucault, Michel. *Discipline & Punish: The Birth of the Prison*. Translated by Alan Sheridan. New York: Vintage Books 1995.

———. *The Archaeology of Knowledge*. Translated by Alan Sheridan. London: Routledge, 2002.

Darnton, Robert. *The Great Cat Massacre and Other Episodes in French Cultural History*. New York: Basic Books, 1984.

Geertz, Clifford. *The Interpretation of Cultures*. New York: Basic Books, 1973.

Ginzburg, Carlos. *The Cheese and the Worms: The Cosmos of a Sixteenth Century Miller*. Johns Hopkins University Press, Baltimore, 1980.

Gunn, Simon. *History and Cultural Theory*. London: Pearson Longman, 2006.

Hunt, Lynn. *The New Cultural History*. Berkeley, CA: University of California Press, 1989.

Jenkins, Keith. *Why History? Ethics and Postmodernity*. London: Routledge, 1999.

Korhonen, Kuisma, ed. *Tropes for the Past: Hayden White and the History/Literature Debate*. Rodopi, 2006.

Ladurie, Emmanuel Le Roy. *Montaillou*. New York: Vintage Books, 1979.

Lyotard, Jean-Francois. *The Postmodern Condition: A Report on Knowledge*. Manchester: Manchester University Press, 1984.

Munslow, Alun. *Deconstructing History*. London: Routledge, 1997.

Nietzsche, Friedrich. *On the Advantage and Disadvantage of History for Life*. Indianapolis: Hackett, 1980.

Schama, Simon. *Dead Certainties (Unwarranted Speculations)*. London: Penguin, 1991.

Scott, Joan Wallach. *Gender and the Politics of History*. New York: Columbia University Press, 1988.

Smith-Rosenberg, Carroll. *Disorderly Conduct: Visions of Gender in Victorian America*. New York: Oxford University Press, 1986.

Spiegel, Gabrielle M., ed. *Practicing History: New Directions in Historical Writing after the Linguistic Turn*. New York: Routledge, 2005.

White, Hayden. *Metahistory: The Historical Imagination in Nineteenth-Century Europe*. Baltimore, MD: Johns Hopkins University Press, 1975.

Chapter 9: World Histories

Bailyn, Bernard. *The Ideological Origins of the American Constitution*. Cambridge: Harvard University Press, 1967.

———. *Atlantic History: Concept and Contours*. Cambridge: Harvard University Press, 2005.

Benjamin, Thomas, et al. *The Atlantic World in the Age of Empire*. Boston, MA: Houghton Mifflin, 2001.

Bender, Thomas, ed. *Rethinking American History in a Global Age*. Berkeley, CA: University of California Press, 2002.

———. *A Nation Among Nations: America's Place in World History*. New York: Hill and Wang, 2006.

Chakrabarty, Dipesh. *Provincializing Europe*. Princeton, NJ: Princeton University Press, 2007.

Christian, David. *Maps of Time*. Berkeley, CA: University of California, 2004.

Crosby, Jr., Alfred W. *The Columbian Exchange: Biological and Cultural Consequences of 1492*. Westport, CT: Greenwood, 1973.

Diamond, Jared. *Guns, Germs, and Steel: The Fates of Human Societies*. New York: W. W. Norton, 1999.

———. *Collapse: How Societies Choose to Fail or Succeed*. New York: Viking Penguin, 2005.

Dirlik, Arif, Bahl, Vinay, and Gran, Peter, eds. *History after the Three Worlds: Post-Eurocentric Historiographies*. Lanham, MD: Rowman & Littlefield, 2000.

Fanon, Frantz. *The Wretched of the Earth*. Translated by Richard Philcox. New York: Grove Press, 1963.

Guarneri, Carl J. *America Compared: American History in International Perspective*. 2 Vols. Boston, MA: Houghton Mifflin, 2005.

Guha, Ranajit and Spivak, Gayatri Chakravorty, eds. *Selected Subaltern Studies*. New York: Oxford University Press, 1988.

Hopkins, Anthony G. *Globalization in World History*. New York: Norton, 2002.

Langley, Lester D. *The Americas in the Age of Revolution, 1750–1850*. New Haven: Yale University Press, 1996.

McNeill, William. *The Rise of the West: A History of the Human Community*. Chicago, IL: University of Chicago Press, 1963.

———. *Plagues and Peoples*. New York: Bantam Doubleday Dell, 1976.

———. *The Human Condition: An Ecological and Historical View*. Princeton, NJ: Princeton University Press, 1980.

Moore-Gilbert, Bart. *Postcolonial Theory: Contexts, Practices, Policies*. New York: Verso, 1997.

Penna, Anthony. *The Human Footprint: A Global Environmental History*. Oxford: Wiley-Blackwell, 2009.

Pomeranz, Kenneth and Topik, Steven. *The World that Trade Created: Society, Culture, and the World Economy, 1400 to the Present*. 2nd ed. Armonk, NY: M.E. Sharpe, 2006.

Said, Edward W. *Orientalism*. Copyright 1978 by Edward W. Said. New York: Vintage/Random House, 1979.

Wallerstein, Immanual. *The Modern World-Systems*. 3 Vols. New York: Academic Press, 1974–1989.

Williams, Patrick and Chrisman, Laura, eds. *Colonial Discourse and Post-Colonial Theory: A Reader*. New York: Columbia University Press, 1992.

Wood, Gordon. *The Radicalism of the American Revolution*. New York: Alfred A. Knopf, 1992.

Young, Robert. *White Mythologies: Writing History and the West*. London: Routledge, 1990.

———. *Postcolonialism: An Historical Introduction*. Oxford: Blackwell, 2001.

Epilogue

Appleby, Joyce et al. *Telling the Truth About History*. New York: W. W. Norton, 1994.

Hoffer, Peter Charles. *Past Imperfect: Facts, Fictions, Fraud—American History from Bancroft and Parkman to Ambrose, Bellesiles, Ellis, and Goodwin*. New York: Public Affairs, 2004.

Linenthal, Edward T. and Engelhardt, Tom, eds. *History Wars: The Enola Gay and Other Battles for the American Past*. New York: Metropolitan Books, 1996.

Nash, Gary, Crabtree, Charlotte, and Dunn, Ross E. *History on Trial: Culture Wars and the Teaching of the Past*. New York: Alfred A. Knopf, 1999.

Windschuttle, Keith. *The Killing of History: How a Discipline Is Being Murdered by Literary Critics and Social Critics*. Paddington, Australia: Macleay, 1996.

Wood, Gordon S. *The Purpose of the Past: Reflections on the Uses of History*. New York: Penguin, 2008.